CLAUDE LA COLOMBIÈRE SERMONS

Image appearing on the frontispiece of Volume 1 of *Sermons prêchez devant Son Altesse Roîale Madame la Duchesse d'Yorck. Par le R. P. Claude La Colombière* (Lyon: Anisson, Posuel, and Rigaud, 1684). Copy housed in the Rare Books Collection, John M. Kelly Library, University of St. Michael's College in the University of Toronto (BX1756 .L22 1684 v.1–4 SMR). Used with permission.

CLAUDE
LA COLOMBIÈRE
SERMONS

✳

VOLUME I
CHRISTIAN CONDUCT

Translated with Commentary
by William P. O'Brien

FOREWORD BY GÉRARD FERREYROLLES

NIU Press / DeKalb, IL

© 2014 by Northern Illinois University Press

Published by the Northern Illinois University Press, DeKalb, Illinois 60115

All Rights Reserved

Design by Shaun Allshouse

Library of Congress Cataloging-in-Publication Data

La Colombière, Claude de, Saint, 1641–1682.

[Sermons. English]

Claude La Colombière sermons / translated with commentary by William P. O'Brien, SJ ;

foreword by Gérard Ferreyrolles.

volumes cm

Includes bibliographical references and index.

ISBN 978-0-87580-472-9 (cloth : alk. paper : v. 1) — ISBN 978-1-60909-092-0 (e-book : v. 1)

1. Catholic Church—Sermons. 2. Sermons, French—Translations into English. I. O'Brien,

William P. (William Patrick), 1969–, editor of compilation. II. Title.

BX1756.L23S4713 2013

252'.02—dc23

2013014980

To my brother Jesuits

Contents

Foreword

GÉRARD FERREYROLLES

Université Paris-Sorbonne

La Colombière is "the ideal Jesuit." In this way Henri Bremond expressed himself in 1922, in his monumental *Histoire littéraire du sentiment religieux*. By thus expressing his own judgment, he anticipated that of the Catholic Church, who went on to proclaim La Colombière "blessed" in 1929, then "saint" in 1992, in recognition of both the exceptional character of his virtues and his decisive role in the promotion, during the seventeenth century, of the Devotion to the Heart of Jesus. But by "ideal Jesuit" it must be understood also that La Colombière realized in his person the humanist ideal that the Society of Jesus, expert in eloquence as in spirituality, worked to spread in the colleges of France and Europe in order to form, in accord with the dictum of Cicero, a *vir bonus, dicendi peritus*—a "good man, skilled at speaking." That La Colombière was a "good man," not only in the sense of natural morality but in the higher, Christian meaning, no one has ever doubted; that he was "skilled at speaking," Fr. O'Brien permits us, by this edition, to assess how far this expression falls short of the truth.

Fr. O'Brien, since his doctoral studies at the Sorbonne, where I had the good fortune and the honor to accompany him in his research, is the foremost expert of La Colombière as orator. He indeed dedicated, in 2008, his dissertation in French Literature to the connections between rhetoric and spirituality in La Colombière's corpus, and especially in three discourses delivered in 1665, 1671, and 1672, in praise of the panegyrist, the age of Augustus, and the French orator, respectively. These Latin discourses show in La Colombière a supreme mastery of rhetorical technique and a virtuosity that verges on the spectacular. The texts that Fr. O'Brien translates in the present work issue from the same author, but they are at the same time altogether different. It is no longer a question of making the powers of eloquence shine for their own sake, in a pedagogical exercise of declamation, but of putting them at the service of God from the pulpit of Truth, in a preaching of which the sole end is the conversion of the listeners.

La Colombière evidently did not forget, when he preached these sermons in 1676, 1677, and 1678, what he had taught his students of rhetoric some years previously, just as Saint Augustine, preaching in his cathedral in Hippo, could not disown his past as professor of rhetoric at Carthage and Milan. And in fact, the texts chosen and presented by Fr. O'Brien are thoroughly those of a master of eloquence, as much on the level of rhetorical invention as on the levels of disposition and elocution. One could go even further and assert that La Colombière, by his psychological lucidity and his sense of the paradoxical and demystifying turn of phrase, proves himself here the equal of the great moralists of the classical age. But he does not seek in his sermons to produce a literary oeuvre—and that may be why it attains such literary merit. He does better than to resist the temptation, denounced by Saint Paul in the work of certain preachers, to "preach himself" (*se prêcher soi-même*) in order to attract the admiration of the crowds: La Colombière preaches Jesus Christ and wants that his own word be nothing but the echo of the Word. Certainly, he resorts to all the rational and emotional means of persuasion, but he knows that these means are useless without that grace capable, with the help of our freedom, to render them effective. While human words echo in our ears, it is in us an invisible master who gives them access to our heart: the true preacher—that is, the Holy Spirit.

Let us not say that the audience of great, worldly people that La Colombière addressed is so different from us, or that his time is so far from ours. We recognize ourselves perfectly in the description he gives of the temptations or desires of his listeners. It suffices to read, by way of example, what he says about the bad habit, which he strikingly calls "a powerlessness that one wants" or "a free necessity," for if it is easy to engage oneself in such habits it is nearly impossible to quit them. Is this not exactly what we name *addiction*, this practice into which one enters for pleasure and which then carries us away by force? And if the era of La Colombière is distant, Fr. O'Brien, by the meticulousness of his lexical and historical notes—not to mention his invaluable scriptural and theological clarifications—brings within our reach these discourses delivered over three hundred years ago. Time passing changes nothing here: if the true preacher is the Holy Spirit, he continues to act through those who have lent him their voice. The texts of the saints are not a dead letter but a living word. And this is why one could not be too grateful to Fr. O'Brien: by passing on to us these intangible relics of Claude La Colombière, he has opened to us a treasury for today.

Acknowledgments

This volume never would have appeared in print without the kind and generous help of numerous mentors, colleagues, and friends, first and foremost Professors Philippe Lécrivain (Centre Sèvres) and Gérard Ferreyrolles (Paris IV), the faculty of the Department of Theological Studies at Saint Louis University, and Fr. Jim Kubicki, National Director of the Apostleship of Prayer (USA), who first suggested to me that I consider providing English-language translations of Fr. La Colombière's sermons.

For the location of a complete first edition of the *Sermons* on this side of the Atlantic, I thank the following people and institutions: David Shahly, Director of the InterLibrary Loan Department, Pius Memorial Library, Saint Louis University; John Buchtel, Head, Special Collections Research Center, Lauinger Library, Georgetown University; Richard Carter, Reference and Instructional Librarian, John M. Kelly Library, University of St. Michael's College, University of Toronto; and his colleagues Gabrielle Earnshaw, Head, Special Collections and Archives, and Remi Pulwer, Academic Librarian. At my request, Ms. Earnshaw had transferred to microfilm the complete first edition of the *Sermons* that belongs to the Kelly Library Special Collections: I have based the translation on this document. Unfortunately, the integral Kelly Library copy of the first edition is missing the engraving of Fr. La Colombière from the frontispiece; however, Ms. Earnshaw discovered in the Special Collections a second copy of the first volume, which copy includes the image. Ms. Earnshaw then digitalized that image for this edition, and Remi Pulwer later verified for me that the image indeed appears in this second copy. Ron Crown, Theology Reference Librarian, Pius Memorial Library, facilitated many of these contacts and operations, all of which have provided the material basis for the book that you hold in your hands.

For technical help, including the checking out of ideas, location of sources, and correction of the manuscript in terms of content, I thank Ben Asen; John Deely; Carl Dehne; Mary Dunn; Harvey Egan; Gérard Ferreyrolles; Scott Granowski; Jay Hammond; Sr. Catherine Thérèse Hubert, VHM; Sr. Jeanne Charlotte Johnson, VHM; Tom Krettek; Mark Lewis; John Markey;

Peter Martens; Michael McClymond; David Meconi; Viviane Mellinghoff-Bourgerie; Geoff Miller; Lloyd Moote; Bryan Norton; John O'Malley; Louis Pascoe; Claude Pavur; Julie Riley; Louis Roy; David Shocklee; Corrine Smith; Nicolas Steeves; Eleonore Stump; Kasia Sullivan; Tobias Winright; and Tom Worcester. Special thanks to Wendy Mayer for tracking down and commenting on a number of references to the writings of John Chrysostom—a kindness occasioned by yet another kindness: that of Cornelia Horn, who first put me in contact with Wendy. In the notes I present Wendy's judgments regarding—and in some cases, translations of—the Chrysostom material. Special thanks go also to my research assistant, Elissa Cutter, for helping to establish the text, looking up references and secondary sources, proofreading the translation, creating the indexes, and performing a number of other essential tasks. On a related note, the hero's award goes to Bill Harmless, who voluntarily reviewed, corrected, and updated the patristic citations, and who graciously put himself on call for my many related questions. While the present volume owes any academic rigor to the efforts of these generous people, I take full responsibility for any remaining errors.

For the correction of the manuscript in terms of form, I am particularly grateful to Karen Clauser; Mother M. Regina Pacis Coury, FSGM; Carl Dehne; Harvey Egan; Garth Hallett; Sr. Catherine Thérèse Hubert, VHM; Sr. M. Anne Maskey, FSGM; Fred McLeod; George Murphy; Steve Schoenig; Sr. M. Rita Severson, FSGM; Kasia Sullivan; and Tom Worcester. I especially would like to thank Bernie Owens, who read an early draft of the manuscript through from start to finish, and Benjamin Parviz, who cheerfully sacrificed several summer days to help me check the page proofs. Just as these people deserve credit for anything that may come across well in this volume, I again will answer for any oversights that remain.

For the publication of the text, I thank the Editorial Staff at the Northern Illinois University Press and their collaborators, in particular Shaun Allshouse, Susan Bean, Amy Farranto, Julia Fauci, and Judith Robey, for their support of the project and for seeing it through to completion. I also thank those scholars who reviewed both the proposal and the final manuscript before publication. Their suggestions and encouragement have directed my work and have made this a much better book.

In closing, a word of gratitude for the Visitation Sisters of Philadelphia, who invited me to preside at a novena in honor of the Sacred Heart in June and July 2011. Given the close relationship between Fr. La Colombière and the Visitation, I feel particularly indebted for the friendship and commitment of these women—religious daughters of Saint Francis de Sales and Saint Jeanne de Chantal, whose spirit continues to animate them just as it influenced the composition of these sermons over three hundred twenty-five years ago.

Thanks go finally to my brother Jesuits—including Fr. La Colombière—who have inspired me with their patience, generosity, and integrity.

Introduction

Devotion to the Sacred Heart has played a major role in modern Catholic culture. For evidence, one need only consider the number of churches, institutions, and publications named either for the Sacred Heart or for Margaret Mary Alacoque (1647–90), the nun whose visions of Jesus launched a renewal of this devotion in late seventeenth-century France.[1] Yet her experience might have gone unnoticed by all but the members of her own religious community had she not met a sympathetic confessor, the Jesuit priest Claude La Colombière (1641–82), whose superior had sent him to direct a grade school in Paray-le-Monial, the town where Margaret Mary lived. Claude met Margaret Mary shortly after arriving in Paray, and in the course of their conversations grew convinced of the authenticity of her unusual prayer experiences. Claude's approval in turn gave Margaret Mary's superiors reason to take her seriously, and her practice of the devotion began to spread. Not surprisingly, Claude himself gained a reputation for promoting devotion to the Sacred Heart under this new form. Such titles as "apostle of the Sacred Heart" often appear associated with his name, and his retreat notes include a prayer of consecration to the Sacred Heart.[2]

Claude was born February 2, 1641, in the French town of Saint-Symphorien-d'Ozon, located between Lyon and Vienne in what is today the Rhône department in the central-eastern region of Rhône-Alps.[3] His paternal ancestry traces back to Gaude, a fourteenth-century nobleman who served as secretary of the Duke of Burgundy. The family home of the Gaudes, named "La Colombière," in turn gave the family its surname. In addition, Claude's ancestors had worked for generations as civil law notaries, further contributing to his mystique as a man of privilege who died a martyr-victim at the age of forty-one.[4] While these considerations have fueled popular devotion to him, culminating in his beatification (June 16, 1929) and canonization (May 31, 1992) by the Roman Catholic Church, they at times have eclipsed appreciation for his qualities as a literary figure. Between 1684 and 1697, there appeared five successive French-language editions of his pulpit oratory, which included one funeral address, ten meditations on the Passion of Jesus, and some seventy-eight sermons, relating to feasts of the liturgical cycle and a wide variety of religious themes.[5] Claude preached primarily in the church of the Jesuit College in Lyon (1673–74) and before Mary of Modena (1658–1718), then Duchess of York, in post-Restoration London (1676–78). Unfortunately, we have neither manuscripts of the sermons nor records of exactly who prepared the sermons for publication, apart from an early indication that Claude certainly could not have edited them himself. Nevertheless, the appearance of multiple editions of the sermons in the space of only thirteen years indicates a sustained interest in Claude among his contemporaries and grounds his reputation as a master of Christian eloquence.[6]

I

Preaching during Claude's lifetime developed under a variety of influences, most notably the thematic sermons of the late medieval period and the humanistic retrieval of classical letters during the Renaissance.[7] As a student at Jesuit institutions, known as *collèges*, Claude received an education in this literary tradition following the systematic approach that Ignatius of Loyola (1491–1556), the founder of the Society of Jesus, or Jesuits, had encountered during his time in Paris.[8] In 1599 the Society formally adopted a *Ratio studiorum* or "plan of study" for training its members.[9] A Jesuit began this structured course with three years of classical grammar followed by a year each of humanities and Ciceronian rhetoric. Taking Aristotle as his guide, the student then would progress to the study of philosophy and metaphysics, which in turn would serve as the foundation for learning Thomistic theology. These three levels correspond roughly to what we know today as grade school, high school, and university or even graduate study. By the end of the program, the man would have acquired the ability to speak about God convincingly and with some degree of eloquence and theological sophistication in a variety of contexts, including the pulpit.

The literary conventions within which Claude composed his sermons thus derive mostly from his formation in classical letters, above all the rhetoric of Cicero.[10] In October of 1650, at the age of nine, Claude entered Our Lady of Good Help, the Jesuit grammar school in Lyon, the building of which today houses the city hall of the fifth arrondissement. The Jesuits had established the school in 1628 to handle overflow from the larger College of the Holy Trinity, for which they had assumed responsibility in 1564. Together these institutions offered a complete classical education following the program outlined in the *Ratio*. Upon completing his grammar studies at Our Lady of Good Help, Claude moved in the fall of 1653 to the College of the Holy Trinity, located on the other side of the Saône

River.[11] There he took one year of humanities and two of rhetoric, the latter consisting of a year each of eloquence and poetics. Upon finishing these studies Claude entered the second course, consisting of two years of philosophy, which covered physics, mathematics, and logic. During these five years he met Jean Papon (1605–72), who functioned as his student monitor and later would serve as his novice master, and François de La Chaize (1624–1709), future provincial of Lyon and confessor of Louis XIV. In the summer of 1676, Fr. La Chaize would appoint Claude to minister in the English court, where Claude probably refined and perhaps even composed the sermons that appear in this volume.[12]

As for Claude's academic formation, one cannot overestimate the influence of Cicero in the training received at the Jesuit colleges.[13] Teachers judged their students' successes primarily according to whether they could write as did the great Roman orator and in so doing become an *alter Tullius*. It thus comes as no surprise that Claude spoke publicly of Cicero as "three times the greatest," even if he did so primarily for rhetorical effect.[14] Recognizing this dedication to Ciceronian rhetoric helps us to appreciate the ample use of rhetorical figures in his discourses and sermons and the extent to which classical literary culture conditioned Jesuit ministry of the gospel.[15] Training in the humanities enabled the students to express their understanding of both the created order, which they studied in philosophy, and the divine plan, which they considered in theology. In this way the unity between knowledge and its expression played a central role in the Ciceronian program of "eloquence joined with wisdom" that the Jesuits appropriated from classical letters.[16]

Rather than outline a list of principles or rules, the humanist project thus emphasized the person of the orator as one who knew something and could make use of it. But for Cicero, as later for Quintilian, the orator must act with integrity. This principle resonates with the Ignatian search for intellectual, social, and moral maturity as well as with Claude's concern to sanctify his audience through preaching.[17] In this sense, the Jesuits taught Latin both to transmit the philosophical tradition and to help students acquire the Latin language itself for practical reasons, including advanced studies in view of a career in the church or in civic life.[18] Again however, both Cicero and the *Ratio* focus on educating the whole person, resulting in a "humanism of formation" more than a "humanism of erudition."[19] By grounding the principle that each person stands responsible before God, this philosophy therefore makes education an enterprise both moral and religious.[20] If the program thus pertains to "the harmonious development of the intellect and of the will, mind, and soul in order to educate well-prepared apostles in view of the Kingdom of Christ on Earth," then the immediate end comes to bear on the *"eloquentia perfecta* [perfect eloquence] that was, for the Jesuits as for the Renaissance educators, the union of knowledge and eloquence, or the proper use of reason joined to cultivated expression."[21] Studying and teaching the classics using a uniform technique would train Claude to maintain this theoretical unity which appears so clearly and beautifully in his discourses and sermons.

II

Having nearly completed his study of philosophy, Claude took a few weeks of vacation at the beginning of September 1658 before leaving on October 23 for Avignon, where he entered the Jesuit novitiate of Saint Louis. King Louis XIV made two visits to the novitiate during this time, once in December 1658 and again in March 1660. Claude, having lost his mother in August 1660, passed in mid-October from the novitiate to the College of Avignon for his third and final year of philosophy, pronouncing first vows at the end of the month. The college was located in the house of La Motte, an ancient ecclesiastical residence that today serves as the municipal library for the city of Avignon. He spent a total of six years there, including his year of philosophy studies (1660–61), four years teaching grammar (1661–65), and one year teaching humanities (1665–66). At the beginning of his final year of teaching, Claude delivered what probably was his first public address, a Latin discourse entitled *Laus panegyristae*, "In Praise of the Panegyrist."[22] This formal exercise given at the beginning of the academic year enlisted rhetorical technique both to encourage the students and to entertain the invited guests. More importantly, it gave Claude practical experience in the art of epideictic oratory, the genre of classical rhetoric that promotes progress in virtue—progress that Trent identified as a primary goal for preachers.[23]

At the invitation of Guillaume Chabrand, rector of the college, Claude delivered his second public address toward the end of the academic year, on the penultimate day of the octave of the feast of the canonization of Francis de Sales, at the first of the two monasteries of the Visitation in Avignon.[24] The visit of Francis de Sales to the college forty-four years earlier, which Francis made at the same time as the visits of both the Duke of Savoy and King Louis XIII, would have remained fresh in local memory. According to a contemporary account, Claude took as the theme of his address the riddle of Samson: "out of the strong came something sweet."[25] Although we do not have the text of this discourse, we can interpret his participation at the event as early evidence of both his devotion to the saintly bishop and his aptitude for public speaking.[26] In accord with Jesuit custom, his superiors may have singled him out already for special training in order to develop his preaching skills.[27] Regardless, the occasion introduced Claude into the ranks of his confreres François Bening, Jehan Pioneau, and Anto-

nio Possevino, all of whom had offered panegyrics on behalf of popes, prelates, and men of state, recalling the Jesuit canonizations of Ignatius and
Francis Xavier (1622) and, during Claude's own lifetime, Francis Borgia
(1672).[28] For the great pulpit orator Jacques-Bénigne Bossuet (1627–1704),
the composition of panegyrics would serve as a kind of "laboratory" for the
delivery of his funeral orations—the only published preaching of his that
he himself had edited.[29] We could presume the same for Claude, although
we have the edition of only one such text.[30]

Having finished his teaching internship or *regency*, Claude received a
mission from Paul Oliva, the superior general of the Jesuits, to study theology in Paris at the prestigious College of Clermont, later renamed Louis-
le-Grand after receiving royal status under its namesake. There between
1666 and 1670 he completed his intellectual formation, established contact
with the literary world, and according to one later account, served as tutor
to the sons of the new finance minister, Jean-Baptiste Colbert.[31]

The decision of the general to send Claude to Paris for studies seems
somewhat surprising, given that Claude's provincial had characterized him
to the general in 1665 as rather mediocre.[32] The public success that Claude
had enjoyed with his discourses in Avignon may already have won him
notoriety in Rome, as a personal letter to Claude from the general himself
suggests.[33] In any case, thanks to his stay in the community of the college, Claude would have had the opportunity to meet two important Jesuit
literary figures: René Rapin (1621–87), who authored a theory of preaching that Claude probably used as a guide for his own pulpit oratory, and
Dominique Bouhours (1628–1702), a grammarian and literary reformer
with whom Claude later corresponded.[34] Evidence also exists that the law-
yer Olivier Patru (1604–81) knew and respected Claude and even sought
his judgment on points of French grammar.[35] In support of this theory, a
thinly-veiled éloge to Patru appears in the discourse *Laus oratoris galli* that
Claude delivered at the College of the Trinity in 1672.[36]

With his academic formation finally accomplished, Claude returned in
1670 to Lyon where he taught rhetoric at the College of the Trinity for three
years (1670–73) and served for one year as preacher in the college church
(1673–74). At the beginning of his second and third years at the college he
again gave the address at the beginning of the academic year to the student
body and invited guests.[37] These two Latin discourses, along with the one
that he had delivered at the college in Avignon, reveal his mastery of Ciceronian rhetoric and introduce the key term *eloquentia* ("eloquence") that
operates in these texts in precisely the same way that *sainteté* ("holiness")
functions in the sermons. Just as the secular virtue of eloquence dwelt in
the orator as hero of the classical world, expressing itself in his words and
actions, so does the sacred virtue of holiness "inhabit" the saint as hero of
the Christian community. In this way, the subject matter of both the Latin

discourses and the sermons falls within the general continuity of the humanist program of the *Ratio* to train students to live and speak well.

III

Upon receiving the charge of church preacher in 1673, Claude began the ministry of the word that would occupy him for five years, up until his return from England at the end of 1678. Forty-eight years after his death, a contemporary wrote the following about Claude's tenure at the College of the Trinity:

> Father Claude de [*sic*] la Colombière, after having done his studies there, before and after his entrance into the Society, taught rhetoric there for several years; he preached there on Sundays, worked there, and owed to [the college] nearly all the sermons that he preached thereafter, during two years in the English court. . . . It is certain that Fr. La Colombière, dead at the age of 41 years, did not place the final hand on his Sermons. But his way of thinking—always apt and often very sensitive—his language—always pure and correct—the feelings that fill his Sermons, and the great success that they have had and still have, all reveal in him a great Master.[38]

According to the author, Claude was not the final editor of his sermons, for which we have no autographs. For this reason, and because his sermons bear no dates, we can say little about whether his style or thought evolved over the years, or how the circumstances in which he preached influenced the composition of any particular sermon. But we can say that the published texts exhibit all the marks of the classic French style, which developed in the second half of the seventeenth century. Note that here, *classic* refers not to the influence of ancient literature but to the fact that this style itself—with its double exordium, division into two or three points, balanced use of stylistic elements and levels (high or grand, middle, and low), and focus on helping the listener to make virtuous decisions—set a standard for subsequent preachers.[39] Yet even apart from these considerations, the sole fact that the publication of his sermons enjoyed success following his death makes them interesting as an index of late seventeenth-century literary and devotional attitudes.

Although Claude lived in community with the professors of the college during this time, he belonged to the group of Jesuits devoted to ministries outside the house—a group that included catechists, preachers, and directors of various confraternities. Beyond the charge of preaching on Sundays and feast days in the college church and elsewhere in Lyon, he certainly held some responsibility for catechism and for working with the confraternities. As such, his role would have resembled that of a modern-day parish priest or, more closely, the pastor or chaplain of a church located on the premises of a Jesuit college or university. Given his apparent devotion to Francis de Sales, it is worth noting that *Monseigneur de Genève* himself preached in the church of the Trinity on December 4, 1622, the Second Sunday of Advent, just three weeks before his death at the Visitation convent in Lyon. Furthermore, at the beginning of Claude's brief tenure as church preacher, he had the occasion to meet his future directee, Mary of Modena, during her visit to the college on Sunday, October 23, 1673. Mary, the daughter of Alfonso IV d'Este, Duke of Modena, had just celebrated, on September 30, her marriage by proxy to James Stuart, the brother of Charles II of England. Note too that her time in Lyon also included a stop at the Visitation convent in order to venerate the heart of Francis de Sales.[40] Given this coincidence, it seems plausible that Claude would have made her acquaintance at the college and that Mary would have heard him preach at Sunday mass.

Claude finished his preaching in the college church on September 8, 1674, and at the end of September moved to Saint Joseph House, on the peninsula of Ainay in central Lyon, where he began his tertianship, or "third year" of probation. This final stage of Jesuit training derives its name from already having completed the two years of novitiate that begin the formation program. During this third year, which lasted from September 1674 until February 1675, Claude went through the novitiate experience of the thirty-day prayer retreat of the Spiritual Exercises for a second time (October 18 to November 21), engaged in pastoral ministry, and assessed his life in preparation for solemn vows. His retreat notes reveal that he had taken a private vow during the course of the retreat to follow the Jesuit rule to the letter, on pain of mortal sin.[41] In a letter dated November 20, 1674, the Jesuit general, still Fr. Oliva, authorized Claude to pronounce final vows, which he did on February 2, 1675, presumably in the chapel of the tertian community.

Claude then left for Paray-le-Monial, located in what today is the Saône-et-Loire department of the Burgundy region, in the east-central part of France. Since 999, Paray had fallen under the jurisdiction of the great Benedictine monastery of Cluny, represented by a prior and a number of monks to whom Paray owes the designation "le Monial."[42] From 1622 on, the Jesuits had tried to counter the strong Protestant influence in the town by giving catechetical instruction to children. During the 1626 Lenten mission of Jesuit Fr. Paul de Barry, a number of girls complained that the lack of a convent at Paray kept them from entering religious life. In response, Barry contacted the Visitation convent of Lyon-en-Bellecour and obtained permission for their nuns to establish a community in Paray.[43] Eventually the town asked the Jesuits to send a grammar teacher to work in the municipal college, and this mission outpost developed into a formal residence.

Upon arriving in Paray in February 1675, Claude took the place of his ex-novice master, Jean Papon, as superior of the Jesuit community and began to develop the small school. Near the end of the month he had made contact with the monastery of the Visitation, where the mystic Margaret Mary Alacoque had been living for nearly four years.[44] The visions of Jesus the Sacred Heart of which she spoke and the asceticism she practiced had raised the suspicions of the members of her community as well as the authorities whom her superiors had consulted about her. Providentially for the young woman, Claude visited the convent between March 6 and 9 of 1675, during which time the two met. Having spoken with Margaret Mary, Claude declared to her superior, Marie-Françoise de Saumaise, that Margaret Mary was "a graced soul." By thus validating Margaret Mary's religious experience, his judgment contributed to re-found devotion to the Sacred Heart in its modern period.

For this reason, most people who have heard of Claude today associate him primarily with this devotion. Yet neither the term *Sacré-Cœur* nor the phrase *cœur du Christ* appears anywhere in his published writings, with the important exception of the famous prayer of consecration. In contrast, *cœur de Jésus* appears a number of times, although mostly in either the greeting or the closing of his letters.[45] In fact, although his sermons speak of dedication to Jesus and confidence in God's mercy, they say little explicitly about the Heart of Christ. Indeed, the central theme in his preaching is not *Jésus* as such but rather *sainteté*—the holiness that appears in the feelings, actions, and thoughts of holy people.

Claude had plenty of opportunities to encounter such people through his ministry in and around Paray-le-Monial. Apart from his principal work as superior of the Jesuit community and director of the little college, Claude established connections at the local parish, Saint Nicolas, and with communities of women religious, including the Benedictines, Ursulines, and Visitandines. Just before Easter he left on mission to the Cistercian abbey of the Bénissons-Dieu, located north of Roanne, where he delivered the funeral oration for Françoise II de Nérestang, abbess between 1654 and 1675. At her behest, the Jesuits had given every three years since 1671 a Lenten mission at the monastery, and Claude would have honored this obligation in March of 1675. The Society had a similar contract to preach three times per week at Saint Nicolas parish in Paray, during both Advent and Lent. In addition to these pastoral obligations, which in all likelihood informed the sermons in the present volume, Claude also served as spiritual director for a number of women in the town and in the various religious communities mentioned above. In some cases these relationships continued for years by correspondence. His obvious affection for the people of Paray and the surrounding region appears both in his letters and in the two visits he made to Paray toward the end of his life.

IV

Sometime in August 1676, Claude learned that his superiors intended to send him to England as chaplain to the Duchess of York. Having settled, on September 16, some outstanding debts concerning the buildings he had bought in April to develop the college in Paray, he left for Roanne, arriving in Paris on October 3 and departing for London two days later. Claude stayed in England for twenty-six months, only twenty-two of which had to do with his mission to the duchess; but after their posthumous publication in 1684, the writings from this period would make him famous.

On October 3/13, Claude moved into Saint James's Palace and preached his first sermon on November 1/11.[46] Thereafter he preached on Sundays and feasts, gave a series of sermons for Lent 1677 and 1678, and regularly visited the duchess for confession and spiritual conversation. He also seems to have collaborated with Mary's secretary, Edward Colman, who had corresponded with Fr. La Chaize.[47] In addition he appears to have engaged in various ministries outside the palace, including with the religious congregation of Mary Ward, which lived secretly at Saint Martin's Lane in London. Claude began his annual retreat the 21st/31st of January 1677, finishing the 29th of January/8th of February.[48] As tradition has it, a provincial congregation of the Society of Jesus took place in London between the 24th and the 26th of April of the same year.[49]

Claude most likely continued his ministry at the court for the following year and a half before the "papist terror" began, in August of 1678, at the instigation of an Anglican priest by the name of Titus Oates (1649–1705).[50] This strange chapter of British history, marked by general hysteria and collective delirium, would have a profound effect on Claude. Essentially, Oates claimed to have evidence of a plot to assassinate Charles II, replace him with his Catholic brother, James, and then carry out a massacre of the Protestants. Coincidentally, Claude began to cough up blood the day the accusations broke, the 14th/24th of August, which marked the beginning of the tuberculosis from which he would suffer for nearly three years. Having finished his preaching sometime after the 8th/18th of September, Claude was arrested in his rooms at two in the morning of Thursday the 14th/24th and taken into custody as accomplice to the conspiracy. Here we see, as Larissa Taylor has shown for the late medieval period, the obvious dangers of preaching in a context where church and state remain very much at odds.[51]

On Saturday, November 16/26, the order was given to transfer Claude the next day to the now-defunct King's Bench prison in Southwark, accused on the sole witness of Olivier du Fiquet, a fellow Frenchman with whom Claude apparently had discussed matters of faith. On Tuesday, November 19/29, a certain François Verdier confirmed under oath the word of Du Fiquet. The sessions that began Thursday, November 21/December 1 at the High Chamber would end the following Saturday, November 23/December 3 with a decree that Claude be banished from the kingdom. After a delay of nearly two weeks, during which Claude remained in prison, Charles gave the order of banishment on Friday, 6/16 December, at which time Claude was put into the custody of John Bradley, one of the king's messengers. Claude's health having worsened considerably in prison, Charles gave him ten days of residence under watch so that he might regain his strength for the return to France.

Claude arrived in Paris in the middle of January 1679, seriously ill with the lung disease to which he would succumb only two years later. He stayed first on rue Saint-Antoine at the professed house of the Jesuits, which today houses the Lycée Charlemagne. There he was welcomed by Étienne de Champs, who had served as his superior at the College of Clermont years earlier. Claude left for Lyon at the end of the month, stopping in Dijon at the Jesuit College of the Godrans for some meetings and visits. Sometime after February 4 he arrived at Paray-le-Monial, where he visited the Ursuline and Visitation convents. On the 14th he again left for Lyon, stopping in Roanne before arriving at the College of the Trinity on March 11. Because of his illness, he departed on or about April 2 for his family residence at Saint-Symphorien-d'Ozon to rest and did not return to Lyon until the end of May. It was during this second stay at the college that he is said to have composed a polemical treatise in defense of a fellow Jesuit whom Étienne Le Camus, then bishop of Grenoble, had accused, in June, of impropriety.[52]

Other than a brief trip to the monastery of Condrieu, Claude stayed in Lyon until the month of August or September, at which time he again was sent to rest at Saint-Symphorien, where he remained for a month. With his health somewhat improved, he returned to Lyon in September or October and served for a year and a half as spiritual father for the Jesuit philosophy students at the *grand collège*. His community included both Joseph de Gallifet, future promoter of the Sacred Heart devotion, and Nicolas La Pesse, preacher in the college church and author of the biographical note in the first edition of the sermons. During this period Claude gave an instruction on the annual retreat, which instruction was published for the first time in the editor's preface to the first edition of the Spiritual Retreat (1684).[53] Claude returned to Paray-le-Monial in April 1681, again coughing up blood. Although he had planned to visit Saint-Symphorien in January of the following year, he remained in Paray at the insistence of Margaret Mary Alacoque and died at seven in the evening of February 15, in the Jesuit community.

V

Claude La Colombière made a lasting contribution to the history of the Grand Siècle largely because he enjoyed a place at the cultural and political centers of his day. Note that he received much the same classical education in Jesuit colleges as did many of his famous contemporaries, including Louis Bourdaloue, who studied at Holy Mary of Bourges; Corneille and Fontenelle at Rouen; Bossuet at the College of the Godrans in Dijon; Descartes and Mersenne at La Flèche; and Fleury, Francis de Sales, and Molière at Claude's alma mater, the College of Clermont. Throughout his life, he appears to have distinguished himself by his exercise of good judgment and his above-average intelligence. And despite rather fragile health, he engaged wholeheartedly in the works of his religious community up until an early death from pulmonary tuberculosis. Without a doubt, Claude owes a debt of gratitude to his religious superiors for enabling him to develop his natural gifts for study, spiritual direction, and public speaking. As a testament to their confidence in him, he left behind a small but impressive body of writings in the areas of classical rhetoric, Christian spirituality, and pulpit oratory, the latter of which he developed in an England torn by religious war and political intrigue. Finally, his spiritual direction of Margaret Mary Alacoque and his chaplaincy to Mary of Modena earned him important footnotes in the histories of the Devotion to the Sacred Heart and the Restoration Stuart Court, respectively.

It must be said, however, that despite his spiritual insight and talent for public speaking, his sermons do not indicate a great deal of thematic or stylistic originality. Preaching on saints and holiness abounds in the seventeenth century, and his oratorical choices closely resemble those of his more distinguished colleagues, notably Bossuet and Bourdaloue.[54] In any case, the present work does not aim to show that Claude introduced new themes or rhetorical treatments into the history of preaching but rather to reveal how he worked within and helped to create the stylistic conventions of the day by drawing on scripture and the Church Fathers in an attempt to convert his auditors.[55] Like most Catholic preachers after Trent, Claude seems to have observed the Tridentine directive that sermons should offer instruction and exhortation so that listeners might make decisions conducive to achieving eternal life.[56] With his contemporaries, Claude followed this intention by taking a hybrid approach to his craft, expounding on scripture but avoiding the line-by-line exegesis of the humanists while incorporating elements from the epideictic genre of ancient rhetoric.[57] In this way he brought a balanced use of rhetorical art into the pulpit so as to please as well as to instruct and move his audience, hereby promoting the development of French classicism in the second half of the seventeenth century.[58]

Given all this, one may wonder why Claude's preaching does not enjoy the same reputation today that it apparently did in the past. Even if we cannot call him a great innovator, certainly we can admire the beauty and integrity of his artistic sensibility. But to approach his sermons only in this way would be to treat them largely as historical artifacts—something like literary museum pieces. The present commentary suggests a different course, by considering the dynamic vision of the human person that emerges from his preaching. How does Claude speak of conversion, and what might this mean for readers today? In reflecting on these questions, I attempt to rethink his insights using contemporary philosophical categories. In short, I aim to transpose his vision into a conceptual frame of reference more clearly compatible with the notion of reality itself as constantly evolving.[59] In so doing, I hope to demonstrate both the relevance of Claude's preaching for contemporary audiences and how this relevance is even conceivable. From this perspective, apart from offering a historico-literary examination of his preaching, this study locates itself firmly in the contemporary quest for a new unity between the theoretical and the practical in Christianity.[60]

Following Peter Bayley, my inquiry starts by making close readings of the texts themselves.[61] This method reveals in Claude's sermons a representational logic that in turn can serve as an interpretive key for understanding their composition, structure, and effect. Taken as a whole, the sermons imply a vision of reality wherein concrete, sensible events establish evolving, law-like tendencies perceptible to the human mind. In other words, what happens in the world—what we do and what is done to us—has real effects that persist through the formation of habits, where *habit* is understood broadly to mean laws of nature as well as virtues, vices, allergies, and indeed any general tendency of reality to act in a predictable way.

The idea of habit formation has a long history in Western thought, appearing notably today in the field of virtue ethics.[62] Claude would have encountered the ethical and moral relevance of this tradition in his study of Aristotle and Thomas Aquinas and so would have composed his sermons with their conceptual grammar in mind.[63] Yet nowhere in his sermons does he offer a systematic account or defense of their principles. Recall that Claude understood his preaching not as philosophical or theological exposition or disputation, but as an effort to convert his listeners. And so, while he may use Thomistic language to present his ideas, his preaching suggests a world that we can conceptualize as the relation among three terms—*quality, fact,* and *law*—where *quality* represents the "how" of reality, *fact* represents the "that," and *law* represents the "what." These categories derive from the philosophy of American polymath Charles Sanders Peirce (1831–1914), whose thought informs both the analysis in this section and the commentary in the notes that accompany the translations.[64]

Peirce's triadic framework can further illuminate Claude's discussions of holiness or *sainteté*—the fundamental Christian orientation that involves the taking of divine habits. When people act or are acted upon in a way that promotes holiness, the habit or principle of holiness begins to govern them, as apparent in their feelings, actions, and thoughts. As a result they manifest the qualities of holiness—e.g., humility, charity, and confidence in God—and are empowered to transmit holiness to others. In this view, the habit or principle of holiness constitutes "what" exists, and the experience of acting or being acted upon assures "that" it exists, while its existence appears according to the "how" of such qualities as humility and charity. Moving out from the moral realm, one could make similar analyses of the tendencies to avoid pain, to laugh at a joke, or to sweat on a hot day. For this reason, I argue that habituation is not just one theme among others for Claude but rather the central concept that orders his whole understanding of the moral life. In other words, habit taking—understood primarily in terms of virtues and vices—forms both the conceptual and the thematic focus of his preaching. Furthermore, these categories can both account for the phenomenon of human conversion and explain how his sermons themselves developed and can continue to affect audiences today.

With these preliminary remarks in mind, I turn to consider the sources upon which Claude most likely drew as he developed his preaching style. Given his devotion to Francis de Sales, it seems probable that Claude had read the letter that Francis wrote in 1604 to André Frémyot, recently named archbishop of Bourges.[65] In this letter, Francis, himself appointed bishop of Geneva just two years prior, presents a fully-developed homiletic theory reflecting the reforms of the Council of Trent (1545–63), which had emphasized preaching as the "chief duty" of the bishop.[66] His emphasis on a brief, simple, direct style, focused on the scriptures and aimed at avoiding vice and cultivating virtue, strongly influenced preaching in the first part of the seventeenth century, and this orientation continues to appear throughout the sermons of La Colombière and his contemporaries. Soon after writing this letter, Francis edited his correspondence to Louise de Charmoisy and published it, probably toward the end of 1608, as the *Introduction to the Devout Life*.[67] A very popular book and apparently a favorite of Claude's, the *Introduction* dedicates the whole third section to the practice of virtue.[68] De Sales's adherent Jean-Pierre Camus (1584–1652), consecrated bishop of Belley the following year, would continue to spread the Tridentine reform in the Salesian spirit through his own widely-published sermons.[69] The choice of appropriate or "correct" topics—above all the appeal to holy models for Christian conduct—would play a major role in both his and Claude's respective styles.

In all probability, Claude also had read and, as Charrier suggests, perhaps even copied by hand the *Réflexions sur l'éloquence de la chaire* (1671) of his confrere René Rapin, with whom Claude had lived at the College of Clermont.[70] From sources such as these and from his studies of classical rhetoric, ancient philosophy, and scholastic theology, Claude synthesized his own *poétique de la chaire* to guide him in the pastoral art of sermon composition. While we have from Claude no formal treatise on preaching, he explains in the first sermon for the Nativity of the Holy Virgin that "a preacher ought to have nothing so much in mind as the salvation of his

auditors."[71] Claude already had introduced this sentiment in the second
sermon for the Feast of All Saints—quite possibly his first preaching at the
English court—when he protested that in obeying the orders of the duchess, he would aim only "to work for the sanctification of his auditors."[72]
He writes elsewhere that in order to attain this end, one must preach "the
truth" and "virtue" everywhere, "even in the courts of princes"—an apparent reference to his mission in England.[73]

This idea that a preacher must proclaim the gospel in all places determines both the content of Claude's sermons and his manner of treating
that content. Moreover, he seems to understand preaching as a universal vocation among Christians, which the Spirit gives to all the baptized.[74]
And he appears to have believed that preachers fulfill their office not only
by attracting others to Jesus through the ministry of the word but also
simply by singing the praises of Jesus: "the task of a Christian orator, if I am
not mistaken, is here to accompany the triumphant Jesus with the praise
due him, and to celebrate the virtues by which he merited the reception he
received in heaven."[75] In this spirit, Claude considered his vocation that of
a *prédicateur évangélique*—an "evangelical preacher."[76] This attitude situates him squarely in the Salesian tradition, in which the charge to preach
the gospel plays a key role.[77] Yet while Claude thus seems to model himself
after the apostles, to whom he refers as the first to proclaim the gospel,
he clearly sees Jesus as the original preacher who sends others on mission
to continue his own work. Ever the Ciceronian, Claude associates Jesus
explicitly with *éloquence* by characterizing his responses to Pilate in terms
that suggest the classical orator.[78] Furthermore, Claude explains that Jesus "teaches, by word and example, a wisdom more excellent than that for
which the Greeks have given so many precepts; and this wisdom is nothing
other than holiness."[79]

La Colombière thus presents his theory of pulpit oratory in terms of virtues both profane and sacred. His sermons reveal that, as he sees it, virtues
and vices, which function as general laws of thought and action, initiate and
reinforce themselves by concrete, reactive events, and manifest themselves
through a variety of sensible qualities. Note however that this fundamental
dynamic does not require an Aristotelian frame of reference, such as Claude
would have learned in the Jesuit colleges, in order to render it conceivable.
In point of fact, Claude himself seems to have recognized certain conceptual
problems arising from the Aristotelian worldview, as when he points out the
difficulty of conceiving the human person as a body informed by a soul.[80] We
can avoid this particular problem by thinking of a human being as the interaction of sensible qualities, concrete reactions, and general habits.[81] Using
these categories, we still can view Claude's pulpit oratory as a poetic expression of his intuitions regarding the graced experience of humanity. But at
the same time we might see more clearly the extent to which his preaching

offered and continues to offer occasions for realizing virtuous dispositions—godly habits of feeling, action, and thought—in his auditors and readers. A coherent anthropology thus emerges from his preaching, which evokes the capacity of human beings to take habits, and uses rhetorical form to bring about habituation in the audience.[82]

My analysis thus far has taken place at the phenomenological level, in the sense that I have been dealing mainly with what actually appears to the mind. The discussion has shown how one might reach a coherent conception of experience, as La Colombière speaks of it, using the categories of quality, fact, and law. In an attempt to broaden and develop this understanding of La Colombière's intuition, I now shift from phenomenology to the normative sciences, which consider experiential phenomena not in themselves but in relation to their ends. As such, the normative sciences divide into esthetics, which considers the ideal in itself; ethics, which studies the ideal in relation to deliberate action; and logic, which deals with thinking in relation to approved conduct.[83] The remainder of the present section will focus on the third normative science, which studies the means of acting reasonably, i.e., how one ought to think. This discussion will enable us to conceptualize clearly and adequately the continuity that makes all representation possible, both in La Colombière's preaching and in every other context.

For the purposes of this study, making the move from phenomenology to the normative sciences involves rethinking the phenomenological categories of quality, fact, and law in logical terms. This move generates the corresponding categories of *sign, object,* and *interpretant.*[84] Within this semiotic (Greek *sēma* "sign") relation, *sign* corresponds to a quality or feeling in that a sign is simply as it is and, as such, is something that needs to be interpreted. More exactly, a sign is a representation of an object according to a general principle that governs both the initial representation and any subsequent representation of that object. According to this logic, an object produces a sign, which in turn generates in the interpreter a second-order sign—the interpretant—in the form of a feeling, action, or thought, thus making conceivable a potentially infinite number of significations, each of which is grounded in the same object.[85] This is to say that the interpretant—as in the case of a rhetorical performance or a virtuous act—is not determined in advance; rather, its determination comes about through a general, evolving principle—for example, *éloquence* or *sainteté*—that governs the artist or the holy person. In this way the concept of interpretant accounts for the appearance of a general principle in various concrete representations.

To illustrate, consider the notion of *éloquence.* In the discourse *Augusti Caesaris aetas,* delivered at the College of the Trinity in 1671, La Colombière argues that the generation of Cicero had perfected the art of oratory to the point that no one ever could hope to outshine it. Yet the following year, in his discourse *Laus oratoris galli* (1672), he turns around and argues that the contemporary French orators had indeed surpassed Roman *éloquence*! What matters here, however, is not that Claude seems to change his mind from one year to the next, at first praising the ancients only later to argue in favor of the moderns.[86] What matters is that, as a reality common to historically different eras, *éloquence* itself functions as a principle of continuity among various expressions in these distinct cultures and worlds.

In this sense, our goal is not to discern what Claude "really thought" but rather to see how the very possibility of a comparison between the Romans and the French requires the notion of continuity in order to put them into relation. This same idea appears in the *habitudes* that give coherence to particular, concrete acts of the same individual and thus assure the integrity of the evolving, emerging reality that is a particular human person. The idea of continuity likewise makes possible the relation between a literary production and the lived experience of the author, i.e., the text and the world to which that text refers. And perhaps most importantly, it renders conceivable the relationship among authors, their writings, and those whom their experience, represented in their writings, affects. In semiotic terms, the interpretant—the third term of the logical triad—preserves the historicity of the literary event while making it significative and therefore efficacious. This approach thus provides a conceptual frame of reference for understanding sermons in terms of both literary and historical considerations.[87] Indeed, the virtue of holiness—grounded in the objective reality of God, signified in the sermon, and interpreted in the listener—constitutes the original bond between preacher and audience.

This analysis of Claude's preaching holds far-reaching implications for contemporary theology and the life of the Christian community. Having exposed the general logical structure of any text, whereby words and groups of words represent some other thing to a mind, we can use this analysis to conceptualize any particular experience of affective, moral, intellectual, or religious conversion. Recall here that "to convert" (Latin *convertere* "to turn around, transform") means simply "to turn" or "realign" oneself with objective reality. Such a turning implies a semiotic chain of effect by which, through their literary representation, the habits of feeling, action, and thought in the preacher come to inhabit (Latin *inhabitare* "to dwell in") the audience as well—which logically presupposes that the self-revelation of divine holiness now actualized in the audience already has represented itself in the preacher, in those who transmitted the gospel to him, and so on, back to the person of Jesus Christ.

We thus can infer from Claude's sermons that the Christian God affects the world by bringing about real habits, and that these habits, through the ongoing process of representation, or *semiosis*, continue to actualize themselves and in so doing to spread continuously. In theological terms, this spreading happens through the third person of the Trinity—the Holy Spirit, who makes God present in the world through the rhetorical virtuosity of the preacher. It is in this sense that Gérard Ferreyrolles describes the Holy Spirit as the "first cause," and the *ars rhetorica* as the "second cause" of faith's persuasive force—a fundamental relation that has defined Christian rhetoric since the time of Augustine.[88]

While Claude did not address these questions systematically, his preaching suggests that he understood the underlying dynamics. For evidence, consider his first sermon for the day of Pentecost, the coming of the Holy Spirit:

> Every Christian, says Saint John Chrysostom, ought to be in the world like the yeast that warms, that makes to rise all the dough in which it is mixed.[89] But a Christian who has received the Holy Spirit fulfills, as though naturally, this obligation.[90] All his speech, all his conversations are edifying; everything preaches in him, up to his breath, up to his habits, up to his silence. He preaches by his alms, by his diligence, and by his modesty in churches; he preaches by the fervent prayers that he offers to God for the conversion of sinners and for the perseverance of decent people; and not only does he sometimes produce more fruit in this way than all preachers together, but it is quite often to his private prayers that one owes all the fruit that one attributes to the greatest preachers.[91]
>
> Who could say in how many ways the zeal of this soul filled with the Holy Spirit manifests itself, and how many occasions [this soul] finds to exercise [that zeal]![92]

Note that the emphasis here falls on the effect of the converted Christian in society. But for Claude, the Holy Spirit operates in the individual in much the same way that "a Christian who has received the Holy Spirit" functions in the world, in that both the Spirit and the individual naturally affect everything about themselves in a qualitatively constructive manner, which is to say, in a way that promotes growth. In this fashion the Spirit, who perfectly represents divine holiness, converts the individual to God and, by dwelling in and effectively governing those who have been converted, empowers them to bring about the conversion of others; or rather, brings about the conversion of others through them.

Having considered the representational dynamic operative in Claude's sermons, we face the inevitable question: would one not encounter the same principles at work in most any religious writings from this period? And if so, then in what consists the originality of La Colombière vis-à-vis his contemporaries? Again, Claude followed the lines that the major preachers of his day—most of them trained in classical rhetoric, scripture, and the Church Fathers—already had begun to trace. This stylistic and conceptual continuity suggests that, were one to analyze other texts from the era, one would find elements much like those that appear in Claude's own writings. Regardless, if we want to appreciate what Claude and his fellow preachers had to say about *sainteté*—if we want to understand how holiness came to expression in and through the texts themselves and can continue to have an effect on audiences today—then it makes sense to think of the world as a network of evolving habits.[93] This fundamental insight underlies the commentary that accompanies the translations in this book.

Finally, a word regarding La Colombière's use of Augustine. Among the many conflicts that characterized the seventeenth-century French church, none surpassed in contention and bitterness the encounters between the Jesuits and the proponents of the theological movement known as Jansenism.[94] Historians in general maintain that the Jansenists sought to revive and defend an Augustinian theology that featured the devastating consequences of original sin, a pessimistic view of human nature, and the likelihood of salvation for only a small number of people, while the Jesuits promoted a more optimistic view of human nature, believing that free will survived the fall of Adam and Eve. From this perspective, it may seem that La Colombière's Augustinianism—as apparent, for instance, in his discussions of "genuine repentance" in the second part of the sermon "On Confession"—seems more resonant with the Jansenist mentality than with what one might expect from a Jesuit. Yet a similar reliance on Augustine appears in the writings of the most celebrated non-Jansenist preachers of the era, including Bossuet.[95] Indeed, Robin Briggs explains that "[t]he austere Augustinian stance is found among clerics of all schools, Jesuits as well as Jansenists, and its hold seems to strengthen as the century wears on."[96] On this note, Jean Dagens simply and famously declared the Grand Siècle "the century of Saint Augustine."[97] Such evidence and commentary supports the thesis that the French Jesuits sympathized with non-Jesuit French spirituality and ecclesiology—including that associated with Port-Royal.[98] And so, La Colombière's use of Augustine need not lead one to brand him a crypto-Jansenist, especially given his supreme confidence in the mercy of God.[99]

Regarding the Translation

The volume you hold in your hands includes twelve sermons, each of which addresses a different issue under the general theme of Christian conduct. I have chosen to translate and publish these particular sermons first because, in my estimation, they present together the notions central to Claude's preaching and general attitude, above all the ideas of habituation and confidence in God. Having studied these discourses, the reader may perceive more easily the development of these ideas in moral, eschatological, hagiographical, and Marian terms in his other sermons, including the Meditations on the Passion.

As a whole, this project represents the first integral English-language translation of the first edition of the sermons, published by the house of Anisson, Posuel, and Rigaud in 1684.[100] In making the translation, I have used the copy of the first edition that belongs in the Special Collections of the John M. Kelly Library at the University of St. Michael's College, Toronto.[101] For the sake of clarity, I have in some cases reproduced the Anisson text either in the body of the translation or in the notes. I indicate this in the body by placing the original word or words, either verbatim or translated, in brackets. In the notes, I use the letter "A" for "Anisson" to indicate the first edition. Thus, the note "A: *absous*" after the word "acquitted" means that I have chosen the word "acquitted" to translate the word *absous*.

For convenience, I made the initial translation from the Charrier edition (1900–01). I later worked with my research assistant, Elissa Cutter, to verify the Charrier edition against a microfilm that I had had made of the Kelly copy of the Anisson edition.[102] Apart from the many typographical errors that we found, especially in the first edition, we noted, not surprisingly, that punctuation, paragraphination, and in some cases orthography differ considerably between the two editions. Furthermore, some passages that appear in the first edition do not appear in the Charrier edition. While I generally have followed the Anisson edition, in some cases I have accepted Charrier's corrections. Regardless, I have noted any deviations from the Anisson text when they involve a difference in meaning.

In preparing the present edition, I organized the seventy-nine sermons into seven thematic groups and reordered them to reflect this division; the Meditations on the Passion constitute an eighth group. I then renumbered the sermons to coincide with this new order, noting both the number of the volume in which the sermon appears and the number of the sermon itself from both the Anisson and Charrier editions. Following this system, the designation "4. On Mortal Sin" with a note indicating "A: *Du péché mortel* (A 4.61/C 4.60)" means that the sermon entitled *Du péché mortel*, the title of which I translated as "On Mortal Sin," appears fourth among the sermons in the present edition, sixty-first in the fourth volume of the Anisson edition, and sixtieth in the fourth volume of the Charrier edition.

Regarding scripture, La Colombière would have referenced the Sixto-Clementine—or simply Clementine—Version, which Roman Rite Catholics of his day used as their official Bible, the four editions of which (1590, 1592, 1593, 1598) are "substantially the same."[103] In fact, most of the Latin-language Bible quotations appearing in La Colombière's sermons accord verbatim with the text of the fourth edition of the Clementine Version.[104] As Richard Challoner's revision of the Douay-Rheims follows the Clementine fairly closely, I have based my translations of the Latin quotations from the sermons on a later revision of Challoner's text.[105] I have done this although Challoner does not seem to have made a rigorous comparison of the Douay-Rheims with the Clementine text, which appeared after the Rheims New Testament, but simply to have focused on making the English of the Douay-Rheims more readable.[106] For consistency, I have used this later revision as the reference for all English-language Bible quotations and references, including the numbering of verses and of the psalms. Note, however, that in some places I have changed Challoner's English, either to reflect contemporary usage or to follow the Latin more closely. Citation form for books of the Bible follows the style of the Society of Biblical Literature.[107]

In addition, I have made every effort to find and to annotate allusions to historical and literary sources, if not to identify the exact editions that La Colombière most likely referenced.[108] For patristic literature, I have cited the most recent editions available and generally have followed the notation style of the *Journal of Early Christian Studies (JECS)*, abbreviating titles and the names of authors in order to save space;[109] I have done the same for classical literature, using the abbreviations that appear in the *Oxford Classical Dictionary*.[110] Note, however, that in some cases these searches have yielded no conclusive results, and this for a number of reasons. First, La Colombière often does not cite source texts directly, instead appearing to paraphrase the sentiment of the author in French using the style of a direct quotation. Moreover, when citing authors who wrote in Greek, he does not provide the Greek text, possibly because he knew these authors only or primarily in translation.[111] To complicate matters further, he sometimes seems to misidentify authors, in some cases perhaps following editions that contain pseudonymous writings or simply relying on his own, faulty memory. Yet despite the many lacunae, I hope that the notes will both enrich the study of his sermons and suggest avenues for further research.

When a Latin text appears in the first edition, I provide a translation of the quote into English and give the Latin in the notes as it appears in the source; unless otherwise indicated, the translations are my own. If the wording of the source quotation differs significantly from that of the sermon, I also provide the Latin as it appears in the sermon or else indicate the variance in some other way. When a French translation of a Latin text appears in a sermon, I translate the French directly into English, providing in the notes an alternate translation of the Latin source text when I think that this might help to avoid confusion. When encountering archaic French words or usages, I have referred to Furetière for clarification.[112] Note too that in some cases, when quoting directly from sources that date from the seventeenth century or earlier, I have preserved the archaic spellings and accentuation, in order to help readers draw their own conclusions as to what the text means.

As for the guiding principles of the translation, I have followed the French grammar and syntax very closely, even when this has resulted in quaint, stilted, or awkward phrasing. In this sense, the translation has tended more toward formal (literal, or word-for-word) rather than dynamic (functional, or thought-for-thought) equivalence.[113] I made this decision for a number of reasons. In the first case, I feel that formal equivalence does a better job of reproducing the exactness of the French. As a result, the translation has the added virtues of maintaining the ceremonial tone of this kind of discourse while at the same time facilitating comparisons with the original text. Furthermore, formal equivalence preserves more completely the rhetorical choices of the author, e.g., periodic sentence structure and the use of anaphora. Recall that, apart from being a spiritual master, La Colombière also was a classically-trained orator, and as such he used rhetorical figures extensively in his preaching. On that account, not to reproduce this feature would both violate the texts themselves and deprive the reader of an important dimension of La Colombière's style. For this reason I also have retained ejaculatory (e.g., *Éh* "hey") and emphatic (e.g., *dis-je* "I say") expressions, as well as expressions of direct address (e.g., *chrétiens Auditeurs* "Christian auditors"; and *Messieurs* "Gentlemen"), all of which contribute to the overall rhetorical effect.

Additionally, such expressions remind the reader that the sermons were meant to be heard—not read—and that the preacher most likely had memorized his sermons for delivery. Nevertheless, I have avoided the use of contractions and have kept most of La Colombière's non-standard capitalization, and I often have changed the punctuation of sentences and the breaking of paragraphs in order to make a passage more readable. This might include, for instance, setting off an apostrophe by en dashes, or placing a word in italics when La Colombière refers to it as a word (e.g., "only those who do not know God treat as minor sins the sins one calls *venial*"). Apart from this, I have tried to keep the original paragraphination from the first edition, even when this has resulted in long, unbroken sections. However, I have taken some liberties with verb tenses, in particular recasting the future, the conditional, and the ubiquitous French subjunctive so that the text might flow more smoothly and might conform more closely to standard American English usage.

Above all I have striven for clarity and correctness, generally following *The Chicago Manual of Style* except where otherwise indicated.[114] If for the sake of clarification I have added to the translation a word or words not appearing in the original text, these words generally appear in brackets. Such additions may serve to specify the antecedent of a pronoun, as in the sentence, "[conversion] is nothing other than an exact correspondence," where *conversion* replaces the demonstrative pronoun *ce*. Moreover, I generally have translated the third-person neuter pronoun *on* by "one," and the impersonal verb *falloir* using either an impersonal construction, such as "it is necessary," or a personal construction, such as "one must" or "he must."

Lastly, a note regarding gender markers. Although the words *homme* or *hommes* sometimes seem to refer to any human being or to people in general, I generally translate them directly as "man" or "men." Likewise, I generally use feminine pronouns (e.g., *she*, *her*) when referring to the feminine *personne* ("person," as opposed to "nobody"). I also use feminine pronouns for the feminine *âme* ("soul") when it functions as a synecdoche for the whole individual, while I use neuter pronouns (e.g., *it*) when referring to *âme* as part of the human person, where the human person is understood as a composite. Hopefully these indications will give some sense of the spirit in which I made the translation.

CLAUDE LA COLOMBIÈRE SERMONS

On the Flight from the World[1]

Jesus was led into the desert by the Holy Spirit. (Matt 4:1)[2]

It is difficult to be engaged in the world and not to
become corrupted there; it is difficult to be converted there,
unless one retreat from it.

AS ALL THE ACTIONS OF JESUS CHRIST are for us appreciable lessons that teach us even better than his words, it is completely evident, by the retreat that he makes today into the desert and by which he begins his public life, that he wants to teach us the necessity that exists to retire into solitude in order to live in a Christian manner.[3] If I were to tell you that this is a happy necessity, I do not know that one would like to take my word for it. Most people are oddly prejudiced against the solitary and secluded life; one barely has less horror of it than of banishment or of death itself. I am not surprised at this; it is that one knows neither the sweet pleasures nor the advantages of it; it is that one knows not that, in truth, one is never less alone than when one is alone, because then one has the pleasure of dealing with oneself, which is to say, with the person whom each one loves most in the world; or, as Saint Bernard said even better, because then one is with God, with whom one cannot say how sweet it is to converse, far from the commotion and the trouble of the world.[4]

Be that as it may, I am convinced that herein lies the most important matter that could be addressed in a Christian pulpit.[5] For, while you still enjoy yourselves in the world, Christian auditors, whatever impression that the word of God have made on your hearts, whatever good desires that you already have formed, I cannot believe there be anything yet done for your sanctification. It will be in vain that I preach and that all preachers exhaust themselves in order to lead you to a great virtue: the seed that falls on the wide paths is a lost seed.[6] If one wants to produce some fruit by preaching, one must address oneself to people withdrawn from the world, or one must lead those who are in the world to withdraw from it. That is what I am going to try to do, Gentlemen, in the confidence I have that the Holy Spirit, who today leads Jesus into the desert, will attract you by his grace, at the same time that I will lead you by my words.[7] Mary will favor us in this, as she does in all things, by her powerful intercession: *Hail, Mary*, etc.[8]

I do not know if what one says about the first human beings[9] is true: that, living in the forests, separated from one another, they had almost only the exteriors and the appearances of men, until, being gathered in places in which nature collected more amenities for life, they found, in society, this politeness and this perfection of reason that, hardly less than reason itself, distinguished them from the animals. But this commerce, by which [their] minds then were softened and civilized, has since contributed not a little to corrupt them.[10] In such a way that, after having left the deserts in order to learn to live, the wisest judged appropriate to reenter there in order to learn again to live well.[11] They discovered that there was less danger in associating with lions than with people and that the passions that the world inspires make us still more like animals than the wild and savage temperament that solitude maintains.

And yet, as depravity is greater today than it ever has been, and that our world, which refines itself every day, seems also to corrupt itself more and more every day, I do not know if there were ever a time in which one had more reason to take refuge entirely from civil life and to flee into the most distant places.[12] It would be without a doubt a very salutary piece of advice, that one there; but after all it is only a piece of advice: even then it is not for everyone. However, we have spoken of necessity, and of a necessity that extends to all kinds of people. Here is, therefore, in what I claim that [this necessity] consist. I say that, in order to effect one's salvation, one must withdraw from the world the most that one can, and above all from what one calls the "great world." And the proof of this is only too evident. One can save oneself only by one of these two ways: either by living constantly in innocence, or by repairing the disorders of one's life by a genuine conversion. And yet I am going to make you see that these two paths are as if closed to all those who have a great deal of communication with people. It is difficult to be engaged in the world and not to become corrupted there: that is the first point; it is difficult to be converted there, unless one retreat from it: that is the second.[13] That is the whole plan of this talk.

First Point

It is certain that there is a world, even among Christians, that is enemy of Christianity, and that Jesus Christ disavows.[14] It is this world that does not know God, as Saint John says,[15] and that hates the Son of God, as the

Son of God complained of it himself: "the world has hated me before you."[16] This world, completely Christian as it is in appearance, has the demon for prince and for chief; it is composed of reprobates,[17] and the Savior of the world does not intend that it have any part in his prayers: "I pray not for the world, but for them whom you have given me."[18] It is this world that the same Savior has conquered, that he has confounded by his cross, that Saint Paul regarded as a villain condemned to be tortured and executed for his sins,[19] against which all the saints have spoken, and that persecuted all the saints.[20]

It is, moreover, certain that to be of this world and to be among the number of reprobates—to love [the world] and to declare oneself enemy of God—is the same thing: "whoever will be a friend of this world, becomes an enemy of God."[21] Yet one asks if one can visit [the world], familiarize oneself with it, have dealings with those who compose it, find oneself in assemblies, without exposing one's innocence and the salvation of one's soul? In order to respond to this question, Gentlemen, it is necessary to tell you what this world is, and by what it can be distinguished. This world is almost completely composed of people vain, ambitious, attached to their pleasures, who dream only of pleasing, of making themselves liked, of spending life in idleness and in pleasure. It is in this world that reign luxury, pride, vengeance, malicious gossip. It is [this world] that invents fads, that makes the laws of false honor and that makes [people] observe them,[22] that assembles itself only in the places where one cannot be attracted except by pleasure, that esteems all the arts, which are made only to flatter and to please the senses.

I do not say, Gentlemen, that all those who are of this world be voluptuous, lascivious, slanderous, libertine, impious; but I say, and it is true, that all those who are the most given over to all these vices are of this world, that they rule there, that there they receive praises and applause. Finally, as the founders of the religious orders have had it in mind to arrange a living space in which everything favored the design that one would have of saving oneself, they introduced there everything that might facilitate the acquisition of virtue, they banished from there all that is contrary to the purity of morals, all that might tempt or lead to evil; the demon, on the contrary, who is the prince of the world, has tried to assemble there all that might inspire vice, wealth, and immodesty of habits: gatherings of persons of different sexes, flattery, laxness of song and of dance, the licentiousness of the theater—in a word, all that could arouse the passions and introduce them through the senses.[23] This supposed, one asks if there is nothing to fear for salvation by living in the midst of this world. And me, I ask if there is the least reason to believe that one will be able to save oneself there in any way?

To whom will we speak in order to be clear on this point? I wish to question only people themselves of the world. We see some of them every day who leave it in order to embrace religious life, and who leave at the same time great goods, great honors, and even greater hopes. If one wants to know from them the motive that has led them to such a strange resolution, I dare to assert that of a hundred there will not be two who have another thing to tell you, if it is not that it is difficult to remain in the world without keeping company with it, and that it is impossible to keep company with it without becoming corrupt.[24]

And not only those who have thus renounced grandly the secular life, but those who are still engaged in it—who take pleasure in it, who cannot resolve to leave it—both of these, I say, still use the same language. When one reproaches them for their continual relapses, their imprudence in giving or taking certain liberties that lead to serious consequences; when one points out to them the danger that there is, both for them, and for others, in initiating or in carrying on talk that harms decency, that harms the reputation of their brothers [and sisters], that harms even religion; in a word, when one proposes to them the maxims of Jesus Christ and when one makes them notice the extreme opposition that there is between these maxims and their conduct—"You are right," they say, "but one then would have to go mute, seeing that all conversations operate today on these three principles: impiety, malicious gossip, and what one calls *charm*[25]. Unless one be of bronze, one would not be able to defend oneself from evil desires in the midst of a world where everything conspires to arouse them. Besides, one finds oneself every day in such disastrous circumstances, such great conveniences to do evil present themselves there, that one might say that it becomes almost necessary there." Here, Gentlemen, is what one hears said every day, and by people who intend by that to justify in some way their faults. But they are mistaken. It is impossible to see the world, to be of the world, without offending God or without exposing oneself to the danger of offending him. You are therefore forced to withdraw and to break this dangerous dealing that you have with it.

"But I am not of this mind," someone might say: "I believe that one can live in the midst of the world, and live there as one lives there, without affecting one's conscience and without running any risk of one's salvation; there are people of great integrity who are of this same opinion; and indeed one knows people whose life, although worldly, is nevertheless quite beyond reproach." To that, Gentlemen, I want to oppose only your own experience. Although that may be, both regarding the sentiments, and regarding the conduct of others, it is to you alone whom I speak in this discourse; and I ask you, if indeed life and dealings with the world have not done you wrong until now; for in vain would you demonstrate to me, by a hundred examples and by the authority of the greatest experts, that one there could maintain innocence and piety, if you there have lost both the one and the other, and if every day your heart there receives fresh wounds.

Tell me then, if you please, in these great gatherings, in these long conversations that you have with the world, which is to say, with men and women who dream only of amusing themselves and of passing the time pleasantly: have you occasionally spent an entire day without making some disparaging remark or at least without hearing one; without amusing yourself at the expense of your neighbor or without taking some pleasure in the mockeries that one makes of him? I am not speaking of the bad desires that you have inspired in others and of which the care that you take to be liked, to dress yourself to your advantage make you only too guilty. But would you dare to say that you always have brought back from the gatherings a heart as chaste, as free, an imagination as pure as you had taken there? There is one thing on which it seems to me that everybody agrees: that is that people who have some principles of piety, some taste for prayer, some desire to please God and to be sanctified feel that these desires weaken, that this taste is lost by dealings with the world. Hardly has one found oneself a few days in these gatherings than this fervor begins to slacken. One returns with difficulty to the exercises of devotion, one feels that God withdraws, and already one becomes accustomed to his absence.[26] What does this mean, Christian auditors? Is it that you are already lost, that all is hopeless? No, but you see by this that you are not invincible and that with time, the world will be able to spoil you like the others. It is not yet death, but it is your stoutness that goes, it is your health that is ruined; it is not death, but it is an illness that leads to it.[27] I know well that you intend to hold yourself to certain limits that the fear of God prescribes for you; but it is a hope that the holiest of all people could not have without an extreme presumption. The world will not be content with what you intend for it, and I do not see how you will be able to resist it in your weakness, since you gave in at the time that the Lord was near you, that you had all your strength, and that you had not yet received any attack.

But when the good and the vicious, when you yourself would not give testimony to the truth that I am preaching to you, I would not fail to be persuaded of it by reason. If we are safe in the world, tell me, if you please: where will there be danger for salvation? There is good reason to fear even in cloisters, from which all occasions [of sin] are banished and where one is protected by a thousand bastions against the tricks of Satan;[28] and we will believe ourselves safe in a place of which all avenues are open to him, in which you have thousands and thousands of occasions to sin! O my God, one doubts that it is difficult to live innocently in a place in which one sees that all the difficulties that could oppose themselves to innocence are quite obviously gathered together!

Besides the objects that attract so powerfully to do evil, and the occasions that lead there as though necessarily, does not the conversation of corrupt people, their examples, their company, even their breath, so to speak, have something contagious?[29] The Wise Man[30] warns us not to associate with a furious man, for fear that he communicate imperceptibly to us his violent temperament: "Do not walk with a furious man, lest perhaps you learn his ways."[31] And nevertheless one might say that of all vices, anger is the one example that has the least malignancy.[32] It seems that the glance of a person who loses her temper is more capable of inspiring horror of this excess than [it is] of leading us to commit it. What therefore will happen regarding pride, vanity, mendacity, and so many other vices that have nothing off-putting [about them, but] that insinuate and convince all by themselves?

I do not intend to expand here on the force of the bad example, or on the danger that exists in keeping company with dissolute people: everyone knows but too well that the friendship of a libertine is capable of perverting the wisest man in the world, that there is as though a kind of necessity to resemble those whose company one keeps. I leave you to consider, Gentlemen, what will happen to that man, to that or woman who throws himself or herself inconsiderately into the great world, which is to say, who spends time not with one person, but with a whole people completely depraved. Sometimes only one wicked man is needed in order to corrupt the entire youth of a city; one woman often has poisoned an entire court; one has seen wretched souls carry contamination into entire provinces and infect even the greatest kingdoms by their actions and by their scandalous maxims. And here is a world of debauched individuals, of people without decency, without religion, who attack a weak and fragile man; and this man hopes to resist them? If a little yeast corrupts a great mass of dough, according to the word of Saint Paul,[33] how is it that a little dough will not become corrupted in a great mass of yeast? A plague victim who would have entered London alarmed the entire city, because in fact the entire city ran the risk of being infected by him;[34] and one sole person, who mixes into a crowd of people all stricken with the plague, sees no reason to fear the illness!

One will, perhaps, present to me as a counterexample the holy man Lot, who, finding himself in the middle of one and even of several completely debauched towns, did not fail to guard himself against infection and to remain resolutely fixed on his duty.[35] But I beg you, Gentlemen, to consider that this example does not favor the recklessness of those who get involved in the life of the world; on the contrary, it ought to make them tremble. It is true that Lot resisted the example of the Sodomites; that was an admirable effect of his steadfast fidelity. But was this not a rather disastrous proof, both of the fragility of man, and of the malignancy of the bad example, that among an entire nation was found but he alone who was either strong enough or lucky enough to resist it? One is encouraged also by the example of Noah, whose virtue was found tested by the general corruption into which the world had fallen in his time, instead of shuddering to think that among all men he was the only one who resisted it.[36]

In addition, these two holy individuals lived, truth to tell, the first in a palace, and the second in an extremely corrupt age.[37] But they had, neither one, nor the other, any dealings with the wicked. Scripture teaches us that Noah was busy building the ark while the whole earth was plunged into debauchery;[38] and Saint Chrysostom affirms that, in the time that Sodom dirtied itself by a thousand obscenities, Lot stayed in his house, where he tried to please God by keeping his family in line and instructing them in the fear of the Lord.[39] I already have told you, Gentlemen, that I do not claim that one be required to flee from the cities or to shut oneself up in cloisters; there is a middle course between the desert and the great world that I esteem scarcely less than the desert itself. It is in this middle course that the two saints of whom we have spoken kept themselves; it is this middle course that I believe to be necessary for salvation.[40]

I conclude this first part by a reflection, after which one no longer can doubt, it seems to me, what I say. All the saints and all the learned men agree that the life of apostolic men, which is to say, of those who devote themselves to the salvation of souls, that this life, I say, is surrounded by a thousand dangers, and that unless one bring great precaution there, unless one be armed with an extraordinary virtue before setting out there, unless one carry out the functions of this life with much caution and self-control, and unless one not interrupt this even from time to time, as in order to take new precautions against the bad air of the world, they cannot fail to perish.[41] Upon which it is easy to form this reasoning. If holy people, who do not expose themselves in the world except in order to sanctify it, run such a great risk of becoming corrupted themselves, how is it that those who do not have nearly so great a store of virtue, who, in seeing the world, dream only of passing the time and of taking their pleasures; how, I say, can those ones believe that they are safe there? Those who see the world only at church and in the confessional[42] have reason to fear it even in those places; and one will not fear it in the gatherings where it displays all its attractions, all its luxury; where it unfolds all that is capable of surprising the senses and of empoisoning the heart!

Do you want me to tell you frankly what I think, Christian company? My thought is that perhaps it is not absolutely impossible to live innocently in the world; but to get through it, one must take such great care, it would be necessary to exercise a vigilance so constant and so difficult, to sustain so many and such harsh battles, that the difficulty would surpass infinitely the pleasure, that it would extinguish it entirely, that there would be much less strain in observing the most austere rule in the world.[43] No, Gentlemen, there is no solitude so dreadful, no efforts, either of body or of mind, that I would not embrace with joy rather than to be forced to spend my days in the world, in the manner that I know, that I see clearly that I would have to live there in order not to perish there.

Why then remain longer in a country where our enemies are so strong and so formidable, in a country where continually one must have weapons in hand, or at each step one must have the difficulty of conquering or the misfortune of being conquered? "Why must you live in a house where you must daily struggle for life and death? Can anyone sleep soundly with a viper near him? No; for, though it may not attack him it is sure to frighten him."[44] These are the words of Saint Jerome: What way to sleep tranquilly close to a viper always ready to bite you? If you are not bitten by it, you at least will be restless, in sensing it so close to you? In such a way that if you are firmly established in the world, either you will live there without anxiety, or you will suffer there the terrible frights that all wise people ought to have among such great dangers of being damned. Everything is to fear for you. I hold you even already to be lost, if you live there without fear; and if you fear as much as you have reason to do, you will not be long without considering the retreat. May it please the infinite mercy of our God to give to you soon the inspiration to do it; for without that you will not keep yourself long in innocence, if you have not yet lost it; and if you have lost it, you never will recover it by a genuine repentance:[45] this is the second part.

Second Point

Gentlemen, conversion presupposes supernatural grace.[46] [Conversion][47] is nothing other than an exact correspondence to this grace that invites us to change. Nothing happens unless God make himself heard in the depths of the heart; and after the Lord has spoken, there is nothing more to do: his plans must be carried out.[48] And yet I say that the commotion, the trouble of the world prevents us from hearing the voice of God, and that, even when one would have heard it there, one would not be able to obey it.[49]

Grace is nothing other than a light that clarifies the mind and that, at the same time, warms the will; a thought that instructs us and that touches us, that reveals to us the good and that leads us to love it. Although God can produce immediately by himself both this good thought and this good desire, he makes use nevertheless, ordinarily, of exterior, sensible objects. A crucifix, a man who battles with death, an example of modesty and of genuine piety are the instruments of which he makes use in order to introduce through the eyes the remedy that will heal the soul.[50] Another time he will take the occasion of a Christian discourse, of an edifying story, of a good and salutary counsel, and will insinuate himself in this manner by the ears to the very bottom of the heart. When only that would be required in order to convert a sinner, his conversion will be difficult, while he is in the world. These occasions of which God makes use in order to call us are extremely rare there; one sees few objects there that inspire compunction; the conversations that one holds there ordinarily are not those that counsel piety.

In addition, if this grace by which God invites me to a more Christian life, if this grace, I say, is not effective, it is evident that I would not convert, although I be able to do it.[51] But what is this effective grace from God's side? It is nothing else, say the theologians, than the choice of certain advantageous circumstances that favor the success of the call—of certain precious moments in which the obstacles that could prevent its effect are found, happily, distant.[52] And yet, how to find these favorable circumstances in the life of a person who is forever either at play or in conversation, whose whole life is spent in receiving and paying visits, who has always before the eyes objects that inspire vanity and love of the world? At what time will the Lord present his Holy Spirit to that person, that [the Lord] could hope that he would be received or that he would not be completely suffocated?

And that, Gentlemen, is the explanation of these words of Scripture by which the Holy Spirit warns us that God is not found in the commotion, that one seeks him in vain in the streets and in public places; that it is in solitude that he speaks to the heart of his spouse, which is to say that he makes her not only to hear, but also appreciate his lessons.[53] It is for that [reason] that Saint John the Baptist, who was a living figure of grace, and who for that [reason] characterized himself [as] the voice of God, preached only in the desert, and that having come to the court he lost there both freedom and life: "I am the voice of one crying out in the wilderness."[54] It is not that God did not desire to save us, if it were possible, even in the world; it is not that he does not seek to insinuate himself, that he does not try all the routes; but this crowd by which one is always besieged, this noise, this confusion in which one enjoys oneself, closes all the avenues to him. It would be to want to waste words to speak to you in these circumstances where you would not take notice of his counsels, or you would not reflect enough on them in order to take advantage of them.

I say, in the second place, that when the life of the world would not close the entrance to divine inspirations, one would always have to retreat in order to begin this holy and Christian life to which we would be led by these inspirations. Solitude is useful at all times and to all sorts of people. But, at the beginning of conversion, it is absolutely necessary, and one could say that it is even a part of repentance. It is only in retreat that one goes out of the occasions of sin, the flight from which is an indispensable obligation. It is only in retreat that one can practice these actions that could atone for our past faults.

Add to this that, in the beginnings, one still does not have enough strength to do, in the view of the world, what the world condemns and what condemns the world itself. A learned interpreter asks what may be the reason why the people of God was for so long in Egypt without making sacrifice to the true God; and he himself answers that it is because the animals, who ought to have served as their victims, were themselves the gods of the Egyptians, who would not have let them be sacrificed to another God. [The Israelites] had to go into the desert and distance themselves from the presence of these idolaters in order to render to the Lord a worship that they had interrupted for so long.[55] One might say that the sinner who considers converting finds himself in completely similar circumstances. In order to reconcile himself with God, he must sacrifice to him all that the world values, all that it loves, all that it adores; he must renounce his pleasures, his conversations, his manners, his customs; he must declare himself, in everything and everywhere, in favor of virtue and against vanity. But to claim to observe this conduct in the view of the people of the world, to distinguish oneself from them in all things, without however separating oneself from them, this would be to attract a persecution too strong for a virtue still weak; this would be to expose oneself to a strange temptation, or to leave everything for human respect, or to lose everything through vainglory.

And it is for that [reason], Gentlemen, that, if it happens sometime that God, by a completely special favor, go looking for a soul even in the middle of public gatherings; if, despite the commotion and the dissipation of her mind, [God] makes flow in her heart some beneficial thought of death, of judgment, of hell;[56] the first movement that gives her this interior grace, it is to withdraw and to begin a more solitary life: "My heart is troubled within me," said David, "and the fear of death has fallen upon me; the sorrows of hell encompassed me, and darkness has covered me, and I said: 'Who will give me wings like a dove, and I will fly and be at rest?'"[57] I have felt some disturbance in my conscience; I found myself as though overcome by the thought of death; I have been frightened in view of the punishments that the outcasts suffer; it has seemed to me that I was already buried with them in the thickest gloom of hell, and from that time I said to myself, "Alas! Who will give me wings, like the dove, in order to draw me as soon as possible from the snares that surround me, to go search quite far from the court a suitable place[58] in order to calm my justifiable fears?"

It is even for this same reason that the first regret that one ordinarily has at death is the regret not to have left the world in the time that one still could enjoy having left it.[59] This is whence come these conversations so common in the mouth of the dying: "Oh, if I had spent my days in a cell! Oh, how much more it would be worth to die Carthusian rather than cardinal," said, not too long ago, a prelate who had been pulled from his monastery in order to be raised to this high rank![60]—"Had it pleased God" (these are the words that a great king uttered at the beginning of this century, when he was on the point of dying), "had it pleased God that I had never been king! If I had spent my days in a desert, I could die more content than I die."[61] It seems, Gentlemen, that they would have had more reason to say: "Ah! How better have I lived, how better have I discharged the duties of my state!" But they go first to the source of all their evils, that they understand then to have been only the company of men and the want of retreat. It is as if they said: "I would like to have lived in a more Christian fashion; but, in order to do that, it was necessary to retreat from the world where I was too committed."

Let us forestall, Christian auditors, let us forestall these useless regrets. Let us flee this world, this impious and dangerous world, this region where the Lord is so little known, and that the Lord seems also to neglect completely, this region where one might say that it comes down continually like rain, like a shower of traps, according to the word of David: "he will rain snares upon sinners."[62] Let us even have little contact with people who are engaged in this worldly life: let us avoid speaking with them and, if it is possible, even meeting them, for fear that we catch some whiff of this poisoned air that they constantly exhale. Do you want to ensure your salvation, Christian soul? Make for yourself a solitude and like a little desert of your own house; busy yourself there to rule your family and to sanctify yourself with them. Converse with yourself there about yourself; study your heart a little and try to discover its passions, its inclinations, its habits.[63] Speak there about God with your children, with your servants, and above all with God himself. Dispose yourself there to die in a Christian fashion, by purifying your conscience and putting order early in life into all that could make your last day less calm; by dying every day, in a sense, by thought and by the desire of a holy death.

My God, that I might make you[, Christian auditors,] understand the sweetness of a life so ordered and distanced from occasions to offend God! What pleasure to see oneself as though on the top of a mountain, beyond the reach of ocean waves, of monsters, of whirlpools, of storms that sweep away, that swallow the majority of people; to see oneself free, from the concerns that worry them, from the desires that disturb them, from the passions that send them into raptures, from the sins that disgrace them, that blind them, that overwhelm them by their number and by their enormity! May one have occasion every day to be pleased with the solitude, when one hears the cries and the moans of those who are in the crowd; may one hear of their disputes, their quarrels, their fits of rage, their confusions, and so many disastrous accidents that happen to them! But, at the hour of death, may one be grateful to oneself for this prudent retreat! May one's accounts be easy to settle, when one has had dealings only with oneself, with God, or with people who fear God! [When one has to confess] only faults reduced by this distance from social gatherings! Of how little consequence are those [faults] into which at times one has not failed to fall—how they are easy to make right! On the contrary, for a person whom death surprises in this secular and stormy life, what difficulty, what confusion![64] How difficult it is to clarify in so little time accounts so muddled and that one has never examined well! How many words, glances, desires, consents slip in a single day! It takes only one word, only one gesture, only one smile to inflict an irreparable wrong to the reputation of a woman; only one wink to scandalize a man; only a moment of time to commit a mortal sin by thought;[65] and when one's whole life has been only a series of distractions and of conversations, and the conversations only a tissue of flatteries and of gossip, is it possible that death be peaceful, that it be even Christian? Go then, Gentlemen, resolve to lead from here on out with Jesus Christ a life hidden in God, as the Apostle says.[66] Your resolution will have, beginning here below, its reward; you will live more innocently, you will die more peacefully, you will reign more gloriously in heaven. *So be it.*

One Should Serve Only One Master[1]

No one can serve two masters. (Matt 6:24)[2]

We are not able to serve God and the world at the same time; and when that
would be possible, we ought not to do it.

FIRST, IT SEEMS, CHRISTIAN AUDITORS, that the Son of God
could not give us a more pointless lesson than this one here. For, people
loving freedom as much as they naturally love it, it hardly appears that they
dream of multiplying their restraints by subjecting themselves to several
masters; and there would be much more reason to fear that they did not
want to suffer even a single one of them than to fear that it took their fancy
to have two of them. Nevertheless, it is only too true that nearly all of us
want to be doubly enslaved; and what indicates a strange blindness is that
it is by this same love of freedom, which is so natural to us, that we look for
this double servitude.

The yoke of the Savior seems regrettable to us, when it is alone; and we
think to be able to lighten it by taking even that of the world[3], as though
a burden added to another burden was capable of diminishing the weight
of the first. Moreover, the yoke of the world is shameful; and in addition,
there is danger in carrying it. And yet, we convince ourselves that in giving
to God a small part of our attention we would save ourselves easily, both
from this disgrace and from this danger. We are mistaken; it is certain that
the service of Jesus Christ, which is so sweet when one gives oneself completely to it, becomes unbearable to [the one] who still wants to depend on
the world in something; and there is no one for whom it be, neither less
honest, nor more dangerous, to serve this same world than for those who
profess to belong in some way to Jesus Christ. But how necessary it is to
know if it is pleasant or painful, if it is shameful or glorious, if there is safety
or peril to share his services in this way, since this sharing out is absolutely impossible: "No one can serve two masters"—no one can serve two
masters at the same time. One must necessarily give oneself completely to
one only. I will make you see it, Gentlemen, in the remainder of this talk.

I will show you that there is a double necessity to that. In the first place, an absolute necessity from which the most rebellious spirits would defend themselves in vain; in the second place, there is a necessity of decorum to which all well-formed spirits ought to surrender: which is to say, in a word, that we are not able to serve God and the world at the same time: this will be the first point; and when that would be possible, we ought not do it: that will be the second. I will begin after having implored the help of the Holy Spirit through his immaculate Spouse: *Hail, Mary*.[4]

First Point

As there are few Christians who truly aspire to a perfect holiness, I dare say that there are not many of them who be determined to spend their life in complete dissoluteness. The great number is of those who seek a temperament between these two extremes and who would like, if it were possible, to reconcile in themselves conscience with concupiscence, and devotion with at least one of their passions.[5] Permit this woman to pull out all the stops, the vanity of finery; to this other a friendship, not exactly criminal, but only dangerous; they will give the rest willingly enough to God. You will find men who deep down want to be good, but who are delighted to live externally as others; who want to have the esteem of decent people and the approval of the most worldly; to pass for devout among the devout and for ladies' men among those who like to think of themselves as such; who claim to have horror of sin, but who enjoy themselves nevertheless and who live in the occasions of committing it.

On the one hand, one practices some good works; and, on the other, one takes part in all the vain distractions: after having attended all the sermons of Advent, one finds oneself present at all the Carnival gatherings;[6] one receives communion in the morning, and after lunch one is in public to be seen; from vespers, this one here goes to the cabaret, and this other to the theater; one hates not being restrained, but neither does one put up with this severe chastity that condemns the least freedoms, the least thoughts—that condemns them, I say, as mortal sin;[7] one has no malicious intent, but one forgets nothing to please, and one would not mind to inspire these same passions that one clearly has decided to renounce.

"It is true," says one, "that I spend more on clothes than I should, taking into account my situation; but at least I stay within my means, and I am not like those women who ruin their husbands by the excess of their luxury."—"I am not miserly to the point of keeping the property of others; I am not generous to the point of giving my own to the poor."—"One does not hear me speak badly of others; but I listen willingly to malicious gossip."—"I would rather die than to take revenge; but I would not be able to love those who wish me evil."—"I am a magistrate; I will not commit injustice; but, for fear of making enemies, one can well postpone or even avoid by some way to fulfill justice."—"I am a shopkeeper; one cannot accuse me of the least deception; but I devote myself completely to my trade, and I do not do more good than bad."—"I am a father; I give neither bad advice nor bad examples to my children; but, apart from that, I get involved in no way in their education; I leave this concern to their nannies and to their teachers." In short, there are certain sins that one must commit from time to time, as though necessarily. Of course, one therefore goes to confession from time to time.

There you have the disposition in which the majority of people of the world live. They want to give something to the spirit and something to the flesh;[8] to live in a Christian manner, but softly, but delightfully; to win the goods of heaven, in enjoying all the goods here below; to please God, without displeasing others and without inconveniencing themselves; in a word, to keep a course that the Gospel has not traced out, equally removed from both the narrow way, and from the broad way—and to build, between Babylon and Jerusalem, a new city, where charity and self-love be equally revered.[9] It is there, Christian auditors, what I call *to serve two masters*; it is thus that one seeks to satisfy God and the world, by sharing oneself, so to speak, with one and the other. But it is in vain that one seeks it, because this sharing can satisfy neither one, nor the other. This is nothing for God but half; this will not even be enough for the world; God wants everything, and the world will want even more.

You are not unaware, Gentlemen, of the virtue to which Jesus Christ, our good Master, commands us to aspire. He wants it to surpass that of the wisest pagans and that of even the most austere Jews. "The pagans have some gratitude," says he, at one place in the Gospel: "they love those who love them; I ask something more of my disciples: I want them to love even those who hate them."[10] The most reasonable among the gentiles share their mind between the study of wisdom and care for their subsistence: that is a lot for them; but for Christians, it is nothing at all; the care for their salvation ought to be their only concern, and to worry about what one will live on tomorrow is to want to secure one's body in losing one's soul.[11] In short, the Pharisees and the doctors of the law profess a life very pure and very regular: however, your justice ought to be more lavish than theirs; otherwise you must renounce paradise. What does all that mean, if it is not that you ought to consider becoming perfect as our heavenly Father is perfect, so the Savior orders us to do, and that whoever is happy with a second-rate holiness would never be able to please God: "Be you therefore perfect, as also your heavenly Father is perfect."[12] And yet the perfection—holiness, and above all that of God—that one proposes to us as a model, holiness, I say, encompasses everything; it is a complete dedication of all that there is in the human person: a sacrifice in which all ought to be consumed, a collection of all kinds of virtues.[13] You would not be able to subtract even one of them from [this collection] without destroying [a person's holiness].[14]

I say much more: if only one virtue is lacking to you, not only do you not have holiness, but all the other virtues are lacking to you. They are all linked together in such a way that they cannot remain separately. This truth is an infallible rule in order to distinguish true piety from false devotion. For piety, when it is sincere, it is even and uniform; it neglects nothing; it has nothing weak, nothing imperfect; if it fails in one sole point, it is no more than hypocrisy and self-love. And so, this woman who appears so humble, so mortified, so attached to prayer, so generous toward the poor, so zealous for the salvation of her neighbor, if she is at the same time, either not very submissive to her husband or not very reserved in judging and in speaking of the behavior of others, not only does she lack discretion and obedience, but, without making a rash judgment, one might say that she has neither humility, nor mortification, nor union with God, nor zeal, nor genuine charity; and if she is not herself of this opinion, she most certainly is fooling herself.

I have said that the lack of one sole virtue necessarily brings about the ruin of all the others. I add that one sole defect—one sole limitation regarding the object or some other circumstance—suffices to ruin a virtue completely. To lose the faith, it is not necessary to believe nothing: it is enough not to believe one sole article; it is even enough to doubt it. Do you hesitate to believe in indulgences or in purgatory? When you would give your life for all the other truths, you would die unfaithful, and you would be martyr only of your own sentiments.[15] It is in vain that you flatter yourself to be chaste, because you are terrified of greater dissoluteness: if your thoughts, if your words, if your eyes, if your ears, if your books, if your habits, if even your rooms—in the paintings and in the tapestries that decorate them—are not as chaste as your body, you might be less immodest than the fornicators and the adulterers, but you have no more chastity than they. You love all your enemies, and you love them very tenderly, with the exception of only one; and you willingly forgive that one there all the evil that he has done to you, with the exception of one sole insult; and still you do not intend to take other revenge for it, if only that you would make for him a little less good and fewer signs of esteem than before. If you are in this disposition, Christian auditors, you have no Christian charity, no love for your neighbor. The authentic virtues are limited neither to certain times, nor to certain actions, nor to certain particular subjects. The one who possesses them is disposed to practice them in all things, in all encounters, with regard to all kinds of people, and in all ways.

If this is true, as one cannot doubt, it is completely obvious that one can satisfy God only by giving him everything without reserve, since the holiness to which he calls us encompasses everything. Furthermore, it is obvious that whoever does not give him[16] everything gives him even nothing at all, because there is no virtue where all virtues are not found, and because they are all, so to speak, infinite by their nature, and one cannot limit them without destroying them.

This truth, Gentlemen, is confirmed by the particular commandments that God gave us to serve him, and above all by the first and the most important of all, which is that of love. You will love me, says the Lord, with all your heart, with all your soul, with all your strength, with all your mind: which is to say you will not love but me alone, and, to give me evidence of this love, you will yearn only for me, "with your whole soul"; you will work only for me, "with your whole strength"; you will think only of me, "with your whole mind."[17] And because one could have been able to doubt if one would have to give a part of one's thoughts to the most necessary things, [God] foresaw this difficulty, in teaching that there is only one sole thing necessary for us, which is to know him and to love him, "but one thing is necessary."[18]

But at least he is happy with the heart, with the mind, with the thoughts—in a word, with the interior and invisible self? No, he wants also that the exterior be consecrated to him; otherwise, the first Christians would have been able to hate—to curse—the false gods of the gentiles at the depths of their soul and to burn before their statues a grain of incense that they would have directed secretly to the God of heaven. Yet they were obliged, under pain of being damned eternally, to suffer the cruelest tortures rather than to resort to this ruse?[19] It was nothing, it seems, that the world asked of them in this encounter. This external worship, devoid of intention, would not have been true worship, but rather a mockery and cruel derision, as was the adoration that Pilate's soldiers rendered our Savior.[20] If we did not adore our God in another way, we would invite all his anger. Furthermore, the horrible torments and the death that one would have avoided by this dishonesty, the peace of the Church that one would have obtained by giving in to these pretexts, were, it seems, quite legitimate reasons; and nevertheless, all these reasons were never able to lead God to relax this point, however inconsiderable it seemed. He always has counted among the rebels and as apostates those from whom the sight of tortures had extracted the least sign of idolatry. And he, who considers the heart above all things, had no consideration for them, all the times that exterior actions did not accord with the sentiments of the heart.

What can they say to that, these timid Christians who believe that, out of fear of what people will say, one can continue to behave in public as one has always lived, to dress with the same vanity, to see the same people, to hold much the same conversations; that, in order to save oneself from the mockery of libertines, one even can affect in their presence a false contempt of the most venerable and the holiest of things? Will they continue stubbornly to believe it after what I just said? There is nothing true, nothing real in all that, I agree; but the Lord demands everything, and, since he challenges empty appearances, I leave you to consider whether he will give over more substantial and more important things?[21]

I want nevertheless that he give over to the world all that you have intended to it for its share. Do you think that the world can content itself with so little? For example, let us say that in order not to appear sanctimonious, one could behave externally with an enemy as if in fact one hated him;[22] that, for fear of having to deal with a person of great reputation and of great standing, a judge be permitted to absent himself from the law court, to postpone judgment, to force the litigant, who moreover has a clear and incontestable right, to force him, I say, shrewdly, to settle out-of-court. I say that it would happen many times that the world would not be satisfied with these sorts of dispositions: for this affront it will call for a cruel and devastating revenge; it will make you a laughing stock, if you continue in these hypocrisies. Not only does this lord not want to be condemned, but he intends that you give a sentence or a decision in his favor.

For you it is a long-established principle that you must make God happy, but that you also must show consideration for people. What will you do then in similar circumstances? Will you renounce this fundamental maxim of your own conduct? Will you start all at once to make fun of yourself and to treat as vain anxiety a fear that would have rooted itself in your heart and that up until then would always have seemed so reasonable to you? At those moments, when your bad policies will be supported by a violent passion, either of fear or of anger; where all nature will help the world to overcome you, you will forget your initial sentiments and trample underfoot all human consideration? Perhaps one could expect it of a saint and of the habit that he would have acquired by repeated actions of the same nature.[23] But you who will be accustomed to these fearful concerns, to these base resignations, whence will come to you so suddenly a courage capable of undertaking something heroic? I know that God has, in his treasury, assistance strong enough to inspire you. But I also know that these great gifts, these miracles of graces, are only for the beloved, and that a person who treats [God] with such reserve would await them vainly from his munificence.

What then will this bad Christian do? He will do, Gentlemen, what Pilate did in the case of the Son of God.[24] Having recognized almost at the same time both the innocence of the accused and the passion of the accusers, he wanted to avoid condemning the former without however displeasing the latter. For that he tried various routes: he attempted to rid himself of this matter and to send it away to the king, Herod, on the pretext that Jesus Christ was a subject of this prince. This ploy did not succeed in the way he was hoping. The innocent was sent back to him; he was pressed to put him on trial; if he condemned him to death, he would be guilty of a horrible parricide[25]; if he sends him back altogether acquitted[26], the whole synagogue will fly into a rage. He chooses a middle course and resolves to spare his life but to take away his honor by having him flogged like a slave: "I will chastise him, therefore, and release him."[27] The hatred of the Jews and the jealousy of the priests are not satisfied with such a small thing; they judge him worthy of the cross, and they intend that the governor confirm their judgment by his sentence. At that Pilate again finds a way out: the sentence will be passed, but afterward he will grant him a pardon. There is, as well, the custom to release a criminal at each Passover festival. Wretched politician, cowardly slave of the passions that you ought to have suppressed and even punished! What will you do, if all that cannot satisfy this enraged crowd; if they demand from you the death of their king and of their God; if you cannot win them over by second-rate injustices; if they reduce you to the necessity, either to offend them or to commit the darkest of all crimes? You know what he did: he finally granted all that one asked of him, he condemned Jesus to be crucified, in spite of all divine and human laws, in spite of the visions and the terrors of his wife,[28] in spite of the reproaches of his conscience.

Yet I confess that there are occasions when the world and the demon himself, who is its prince, initially appear more moderate and seem to be content with little enough. But that is a trap, against which all the saints, against which all the Fathers [of the Church] advise us to guard ourselves. [The demon] is happy with little only because he knows very well that, of your own accord, you will grant to him all the rest. It is enough for him that you have received a spark in your heart, because no more is necessary to set you afire. He only asks of you a few steps; but it is on a slope so steep that, once you have started out there, you will not be able to stop yourself until you arrive at the bottom of the abyss. That is why this "little" is not so little, says Saint John Chrysostom—one can say that it is almost everything: "As regards this little, it is not a little. Rather, it is truly almost everything."[29]

"I will keep company with the world, however corrupt, however libertine it be today; but I will guard myself well from adopting its sentiments." How naive you are! Are you wiser than Solomon? When he allied himself with the Sidonians and the Moabites, he was quite far from thinking about the worship of their false gods; and yet he worshiped them subsequently; he built them temples and offered incense to them.[30] "I may permit myself some glances, but I will forbid myself every kind of desire." Who is the man presumptuous enough to promise himself this moderation in such precarious circumstances? Job, as holy as he was, did not feel himself strong enough for that; he had made a covenant with his eyes that he never would look a woman in the face.[31] It is true that David distrusted his virtue less; but also in what abyss of wickedness was he not thrown by his confidence.[32]

Yes, Gentlemen, Jesus Christ is a loyal and sincere Lord who cannot practice dissimulation and surprise. He will state to you frankly either that he wants all of your services or that he does not want them at all. The world is deceitful and cannot be happy with less, although initially it does not ask for as much. But why do you worry so greatly to make these two irreconcilable enemies agree with one another? Since you love the world and since it attracts you so powerfully, why not come out in favor of its interests and its principles! Why not give yourself over to it without reserve?—Without reserve, good God, to this traitor, to this tyrant who pays only with wind and with smoke, who abandons to death all those who have followed him during their lives, who strips them, who hands them over to cruel and to everlasting tortures! That I give myself to it without reserve!—But, if the world is as you say it is, are you not so wretched as to waste a great part of your cares and of your labors in the service of so wicked a master? What madness to hold in esteem, to treat considerately a traitor, to give half of your goods to a wretch from whom you can expect nothing but tortures!

Moreover, I see that in your greatest freedom you fear to cross certain lines; you would like not to continue to the point of mortal sin;[33] you fear to anger God by satisfying your passions. Why these considerations and this troublesome fear? Why not shake off entirely this heavy yoke?—"How," you say, "could I break off relations entirely with my God! Well! What would I become, if I were his sworn enemy? Who would protect me amid the perils of this life? Who would receive me at the entrance of the next? Who would deliver me from the hands of the demon? Who would make me happy during all eternity?"—What, Christians, you expect all of that from God, and you do not give yourself completely to him? You hope for nothing except from him, and you want to serve another one with him? You believe that for the little that you do he will give you infinite rewards, and you do not consecrate to him all that you do? You have such a good Master, and you look for a second one? Go, weak and imprudent as you are, you well deserve that Jesus Christ reject you forever from his service and that he disown you for his servant in the presence of his Father. After that, I no longer tell you that it is impossible that you serve two masters both at the same time. I say that, when you would be able to do it, you ought not to do it. This is what I am going to prove to you in my second part.

Second Point

When one could share his services with God and with the world without offending one or the other, one could not do so without committing an enormous injustice and without making oneself guilty of a horrible ingratitude; and it is for these two reasons that I say that one ought not to do it. We belong to God, Christian auditors; it is he alone who has brought us out of nothingness; it is he alone who prevents us to fall back there; it is in him, it is by him alone that we live, that we think, that we speak, that we act.[34] What right, therefore, can the world claim over all these things, in order to share them with the Creator? Is not God alone master of the land, and the tree, and consequently of all the fruits? And yet you give him [a][35] part of his own property and you think to be able, despite him, to make use of the rest without doing him wrong.

In addition, besides that he is the sole Master of all things, the excellence of his nature and of his splendid perfections demands that all things be offered up to him. You are happy to give him half of your heart. Is he not so worthy as to possess it completely? You do not like it that one thinks this way, and you treat him in fact as an imperfect and limited being who, far from being able to claim infinite love and honor, merits only a part of these small services that you are able to render him. Do you understand well the injustice you do to God in serving him thus by half-measures? You strip him of divinity; you degrade him; you destroy him, to the extent that it is possible for you.

And it is even more outrageous to him that it is in order to give to the world that you take something away from him; to the world, I say; to that impostor; to that tyrant; to that villain, to that horrible monster, dark and composed of all kinds of sins. For in this way you make God equal to that loathsome creature; you reduce him to the point of making him go hand in hand with it. And not only do you put God on the same level with the world, but, what is an even stranger injustice, you even prefer the world to God, since in order to satisfy the former, you are happy to risk the friendship of the latter. This is even more evident by today's Gospel, where the Savior of the world ensures that, of two masters that you undertake to serve, it is necessary that you esteem one of them and that you hate the other: "he will sustain the one, and despise the other."[36] But I ask you, Gentlemen, which of the two do we despise in these cowardly engagements? Is it the world whose contempt we fear so strongly, whose judgments and conversations we dread so strongly, whom we want to please at any price? Can one give greater signs of esteem and of respect than those? It is therefore God who is despised and who, evidently, gets the worst of it.

O you people, who naturally love reason and equity and who like to think that you are just to everyone, will you never act this way toward your God? But will you always be inconsiderate toward him, you who hate ingratitude so strongly and who cannot forgive others for it? What greater ingratitude! God has given everything to you; you have received nothing from the world; and you honor them equally, and you share your services equally with them! What do you have that you not have received from God? And not only that, but what has God had that he not have given you?[37] He himself has given himself to you without reserve, and you quibble with him over a part of your rigid and narrow heart, a part of a moment of time that is at your disposal! If you find a day, an hour, an instant in your entire life when God does not think of you, when he suspends the exercise of his loving providence toward you, when he does not act for you and with you, at the right time, I grant that, during that time, you interrupt the service that you owe him. But if he is eternally attentive to support you, to guide you; if he never ceases to do good to you, why will you stop acknowledging the good that he has done for you?

If God behaved with you as you do with him! Would you not be the most wretched of all people if, as you pardon only certain insults, he pardoned you only certain sins; if, as you content yourself not to take revenge on your enemies without wanting to do them some good, the Lord no longer gave you actual graces, even though you have recovered sanctifying grace?[38] You want to avoid great sins, but you do not trouble yourself about the smallest; and if God gave you, for his part, only small assistance, only ineffective assistance, what would become of you?—"I will be happy to see, and I will abstain from unrestrained and lustful touch."—And if God took sight away from you, as he could, and he was happy to preserve the other senses for you, would you be happy with him? If, in order to recognize the innumerable and infinite favors with which he showers you, you had infinite time, infinite strength, a heart immense and capable of loving him infinitely, all that ought to be used to give marks of gratitude to him. But you have only a moment of time, only a breath of life, only a small mind, a small heart; and still you take away from him half of this little bit that you are able to give him!

But if there is so much injustice and ingratitude in thus sharing your services between God and the world, what will we say of those who make the share so unequal and who give to God such a small portion? What will we say of those who, of all the thoughts of the day, hardly offer to him the first; who, of all the days of the week, dedicate to him only Sunday, and who, of the whole Sunday, quite often give to him only the time that they need in order to hear the shortest mass? What will we say of others who, having spent the whole year either in business or in the pleasures of the world, consider themselves to be no longer in God's debt for having come to the Easter celebrations to perform I know not what devotions? And those who, of all their life, reserve for the Lord only the last years, or even the last hours of life? What do you think of them, Gentlemen? Are these very grateful and very reasonable Christians? Can they say that they love God with all their heart, with all their soul, with all their strength?[39] Can they boast of being servants of Jesus Christ? Can they hope that their services be pleasing to him? I have made you see that he cannot be content if they take away from him. And these people believe that he will be happy if they give to him!

When you would be [happy], Lord, I will not be [happy] unless I have given all things to you and unless I have given myself to you without reserve. As I am obliged to serve only you, therefore I want to serve only you. All other servitude is shameful to me, is unbearable to me. I will obey willingly the one who commands nature; but I never will be the slave of another slave: "My Lord, and my God."[40] If I necessarily must choose a master, I want no other one than you, O my God, who have deigned to choose me, among so many other people, in order to number me among your servants; who have delivered me from the tyranny of the demon; who have been pleased to descend even to the condition of slave in order to free me.[41] Hey! What yoke could I embrace that were lighter than yours, since you yourself help to carry it;[42] since, quite far from overwhelming by its weight, it even has the power to make all other burdens light? What could be gentler than your authority! You give everything that you require; you yourself accomplish, by your grace, all that you command, in such a way that, although your rewards be very magnificent, all the same you never reward but your own gifts. You are not content to facilitate the execution of your wishes; you execute in turn all the wishes of those who obey you.[43] Either you make everything you do suit them, or you do only what pleases them. So that if we still want to seek glory in servitude, this raises us above all the miseries of the world, above all the grandeurs of the world; it subjects to us all that is subject to God and makes us free in the freedom of God himself. Let us then love it, Christian company, this gentle, this glorious servitude. Let us bind ourselves exclusively to the only master who has the right to govern us. He is good; he is faithful; he is rich; he is generous; he is immortal. To serve him, that is to reign beginning in this life and to assure ourselves for the next life a kingdom that will never end. *So be it.*

3

On Care for Salvation[1]

The children of the world are more prudent in the conduct of their affairs than are
the children of the light in that of their salvation. (Luke 16:8)[2]

One lacks prudence in temporal concerns, because one counts for naught
the most necessary and sure [means] of succeeding in them, which is God;
one has still less prudence concerning salvation, because one does not
even think of it as a concern.

IT IS AT ALL TIMES, CHRISTIAN AUDITORS, that men have prided
themselves on prudence.[3] One has never seen people who wanted to admit
they were lacking in it, either because it is such a great distinction to appear
wise that one could not resolve to give it up, or because it is as shameful not
to be [prudent] as to recognize [that one is not prudent], which is like confessing that one is not a man.

Be that as it may, one can say that of all good qualities, that which one
feigns most universally in polite society is that of the prudent man above
all in this age said to be the age of wisdom, and in which one boasts of
knowing and following so closely all the rules of good sense and reason.[4]
For myself, according to the little knowledge I have of things, I agree that
besides the well-refined taste one has for judging all the works of the spirit,
I agree, I say, that things were never done with such skill that they are done
in these times. It is a wonder to see to what extent one discovers every
day new ways for arriving at one's goals, with what dexterity one hides the
means that one uses to succeed, and with what subtlety one makes them
work. One would say that ambition, avarice, love, even anger and the other
passions, which once were so unreflective and so rash, all have become
judicious. In place of this commotion and of this noise that [the passions]
had custom to make, [the passions] all have learned to conceal in order to
reach their goal both more surely and more quickly. But, quite far from
inferring from all this that one is more reasonable today, it seems to me
that one would not be able to give a more obviously contrary conviction.

For in short it is completely obvious that therein lies what Saint Paul calls the prudence of the flesh—that which, being the enemy of God, as the same apostle says, cannot miss destroying that [prudence] of the spirit of which God is the source.[5] In effect, Gentlemen, this false prudence has nearly smothered the real thing. Even the majority of these quite enlightened people, who think to improve upon all the precepts of ancient morality, sin constantly against the first principles of this knowledge. I will make you see it, after we have implored the assistance of the Holy Spirit, by the intercession of Mary: *Hail, Mary.*[6]

The Savior of the world tells us, in today's gospel, that men reveal more attention in temporal concerns than concerning their salvation. That is the meaning of these words that I recalled at the beginning: "the sons of this world are more shrewd than the sons of light in dealing with their own generation." I do not think that there is anyone who would want to contradict this truth. Besides the sovereign authority of Jesus Christ, to which every created spirit must submit, the thing is so evident by itself that, unless one is completely unaware of how it is that one lives in the world, one cannot doubt it. But I go further and I do not know if what I am going to say will find at first some credibility. I do not say only that the people of the world are more prudent in temporal concerns than in eternal things; I say that, for the most part, they are very badly informed, both in the one and in the other. There is my thought, Christian auditors, and maybe that also will be yours, when you will have understood the reasons upon which I base myself. There are two parts to my proposition. The majority of Christians are very imprudent in the conduct of their temporal concerns—that is the first; they are still more imprudent in those of their salvation—that is the second. For each part I have only one reason: one lacks prudence in temporal concerns because one counts for naught the most necessary and sure means for succeeding there, which is God: this will be the first point; one has still less of it in what concerns salvation, because one does not even consider it a concern: that is the second. There is the subject of our discussion.

First Point

Whatever plan a man forms, be it for his fortune or for his reputation, no one could say on how many things it depends for success. The number of these things is in a sense infinite—and quite far from human prudence being capable of bringing them all together, I argue that the human mind would not even be able to count them. When, in order to succeed, we would need only health or life, who can say by how many accidents the one and the other can be taken from us? We are composed of an infinity of parts of which each is subject to an infinity of evils; each of these evils can come to us from an infinity of causes; we depend upon all of these causes in our smallest concerns; only one suffices to turn everything around. I do not speak of the aid of material and non-thinking things, as of the stars, of the weather, of the seasons, of gold and of silver, of plants, of animals, of insects—all of that can either help us or harm us. I speak only of people[7], some of whom we need in order to advance our designs, and others easily can oppose them. Who can account to us for so many intentions, so fickle by their nature? By how many paths can [these intentions] become removed from our interests and become even contrary to us!

Moreover, not only does the success of our undertakings depend upon an infinite number of creatures, causes, accidents, circumstances; but none of these things depends on us. Quite far from being able to bring together, to dispose, to govern so many means, there is not even one of them of which we are the masters; there is neither credit, nor authority, nor precaution that can assure us of anything. The Sage therefore was quite right to say that the providence of men was irresolute and uncertain: "Our counsels are uncertain."[8] There is only that [providence] of God that is infallible. Because all things depend on him, he alone can move everything, stop everything, when it pleases him and as it pleases him; he alone can make free causes act to his pleasure without forcing them, and necessary causes without making any effort himself.[9] At one moment he approaches the most distant, he distances the closest, he joins them, he separates them, he opposes them to one another, and by completely opposite movements he makes all of them conspire to one same design. Be forever praised, O my God, that you are the only one who knows everything and can do everything. How well this infinite force fits this infinite Wisdom! How happy we are to be ruled by so great a Master above all if we let ourselves be ruled by him.

But, if it is true that, of this infinite number of causes that ought necessarily to come together for the execution of our thoughts, there is not even one that depends entirely either on us or on our care; if it is true that all [of them] are uniquely and entirely at the disposition of the Lord, can one imagine an imprudence equal to that of men who, in all their concerns, make such a great foundation on their mind, on their forethought, and who neglect to have recourse to God, as if they were able to manage without his help?

What would you say of a man who, having the intention to build a magnificent palace, would content himself to make a great pile of materials, instruments, and machines, and who would not dream of looking for an architect and workers to budge these instruments and use these materials? That is what we do, Christian auditors, when we fail to have recourse to God in our temporal concerns. One looks for money, one makes friends, one tries to acquire some authority and some reputation; these here are only the materials. Besides that is required a sovereign wisdom that directs the project and an infinite force that operates under this wisdom. What madness to content oneself to accumulate sand and stones, as if these stones could place themselves by themselves and bind themselves together by the plan that we have outlined for them.

You admit in good faith that it is difficult to do anything by oneself— that one cannot manage without the advice and service of others; you confess that you need a hundred things without which you would not be able to reach the end of your plan. Are you unaware that God is the Lord of all these things? Do you think yourself able to make use of them, if he does not agree to it? Is there one sole creature who acts for us, if it has not received the order from its Creator to do so? See therefore what your good sense is in assuring yourself regarding things that do not belong to you, without having dealt with the master, without having asked him for his consent that you make use of them, like a deluded soldier who, having placed himself in charge of conquering a kingdom, would insanely count on the troops and ships of a foreign king, without bothering to win over this prince, without even having begged him to send him his forces. Prudence, says Saint Augustine, is a kind of love that disentangles in a subtle way the means by which it can draw some advantage for its plans from the obstacles that would be capable of ruining them: "Prudence is love that wisely separates those things by which it is helped from those by which it is impeded."[10] It is for that [reason] that a wise man no sooner has formed a resolution than, glancing to all sides, he tries in particular to discover who are the people who can harm or serve him, in order to engage them, if it is possible, in his interests. And yet one does not think of the Lord without whom men can neither harm nor serve, who himself alone can truly reestablish in an instant the most hopeless and topple the best established affairs. In that we are all the more imprudent because we are not unaware that he is extremely jealous of his[11] glory; that, as he takes pleasure in protecting exceedingly and entirely those who have recourse to him, he also is accustomed to confound the vain confidence that others have in their wisdom. It is for that [reason] that he reproves the projects of monarchs, according to the word of David: "he casts away the counsels of princes."[12] Not that he repels kings, when they go and see him in order to have his protection, but as they always are surrounded by a great number of human means, they consider more rarely than other men to take recourse to the King of kings; and God who wants everyone to understand that nothing is done without him, God, I say, is pleased to break all their arrangements and to render useless their greatest preparations: "[the Lord] rejects the devices of people, and casts away the counsels of princes."[13]

But our imprudence goes even further still. We believe we are able to succeed not only without imploring the aid of heaven, but even [with] heaven being against us. There is no one even among the infidels who does not know that, when we are on bad terms with our God, we are as stricken by all kinds of misfortunes. Find out, said Achior to Holofernes, how those of Bethulia are with the God whom they adore. If they have irritated him by some sin, let us go brazenly attack them on the peak of their highest mountains, for they cannot get away from us. "Search, if there be any iniquity of theirs in the sight of their God, and let us go up to them, because their Lord will surely deliver them to you."[14]

In effect, when we have displeased God, it happens, I know not how, that everything goes against us. We work in vain; everything resists us; we find at each step a new obstacle that we are incapable of overcoming: "the king is not saved by a great army."[15] There is no monarch so powerful who is therefore safe. Saul, though in the midst of his army, fell twice into the power of David whom he was persecuting. "Nor will the giant be saved by his own great strength."[16] Goliath was a giant whose presence alone made the whole camp of Israelites shudder; he was fully armed and yet a child brought him down and cut off his head with his own sword. "Vain is the horse for safety," continues the same prophet.[17] What did it serve Absalom to be the most skilled of his horsemen? This advantage was an obstacle to his flight, quite far from helping it. He was carried off by his horse with such swiftness that, passing beneath an oak, his head got caught between two branches:[18] "Vain is the horse for safety." The reason that one can give for this is that creatures have been made only for the use of the innocent man. That is why one need not be surprised if, as soon as he has revealed himself guilty of some sin, [those creatures] all abandon his service—if they themselves, from whom he promised himself more help, are unfaithful to him and revolt against him.

Prudence would dictate therefore that before getting involved in any matter, if one is in mortal sin, one try to enter back into grace with God, so that he not oppose himself to our plans. Do you do it, Christian auditors? This man who passes for clever and who himself believes himself so competent in all kinds of affairs, this man who anticipates from so far the smallest difficulties, who anticipates them with such skill, who takes such just measures, who omits no precaution, who has for maxim to bet only on sure things—when he advised those who came to him as to the oracle, did he advise them to begin by putting themselves in a good state? When did he himself make use of this advice?

There is a strange blindness for the people who pride themselves on some wisdom. But here is the height of foolishness. In order to succeed in temporal concerns, one makes use of paths directly opposed to God. One thinks it possible to manage not only without having first appeased [God], but even in irritating him again, in offending his interests and taking him, so to speak, to task. It is what is done, not only by this policy that makes religion give way to reasons of the state, this courtesan who is happy to owe her fortune to her treachery, this judge who hopes to make himself friends in making unfortunates;[19] but even this tradesman who, in order to enrich himself or, if you want, even to survive, sells on feast days to all who go and come, and sells at false weight, at false measure, who adulterates his merchandise, who lies and who betrays his promise in order to make [his merchandise] worth more, who disparages his neighbor in order to attract his patrons; this laborer who works on prohibited days; this servant who is not faithful; this girl who, intending to establish herself, dresses indecently, keeps dangerous company, has recourse to vanity and to artifices that the law of God prohibits.[20] In truth, Gentlemen, do we believe that such paths can lead us where we aspire? Is it possible that the human spirit presumes to be able to do something not only without the aid of its Creator, but even despite him? Will this Providence, so wise and so strong, allow it? Would you allow it, my God? You, who dash the plans of those who trust in their own strength, will you facilitate the desires of those who offend you in satisfying themselves? Will you bless the means that you prohibit, that dishonor you? Quite far from that, Christian auditors, he will turn these means against those who put them to use; he will take revenge on them by themselves and will make them find their punishment in their own sin. It is thus that he has done since the beginning of the world until today.

Adam wanted to raise himself through his disobedience, and it threw him into all kinds of difficulties.[21] The brothers of Joseph sold their brother for fear of finding themselves one day forced to obey him, and through that itself they prepared for themselves the yoke beneath which they finally had to yield.[22] The people of Israel multiplied all the more so in Egypt because Pharaoh imposed greater works upon them in order to overwhelm them: "But the more they oppressed them, the more they were multiplied, and increased."[23] Saul wanted to ruin David in order to retain the kingdom for his children, and the persecutions served only to render his enemy more renowned and to move him closer to the throne from which he had the intention to distance him.[24] The Jews feared losing their city and their temple if they did not have Jesus Christ killed, and this injustice attracted to them all the evils that they hoped to avoid in committing it:[25] "They were afraid of losing their temporal possessions, and thought not of life eternal; and so they lost both."[26] Something similar happens all the time to our false sages. God allows that these unjust dealings ruin this man who promised himself immense profits. You thought to enrich yourself by retaining this good that is not yours; you will see that after all you will lose even what you acquired by very legitimate means. The Lord will make it so that this calumny will fall back onto you yourself. The excessive care that you take to please men will disparage you and make you fall into confusion. You congratulate yourself in secret for your malice, says David;[27] you think to be able to accomplish your plans by force of sins; every day you dream up some new surprise; you are skilled at cheating your neighbor; you have preferred violent paths to those that gentleness and charity recommended to you; you loved more to make use of prohibited [rather] than legitimate means: "Therefore God [will destroy] you forever: he will remove you from your dwelling place, and your root out of the land of the living."[28] Maybe God will put up with you for a little while; but at last he will destroy you, he will strip you of all your goods, he will reduce you to not have even a refuge on the earth. These grand designs of elevating, of immortalizing your family—these designs, I say, will go up in smoke and will perish with the children on whom they were based: "The just will see and fear, and will laugh at him."[29] The good people will be witnesses to your fall; you will be for them at the same time a dreadful example to confirm them in the fear of their God, and a subject of ridicule: "And [the just] say, 'Behold the man that made not God his helper, but trusted in the abundance of his riches and prevailed in his vanity.'"[30] There you have this man who thought to be able to manage without God, who did not judge that he ought to implore, not fear, his strength[31]. "Behold the man!"[32] See this poorly-advised one who established himself at the expense of his conscience and who thought that riches would place him above all setbacks. What do you say of this change? To what has the poor wretch been reduced? What difference between this radiance and this pomp that dazzled us not long ago, and the misery in which we see him today? "But I, as a fruitful olive tree in the house of God, have hoped in the mercy of God for ever, and for ever and ever."[33] For me, I am in the house of God, as a fertile olive tree, always green and laden with fruit, fearing neither lightening nor the storm, because I have put all my hope in the Lord and he will be eternally my only support.[34]

Do you then want, Christian auditors, to govern yourselves prudently in the conduct of your temporal concerns? Disabuse yourself of this error: that one can ever win something in losing God. You can be sure that sooner or later you will regret having sacrificed his interests to yours, and you will regret it all the more because it will have taken more time from you to repent of it. Furthermore, never begin anything significant without having tried to get on God's good side. You undertake a voyage, a company, a trial; you have to negotiate an estate or a responsibility; one speaks to you of a marriage or a job: go confess before taking any step, before hearing any proposition; fear all things, beware of everything, until you are morally assured that God loves you. What fruit can you expect from your works, while you will have on your hands such a powerful enemy? After these precautions, it is permitted to you to make use of all the human means that offend in no way the law of God. But in this there are still two important rules to observe. The first is not to put all your confidence in these means, in such a way that you neglect however to take recourse to God at all times. I at least would want that one divided these cares between heaven and earth: I am certain that things would go much better. You think night and day of your [earthly] concerns: I admit that it is some prudence to think of them; but remember the advice of the wise man: "set bounds to thy prudence"[35]—put limits on your prudence; release some of this constant attention; use for prayer a part of this time that you consume in consulting and examining your plans: this prayer, which seems to have little to do with these concerns, will not advance them less than your long consultations. You make generous gifts to those who can serve you, either from their credit, or from their hand; if you gave to the poor a part of what you distribute to these people, your gifts would be without fail still more effective: employ fewer solicitors on earth and try to enlist some saint to speak for you in heaven. You have to see your judges, your patrons, your friends; but must you make yourself a bore by your regularity? Omit some of these visits and multiply those that you pay to Jesus Christ in the Blessed Sacrament of the altar, and you will see that your appeals, though less frequent, will become imperceptibly more profitable.

The second rule is that you have no confidence in these moderate cares that you henceforth will bring to your [earthly] concerns. You need not neglect them; but you ought to consider them as instruments that can serve equally to build and to destroy. It is up to the Lord to make that they be useful to you; for, if he does not lend a hand there, neither this work, nor these friends, nor this money, nor this doctor, nor these remedies would be able to give you what you expect of them. Say therefore to your God, when you use [these things] in this manner, "My God, I know the uselessness of all these things; I make use of them because you want it so and because I know that you can make use of them to help me; but it is not upon this that I base my hope. I expect an aid much more strong and more powerful: "My help is from the Lord, who made heaven and earth."[36] It is from you, O my God, who created heaven and earth, it is from you that I hope for everything; it is you whom I want to thank for all things. I would be quite insane to believe that, without you, your creatures were able to do anything in my favor, since they would not even exist without you. However, Gentlemen, this is an insanity that is only too common in the world. It is in this, it seems to me, that we lack prudence even with regard to temporal concerns. Let us see if it is true that we have still less of it in the matter of Salvation.

Second Point

It is to be quite imprudent, in the management of an important concern, to count for nothing the surest and most essential means that one have to make it succeed. But one commits an even much

more considerable imprudence when one neglects [that means] entirely and does not even count it as a concern. I am convinced that
it would be difficult to find a person in this assembly whom one can
criticize for such conduct in the matter of her Salvation. But alas!
there are Christians in the world to whom this criticism applies in
all its scope! You will judge it, if you please, Gentlemen, after two
small reflections that I am going to propose to you.

The first: when a matter arises that one judges of some importance for
the temporal realm, is it not true that one thinks of it very often and that,
until it be finished, one has difficulty to think of another thing? Is it not
true that one searches in one's mind for all the means that can help us
to get out of it happily, that one does not rely on oneself for it, that one
still takes counsel of others and that for this one takes care to do and see
the most skilled and most experienced? Even more: after having devised
several means capable to make the thing succeed to our taste, does one
not have the custom to compare these means with each other in order to
discover those that will be able to be the most appropriate? And when one
finally has recognized them, is there ever found a man senseless enough to
prefer, calmly and with complete understanding, the weakest to the most
effective, the most complicated to the shortest, the most perilous to the
most safe, to the most certain? I blush, Christian auditors, when, after this
reflection, I glance at the conduct of Christians concerning Salvation. No,
I say to myself, no, without doubt, one does not know the importance of
it; one does not even know what it is about. For it must be confessed that
there are only too many people who, in all their life, have not thought seriously of this one single time. One dreams of a trial, both during the time
of rest, and during that of sleep; one remembers it at prayer; one is completely occupied with it, even at play. Alas! If one gave to the care for Salvation at least idle time, if one considered it when bored and when one thinks
of nothing at all! But no; that is a care that occupies very few people; the
majority of people find no leisure for that in all their life.

That supposed, one need not be surprised that one troubles oneself little
to take the advice of anyone regarding this concern, since one does not consult oneself. But it is strange that, when one advises himself to ask counsel
on this, it seems that one have the desire to be misled. One confesses to a
confessor whom one has not chosen, but whom one has encountered ran-
domly: it is today this one, it will be tomorrow another; or if one makes the
choice of someone, that will be of him whom one hopes should be the most
indulgent or by whom one thinks that one will be the least known. Finally,
one cannot deny that one sometimes compares the means that can lead us to
heaven; but is that to take the best and the most certain? This is what seems
incredible and what is not practiced in any other concern: no, it is not to
choose the best means that one deliberates; it is most often in order to follow

the most uncertain and weakest. Can one save oneself in seeing the world, as well as in keeping oneself on retreat?[37] Solitude is a sure and easy way; the business of the world is full of dangers—a kind of miracle is needed to live there in a Christian manner; nevertheless, it is not absolutely impossible: that is enough; one does not ask more of them?[38] Can one go to the theater and dance hall without sinning mortally? If one could do it, it is only with great difficulty; maybe that is possible, as it is possible for a vessel without masts and without rudder to resist the most horrible storms: that is too much; one exposes oneself at that point with the same assurance as if one were certain to escape. A man who, in every other concern, would fix himself upon a choice of this kind, would he not pass for the greatest fool in the world?

The second reflection: when one has a very significant matter, one thinks of no other matter of lesser importance unless one have examined whether it will be able to serve or to harm the main one. For example, a man has the intention to establish himself. Not only does he always carry this intention in his mind, but in all the other matters that present themselves, he hardly resolves to put them off or to undertake them except as he judges that they might be obstacles or means for his establishment. It is thus that one would behave with regard to Salvation, if one counted it for something; it would enter into all our deliberations; nothing would be determined until after having consulted the interest of the soul; its advantage would be a motive to make us act; and to stop us in our encounters, it would suffice to know that [the soul] ran some risk. Speak to me frankly, Christian auditors; you know in what manner one lives in the world; is this here the conduct that one keeps there? How many people have chosen the state in which they ought to spend their life, without having examined if they were called there, if it would be easy or difficult for them to gain heaven there!

When that man has deliberated about the work that he has chosen, he has considered if it was honorable, if he could draw from it the means to live glamorously, if it did not demand too much regularity and too many tiring works. But has he considered if he could easily discharge his duties according to God, if there was nothing to fear for his conscience? This child must be enlisted in the ecclesiastical state; that is a state which has nothing too bothersome, in which one easily finds the means to live with honor; one even can arrive there at very significant dignities; finally the family will be less burdened with him and his elder brother will be wealthier because of it. But he is not called there; he has a nature and inclinations that bear little resemblance to the holiness of this state; he runs the risk of losing himself. That is what one does not consider. One would say that Salvation is an illusion,[39] that it happens without thinking of it, that this life is not the time to deal with it; in a word, either that it is not a concern, or that it is not our concern.

What does it serve us, Christian company, that God has given us reason, if it is useless to us in the only thing for which it was given to us, which is to gain paradise? Alas! We use it, so to speak, this reason—we squander it to develop and to guide the plans of children. We make ingenuities where it is a matter of nothing.[40] Each one prides himself on giving wise advice and on making an extraordinary prudence shine out in all things. And yet we lack the main thing, and when it has to do with eternity one would say that we do not even have common sense. Herein lies quite enough to disabuse you of these false measures, which expose you to such a great misfortune.

Let us conclude, Christian auditors; but before finishing let us all make a firm resolution to be more prudent than we have been up to this moment in the thing that matters to us most in the world. First, may we take time to deliberate on the matter of our Salvation. Would a quarter of an hour, every day, be too much to examine its condition, and what stops it at present, by what obstacles it may be blocked in the future, by what means one can raise these obstacles and in some way assure oneself some success; in a word, to ask oneself seriously: "What must I do to possess eternal life?"[41] How could I act in order to save myself?

Let us have zealous people, but wise, clear-sighted, unselfish [people], whom we can consult often and whose advice holds the place of rule and inviolable law for us. In the second place, in the other deliberations, may the reason of Salvation be always the strongest in our mind and may it win out over all the other reasons. Yes, in all the concerns that present themselves, let us make use of the practice of a great saint from the last century who, before undertaking anything, had the habit of making this brief reflection: "What does this serve for eternal life?"[42] What rapport has this with blessed eternity? May we place ourselves in the presence of God and try to adopt the same sentiments that we will have at the hour of death; let us see what one proposes to us—if what we desire, if what we are about to do is either useful, useless, or harmful to the afterlife. If the thing is of some use for our main intention, however painful it might be to nature, although human reason can argue in order to render it horrible to us, let us embrace it, and let us embrace it with joy, since in truth it is a treasure that has fallen into our hands. If it is useless, although it otherwise be either pleasant or worthwhile according to the world, let us make little of it—let us even hold it in contempt; but above all let us be very careful not to have for it this enthusiasm, this overzealousness that we ought only to have for the Sovereign Good. That if it is a question of something that pushes back, that hinders our Salvation, that puts our soul in some danger, when it would have to do with gaining the whole world, let us flee, Christian auditors; let us be horrified with this thought and not hesitate one minute to reject it.

"For what does it profit a man, if he gain the whole world, and suffer the loss of his own soul?"[43] What would it serve us to have gained the whole world, if after that we lose our soul, this soul for which the whole world has been created, this soul that ought still to live on after the whole world will have been destroyed, this soul for which God would give, God would sacrifice a thousand worlds? The soul [being] lost, can we retain something of all the rest? Will our wealth and our pleasures accompany us in the other life to console us for the immense loss that we will have made, if we have lost our soul? "For what does it profit a man, if he gain the whole world, and suffer the loss of his own soul?" To lose his soul, and to lose it with no means of support, and to lose it forever! Ah! There is nothing that is not worth risking in order to prevent such a great misfortune.

Every day we see virtuous people who renounce all the goods, all the sweet things of life, who think to gain much if, in stripping themselves of all things, they dispose themselves to go save the soul of a savage.[44] And you think that there are goods that can compensate you for the loss of yours [i.e., your soul]? The Son of God rejoices in happiness: he wants that heaven and earth be pleased with him, when, on account of the paradise that he left, on account of the blood that he shed, he won the soul of a sinner, of a villain; and I would attach so little importance to mine [i.e., my soul] to consent to lose it for something earthly and passing! Do not permit it, O my divine Redeemer. Since this soul is yours as well as mine, since it is incomparably more yours than mine, since it has cost you so much, since it is precious to you, make that I value it, if it is possible, as much as you value it, that I love it as much as you love it, so that I give everything for it, and[45] that I not give it away for anything in the world. *So be it.*

On Mortal Sin[1]

We are going to Jerusalem where the Son of man will be delivered to the priests
and to the doctors, and condemned by them to death. (Matt 20:18)[2]

The cause of Sin, in the man who commits it, is a mortal hatred against God;
the effect of Sin, in God against whom it is committed, is an infinite
hatred against man.

SOME DAYS BEFORE THE SON OF GOD was to die, he took aside his
disciples and told them in secret everything that had to happen to him at
his Passion. The Son of Man is going to be sold to the Jews, judged worthy
of death, then handed over to the power of the Romans, who will mock
him, scourge him, and fix him to the cross: "And will deliver him to the
Gentiles to be mocked, and scourged, and crucified."[3] What do you say
of this prophesy, Christian auditors? Is there nothing more clear, nothing
more precise, better indicated than these circumstances? However, if we
believe Saint Luke, the apostles understood none of this; it was for them an
unfathomable mystery: "And they understood none of these things."[4] You
are amazed at this, undoubtedly. For me, I am not surprised in the least.
And who would have ever thought that such a great innocence, a holiness
as recognized as that of Jesus Christ could be open to the least doubt; that a
man so beneficent, so amiable could be the object of such a furious hatred?

But is it really true, Christian company, what one has preached to us so
often, what Saint Paul himself teaches us in his *Epistle to the Hebrews*, that
whoever commits a mortal Sin makes himself guilty before God of an injustice as cruel, as appalling as that?[5] If that were [so], would there be found
a man in the world who consented to sin mortally? Can one love a pleasure
or his interest to the point of hating God who is nothing but love, who has
nothing in him that is not infinitely worthy to be loved? This is only too
true; but it is also true that one hardly reflects on it, when one sins. The
Jews, completely wicked as they were, would never have crucified the King
of glory, says the Apostle, if they had known it.[6] How much further would
the Christians, in whom the Gospel has inspired such humanity and such

sweetness, be from offending God if they knew how much God is offended by their sins! It seems to me that it will not be pointless to devote one of our discussions to a subject of such great consequence. If we do not say things strong enough to convert the sinner, I hope that the Holy Spirit will inspire us with things reasonable enough to confirm the good [people] in the horror they have of Sin. It is on your intercession, Holy Virgin, that this hope is based; you will not refuse it to the prayer of the Church. *Hail, Mary.*[7]

I see only two rules by which one can properly judge the malice and the shamefulness of Sin. We must try to untangle the sentiments that arouse it in the heart of the creature; we must, if possible, discover the sentiments that it arouses in the heart of God. I say that the cause of Sin, in the man who commits it, is a mortal hatred against God; I say that the effect of Sin, in God against whom it is committed, is an infinite hatred against man. There is nothing so appalling as to hate that which is infinitely lovable; there is nothing so appalling as that which is hated by the One who is infinitely good. It is by this double hatred that I hope to give you today a perpetual loathing of mortal Sin. I will speak, in the first point, of that [hatred] which [mortal sin] contains in itself against God; and, in the second, of that which [mortal sin] attracts to itself on the part of God. Let us begin.

First Point

There is a saying which the force of truth has torn from the mouth of the most impious of all princes: that it is just that man be submissive to God—"It is just to be subject to God."[8] Indeed, if nature inspires in us some respect for those who have given us life, [nature] teaches us to submit ourselves, as though blindly, to their wills. God being the Father of our own parents, having drawn them out of nothingness, having formed us in the womb of our mothers and having created from nothing this soul that distinguishes us from the animals and that makes us to be what we are, to whom can we owe a more respectful and more complete submission? Moreover, this obedience that all wise men, [that] all the nations on earth, have judged that one owes so justly to the rulers is based only on the protection that they give to the peoples—on the care that they take to procure for their subjects an easy and peaceful life.[9] But, Gentlemen, it is the Lord who provides us continuously all the necessities of life, who watches around us to ward off the dangers that threaten us, and without whose protection all the vigilance, all the weapons of kings could not secure us one sole moment from death: "Unless the Lord keep the city, he watches in vain that keeps it."[10] Consequently he has the right to command us—he has the right to establish laws by which he declares to us his good pleasure; and the resistance that one make to him ought to be taken as criminal disobedience—for a completely apparent rebellion.

This principle set down, Christian auditors, do you want to know what Sin is? It is a word, an action, a desire that offends the law of God. So it is that all the doctors define it, after the master of doctors, Saint Augustine: "It is a word, deed, or desire contrary to the eternal law."[11] Therefore, from the assent of all peoples and according to all the most natural wisdom, Sin is a brutal revolt—an unjust refusal that we make to recognize a very absolute and very legitimate power.

This act of treachery is all the more appalling that, God being truly the master of our goods, of our lives, of all our actions, and being able, without doing us wrong, to demand all things of us, and even the most difficult things, he demands of us only very little, and all very reasonable things.

Human laws impose on us many other obligations! They, as well as God, keep vengeance for themselves: they punish adultery with death and fornication with disgrace, which is something worse than death itself; but in addition, they oblige us to give our goods—the fruit of our efforts and of our sweat—to risk our lives for public service, to banish ourselves from our birthplace to go carry out, in other worlds, through a thousand dangers, the orders of our monarchs. Add to this that, being able to use violence and to force us to obey him, [God] demands nothing but by love; that, although we be his slaves in a thousand ways, he does not want to be obeyed free of charge, but only in paying and giving, for the smallest services, infinite rewards. Finally, all that he commands us has only our own interest for goal. He has no use for our regards or marks of respect; he wants only to make us happy, he offers us the means to become [happy], and he uses his sovereign authority only in order to make us put these means in use.

Whence does it come then, Gentlemen, that, God being truly our King, having over us a power that has no limits, we refuse to obey him in such little things although he demands them with such sweetness, although they be all for our good and that he promises to leave nothing without reward? Is it thus that one treats the most vicious princes who have for all their merit only a crown of which they are unworthy? I see well what this is, Christian company: it is that we do not love God—it is that we really hate him; and it is for this that one does not content oneself with neglecting his wishes; one goes so far as to despise them, so far as to violate them with insult. The least interest, the least pleasure is more than enough to resign us to displease him; still more, we do it even often without being brought there by any reason of pleasure or self-interest—it seems that it is enough that he has made a law, to give us the desire to break it. You will think of it as you please; but if this is not the sign of an empoisoned heart, full of hatred and of loathing, I confess that I do not see what it can be.

"This is not by a movement of hatred," you will tell me, "it is rather lack of reflection." One does not consider it [hatred], I admit, but it is for that very reason that I say that one does not love him. When one loves the one who has authority in hand, one receives blindly all the orders that come from him, one executes them with warmth, with joy, without considering if they are unjust or difficult. When it is on behalf of an indifferent person that one commands us, one examines the thing dispassionately, completely ready to obey or to refuse to do it, as one will find some justice, profit, or readiness there. But from an enemy, one does not deign so much as to dream of it; one prefers to give up these genuine benefits than to submit; one prefers to risk everything than to purchase his safety and his fortune by the least accommodation.

In the second place, Sin does not contain only an outrageous disobedience but, in addition, an extreme ingratitude; and I claim that this ingratitude can only be the effect of a great hatred. My intention is not to place here before your eyes the benefits of creation and redemption, all the particular graces that we have received and that we still receive every day of his divine mercy. What do you have that you have not received from God, says Saint Paul?[12] Not only are you completely laden with his gifts, but you are, so to speak, completely constructed of them. I would not be able to bring myself to a more precise description: it is an ocean without bottom and without limits; I get confused, I get lost as soon as I try to think about it.

That being so, Christian auditors, how do you want us to call the offenses that we commit against our God? When one does not recognize the graces of which one has been informed, when one forgets them, it surely is a very appalling ingratitude. But, when one comes to the point of doing harm to his benefactor, does one not mock both him and his benefits? Is this not a hatred all the more strong that it cannot be conquered by the memory of goods received, that it seems to get aroused by those that one actually receives, that it even uses these goods to offend the One who is their author?

How is it, said the chaste Joseph to the wife of his master, she who solicited him to sin, how is it that I can do this wrong to your husband?[13] I now have in my power everything he possesses in the world; he has left all to me, save you who are his wife. What reason could bring me to dishonor him in this way? What cause do I have to hate him to that extent? I could have forgotten the ancient obligations that I have to him; but here I am still completely laden, completely surrounded by his favors. "How then can I do this wicked thing, and sin against my God?"[14] Joseph finds impossible a sin that he could commit with impunity, to which one presses him to consent, in an age when one has so little strength to resist similar temptations: he finds it impossible, I say, because he loves his benefactor. Whence does it come therefore that a man who sees himself in the world as in the house of

God, master of all creatures, neither living nor breathing but by his sheer mercy, can consent to the sin that dishonors the author of such benefits? It is completely apparent that he does not love [God]. But when instead of resisting sin, he seeks of his own accord the occasions to dishonor him by committing it, when, not only does he not defend himself against those who solicit him, but he solicits even those who defend themselves, who can deny that he does not hate the One who has given him so many reasons to love him?

I know that often we excuse our dissoluteness by our wicked inclinations, by our natural weakness. But one cannot say that ingratitude be a vice that begins with us, given that naturally we have such leaning to the opposite virtue. Although Rome desired the death of Caesar who had brought it into subjection, although for a long time Rome looked, so to speak, among its citizens for someone who was tired of the servitude and who broke the chains under which it groaned, yet [Rome] hated to receive this service from the favorite of the dictator.[15] After Augustus, his successor, had forgiven Cinna the plot that he had formed against his life,[16] the Romans felt so indebted for this grace made to their liberator that the gratitude that they had for it smothered instantly in their soul this hatred of the monarchy that they all had taken in with their mother's milk, and which seemed ought never to pass away. This sole grace habituated them to the yoke—they loved better to be slaves than to seem ungrateful. It was pagans, Christian auditors, who had these sentiments; and nevertheless the goodness of the Lord—his readiness to forgive us a thousand times our own faults—could not make a similar impression on us. Gratitude makes [one] love those whom one has cause to hate: O God, is it that the hatred we have for our good Master is stronger than was that of this people for their tyrants?

Although sinners do not deserve that one show consideration for them in any way, still if the great Saint Ambrose had not first made use even of the example of a dog in order to teach us gratitude, I would not have dared mention what I am going to say.[17] About two years ago, [while] in a town in France,[18] someone recounted to me that, shortly before, a dog had bitten his master, who was entering his house in disguise and very abruptly. This poor animal developed such a great regret of what he had done that it was impossible to console him of it. He went to hide himself under a vat from which [the master] tried in vain to withdraw him, what little he could pet him. He presented him to eat and to drink everything that could be most to his taste, without ever being able to get him to touch it. Finally, [the dog] died three days later of pure sadness, unable to withstand the distress that he had of having been mistaken in the person of the one who fed him and who himself had despaired of not being able to save this beast who was made lovable in his gratitude.

"Man when he was in honor did not understand; he is compared to senseless beasts, and becomes like them."[19] That was the complaint that David made, Christian auditors. Man, whom God had established king and lord of all the animals of the earth—whom he had so strongly distinguished from them in making him reasonable and immortal—this man, I say, has lost human feelings; he has debased himself to the condition of beasts; he has become completely like them. But alas! Lord, things have gone even further still. This man has so degenerated, he has so greatly corrupted all the natural inclinations that there is reason to hope today that he might resemble the animals a little more and that, in his fury, he might spare at least, just like them, the One who has done such good for them and who has done nothing but good for them.

But this still is not enough. Not only does the sinner give signs of his hatred against God by his disobedience and by his ingratitude, but one can say, with Saint Bernard, that he hates God truly and with a formal hatred, not only because he does harm to him to the extent that he can, but because he wishes to do to him much more harm than he is capable of doing. Whoever can make up his mind to offend the Creator, the Master of all things, if he wants to examine the sentiments of his heart, will find that he would wish that there were no God or, at least, that this God lacked either justice or the strength to punish him, which is to desire his entire destruction. And, more to confirm this truth, I observe in the majority of sinners certain dispositions with regard to God, which can only be the effects of the extreme aversion they have of him.

They have all the trouble in the world to give some credence to his words. He explained himself as clearly as was possible; he confirmed by an infinite number of wonders what he said; the Greeks, the Romans, the Jews, the gentiles, the idolaters—the whole land believed the truths that he taught. But a sinner still cannot give credence to them. He has no reason to doubt, and it pleases him to doubt everything rather than to confess that God has spoken the truth: he will have the boldness to maintain that the whole universe has been blinded—that it has been taken for a fool—and that he alone has protected himself from such widespread illusion. It is that, in order to make a point unbelievable to us, it is enough that it be put forth by a person whom one does not love, whatever likelihood that the thing might be able to have otherwise. It is for this reason that the theologians say that, in order to have actual faith it is not enough to be greatly enlightened in the understanding; the heart still must be favorable to the one who reveals the object of faith and [the heart must] move the mind, which is only weakly attracted by obscure truths in themselves.[20]

But what do you say of the ease, or rather of the readiness, that they have to blame the Lord and to quibble constantly over the orders established by his infinite Wisdom? Now he has made man too weak for the commandments that he had to give him; now he demands tyrannically a submission that he is not unaware to be impossible for us; he has not made himself sufficiently understood to man; he would have been able to give us more knowledge on the subject of religion and not to leave us in the cruel uncertainty that exposes us to so many dangers. If [men] have nothing to say regarding what touches them, they are scandalized, they complain about the manner he employs toward the infidels who have never known Jesus Christ, toward the children who have died without having received baptism, toward the good who suffer and the wicked who prevail. Is it not a very ridiculous thing that blind, ignorant little creatures, such as we are, want to give advice to God and to comment on his behavior? Is it that we can be persuaded that in fact the Creator is unjust, that he has lacked goodness or counsel, that he would have done better if he had taken our advice, that he is less enlightened than a mole that he formed out of earth by a word and that returns to earth some days after it has been drawn from there? No, Gentlemen, no man is crazy enough to say that seriously or thoughtfully. But when one has hatred for a person, one can approve nothing of what she does, one finds fault with everything without reason, without even the appearance of reason, despite the clear and evident reasons that one would have to make more favorable judgments. And, to make clear that their complaints and their mutterings are the effects of their bad will, [note[21]] that those who love God are in sentiments most contrary to the sentiments of libertines and even seem sometimes to form completely opposing complaints. They find that the knowledge of God is as natural to us as reason and feeling: "It is signed, etc.;"[22] that he has given only too many proofs of the truths that it has pleased him to reveal to us: "Your testimonies have become exceedingly credible;"[23] finally, that the way of his commandments is too wide, that there is no difficulty to observe them: "your commandment is exceedingly broad."[24]

Gentlemen, Saint Augustine, in the first book of his *Confessions*, cannot be surprised enough that God commanded him to love him and that he commanded him to do it under serious penalties. Hey! What, Lord, he said to him, did I not already have enough reason to give you my love? You threaten me with extreme hardships, if I refuse to love you! Is there some hardship in the world more terrible than not to love you? "What am I to you [Lord,] that you command me to love you, and that, if I fail to love you, you are angry with me and threaten me with vast miseries? If I do not love you, is that but a little misery?"[25] But, if that is such a great hardship not to love God, Christian auditors, what ought one to say of those who hate him, of those whose hearts are full of gall against this inexhaustible source of sweetness, who have repugnance for this such perfect being who is the principle, the end[26], the center, the goodness of all creatures, who is the beauty of beauty itself and the goodness of all that is good in the universe?

What blindness, what frenzy can carry one of your creatures to hate you, O my God—you who are their Father and their King—and to hate you as far as to revolt openly against this infinite authority, which you exercise in such a paternal manner, as far as to forget all your benefits, as far as to make use of them even to insult you, as far as to desire your absolute destruction, as far as to destroy you, in as much as possible, in his mind by the thoughts of complaint and of blasphemy that [he]²⁷ entertains there!

Spirits of darkness, and you, reprobate Souls, who suffer in the underworld so many different punishments, how miserable you are to hate the One who formed you, the One whose love makes the seraphim so happy above the firmament! Oh, how all your tortures would seem easy to me, if you could suffer and love at the same time! What difficulty I have to understand how they can be sufficiently violent, these same tortures, to obligate you to wish evil to the One who has loved you so and who would love you still, if you had not forced him to hate you! But finally he does not love you anymore, his mercy has changed to hardness regarding you, he is to you a cruel and ruthless God. But what reason can we have, we others, to hate God, at the time when God showers us with goods, when he offers us his mercy, his grace, his paradise and, what is, to my mind, still more amiable, at the time when he offers us his divine love? You will not be surprised after that, Gentlemen, when I tell you that the Lord hates Sin in turn. But maybe you will be [surprised] to learn how much he hates it and what signs he has given of this hatred. That is the second part [of this talk].

Second Point

Origen, speaking of the death of Ananias and Sapphira, reported in the *Acts of the Apostles*,²⁸ says that the cause of this tragic accident was a ray of light by which God made known to them the sin that they had committed, and which depicted it to them so deformed and so dreadful that they could not stand the sight of it a single moment.²⁹ I do not think that Sin can be considered from any place more capable of making such a great impression than from the infinite hatred that God brings to it. And it seems to me that it is not thanks to a simple ray that this hatred can be perceived, but that we are completely surrounded by lights³⁰ that reveal it to us.

The first sign that God has given of the boundless loathing that he has for Sin is the condemnation of the first angel and of this countless number of spirits who were accomplices in the revolt. It is certain that Lucifer was the masterpiece of the Creator; that among his other works he shined like the sun among the stars; that God commended himself to have formed such a perfect creature; that he regarded him with a particular self-satisfaction. And yet this wretched angel had no sooner consented to sin that he became appalling in the eyes of God, that God could not resign himself to bear it a single moment in his presence, that [God] resigned himself to lose him, that there was no place far enough from heaven, dismal enough, in which to sink this object of horror, did [God] have to dig intentionally a hell at the center of the world to bury him there in the eternal darkness.[31]

I imagine a great vase of gold enriched with a thousand diamonds and of the most exquisite workmanship that ever indicated the skill of the first master of the world, into which falls by accident a drop of a liquor so vile that the worker smashes it, breaks it at once into a thousand pieces, has it thrown so far from him and into a cesspool so deep and full of so much filth that he can never see it and that it can never be seen by anyone without horror. It could be washed or even purified by fire. But after this infection, all the waters of the sea, all the sphere of fire do not suffice to have vanquished for him the loathing that he has developed of it. Neither the richness of a metal so precious, nor the brilliance of so many diamonds, nor the excellence of the work gives him any desire to keep it. He would have had a great deal of pleasure to see this masterpiece shine on a sideboard or in a royal hall. But, after it has been so polluted, he can no longer use it to any purpose; he loses it without regret and without hope.

What must this poison be, Christian auditors, that from the most perfect of creatures—that from so many creatures so perfect, full of so much wisdom, adorned with so many natural and supernatural gifts—could make, in such little time, objects so horrible even to that one who had formed them and of whom they were the most lifelike and sumptuous representations? He does not even want to hear either atonement or repentance discussed; there remains for him no movement of tenderness or of mercy for them; it is nothing but an infinite hatred that cannot be either extinguished or softened.

But, Gentlemen, if only one Sin was able to render appalling to God creatures so excellent, so spiritual—and who gave him such honor—alas! What will be of you, scrawny Creature, little Earthworm, Man molded of mire and mud—what will be of you, when you have received mortal Sin into your soul? Do you believe that he can put up with clay vases after such a horrible infection—he who has sacrificed vases of such great price?[32] What will be of these souls who have committed a thousand Sins—who wallow in filth, who are plunged in it and as though buried for so many years—who have all their senses infected with it—all the faculties of their bodies, all the powers of their soul![33] Who can express the horror that they embody to God and to the angels?

The second proof is in the punishment of Adam. I do not know if you have ever examined what anger his disobedience aroused in the heart of God, in the first place against Adam. But that is nothing: his whole race, all that carries a single trait of this disobedient man, as long as there will be a drop of his blood on the earth, the Lord will be angry and he will exercise a cruel vengeance. There has been no forgiveness for anyone. He has armed all creatures, all of nature. The animals, the smallest insects, the air, the water, the winds, the earth and the fire; the wars, the plagues, the fires, all that we suffer from poverty, from sickness, from heat, from cold—all that is an effect of this anger. It is already six thousand years that he has taken revenge[34]; his vengeance still is not assuaged: "A fire is kindled in his wrath, and will burn even to the lowest hell."[35] It will not end until the world end, until the whole universe be consumed by the fire of this anger, so that no trace of the Sin that ignited it remain.

How is it that this does not terrify you? What is our numbness, not to mention our arrogance, to dare sin in the sight of a God who carries such hatred for sin; and in the time itself that this hatred breaks out with such a terrible vengeance, that [God] goes everywhere, sword and torch in hand, burning and rooting out the remains of such an ancient rebellion!

I have said that his vengeance will last until the end of the world. But hell, which is the punishment for our present sins, will last a whole eternity. When I said "hell," "eternity," that is more than one could explain in several discourses;[36] all the evils, a duration that goes beyond all time. What I had to say above is that God is not unjust, that his hatred is not, as in men, an effect of his whim or of a blind antipathy. On the contrary, he is infinitely good and he loves infinitely all that he has made; he has an infinite inclination to gentleness, to do good; nothing is found in him that drives him to anger, says Saint Augustine, that carries him to revenge.[37] If something can carry him there, it must come from us, and then there is nothing more just than his hatred, nothing more proportionate to the merits of the thing that he hates. Judge therefore how much sin merits to be hated, since God will hate it, will persecute it, will punish it eternally!

That is what God does to take revenge on sin. But nothing makes more visible how much he hates it than what he has done to destroy it. Is it not too much to say that he wanted to descend from heaven and die himself to wipe it out? Did Samson not need to have a great hatred for the Philistines, to resolve himself to die himself, so as to ruin them at the same time?[38] One speaks of certain persons who poisoned themselves, who stabbed themselves, who had themselves burned alive in order to have the pleasure of seeing their enemy burn. I say that this is the effect of a strange hatred, since it is stronger than the love that each one has for oneself. The Son of God has hated sin as far as to want to die in order to destroy it. What is surprising is that less than that was not needed in order to prevent the effect of sin in only one man. God had to become man and die. All the penances, the austerities, the death of all creatures. . . .[39]

On Venial Sin[1]

A man fell into the hands of robbers who stripped him, and having covered him
with wounds, went away, leaving him half-dead. (Luke 10:30)[2]

The minor Sins are all dangerous in the sense that they lead to the death of the
soul, that they incline toward mortal sin: they oblige God, whose graces they bring
to an end, to permit [mortal sin]; they incline man, whose strength they weaken,
to commit [mortal sin].

THIS MAN, STRIPPED BY ROBBERS and left half-dead on the road, is a
figure and like a riddle proposed by Jesus Christ, to which the Holy Fathers [of
the Church] and the other doctors give various meanings. I have the intention
of explaining it today from the deplorable state[3] in which venial Sin reduces a
soul who abandons herself willingly to it and who gives it a free entrance into
herself. Perhaps one will tell me at first that this nudity, these wounds, this
fall, this mortal weakness are traits a bit too strong to express such a minor
evil. For it is thus that one commonly speaks. One treats as minor evil an action that offends God—that, to tell the truth, attracts not his hatred to us, but
at least his indifference, which makes us lose goods more precious than all
the treasures of the universe—that causes us damage in comparison to which
miserable eternity would not be a great difficulty, if [miserable eternity] could
be separated from the sins for which it is the punishment.

I admit, Christian auditors, that venial Sin is a minor sin; but I am quite
distant from acknowledging that it is a minor evil. It is minor with regard
to mortal sin, which is the greatest of all evils; but, considered in itself and
outside of this comparison, there is neither suffering, nor infamy, nor
torment—however cruel, however despicable it may be—that not be pref-
erable to the least of these faults that we call "slight." They are slight only
because one commits them thoughtlessly[4] and without considering enough
what one does. Venial Sin is, with regard to mortal [sin], what sickness is with
regard to death. I confess that death is something dreadful; but that does not
prevent that leprosy, epilepsy, paralysis, gout, kidney stones, a raging and

continuous fever, be strange curses of God, and that one avoid them with great care. Please God, Gentlemen, that I can make you see, in this discourse, how significant is this sin! The fruit would be greater than one thinks. But this is absolutely impossible: the most enlightened of all the angels would strive in vain to makes us to imagine all its greatness [i.e., of venial sin], since he does not understand it himself. I will try only to show you that this is not so minor a sin as people convince themselves; and that seems easy to me with the heavenly aid that I expect from the intercession of the Holy Virgin: *Hail, Mary.*[5]

When I say that a venial Sin is a great evil, I speak not of these sins of pure frailty that one commits rarely and that one effaces by penance almost as soon as one has committed them. The just, according to the word of the Holy Spirit, are not exempt from these kinds of woes, and all the theologians teach that they are in some way unavoidable.[6] I speak of the faults that Christians who live in half-heartedness are accustomed to commit deliberately and of which they make for themselves habits that they hardly bother to correct.[7] Such are the minor angers, the minor swipes, the words of contempt, the slight gossip, the mockery, the lies, the irreverence and the voluntary distractions in prayer, the desire to please people, the humorous talk that can produce nasty thoughts, the curious looks, too great a love of neatness in dress, laziness, the minor overindulgence in drinking and in eating, the negligence in things that pertain to duty, as in the instruction of servants and in the education of children; in a word, all sins of whatever kind they may be, when the issue is slight or there is more lack of consideration than malice. I say, Christian auditors, that these faults, above all when they are actual[8]—when one often falls back into them, when one neglects to mend one's ways from them, when one counts them for nothing—I say that these are the greatest evils.

Of many reasons that present themselves in order to prove this, I choose not but one sole of them, which will be the whole subject of our discussion. The little Sins are great evils, because they are great dispositions to the greatest Sins; they are all mortal, in this sense that they lead to the death of the soul, that they dispose to mortal sin; they dispose to it, both from the side of God whose graces they deplete, and from the side of the individual whose forces they exhaust. They oblige God to permit it: this will be the first point; they dispose people to commit it: this will be the second. That is the whole outline of this discourse.

First Point

It is only those who do not know God who treat as minor Sins, the Sins one calls "venial." It is true that [venial sins] are not punished with an infinite and eternal penalty. But, in the opinion of the great chancellor of Paris,[9] they merit [this penalty], and the Lord could not be accused of injustice if he damned us for having committed only one of them.

In effect, Christian auditors, the same God who is offended by mortal sin—this infinitely great and lovable God, this God to whom we owe everything, who has drawn us out of nothingness and who prevents us from falling back there—this same God, I say, is offended by venial Sin. It is true that it is as a slight thing; but the slightest offenses become infinite in some sense, when they are done to an infinite Majesty and Goodness. I know well that the faults that a subject can commit toward his prince are not all equal, but it is certain that none of them are minor. It would be an assassination attempt to conspire against his life—I admit that there is nothing darker than that; but he who would be happy to raise a hand to strike him on the cheek would not fail to have committed a great sin and to have deserved the severest tortures. We would regard as a freak of nature a child who would have stabbed his own father; but the one who only would have scratched his eyes out, wounded him, or thrown him to the ground—would he still not be the loathing of everyone, held just the same to insults and gestures of contempt? Who would dare say that a child who scorns his father—who insults him verbally—is not apart from that guilty and that he deserves some pardon? My God, how blind we are! Our dissoluteness horrifies us in these examples, and we are not affected by them when we consider them in themselves, where they are infinitely more horrible![10] Must we, Lord, forever return to these parables that point out to us so imperfectly your glory and your benefits?[11] What is a king—what is the greatest monarch in the world—in comparison to God who has drawn all monarchs from the mud—who strikes them, who throws them down, who kills them, who damns them—when it pleases him!

Can the obligations that we have to our parents be compared to those that we have to our Creator, to the Redeemer of our souls, to the perpetual Preserver of our goods and of our lives? And nevertheless it is even to this One here that we think ourselves able to lack respect and obedience, without doing anything that be greatly reprehensible and that one ought not easily to excuse. So it is that we judge it, Christian auditors. But God, who laughs at our thoughts and who judges our judgments, God, I say, is of quite opposite sentiments. He regards a venial Sin as an action worthy of the most severe punishments and indeed he punishes it with an extreme severity: witness the wife of Lot who was changed into salt for having turned her head slightly.[12] The defiance that Moses made apparent in striking twice the rock that was to give water to the people of Israel, this defiance, I say, cost him his life.[13] God struck with death seventy thousand soldiers in order to punish a vain indulgence that David had taken in making the review of his army.[14] A prophet was torn apart by a lion, simply for having been too gullible.[15] Forty-two young children were devoured by bears for having lost respect for Elisha.[16] We have in the Holy Books a hundred other examples of similar punishments for faults of the same nature. In the next life they are condemned to the same flames as the most enormous sins.[17]

There is no difference except in the duration of the torture, but of all the punishments with which God customarily punishes them, there is none of them more terrible than the removal of his graces, which is ordinarily followed by more grievous faults and often even by mortal sin. It is true, Gentlemen, that the minor faults do not attract the hatred of God; but it is a Catholic doctrine that they cool his heart and, consequently, that they put a stop to his liberalities—that they break off this particular providence that he exercises over his favorites and that shields them from all the abuse of the demons. He grows weary of putting up with an ungrateful soul, who thinks to acquit herself sufficiently of the infinite obligations that she has to him, by sparing him the final insults, although for the rest she gives him every day a thousand little annoyances. He gets imperceptibly sick of her services, he cuts off his favors from her, he breaks this narrow commerce that he entertained with her, he no longer takes such a great interest in what concerns her; finally, he abandons her to her enemies who, finding her thus deposed from such powerful protection, unload on her all their rage and give to her a thousand deadly blows.

You know the reproaches that Saint John makes in the Apocalypse to the bishop of Laodicea, in the name of the Savior: Please God, he says to him, that you were cold or hot; but because you are lukewarm, I will begin to vomit you from my mouth, like a piece of insipid and disgusting meat that my heart can no longer bear and that I am forced to reject.[18] This state of tepidness is the state of a Christian who is content to flee serious sins, who refrains only from what is mortal, who commits in all encounters a thousand slight infidelities and who neglects to mend his ways from them. It is the disposition in which Saint Teresa found herself for some time and which nearly ruined her without recourse: during that whole time there, she never lost grace; and nevertheless, her place was marked for her, from that time, among the damned, as she knew from revelation, God having resolved, if she finally had not awakened, to withdraw from her and to deliver her up to the passions that soon would have made her worthy of hell.[19]

There may be someone who will find severity in this behavior. But I beg you, Gentlemen, to consider that there is no one in the world who has not treated another in this manner. I am not speaking only of the great ones, whom only one reckless mistake often makes forget several years of very scrupulous and very useful service. I am certain that of all those who hear me there is no one who could bring himself to keep for long a servant, faithful to the truth, but who, apart from that, would have all kinds of faults, who never would obey except in grumbling and with slowness, who would speak always without respect, who would do everything grudgingly, who would be absentminded, unclean, indiscreet, who would break everything, who would dirty everything, who would spoil the whole job that one would put into his hands.

There, Gentlemen, is the picture of a man who scorns minor Faults. From morning to evening, he hardly does one sole deed where there not be something with which to find fault: one thing is corrupted by pride, the other by laziness, the other by sensuality and love for pleasure; if he prays, it is without attention; if he gives alms, he listens to the vanity that delights him; if he corrects his brothers or his children, he does it with anger and with harshness. He is soft in his pleasures, too greedy, too self-seeking in his affairs, weak and sluggish in his devotional practices. Finally he presents nothing to God that be good and straight, that does not offend his eyes in some way; he does nothing for him that there not always be something to hold against him. And you think that God should put up with him! You want him to keep a servant that you yourself would not want! You want at your service only flexible, clever, hard-working, industrious, watchful people; and you claim, says Saint Augustine, that the Lord will keep you before him, although you have all the vices opposed to these good qualities! He will not do it, Christian auditors; on the contrary, he will take measures to rid himself of you—he will let you get involved in dangerous circumstances, he will allow the demon to tempt you strongly, he will give you only weak graces that he will know ought to be ineffective; in a word, he will take from you this same grace, to the preservation of which you have committed all your care, just as the master of the Gospel took the silver coin from the servant who had contented himself with not squandering it.[20]

If you add to this that a Christian who contents himself exactly with retaining the friendship of God attaches hardly any importance to this same friendship, can one doubt that he soon obliges the Lord to deprive him of such a great good? Yes, Gentlemen, I maintain that whoever thinks only of saving himself from mortal sin, committing minor Sins without number and without scruple, I maintain, I say, that he truly fears having God as an enemy, but that he does not trouble himself with anything less than having him for a friend. When one appreciates the friendship of a person, one tries to insinuate oneself or to stay in her good graces by all kinds of politeness and indulgences, by a thousand services to which one is not even obligated, by a particular care to avoid everything that could displease her in the least; one refrains, for fear of torture, from mortally wounding even those whom one hates to death; one does neither good nor evil to those by whom one wants to be neither loved nor hated. But, for the little that one offends a man, above all if one does it often and with foresight, it is completely apparent that one also scorns both his love and his hatred and that, if one does not move on to great insults, it is for fear of his power rather than of his loathing. Indeed, if these people who are determined to do everything with the exception of great sins, if, I say, they themselves want to examine themselves a little, they will recognize that they avoid the serious sins only because of the serious penalties with which God punishes them—that they willingly would lay themselves open to displease him, if they had not been stopped by the vision of hell, and that they would wish with all their heart that one could offend him with impunity. But this disposition, Christian auditors, is in no way pleasant to God. This motive for refraining from sin is a motive in which he has no part and which, consequently, commits him in no way to help us. This is why I consider it morally impossible that a person who wants to avoid precisely only mortal sins can avoid them for long.

Beyond this negligence, which chills God's friendship and repels him—beyond the contempt we have for this same friendship, which makes us so worthy to be completely excluded from it—venial Sins, says Saint Augustine, cause in the soul a deformity that makes it ashamed of itself, that prevent it from reaching its Spouse with this tenderness and confidence that a pure and stainless heart feels.[21] [The soul] no longer has this sweet tenderness to pray that inspires perfect fidelity and to which the Lord refuses nothing. From there it comes that prayers are cold and listless, that one dare not demand nearly anything, that, at least, one dare not hope to obtain anything. One cannot believe that one can sway a Master who has so many little things about which to complain. This timidity—this defiance—renders our prayers ineffective, or, at least, makes that we attribute to them only very little help, which does not prevent us from perishing. I call all those who find themselves in this state to witness to this by the other good works that they practice—the confessions, the communions, the masses—all done without taste, without fervor and, consequently, almost without fruit. Much more, in this state of half-heartedness, it is nearly impossible that all the actions, although holy by themselves, be not mixed with other venial Sins, as with willful distractions, vain indulgences, laziness to rebuff thoughts of vengeance or of impurity that come to mind, curiosity, irreverence, and other similar ones. They are done therefore without merit, according to the maxim of Saint Chrysostom, who says that one cannot by the same action [both] gain merit and show oneself unworthy.[22] Such that, thus rendering useless to us the sources of graces and heavenly blessings, we often remain reduced to our strengths alone with which we would not be able to withstand the least temptations.

But if minor Sins have such disastrous consequences—if they lead God to abandon us to fate, if they dispose him to refuse us all help in the most pressing needs—whence does it come, you will ask me, that one calls them *venial*, since quite far from forgiving them willingly, he punishes them so severely? To this difficulty I have two things to respond. The first is that, although God easily enough grants forgiveness for these sins, yet the persons of whom I speak obtain it very rarely. It is true that God does not have to be persuaded much to deliver them; but he wants us to ask it of him as we should. He wants that one have a sincere distress to have fallen into [venial sins] and a firm resolution not to fall back into them in the future.[23] It is certain that without this there is neither holy water, nor prayer, nor even sacrament that can erase them.[24]

And yet I ask you if it is very easy to have this genuine regret, for one who disregards all that is not deadly—who customarily allows oneself all that God does not prohibit under pain of damnation? Who will persuade me that in your confessions you promise in good faith a prompt and perfect amendment, if you are of the mind that, for these minor faults, it is not worth the trouble to avoid them, and, if you lack these dispositions, quite far from being absolved, do you not commit a sacrilege? How often that happens, Christian auditors, to lukewarm and negligent people! And when there would be no other danger than that of passing from venial to mortal, I would have only too much reason to say that the one serves to dispose to the other, and that one does not go long without losing grace when one puts oneself in the mind that it is enough not to lose it.

I respond, in the second place, that although the fault and even the punishment of venial Sin is easily made right, it does not follow from this that one easily obtains the return of the graces that our negligence has diverted. As they were rewards prepared for our fidelity, it is quite necessary to make other efforts in order to call them back as to erase the stain with which our soul polluted itself. However, these graces will be necessary for us in certain encounters, in which they will be missing. I say necessary, because those that we will have for the time being will serve only to make our fall inexcusable.

This is what makes it that the saints consider that all sins are great; this is what renders [the saints] inconsolable when it happens that they willingly fall into the most minor [sins]; this is what carries them to make such long and such terrible penances for them. They are right, Christian auditors, not only because of the enormous brutality and intolerable ingratitude that there is to shock coldheartedly a God as kind and beneficent as ours; but still because of the horrible consequences that these minor Sins might have. That is also, Gentlemen, what ought to obligate us to live in a continual contrition and to take all the means that God and the Church offer us to expiate without ceasing these slight infidelities. One hardly puts oneself in danger of avoiding purgatory; one prefers to burn twenty and thirty years than to make either a fast or an alms; one worries little to be raised very high in heaven; one still manages very easily without all the strokes that God gives here below to his favorites. It is a blindness that should elicit great pity from the angels and the saints who know the grandeur of these goods that we despise.

But patience: it is not for all these things that I exhort you to purge your-selves without delay of even venial sins. It is a matter of your salvation; it is a matter of saving this grace that you yourself recognize to be a very great good. You know that you would lose everything in losing it. I have made you see that God often permits that one lose it in order to punish some faults that we consider slight. Let us ask him therefore for forgiveness, a thousand times a day, for these faults into which we fall every day. Let us tell him with a great feeling of pain and of humility: Lord, I recognize all my miseries in your presence; my life is nothing but an endless series of sins and acts of ingratitude; I forever fall from one into the other; I commit them at all times and in my holiest actions; I would be incapable of doing anything that does not give you some reason to complain; and God wants that even this prayer, that I offer you at present, draw to a close without my having displeased you in anything! I do not know how you can put up with me for so long; for it begins again every day, at every hour. However, I hope in your mercy and I dare to ask you for one more grace. I do not refuse to be punished; but, my God, you have thousands and thousands of scourges in hand with which you can strike me: "Many are the scourges of the sinner."[25] Punish me, my God, either by sorrow or by confusion, or by the loss of those whom I love, or if you want by all of these together. But do not punish my sins with other sins, my slight faults with serious faults; I fear only this from your justice; all the rest seems to me rather to come from your mercy.[26]

That is enough of it, Christian company, for this first part. Venial Sin is a disposition to mortal sin,[27] because it obliges God to permit that we fall into it; and, when that would not be, it imperceptibly disposes us ourselves to commit it. That is the second point.

Second Point

Saint Thomas says that venial faults dispose us to mortal sin, a little like accidents prepare a subject to receive a form that they did not have[28]—which is to say that [venial sin] is in our soul, with regard to great sins, what dryness and heat are in combustible materials regarding fire; so much that, as straw dries out and warms up little by little in such a way that it takes only a spark and a moment of time to set it ablaze, likewise our heart, by force of letting minor Sins enter, becomes imperceptibly so sensitive to the most enormous [sins] that it consents to them at the first temptation.

Experience teaches us this truth so well that it seems unnecessary to ask for more proofs of it. Every day we see that the most reserved people, for having first given to themselves some not very sinful liberties, have aban-doned themselves finally to disorders of which only the thought had long horrified them. A man who is habituated to lie in very slight things has trouble refraining, on occasion, from a more serious lie. A greedy person, who for a long time only committed petty thefts, if a considerable amount presents itself, is very tempted to keep it; the fear of losing the grace of God fights a moment in her heart against the corrupt desire; but it is a wonder if avarice does not win out over all otherworldly considerations. Whence does this come, Christian auditors? It is that the minor Faults, as slight as they may be, do not fail to form a habit that also leads to minor and to great sins of the same kind, and sometimes even more strongly to the great as to the minor, since the object of [the great ones] is ordinarily more attractive and more capable of satisfying the passion.[29]

And this habit is contracted with even more ease that, as one pays it little mind, one takes no care to impede its progress, such that it is strengthened in little time, and makes itself entirely incurable—like a minor illness that becomes deadly if one does not hurry to cure it, or like a slight wound that festers, that becomes infected and that then infects the whole body for having been ignored.[30]

Moreover, there is sometimes so little difference between mortal and venial sin that, when one is habituated to the latter, one even commits the other without thinking of it: all the more so since one often is unaware to what point one can go without sinning mortally. Every day it happens that a piece of scandal that one believes slight is in fact very significant because of the circumstances; that a sum that one considered small is more than enough to commit a theft that deals death to the soul; finally, that a thought or an action, which seemed innocent enough to you, is nevertheless exceedingly sinful. In all of these encounters, the soul who is not instructed—who doubts, who flatters herself, who does not want to take the trouble to examine herself—follows habituation, which carries her away and involves her in great sins.[31]

But when these sorts of lapses and relapses would not be able to produce in us a vicious habit, at least one cannot deny that the habit that one would have acquired from the opposing virtue receive some attack from it, in such a way that [the virtuous habit] always makes less resistance to the second attack than to the first. This young person could not hear yesterday, without blushing, certain stories that offend decency; she listened to them nevertheless. Today, one began the same discourse in her presence, and that did not bother her at all; she will laugh at it tomorrow, and I know not if, soon after, she will not let herself go to the point of holding similar conversations herself.

Finally, everyone knows that, as soon as one grants something to passion, it becomes more avid and more insolent, and that it always presses to the point that one have given it more. It is thus, Christian auditors, that all the villains among men are lost. No one among them began with a great sin. It is certain that if they had held themselves to their first actions, they would have been, for the most part, innocent enough. But, when one has taken to the route on a very steep incline, it is morally impossible to stop oneself until one be entirely at the bottom. That is why the demon, who would not be satisfied if he did not take from us the grace of God, still never begins by carrying us to commit a grave sin. At first he demands of this young man only simple glances; he will be happy if he can inspire some vanity in this girl, and in this woman the fantasy of fashion and of vain finery, because he knows well that this could not fail to go further and that, even without involving himself in it, one will come to something more serious. Believe me, Christian company: a person who wants to avoid only mortal sin does not really want to avoid it. It is an illusion, this life project in which one intends to permit oneself, against the law of God, all that [this law] prohibits only on slight penalties, and to miss nothing of the essential things. If you think you know someone who models himself continuously on this basis, be assured that you know him little and that he is either more wicked or better than you think. Otherwise he would have found the secret of reconciling God with the world—that which the Savior has judged absolutely impossible.[32]

To all these reasons one still can add that we naturally love rest, and that it is that [rest] that we seek by all our cares and by all our efforts. And yet there is no rest in the middle, says the devout Saint Bernard: it is found only in the two extremes—either in the most exact virtue, or in the final dissoluteness; either in the height of love, or in the abyss of insensitivity: "on this side, love; on that side, apathy."[33] Those who are completely for Jesus Christ are happy, because they possess the source of all goods; those who are entirely devoted to Lucifer believe themselves also happy, because they do not feel their sorrow. In perfect love, the conscience is calm and the concupiscence subdued: in developed insensitivity, the concupiscence is assuaged and the conscience mute. But whoever hopes to manage these two enemies, in giving the minor things to the concupiscence, the great ones to the conscience, he suffers equally from the one and from the other, because neither the one nor the other is satisfied. Concupiscence, which is insatiable, is irritated by the little that one gives to it, in place of being satisfied with it; the conscience, which is delicate, is wounded by the lightest yokes that one imposes on it and disrupts the peace of heart by its cries. Such a painful state is intolerable to man, such that, if he does not resolve himself to remove the most minor Faults, he is as if constrained to plunge himself into the most horrible disorders.

You will tell me perhaps that it seems to follow from this discourse that, for whoever wants to be saved, it is a necessity to be holy. I do not say that, Christian auditors; but I am convinced that it is an indispensable necessity to aspire to holiness. When everything I have said up to here would not prove it sufficiently, Saint Paul does not permit us to doubt it: "This is the will of God, your sanctification."[34] "My Brothers," says this great apostle, "God does not content himself with a mediocre and imperfect virtue; he wants that you sanctify yourselves: you have vowed it on the fonts of your baptism; the Church has received you[35] in her bosom only on this word that you have given her to work without rest to imitate the holiness of the Son of God and of his heavenly Father. To be baptized and to be clothed with Jesus Christ is the same thing:[36] 'This is the will of God, your sanctification.'" I know that all nature shudders at this sole thought; that it fights, with all its might, such a generous resolution; that it places a thousand obstacles that appear invincible.[37] I know that it conjures up monsters and chasms on the road to holiness. But nature is blind and demented; [nature] has made the same difficulties for all the saints who ever have undertaken to destroy it.

Ask them if [nature] was right to tremble and to become so strongly alarmed. Is there a single one of them who have repented of not having listened to it? Is there a single one of them who have not blessed God, a thousand and a thousand times, to have despised all these oppositions and to have forced [nature] to yield under the lovable yoke of grace? Should we then always listen to our imaginations and to our false terrors, rather than to the witness of so many faultless people, who were convinced, by their own experience, of the vanity of our anxieties? Courage, then, Christian souls! It is not to work and to efforts that I invite you; it is to rest, it is from this life to paradise, it is to early paradise, it is to true bliss. Just resolve yourself, say once and for all, "I want to be holy, although it cost me." This step being taken, there you are beyond the thorns. There are only flowers, only lively sources of pleasures; there remain only peace, only tranquility, only unspeakable delights. Let us take it today, this great step, Christian auditors.

Let us go see if one has deceived us or if one has told truth to us, when one speaks to us of the happiness of decent people. If we find less than promised us, that will make us retrace our steps, if we want, and dive back into this mud that has such great appeal for us. But it is in vain, O my God, it is in vain that one pushes us to clear this important step; we will never do it, if you do not stretch out your hand to us in order to help us there. It is for you to attract us into the garden of your perfumes and of your chaste pleasures. Happy are those to whom you deign to make such a remarkable favor. What praises, what acts of thanksgiving, what love do they not render you, beginning in this life, for having set them on a path that directs them so surely, so gently, so exquisitely to the end and to the summit of all their desires that I wish for you,[38] in the name of the Father, and of the Son, and of the Holy Spirit.

On Conscience[1]

This is the voice of the one who cries in the desert: prepare the way of the Lord
and make straight his paths. (Luke 3:4)[2]

The Conscience continuously makes very great trouble for the sinner, by its bitter
criticism, and causes him a deathly fright, by its awful threats.

ALTHOUGH THE PROPHET ISAIAH WANTED to indicate by these
words the preaching of Saint John the Baptist,[3] and Saint John [the Baptist]
himself applied them to himself,[4] yet if one wants to take them in a figurative sense, there is nothing to which they can apply better than to the Conscience. For at last, one cannot deny that the Conscience be the voice of
the Lord that makes itself heard in the depths of the soul, in that desert so
remote from the sight of all, in which we have only God alone as witness,
both of our virtues and of our sins.[5] As the voice has been given to us to
be the interpreter of our feelings and of our desires, God makes use of the
Conscience in order to let us know what he thinks of each thing and what
he expects of each of us.[6]

This secret voice forms various interior words in order to express the different lessons and the various orders that it pleases God to give to his creature. [This voice] even has several tones and several accents to represent to
us the different dispositions of his heart toward us. It is sharp and explosive
in his anger, it becomes milder to explain his love to us, it humbles itself to
indicate his indifference to us; in a word, one can say that it is the link for the
interactions that God wants to have with us—the most ordinary instrument
that he uses to touch our hearts and to open his. It is this, Christian company,
that serves today as precursor to Jesus Christ and that invites all sinners to
prepare the way for him by a prompt and sincere penance: "Prepare the way
of the Lord, make straight his paths."[7] If they refuse to listen to him, if they
do not dispose themselves to reconcile themselves to these celebrations, according to the advice that it gives to them, they oblige it to cry out; or, which
is worse, they oblige it to be silent. We will speak another time of the awful

silence of this repelled Conscience; today, I intend to speak to you about its clamors. But I take good care not to set about anything before having addressed myself to the One who was so prompt to obey the voice of the angel, when he greeted her with these lovely words: *Hail, Mary.*[8]

Gentlemen, there is no peace for the ungodly: "'There is no peace for the wicked,' says the Lord"[9]—it is the Lord himself who has said it and it is he himself who has declared to them an everlasting war without rest. Do not believe them, when they want to delude you into believing that they are happy and that they enjoy the pleasures of this life with a great tranquility: that is impossible; they have to deal with a very powerful enemy. When one has a God to fear, what rest is one capable of taking? And where are the sinners who do not fear him, if it is not those who do not know him? In order to lead a sad and miserable life, one need not be deprived of all goods and overwhelmed with all kinds of evils—one sole evil is capable of removing from us the feeling of a thousand goods; even the privation of one good deprives us of the pleasure that the possession of all the others would cause us. And yet, what few glories, what few riches that the ungodly possess, they cannot avoid their Conscience, which God awakens and which he arms, so to speak, against them, in order to avenge himself for the insults that he has received from them. More than this is not necessary in order to disturb their happiness—even to make them completely miserable. I would not tell you, Gentlemen, with Saint John Chrysostom, "that this conscience is a cruel torture—a pain that one would be unable to explain; that it is the worm of the mind, the poison of the heart, a ruthless torturer, a gloomy and dreadful night, a tempest, a storm, an internal and malicious fever, a combat that never ends."[10] I content myself to say that it is a voice that never ceases to complain and to terrify us—a voice that stings by its reproaches and that frightens by its threats—a troublesome voice—a baleful voice—a voice that forever places before our eyes our sins, the tortures that are due for them—that exaggerates incessantly for us the enormity of the former and the harshness of the latter, in order to confuse us with the memory of the evil we have done and to alarm us with the sight of the punishments we have earned. This is, Gentlemen, what we will discuss in the two parts of this discourse. We will see, in the first, what trouble the Conscience constantly makes for the soul by its bitter criticism; and, in the second, what fright it causes it by its terrible threats; this is all that I have to say today.

First Part

No sooner has the sinner contrived the wish to offend God than he begins to suffer the punishment for his sin: "he has been in labor with injustice; he has conceived sorrow,"[11] said David: he has received in his soul the seed of pain, as soon as he has formed the desire for the sin; and, as this sin and this pain were generated at the same time, it is completely obvious that they should be born at the same hour, or at least follow one another very closely. Enter, if you please, says Philo the Jew, enter a little into the heart of this man who gives false witness: "Take a look, if you please, into the mind of the perjurer."[12] You will find that, even in the time that he betrays his promise, his mind becomes flustered, rebels against itself; that he criticizes himself for his weakness and his treachery: "You will see him not at peace but full of disturbance and alarm, accusing and insulting himself."[13] But without penetrating into the secret of his Conscience, put only your hand on his heart, and see how it is moved, how it stirs by its frequent palpitations; consider his eyes, his face, his lips, his voice, his hand that he raises only in trembling: all that will reveal to you the commotion that is in this soul. It seems that all the parts of his body, revolted by the Conscience, refuse to serve him in this sacrilege. There is nothing even to his tongue which, becoming heavy and cleaving to his palate, witnesses against him by the same words he used to disguise the truth.

I say the same of the other offenses. From the time itself that one commits them, the Conscience, which at first advised against them, openly condemns them; it begins to cry out against the malice of the villain, to demand justice of the violence that one does to it, to itself take revenge for [the violence]. But, when the sin is accomplished, it is quite another noise, another torture, for the passion, which leads to the sin, being slackened, and the little pleasure that is found there having ceased completely, the soul remains prey to distress and to regret. Passion makes that one take the poison without considering it; sensual delight waters it down with some pleasures that disguise it to the mouth; but, once it is swallowed, and it is spread throughout the innards, it makes itself only too well known by the horrible pains it causes us. Saint John Chrysostom notes that it happens to us here completely to the contrary from what mothers experience in childbirth: they give birth with pain, but this pain is immediately dispelled by the joy that they have to have brought a child into the world.[14] The sinner, on the contrary, does evil with some pleasure; but, no sooner has he given birth to this monster than he begins to suffer from torments that surpass everything most painful that cruelty has ever invented.

One says, and it is very true, that one cannot understand the peace and the interior delights that a fervent soul tastes in the practice of the good, unless one have learned it by experience. I say the same thing of the distress and of the pains that a wicked Christian endures from his irritated Conscience. Firstly, it pursues him everywhere by continuously putting his sin back before his eyes, and not permitting him to divert his thoughts from it whatever he do to forget it. This is what the prophet David wanted to express by these words: "For I know my iniquity, and my sin is always before me."[15] I see the evil that I have done, and my sin presents itself to me at all times and in all places. Without a doubt, this would be nothing if [conscience] represented [the sin] such as greed made it appear before it had been committed.[16] But [conscience] removes from it this mask that had disguised it to passion; [conscience] paints it as it is, with this dreadful ugliness that disfigured Lucifer and that in an instant made of the most beautiful work of God the most hideous and the most horrible of all creatures. It is no longer so sweet, this vengeance; so charming, this sensual delight; so necessary and of such great use for all kinds of intentions, this money: it is no longer anything but cruelty, but filth, but shameful brutality, but an unjust and barbaric thirst for human blood; it is an ingratitude, an ungodliness, an open rebellion against God, which makes us unworthy to live and worthy to be shunned, to be hated, to be scorned and cursed by all people.

Kedrenos, a Greek historian, recounts that, the emperor Constans having had one of his brothers, named Theodosius, who was a deacon, killed, this brother appeared often to him, during the night, dressed in sacred vestments and carrying in his hand a cup full of blood that he presented to him with these words: "Drink, my brother," in order to make him remember, at the same time, the sacrilege with which he had soiled himself, the fratricide that he had committed, and the brutal and bloody temperament that had led him to this fit of rage[17].

It is thus, Gentlemen, that the Conscience continuously offers to the mind the image of its sin with all the most appalling traits—with all the circumstances that can either increase or reveal its wickedness. There you are, finally satisfied, it says to this vindictive one, you have made yourself drunk on the blood of your brother, you have trampled underfoot that of the Savior, you have scorned the voice of God that demanded pardon from you for this poor wretch, you have preferred to renounce the forgiveness you needed for yourself rather than to forgive for the love of Jesus Christ.[18] Oh, but it would be a fine thing for you, with these passionate eyes and this hostile expression, to do violent actions—to sting like a serpent, to roar, to bite, to tear apart like a tiger or like a lion! Barbarian! You had then forgotten you were a man and that it was another man whom you were abusing; you had forgotten how many times your Judge had forgiven you, and for how many things it was still necessary that he forgave you.[19]

Ah! Unfortunate one, [the conscience] says to this woman, there you are, dishonored for the rest of your days! One moment of pleasure has taken from you what constitutes all the glory of your sex and has numbered you among the prostitutes! Do you really dare from now on to show yourself to your friends and to mix with such virtuous people? You were able then to consent to the loathsome desires of this debauched individual and to sacrifice to him a husband who was so worthy of a more virtuous spouse! There is your reputation, and maybe even your life, in the hands of a libertine, who maybe has already confided about your weakness and who, at least in an act of debauchery—where wine makes the most reserved speak—is capable of making it public. But when that would not be, you have sinned in the presence of your Creator, you have dared make in his eyes a thing of which he is horrified and for which he will not fail to criticize you one day in the eyes of the whole world!

That, Gentlemen, is what this wounded Conscience cries into the ears of the sinner. But with what steadfastness and what impunity? Judge it, if you please, by what I am going to tell you. [The wounded conscience] takes advantage of all occasions in order to renew its complaints. If he looks to heaven: "There is," he says to himself, "what belongs to me by right of my innocence and which I have renounced for the goods I no longer possess." If he sees a pious person, he criticizes himself for the little resemblance he has with her. If he encounters a public sinner, he blushes to see in himself what makes this man vile and appalling to the whole world. If one praises him, his Conscience makes him recall that he owes these praises only to the ignorance of people and to his hypocrisy. If one blames him, it supports with harshness [the one who blames him], it holds against him, as to his face, what one says of him; it ties his tongue, it hinders him in such a way that he defends himself only weakly and that, in the eyes of persons a bit enlightened, he reveals himself in wanting to justify himself. If in his presence one praises the virtues that he has lost—if one accuses others of the vices to which he is subject—these are as many lashes, says Saint John Chrysostom, that he himself receives secretly.[20] Much more: it even uses the good that one did in the past, in order to persecute us in our dissoluteness. It compares us to ourselves, it exaggerates to us the glory and the reserve of our youth, the esteem that we had acquired for ourselves by the regulation and the purity of our manners, the unassailable faithfulness to God that we had kept during the space of several years and the interior peacefulness that had been the sweet fruit of this fidelity. There is nothing so bitter, nothing so unfortunate as this memory to a soul who is torn from this happy state: "There is nothing," says Saint Ambrose, "that causes such great grief as when anyone, lying under the captivity of sin, recalls whence he has fallen."[21]

It is in this view that one cannot refrain from saying with Job: "Who will grant me that I might be, according to the months past, according to the days in which God kept me, as I was in the days of my youth, when God was secretly in my tabernacle, when the Almighty was with me?"[22] Alas! Who will restore me to that glorious innocence that I had preserved with such happiness! How I can recall those lovely years, in which I lived under the protection of my God and in which God himself made his dwelling in the depths of my heart! "The young men saw me, and hid themselves: and the old men rose up and stood."[23] The most dissolute composed themselves in my presence, and the wisest revered in me an ordered and faultless youth. "The ear that heard me blessed me, and the eye that saw me gave witness to me."[24] It was a time that those who heard speak of me gave me a thousand blessings and envied the happiness of those who had brought me into the world; and, when one would come to examine closely my life and my actions, one recognized that I deserved the praises that one would give me, and that the fame did justice to me. But alas! That time is no more. I have become the subject of chatter and of mockery; the young people, and the most discreet, loathe me; they dread my company; one prohibits them from it, for fear that it corrupt or dishonor them: "But now the younger scorn me, now I am turned into their song, and have become their byword; they abhor me."[25] You need not be surprised, Christian auditors, if the people who have abandoned God appear sometimes so starved for pleasures and new distractions. It is as if they are forced by the troublesome cries of their Conscience, which they hope to be able to charm away by the constant use of all that is most pleasant in life; they try to keep up with, as closely as possible, the festivals, play, dance, the theater, for fear that, if the Conscience found a moment of silence and of idleness, it would condemn them with its criticism. Nothing acquaints me so well with the magnitude of their agony as this insatiability and this fickleness. To me it seems like seeing sick people who are tormented with a cruel edema. I have refrained from carrying any envy against them, however delicious be the drinks with which they try to quench their thirst: on the contrary, the more they drink, the more they make me feel compassion, because it is a sign that their illness is greater, and that they endure more.[26] I even compare them to certain people for whom it seems that blessed Arabia cannot provide enough perfumes, and who always have all sorts of them, and of the most exquisite. One accuses them of sluggishness and of sensuality, and quite often they load up on musk and amber only to combat the stinking air that they breathe and that infects them. It is the same way with sinners: they plunge themselves into all kinds of delights in order to try to soften their internal pains; they make use of them as of perfumes in order to resist the contaminated fumes that their Conscience breathes out. They need pleasures to find relief, and they always need new ones, because no pleasure relieves them. There is nothing more true and this point is quite worthy of consideration.

David's harp pacified the demon that possessed Saul;[27] but no chorus, no wind section is able to pacify a guilty Conscience: it follows the sinner everywhere, it disturbs him everywhere. One of the most regrettable scourges with which Moses struck Egypt was the horrifying number of frogs or, as some authors maintain, of toads with which the hills were covered and the cities themselves filled.[28] These nasty animals even crept into the palace of Pharaoh, even into his bed; they came to defile with their spittle both the precious furniture and even the meats of the table; they never ceased to disturb his peace with their horrible croaking. It is the image of the wicked Christian and of the torture that his own sins cause him; they present themselves to him at all times and in all places, and always under a hideous form; they spare neither working hours nor those of leisure; they spoil, they poison the most delightful stews; they blend their awful cries with the sweetest choruses; they interrupt his sleep and his most pleasant conversations.

It is for this reason that Epicurus, the most sensuous of all men, nevertheless always excluded the sin of his savage bliss, although he had [his bliss] all composed of earthly and sensory pleasures.[29] He did not think that one could be both happy and wicked. It is about this that David said that innocence and peace had combined and that they had made such an intimate union that one would not be able to separate them: "Justice and peace have kissed."[30] It is in vain that the sinner yearns for a peaceful life: all that is most able to delight the senses will not deaden the worm that gnaws away at it; he must become good, if he wants to stop being miserable: "Justice and peace have kissed."

And if the Conscience makes itself so inconvenient and so troublesome to the sinner, even in the midst of his pleasures, who can say how much it is cruel to him during times of adversity? With what harshness does it not abuse him in his misfortunes? In these engagements, what advantage does it not take, either of bodily pains, or of despondency of spirit, in order to avenge the contempt that one has made of it? The brothers of Joseph thought themselves on the point of being overwhelmed by slander: the first thing that comes to their mind, that is the cruelty that they practiced toward their own brother, although several years already have passed. It does not help them at all to be innocent of the new sin with which one charges them: their Conscience takes precisely that time there to criticize them for their former hardness, and it criticizes them for it with such strength and passion that it covers them with confusion and obliges them to keep quiet at a time in which they had such reason to complain: "We deserve to suffer these things, because we have sinned against our brother; behold, his blood is required."[31] Justice is done to us, they say, we are asked again for an account of the blood of Joseph; it is the voice of this blood that cries today against us and that demands revenge; such a great sin cannot go unpunished. Look at the miserable Antiochus, overwhelmed with shameful illnesses, completely covered with ulcers and awaiting a hasty death: it is in these circumstances that his sins rise up against him in order to bring his misfortune to a climax: "Now I remember the evils that I have done in Jerusalem"[32]—it is precisely at this time that my Conscience returns to me in memory all my acts of irreverence, that it criticizes me for the violent acts that I exercised in Jerusalem and the acts of desecration that I did there: "Now, now"; it is at this moment that [my conscience] spreads before my eyes the holy vases, that it unfolds the furniture that I stripped from the Temple of the Almighty: "Now I remember the evils that I have done in Jerusalem."[33]

Gentlemen, the condition of the sinner, in whatever state he may be, always seems to me very wretched; but it is never more to pity than in these encounters. A distressing illness keeps him in his bed, as on a wheel or as on a burning grill;[34] he unjustly loses his goods; his enemies blacken his reputation and mistreat him; death takes from him what he holds most dear in the world; he is beset by crosses; and if he wants, either to raise his eyes to heaven, or to retreat a bit into himself in order to take some consolation, he finds only subjects of pain and of despair. What disgrace, says Saint Augustine! And where can this poor wretch find a retreat? Adversity attacks him in the country; it follows him in the city, it enters with him into his house, into his bedroom, into his closet; nothing remains to him anymore except the tiny room of his Conscience. But, if even there everything is on fire, if turmoil and disorder reign there, if his enemies have made themselves the masters of it, he will have to take flight. But where will he flee, where he himself does not follow? And, in his present state, everywhere he finds himself, will he not find his torturer and his torture? "To whatever place he flees he draws himself after himself, and to whatever such place he draws himself, he torments himself."[35] How happy you are, holy Souls, how happy you are, even in the greatest misfortunes of life, always to have in yourselves a faithful friend and a refuge impervious to all afflictions!

Yes, Christian auditors, a good Conscience is an impervious retreat against all the enemies of our happiness; it is a very pleasant friend in all seasons, but very helpful and of great assistance at times of adversity. It is at that time that a soul, afflicted outwardly and persecuted by creatures, finds in herself grounds for sound comfort. She finds there an unerring witness of her innocence and consequently a certain proof that what she suffers is not an effect of the anger of God, but on the contrary a sign of his love. It is there that one gives her assurance to see the end of her difficulties, to draw from them much fruit, to see them transformed into unchangeable goods that will never end. I remember poor Anne, mother of Samuel, who, in the extreme distress that her sterility caused her, received from her good husband such tender caresses and such reasonable comfort: "Anna, why do you weep? And why do you not eat? And why do you afflict your heart?"[36] Why do you cry, Anne, and why do you not eat? What reason do you have so to drift into grief? You have no children. But what does it matter to you, since I am happy and I love you no less for it? Can I not, myself alone take the place of several children for you? "Am I not better to you than ten children?"[37]

This is just about what the voice of the Conscience—or rather the voice of God—is, when he speaks to a faithful soul who is in desolation: "Why do you weep, and why do you afflict your heart?" What reason do you have to afflict yourself, my Beloved, since I love you and I am happy with you? It is myself who has given you the blow of which you complain, and since you have offended me in nothing, you well can think that it is not in my anger that I strike you. Regarding the manner in which you live today, paradise cannot escape you. Let the outcasts enjoy this false and short happiness. Consider that the evils that you endure serve not a little to increase the glory that I prepare for you: "Am I not better to you than ten children?" You have no sons; you have lost the one upon whom you had based such great hopes and whose birth had caused you such joy. But do you think that this happened without my permission or that I permitted it unintentionally? And, loving you as I do, can I have an intention that be not for your benefit? I want to take the place for you of father, and of son, and of everything. No, you ought not to afflict yourself, whatever loss you might be able to suffer, while you will not lose my friendship. These are the interior consolations that cause true Christians this evenness of spirit, this wonderful constancy that edifies us and that delights us; this is what sustains them against setbacks under which we hardly doubt that they ought to give way; this is what makes that they have in their mouths only words of submission, thanksgivings, in encounters where sinners give such visible and such scandalous signs of their despair. But this is enough spoken of the sadness that the Conscience causes the sinner by its constant criticism; let us say a word about the fright that it causes him by its threats. This is the second part.

Second Part

Although the Holy Spirit spoke in different passages of Scripture about this mortal fear that forever afflicts the soul of the sinner, and though he expressed himself everywhere in a very forceful way, it seems to me nevertheless that he has said nothing about it stronger than these words that we read in the book of Job, fifteenth chapter: "The sound of dread is always in his ears":[38] the ungodly always has a terrible sound in his ears, or rather the voice of terror itself that frightens him and brings him down with fear. "He does not believe that he may return from darkness to light, looking around about for the sword on every side":[39] if it is during the night, he would not be able to believe that he should live until day, because it seems to him to see on every side the sword of the justice of God that pursues him and that he cannot avoid.

It is true, Gentlemen, it seems to him that all that he hears foreshadows to him a certain death and that all that he sees threatens him with it: a cloud that covers the sky, a flash of lightning that appears, a thunderbolt happens to chill him to the bottom of his soul. The sound of a bell, the sight of a funeral cortege fill him with a thousand baleful thoughts. If he sees a shadow, it is a demon that is going to take hold of him; if he hears the least noise, it is the house that is going to collapse, either under his feet or on his head. He thinks to die from the slightest illnesses, and for the little that he totters or that he sees himself about to fall, he imagines that it is the hand of God that pushes him in order to hurl him into the depths. As he is already condemned by his own Conscience, he expects at each moment the execution of this fair judgment. It is like a robber to whom the death sentence has already been pronounced: he is always in the cruel expectation of his execution; for the little that one rattles the bolt of his cell, he imagines that one is coming to get him out of it in order to lead him to the gallows.

And not only does his Conscience make him dread the anger of his Judge, but it frightens him to the point that he mistrusts all people—all creatures—all of which he believes to be interested in avenging their Creator. Although no one considers him, he thinks, says Saint John Chrysostom, that everyone knows his sin, that one reads it on his face, that one discusses it in all the gatherings, that there are ambushes set in every corner to surprise him.[40] If someone flatters him, it is that one wants to hide the intention one has to ruin him; if one greets him more coolly, it is that one is informed of his disgrace. He distrusts his own servants—even the accomplices to his sin. It is for this [reason] that Cain wandered in the woods, that he even fled his children and that he thought that all that was human on the earth had plotted his death. "For whereas wickedness is fearful," says the Sage, "it bears witness of its condemnation, for a troubled Conscience always forecasts grievous things."[41] It is that iniquity is extremely fearful and, as it feels worthy of the hatred of everyone, it persuades itself in its distress that everyone really hates it.

What is very strange about this fright is that it is not like these panics from which one can recover with the aid of reason. It is reason itself that forms the fear of the sinner: the more he consults it, the more he finds that there is cause to tremble. "For he has stretched out his hand against God and has strengthened himself against the Almighty":[42] indeed, says the holy man Job, he has brought upon himself a formidable enemy; he has been crazy enough to place the blame on God and to attack the Almighty. What more reasonable, Christian auditors, than the fear of a puny creature who has so cowardly, so cruelly offended the One who can punish him forever? The One who has in his hands the life of all men, who has made everything, who can destroy everything, whom everything obeys—the angels, the demons, the elements, in a word, all sentient and insentient beings! One has seen poor wretches who, having offended some people of high worldly status, have lost their minds by the constant anxiety in which they were of not being able to escape the authority and power of their enemies. What therefore should a man not fear who has had the arrogance to despise, to offend gravely the Lord of both heaven and earth? To be confident, when one has sinned, one by definition either already must have lost one's mind, or think that there is no God. One finds people who, to live more peacefully, try to persuade themselves of it; but do they manage to do so? That, to my mind, is impossible. The most that they can do is to doubt that there is [a God]. But, in this doubt, I leave you to consider whether one can be free from all fear, when one considers that one risks everything on an opinion contrary to the opinion of the whole world—on an opinion that has never occurred except in the mind of a very small number of men[43], ungodly and corrupt in their habits.[44]

But what torture, Christian company, thus to be always anxious, always seized with a mortal fear! Saint John Chrysologus says that death is a lesser evil than the fear of death.[45] One also sees only too many sinners who, unable to endure any longer the terrors that their Conscience causes them, themselves have themselves killed, as did Judas.[46] One sees some who go to confess their sins and give themselves up willingly to the judges, preferring to end their life by the cruelest tortures than to listen any longer to this terrible voice. When I see a man who has a kidney stone and who, in order to relieve himself, agrees that one go search for it with the knife even into his entrails, I say that this illness must be quite painful, since it makes one desire such an odd cure. What will we say therefore of the frights that a bad Conscience produces, since one sees criminals who, in order to free themselves from them, offer themselves of their own accord to be put on the wheel and burned alive![47] Finally, Gentlemen, this evil appeared so great to Origen that he believed—albeit falsely—that even after this life there would be no other hell for the reprobates;[48] and Saint Jerome, who criticized this opinion of [Origen's] as an altogether stupid error,[49] does not fail to mention, in support of the truth that I am explaining, that there is a greater hell that one can oppose to that inferior hell that David mentions, and that the first [i.e., this greater hell] is nothing other than the guilty Conscience.[50] The pleasure of the sinner, says Saint Ambrose, is like a dream that vanishes upon waking. One still must recognize that what seems like sleep and repose, to judge it by appearances, is a genuine hell into which they fall completely alive and where their Conscience completely alone takes the place of flames and demons for them. "They may appear to live a life full of repose, but it is the repose of the wicked in hell, for even while they live they are plunging deeper and deeper into hell."[51]

If that is so, Christian auditors, who will ever be able to marvel enough at the stupidity and the blindness of the sinner! I always am extremely surprised that there were men who had neither respect for the infinite grandeur of our God, nor love for his goodness—who were touched neither by what he has done, nor by what he has endured for us. I still cannot understand how, with the belief that we have, one can live in the manner that one lives in the world, with so little concern for death and in such a great forgetfulness of eternity.[52] What such powerful appeal sensual de-light must have, I often have said to myself, in order to lead us into evil despite the threats and the promises of a God, despite the hope of paradise and the fear of hell, in the sight of these, such pure joys and of these cruel flames! But here is something much more surprising, Christian company. The life of the sinner is a discomfort—an endless torture; it marches un-ceasingly on thorns and on burning coals; his sins guide him not only to hell: they make for him a hell of this world here; and nevertheless he loves them, he renews them every day—he cannot resolve to renounce them! "Be astonished at this, O you heavens, and you gates thereof, be very deso-late! My people have done two evils: they have forsaken me, the fountain of living water, and have dug for themselves broken cisterns that can hold no water."[53] Stop, O Heavens, and remain motionless with surprise! And you, O Gates of the heavenly Jerusalem, give yourselves up to mourning and to tears, in the sight of such a phenomenal blindness! My people have abandoned me, I who am the fountain of living water; they have scorned me for muddy cisterns that cannot even hold the dirty and bitter waters that they collect there!

Alas! Christians, when we renounced the world in order to avoid the danger of falling into sin, we had thought we were making a great sacrifice to God, and you thought you were offering up to him all your joys and en-tering a hard and narrow path.[54] And however it is found that you have fled work and pain, you have broken heavy chains, you have taken the softer way, the way of freedom and of peace. If someone therefore still hesitates to make the same choice, I hope that he will resolve to do it after these thoughts: "Today if you will hear his voice, harden not your hearts."[55] It is too much to resist this voice of God that calls us to an authentic conver-sion. Why push back to Easter that which can be done at the impending celebration? Have we still not suffered enough on this rack where our Con-science has held us for so long? Have we not moaned enough under the weight of iniquity that overwhelms us? I know that this word of *penance* frightens several of you. But what is the most rigorous penance in com-parison with what one must endure in bondage to the demon?[56] Believe me, Christian auditors, it is neither to work, nor to suffer that one invites us; it is not in order to become unhappy that one presses us to change; on the contrary, among the motives that awaken and that further enkindle the zeal of preachers, one of the strongest is the genuine compassion that they have to see us languish under an unbearable yoke—the desire to make us pass to a calmer and softer life and to obtain for us an eternal one. *So be it.*

On the Relapse[1]

The last state of that man becomes worse than the first. (Luke 11:26)[2]

Whoever relapses has reason to believe that he had not recovered well; he has reason to fear that he will never recover.

IT SEEMS TO ME THAT IT IS WITH much reason that Saint John Chrysostom, speaking of Lent, says that it is the spring of the Church.[3] Indeed, just as in the new season it seems that the earth appears younger and that the whole universe comes back to life, likewise one can say that in this holy time the Church renews itself, that it recaptures its first beauty and all its children their first life. Oh, the lovely time, Christian auditors, and how it causes joy to all those who have some zeal and who work in the vineyard of the Lord, not only because they have the pleasure to see there the greenery and the flowers of spring, but more because they gather the fruits of summer and of autumn, that the word of God is sown then, that it germinates then, and that, in the space of forty days, the harvest ripens and abundantly rewards the works of the laborer.[4] If the angels make such a great feast in heaven for the conversion of only one person,[5] what reason do we not have to rejoice, seeing so many sinners who think to reconcile themselves with God and who dispose themselves by abstinence and by fasting, by the removal of debauchery and even of permissible pleasures, who dispose themselves, I say, to a genuine repentance![6]

These are some thoughts, Christian auditors, which, since Carnival,[7] often have returned to my mind and have given me plenty of consolation. But one must admit that today's gospel has blended a little bitterness with this sweetness, in making me recall our fickleness and the Relapses by which this repentance can be followed. It is true, I said to myself, that nearly all Catholics think presently to atone for their faults by confession, and that from here to Easter the majority will discharge this duty. But what will this sacrament serve them if, immediately after, they trample underfoot the blood of the covenant by which they will have been sanctified—if, renewing their disorders, they relapse into a state even worse than that from which they will have emerged, according to the word of our gospel: "And the last state of that man becomes worse than the first." My God, if we could anticipate such a great evil! If we could give a little more firmness[8] to these resolutions that one is going to form at these celebrations! If we could make them unchanging! Divine Spirit, you alone can stabilize the fickleness of the heart of men! For myself, I only can spread sterile words and make prayers unworthy of being answered. But I hope that you will accompany my words with your grace and that our prayers will be supported by the intercession of Mary: *Hail, Mary.*[9]

To collect in two words what is most important in this matter, it seems to me that the Relapse into sins has much to do with the relapses that happen in illnesses, whether one investigate their cause, or consider their effects.[10] It is a certain thing that the relapses into illnesses are caused, most often, by the same humors that had altered the body the first time—those that have not entirely been purged. I say the same thing of those sins into which one relapses after having been to confess—it is to fear at least when they are significant sins;[11] it is to fear that these new sins were the effects of the former ones from which one had not received absolution, and it is true that the more I examine this thought, the more it seems true to me. In the second place, everyone knows that the return of illnesses is very dangerous and that it is ordinarily deadly, because nature, weakened by the first attacks of the illness, has less force to sustain a second assault and to assist the art of the doctors who can do nothing without it. It is again the same thing with repeated sins: one recovers from them with difficulty, and it is a wonder if they do not lead to death.

I do not think that on this subject one can say anything more dreadful. You will judge, by the proofs of this that I will give you, if these are solid or poorly-founded truths. Here then is what the division of this whole discourse will be. We will speak, in the first place, of the cause of the Relapse, and, in the second place, of its effect. I say that its most ordinary cause is feigned repentance and that impenitence is an effect that it produces only too often. Whoever falls again has reason to believe that he had not recovered well: that is the first point. He has reason to fear that he will never recover: that is the second.

First Point

For a long time I have been of the mind—and may it please God that this were an illusion—that very little genuine repentance happens. The reasons that I have for believing this are that, in having envisioned a great idea of this virtue, I see nothing in the ordinary repentance of Christians that

matches this idea. "Repentance," Tertullian says admirably, "is the shortening of eternal fires,"[12] which is to say, either that it makes the soul suffer a
distress that by its violence equals the eternal duration of hell, or that in a
moment it settles with God, by its value, for all that his justice would have
been able to demand[13] of us by a torture that would never have had an end.
"Repentance," says Saint Gregory of Nyssa, "is the ruin and the reversal
of sin"[14]—of this sin, I say, that had ruined the angels, that had distressed
the whole universe, that has dug the abysses, that has destroyed the most
beautiful works of God, and that Jesus Christ has finally destroyed[15] only
by his death. "Repentance," says Saint Bernard, "is the feeling of a man irritated with himself";[16] and I add, Gentlemen, that this anger has the virtue
of extinguishing that of God and of making him change into love an infinite hatred, similar to that merciless hatred that he has conceived against
the demons, and from which he will never return.

However, Gentlemen, you would have me believe that, to make this repentance so effective—so wonderful—after a year of debauchery, it suffices
that there be a quarter of an hour of time to prepare oneself enough to tell
the sins that one has committed, perhaps less to satisfy the justice of God,
and all that without emerging from the occasions [of sin], without chang-
ing [one's] life, without reconciling oneself with one's enemies, without renouncing the world or the vanity of the world, without detaching one's heart
from the objects that have led us to evil, with less feeling to have lost God
than one sometimes would have for having lost a dog or a pair of gloves. I
admit that this seems almost unbelievable to me. I would believe it nevertheless if, after such a cold and such a short penance, one actually mended
his ways. But, when I see that, after some days, one falls back into the same
faults—that no sooner has one received absolution than one dirties oneself
with new mortal sins, Gentlemen, I doubt that with absolution one has received the grace of God, and, to speak more sincerely, I believe firmly, outside of certain extraordinary cases, that one has not received it at all.

On what do I base myself? First, for a genuine repentance, all the theologians agree that it takes a distress that surpasses all other distress—of
the kind that there is nothing in the world that were capable of causing you
a regret equal to that which you have, having violated the law of God.[17] I
know that this regret need not be such in feeling; but no one doubts that it
ought to go as far in the effect as I say.

A regret is extreme in feeling when it goes even to smother the one
who is seized by it, as happened to that woman who expired at the feet of
Saint Vincent Ferrer, of the order of Saint Dominic,[18] and to this patriarch
of Constantinople who, having let himself get enlisted by human reasons
to favor the heretics of his time, died of grief at the memory of this sin, in
the presence of the great men of the court who had gone to find him in
his seclusion, to hear from his own mouth the motives of his conversion.[19]

This criticism awoke in him that of the conscience and gave such sharpness and such force to the grief that already had pierced his heart, that he could not withstand it, that he was smothered by it in the eyes of those who had asked him this question. This regret is extreme as to the effect, when, right to the feeling,[20] it produces in us all the effects of the most excessive grief. Regard this young woman whose husband just had his throat cruelly slit. Who can express the hatred and the horror that she feels for this barbaric action? The mere sight of the dagger that struck the blow is capable of making her swoon with grief. It is necessary to remove from before her eyes this bloody shirt, this coat that was the first penetrated, and everything that can make her remember her misfortune. She never will resolve to pass by the place where the crime was committed. She makes an eternal break with all the relatives of the killer, with everything that belongs to him; his wife, his children, his friends, even his house are for her such hateful objects that she cannot consider them without being shaken to the core—without being as if beside herself. But above all she forgets nothing in order to ruin the man himself—to destroy even his name, even his memory, or at least to make it despicable to all of history.

Gentlemen, sincere contrition ought to produce in us the same effects with regard to the sin from which we want to be absolved. Everything that makes us recall our misfortune ought to renew and increase our displeasure; everything that has contributed to make us offend God—this house, this game, this company, this money, this wine—ought to be for us objects of horror. To see this person who has been the cause of our fall—even to hear speak of her—this ought to be for us a pain that equals the pleasure that before we took at his conversation. O God! There is the trap that made me fall into your disgrace and that nearly threw me into hell; there is the enemy who wanted to ruin me without means of support; there is the instrument of which I made use in my fit of rage to pierce Jesus Christ and to pierce even me; there is the place where I gave myself over to the demon and where all of heaven was witness to the offense that I dared make to God in his presence! How is it that I still can withstand the sight of it, that I do not die of shame, of grief, of despair at this memory!

Now, I ask you, Christian company, if one person, who is in these sentiments, is capable of surrendering a second time and without resistance to the first temptation. If this woman, so distressed, who breathed only vengeance yesterday, today consents to marry the murderer of her spouse, will you not say, either that she has lost her mind, or that her grief was feigned and that she rejoiced in her heart at the time she was shedding the most tears? I say the same thing of you, if you fall back so soon after having had such a great regret of having fallen. It must necessarily be either that you have ceased to be reasonable, or that the sin has ceased being hateful, or that you never really hated it. "But I have sighed," you will tell me; "I have wept, I have been inconsolable for some time." That may be; it may happen that you wept, but it cannot be that these tears were sincere. You wept that you could not, at the same time, take your pleasures and save yourself. You wept at the sole thought of leaving that which is dear to you, although you have never had the will to do it. These tears were effects of your attachment—and not of your aversion—to sin; it is nature and not grace that has pulled them from you.

But, even when they had they been supernatural, if they are not followed by amendment, there is place to presume that they have been useless. You know, Gentlemen, that the most virtuous and chaste people in the world are sometimes tempted, like Saint Paul, with such persistence and violence that they are in doubt if they have consented to the suggestions of the demon—that they even believe to have consented in fact and fall into incredible sadness and desolation from it. However, it is certain that they are never so pure as when their imagination is so attacked by a thousand impure phantoms and when their body itself is in passions by which it seems that they ought to be consumed. The reason that one has to make this judgment is that one sees nothing on the exterior that can make believe that there be infidelity in the interior: no liberty, no dissolute action—always the same reserve, be that in words, be that in looks—no fault against the virtue that is attacked in their imagination. What happens in decent people, with regard to temptations, happens only too often to the wicked with regard to the movements of the Holy Spirit.[21] You have moaned at the feet of the priest; you have felt moved and shot through with regret for your sins; that has gone to the point of sobs, to the point of tears. This is to say that grace has been strong—that the Spirit of God has pushed you extraordinarily. But I maintain that you have not given yourself to this grace—that you have resisted; that you have smothered the spirit of God. I judge this by your actions which are proofs that do not deceive. You immediately have reengaged in the first occasions [of sin]; you right away have resumed the same life; you have not taken one sole step to withdraw from evil—not a move to follow Jesus Christ who was calling you. Know that, as the saints suffer temptation without succumbing to it, the wicked feel contrition without consenting to it: "evil men," says Saint Gregory, "are frequently compelled in vain to righteousness, just as the good are typically tempted unsuccessfully into sin."[22]

In the second place, for a genuine repentance, a genuine resolution to commit no longer the sin that you want to erase by repentance is needed. The intention one has no longer to offend God must be absolute, say the theologians, which is to say that one be ready to resist sin, whatever pleasure invites us there, however great be the interest that can attract us there, whatever threats that one can make to us, however long, however insistent be the temptation that leads us there, at all times, in all places, in all the circumstances that one foresees or that one does not foresee. Is it possible that, if one had this will, one were capable of succumbing to the first occasion [of sin], to the slightest temptation, for an interest of nothing? This intention ought to be effective, which is to say that one must desire to flee sin, as a greedy person desires gold and silver, as a sick person has the desire to get well, as a poor person wishes to be relieved in his destitution. Still we must carry the thing further. One must desire a holy and Christian life with more ardor than one desires either health or goods, since one has to be prepared to lose everything rather than to lose the grace for which one hopes. Gentlemen, I leave you yourselves the judges of this: do you believe that a penitent who, the day after his confession or a few days later, returns to his first dissoluteness, has wished more to correct himself than to live and to enrich himself? What would he do, if he had had a contrary desire? Would he be, at least, on guard or more prompt to surrender, being attacked? For myself, I am persuaded that, in the bottom of his heart, he has had this totally contrary intention; that at least he felt that he would regain his first way and that it was only for little time that he would retreat. It is for that [reason] that he approached the sacrament with the same indifference, with as much calm[23] as if it was a question of nothing and that his confession ought not to have any continuation. What! Young man, you go to penance and you do not shudder in going there? And how will you be able to renounce forever this sensual delight, this creature, this gambling? Are you therefore resolved to suffer and to forgive? What! These habits that keep you bound—that have delivered evil to you as necessary—are there for you more fearsome enemies? Oh, if you truly believed that this is for always, there would be many other combats, and the resolution would not be taken so abruptly.

Do you want to see a man quite convinced that he must change, when he wants to reconcile himself with God? That is Saint Augustine. But you also see what resistances he finds in himself, what efforts he must make in order to resolve himself! If, for a perfect conversion, one had only to weep, he already has shed more tears, he has sighed more, prayed more than you have done in your whole life; but he believes to have done nothing, if he does not have the intention to live better. Quite more: he desires it, he criticizes himself for his weakness and his slowness, he would like to be able to do violence to himself and to say farewell to sensual delight. But he does justice to himself; he feels that despite all his tears, all his desires, his will is still enchained, that he still is not resolved to renounce forever these criminal pleasures, and that in this way there still is nothing in fact, and that God and his conscience still have the right to torment him. One must intend effectively. He fought for ten years before being able to form this effective intention; but also, when once he will have conceived it, he will make a whole and eternal divorce with sin.

In the third place, as genuine repentance makes us enter back into the friendship of the Lord, it brings us a powerful protection that makes us formidable to outside enemies—that distances them from us—that disarms and weakens our household enemies. In such a way that, in what follows, one is tempted much more weakly and one feels much more strength to resist. While we are enemies of God, the tempter does not bother to engage us every day in new sins. That is why the great Saint Gregory says that, when one postpones erasing a sin by repentance, this sin soon attracts us into another: "A sin that penance does not blot out, soon by its weight leads to another."[24] It is that the demon is the master of the place: everything bends, everything is in his hands. But, if a more powerful warrior comes to attack him, if he makes himself master of the fort, he removes from the defeated one all the weapons in which he placed his confidence and renders him harmless—just as Jesus Christ himself says it today in the gospel.[25] If therefore, after your confession, you let yourself be conquered—if you fall back with the same ease as before—if you do not feel more horror for sin, not more strength in the occasion [of sin]—if you surrender at the first attack—it is completely obvious that the tyrant is not disarmed, that he is still master of your heart. What! Your soul will have been unburdened of a thousand heavy chains; it will have received sanctifying grace with this great number of actual graces and of supernatural gifts with which it is always accompanied;[26] God himself will have descended into you, and all that will not have made any change! You will feel as weak—you will fall with the same ease as if you were relieved of all these aids! Gentlemen, this is, to my mind, absolutely impossible; and it seems to me that this here is what one calls a demonstration, for whoever believes in Jesus Christ—in the merits of his blood and in the virtue of grace.

Saint Paul, writing to the Hebrews,[27] says a strange thing on the subject of the Relapse. He says that it is impossible that those who once have been enlightened by God—who have tasted his grace and received his Holy Spirit—and who, after that, have fallen—that it is impossible, I say, that they renew themselves by repentance![28] These words give terror to many people. For me, I have no difficulty to add a complete trust to that. Yes, I believe that a person who, truly touched from on high, has conceived a sincere aversion for his disorders and that great intention that one must have in order to abandon them forever and without reservation—a man who, by the force of his distress, has driven the demon from his heart and bound the Holy Spirit to come make his dwelling there—I believe, I say, that if this person were unfortunate enough to fall back, he would close for himself, by his fall, all return to mercy; it would be morally impossible for him to recover.[29] But also, for whoever has made a similar repentance, I consider the Relapse morally impossible.

To do penance, Christian company, is to die to sin, according to the expression of Saint Paul.[30] And yet, as after death there can be no return to life except by a miracle, likewise, after one truly has died to sin, a kind of wonder is needed in order to make sin come back to life in us: "We who are dead to sin, how will we live in it any longer?"[31] How could it happen, says the great apostle, that we reawakened to sin, we who truly have died to it? But permit me, Christian auditors, to change these words a little and to say, in applying them to us ourselves: if we truly had died to our sins, how would it be possible to happen that we were so soon and so easily reawakened to them? If the repentance that we made at Easter the preceding year had been done in the required forms and in all the required circumstances; if it had been of the same nature as that of Saint Augustine and of Magdalene, by what diabolical miracle would we have been, this year, subject to the same vices as before? How could it happen that we still had the same sins to confess, and perhaps still greater ones? What monster, if Magdalene, after the Ascension of the Savior, had reengaged in her licentious life, if Saint Augustine was returned to his debauchery after having rendered both his sins and his repentance so public! "We who are dead to sin, how will we live in it any longer?" No, no: experience makes us see every day that genuine repentances are followed by an eternal divorce from sin. That if it happens sometimes that one relapses into the same state from which one actually had left, that is never all of a sudden, nor at the first step. Some time is needed to erase the memory of this bitter contrition—to destroy this great intention of which I have spoken—to ruin this treasure-trove of graces and to drive out the Holy Spirit who has made himself the master of the heart. One does not resume by the greatest sins; one lets up little by little on the exercises of piety; one permits oneself small liberties that open the door to temptations; one makes oneself unfaithful in a thousand encounters of little importance that habituate the soul—that dispose it to greater infidelities—before coming to mortal sin. One must smother many inspirations, many criticisms of the conscience. But that, in the space of eight days' time, beginning the following day, this extinct sin—this dead sin—comes back to life:[32] this enemy—weakened, defeated, disarmed, driven from the heart, destroyed, annihilated—finds itself, a moment after, as strong, as formidable, as master of the place as if God had not seized it—had not entrenched himself there and fortified himself against all the efforts of Satan. I confess that I cannot understand how this might happen: "We who are dead to sin, how will we live in it any longer?" This grief therefore must have been feigned—this intention imperfect, this reconciliation false, this repentance useless. Only if it was genuine and nevertheless one be weak enough to relapse does one have reason to fear that this be never to recover. This is the second point.

Second Point

Saint Luke quotes, in the ninth chapter of his gospel, a saying of Jesus Christ that seems to me quite strong and quite expressive: "No man putting hand to the plough, and looking back, is fit for the kingdom of God."[33] Whoever has put his hand to the plow and looks behind himself is not fit for the kingdom of heaven. Hey! What, Lord, have we not all been made for your kingdom? Have you not given to our hearts a secret desire to possess you? Have you not formed them all for your love? Yes, without doubt, Christian company. But it seems to me that by this expression he wanted to indicate the difficulty that there is to regain a better life when once one has abandoned it, by making us understand that it is as difficult to return as it is difficult for a man to succeed in an art of which he is naturally incapable and to which he has no disposition. But still, whence can come such a great difficulty? Alas! Gentlemen, I do not know whence it is that it does not come. It seems to me that everything contributes to render it insurmountable.

The Savior of the world seems to want to make us understand today that [this difficulty] comes especially from the demon who, having once been driven out from the heart of man, does not return there unless he be accompanied by seven other spirits more wicked than he, to be in the state to make a longer and more rigorous resistance.[34] Without doubt he is much more careful and more vigilant, after having won back this post, than he was before he had lost it. He has learned by experience whence it is that grace can have access; he does not fail to close—to the extent that he can—the avenues and to strengthen himself in the places that he has found weakest. In a word, he employs all his strength and all his tactics in order to avoid the confusion of a second surprise.[35]

In addition, we find in ourselves great obstacles to a second conversion. For it is true, Gentlemen, that, by this Relapse, the inclination that you have to evil is more increased in you than it could have been able to do by a hundred and by a thousand repeated acts before your repentance. One can say that [relapse] is, with regard to vice, what a heroic act is in the matter of virtue: only one of them is needed to produce a very great habit.[36] For example, a woman who, at the strongest moment of her grief, will have the courage to kiss her enemy [who is] still completely covered with the blood of her son or of his father—this woman, I say, will gain by this action such a great readiness to suffer and to forgive injuries that she will appear impervious to them.[37] Those saints who, to overcome the extreme disgust that they felt to dress wounds, have even sucked the sludge that came out of them—these saints, I say, have never had since any difficulty in the service of the sick.[38]

But I say that a sin, committed after a genuine repentance, is a heroic sin, if it is permitted me to express myself in that way. In order to commit it, we had to smother all the insights that had drawn us from evil—all the graces that one had received—all the good desires that one had formed with such fervor. One has sinned in the sight of all that can make sin difficult; one has rendered useless all the obstacles that can block a malicious intention. Given that, who will be capable henceforth of stopping us? What devastation will not be made by a torrent that was able to break such strong dikes? And if it is true, as the doctors [of theology] assure it, that after an action of a strong and magnanimous piety it is difficult to be damned, cannot one say that, after a similar Relapse, salvation is as if impossible?

All that could remain of hope, that would be in you, O God infinitely good, infinitely compassionate! But, on the contrary, one can say that it is from your part that the greatest difficulties come to us. Gentlemen, although it be very true that the Lord is full of mercy, it is certain, however, that he does not always forgive, nor [does he forgive] all kinds of sins— otherwise hell would not fill every day with the souls whom he sacrifices to his justice.[39] There is a limit of graces. A time comes when one cries and is not answered. But toward whom can this rigor be exercised with more justice than toward a Christian who, after having made his peace with his God and having promised him an eternal fidelity, makes himself guilty of a second rebellion?[40]

For, in the first place, he no longer can excuse himself on account of his ignorance: the confusion that he suffered in confessing his sins shows sufficiently that he recognized their enormity.[41] He admitted that he had need of a great mercy and even that he was completely unworthy of it. He had taken the trouble to defend himself from despair; the confessor had to console him, to raise his spirits—to place before his eyes all the riches, all the treasures of the infinite goodness of our[42] God; he has criticized himself a hundred times for his blindness, his obstinacy, his past ingratitude. He falls again after all that. Here is a sin committed with a complete malice and, consequently, very worthy of all the rigors of the justice of God.

Why do you think that there has been no grace, no time of repentance for the demons, if it is not because they had offended God with a perfect knowledge of the evil that they were doing? If that is so, who among men has more reason to dread a judgment similar to that of Lucifer than those who relapse into their disorders, after having been drawn out of them by force of supernatural insights and visions—by the distinct knowledge that they have had of the greatness of their errors and of their duties? "If we sin willfully after having the knowledge of the truth, there is now left no sacrifice for sins."[43] If all Christians are saved, I no longer have anything to tell you. But if there must be some, even among us, who will test the eternal severity of the divine justice, who will it be, once again, if it is not this man who—after having accused himself with such confusion—after having demanded grace with this regret and this horror of his sin—this resolution to sin no more that moved the depths of the confessor—that touched the heart of God himself and without which he cannot have obtained any forgiveness—and who, after all that, I say, returns coldly to his first life and to the disorders that he took such care to make right?

In the second place, this Relapse contains a scorn for God that cannot fail to attract his anger to us. That is why Saint Paul calls it an insult made to the spirit of grace whom one shamefully drives from his heart, after having called him there by great cries and with great entreaties.[44] It seems, says Tertullian, that you wanted to put yourself right with the Lord only to test if you would find your account better in serving him than in serving the world and that, having made a comparison, you gave preference to the enemy of Jesus Christ.[45] Before your reconciliation, you did not know, in fact, what you were doing; the attachment that you had to the bad part was rather an effect of your unhappiness than of your choice. If you preferred the creature to its Creator,[46] it is that you knew neither the one nor the other, and so your judgment did not cause great harm to your God. But, what does this second change mean—this second repentance? What! You have tasted God and you look for another master? You repent of your having reconciled with God, of having asked forgiveness of him? Know then that he will repent of having forgiven you and that he will never repent of this repentance. He repents of having made Saul king, of having drawn him from the dust: "I regret that I have made Saul king."[47] But Samuel begging him to receive this prince with mercy, [God] declared to him that he was not capable, like men, of these second repentances. "Then the one who triumphs in Israel will not be sparing: for he is not a human being that he does penance."[48]

Therefore, when at these Easter celebrations you will go to present yourself at the sacrament of penance,[49] when the priest, in the name of Jesus Christ, will remit for you the sins that you will have declared to him, imagine that Jesus Christ himself says to you as to the man paralyzed for thirty-eight years:[50] "Go and sin no more, lest some worse thing happen to you":[51] "Go, sin no more, for fear that some evil happen to you, still worse than that from which I just healed you." But to a paralytic—to a poor wretch who is deprived of the use of all his limbs—and who, for so many years, is as though dead among the living—what worse can happen to him: death, or a sickness from which he will never be cured? "Sin no more, lest some worse thing happen to you." Believe me, Christian soul, guard yourself against a Relapse that could be deadly and from which perhaps you could not recover.

This is not the first time that you have fallen back. This may be; but perhaps also you have yet never recovered as is necessary, and all your penances to this point have been feigned and useless. But, be that as it may, take care that you expose yourself so often to the same danger, lest you finally perish there; take care that the demon does not become established with you in such a way that you contract such a strong habit of offending God that even God find himself so offended by your first Relapse that your salvation becomes entirely impossible because of it. Go: one forgives you for this time; but consider that perhaps this is the last pardon that you can expect from the divine mercy. It is too much; it is a marvel of goodness that, having been offended so cruelly by a creature so vile and miserable, he condescends today to forget your ingratitude and to offer you the kiss of peace. But believe me, do not risk a second time to displease him; it can happen that from now on nothing will be capable of swaying him in your favor and that it will be in vain that you fast, that you pray, that you try to soften him by your grief and by your tears: "Go and sin no more, lest some worse thing happen to you."

But, what therefore must one do in order to prevent this Relapse? One must behave, above all in the initial stages, as the sick who emerge from great illnesses and who go into convalescence: never [should you practice] more care or reserve—never more temperance, more fear of bad food or of bad air[—than you practice at this time]. Remember that the demon never sets so many traps for us than when we have recently left his bonds, and that unless you exercise an extreme vigilance he soon will have re-engaged you there. Your fall has taught you of what you are capable; you see how weak you are in the occasion [of sin]—what effect the world and social groups can have on your heart and on your mind; the cause of evil is known to you—it is for you to remove it. You must tear out this eye, cut off this arm that has given you occasion to sin,[52] otherwise you have done nothing—you have left the source of evil deep within you—you soon will be in the same state that you were two days ago.[53] Know that no one ever will live a truly innocent life unless he completely change his life and aspire to nothing more than to avoid sin. While you visit the same world, frequent the same places, take the same entertainments, you always will make the same mistakes.[54] It is almost impossible not to fall on a path so narrow and so slippery; you must take a route more sure and further from the abyss.

Finally, the last advice that I give you is to have often—and very often—recourse to God with an entire confidence.[55] Tell him with the apostles, above all at the time of temptation: "Lord, save us, we perish."[56] Ah! Lord, I am lost, if you do not come to my aid. I am, by your grace, full of good resolutions and of good desires; but I am beset by enemies who have no less desire to ruin me than I have to save myself, and who make all their efforts to take from me the treasure that I just received. I have given up sin, it is true; but still are left to me some passions, an extremely spoiled nature, a great inclination to vice, fortified by long habits. "We perish." Alas! I feel already that this first fervor slackens, that this great intention, which seemed to make me invincible, loses every day something of its fervor; I feel this mortal weakness return. If you do not support me, O my God, I cannot promise you an hour of steadfastness.[57] The first temptation is going to overcome me. I will escape you, Lord; you will ruin me without fail, if you do not have your eye on me unceasingly, if your hand abandons me only one moment to myself: "Lord, save us, we perish." Preserve your work, O my God, the work of your infinite mercy. Make—for after all you can do it—make that I, having served you continuously here below, can love you eternally in heaven. *So be it.*

On the Vicious Habit[1]

You will find an ass tied and her colt next to her: loose her and bring her to me.

(Matt 21:2)[2]

Whoever engages himself in a vicious Habit will not come out of it when he wants

to do so; nevertheless, whoever engages himself there would come out of it if he

really wanted to do so.[3]

SAINT BERNARD, IN THE THIRD DISCOURSE that he made on our gospel, teaches us that the conversion of the sinner is mysteriously expressed in the words I just quoted. He says that these animals that Jesus Christ has unleashed to be led to him are the figure of the souls whose bad habits enchain in such a way that they cannot—or at least that they do not want to—do the good, or rather that they cannot and do not want at the same time: "He was released at the Lord's command, the one that was previously held, either not able or not willing to grant a favor; or perhaps rather bound by both chains, namely, neither willing nor able."[4]

I do not think that one could say, either more clearly or in fewer words, all that regards the subject of bad Habits. It is true, Gentlemen, that, when one has contracted them, one ordinarily rots there, both because one cannot conquer them and because one does not want to fight against them. I want to say that it is nearly impossible to get free from them and that nevertheless it is not absolutely impossible; that the difficulty is so great that it seems insurmountable; that it is not so great however that one be deserving of some excuse when one does not overcome it.

And it is by this doctrine that I intend to destroy today two illusions, both very hurtful and very common among bad Christians. The first is of those who get engaged in a vicious Habit in hope that they will be able someday to withdraw from it. The second is of those who remain there, under the pretext that they no longer can withdraw from it. When the demon attracts a soul to relax and to give admittance to love of the world, he does not fail to make her understand that this is only for a time, and to depict to her the return from the evil to the good as easy as is the fall from the good into the evil. But when God urges us to return to him, the same enemy of our salvation tries to persuade us that this return is as impossible as the fall has been easy for us. He deceives us, Christian auditors, and I want, with the help of the Holy Spirit, to reveal to you today his tricks. I will make you see, in the first point, that whoever engages in a vicious Habit will not come out of it when he wants to do so; and, in the second, that whoever engages there would come out of it if he really wanted to do so. It is not so easy to get rid of it as one imagines it to be, when one begins to contract it; and it is not as difficult [to get rid of it] as one wants to believe it, when once one has contracted it. This is the whole subject of this talk. My God, I see the fruit that these two truths could produce, if they were well-understood. I sense the powerlessness in which I am of making them enter into the soul of my auditors, but I know that you can [do] everything and that you refuse nothing to Mary. That is why I make use of her intercession before you, and, before her, of the prayers of the Church: *Hail, Mary.*[5]

First Point

One would not be able to say how difficult it is to reform nature, when unfortunately it finds itself defective. Those who are born with wicked inclinations and who apply themselves to correct them can tell how much vigilance this study demands and the little progress that they make with all their care and all their efforts. If someone is slow by his nature, whatever means that one takes in order to arouse him, one will have much difficulty to make him effective and industrious. A lively mind cannot be restrained, either easily or for long, within the limits of perfect moderation. It takes a miracle—and a great miracle—in order to soften a heart that has some inclination to anger, or in order to inspire the love of mortification in a soul [that is] lax and that naturally loves pleasure. This is so difficult that grace itself—as powerful as it is—does not dare, it seems, to hope to overcome it.[6] That is why, in place of undertaking to change our natural passions, [grace] is as if obligated to follow them and to find for them objects to which they innocently can attach themselves. For example, for a quick-tempered man [grace] will inspire feelings of repentance, which is to say of harshness and of revenge against oneself; it will lead a miserly person to accrue riches for the next life, an ambitious person to walk in the steps of the most holy, a heart amorous and sensitive to the most tender passions to love the One who deserves to be loved above all things and who responds so faithfully and so generously to our love.

This assumed, Gentlemen, in order to make you understand how difficult it will be for you to break free from a vice—whatever it may be—when the habit will have formed itself in you,[7] it suffices to tell you that habit is a second nature—a nature added—so speaks Saint Augustine—and as though grafted on to our inclinations: "a second nature, as if added by art."[8] In such a way that, if you habituate yourself to vanity, to luxury, to malicious gossip, to gambling, to sensual pleasure, to an idle and worldly life, it will be as difficult for you, in little time, to reform yourself as it is difficult to win over a gloomy mood and to soften a rough and harsh spirit.

Much more: I say that habituation is still stronger than nature, since it can overcome it—it can bend it, so to speak, as unyielding as it is. In this way we see that the weakest bodies become hardened little by little at the greatest efforts—that the most timid learn to despise dangers by force of being exposed to them, and that, often making use of the most deadly poisons, one at last makes of them a food.[9] And this destroys the vain presumption of those who, feeling financially stable or having had a profitable education, believe that they will be able to resist the malignancy of the bad Habit and find in the first impressions an aid to return, when it will please them, to a better life. But alas! It takes little time for vice to destroy such weak advantages that we have brought to the world or that we owe to the zeal of those who have taken care of our first years[10]! One no longer recognizes a person after six months of a slightly dissolute life, and she no longer recognizes herself. To me it is like seeing poor Samson, who falls asleep in the bosom of Delilah and lets himself get tied up, in the confidence that he has in his natural strength. But the poor wretch does not consider that all this strength is in his hair, which is the slenderest thing in the world and the easiest to cut, and that treachery will not fail to shear it in order to weaken him.[11]

If habit is so powerful, when it has even nature to fight against, what will it be, Christian auditors, when it joins itself to [nature]: when their forces will be united—when one will be habituated to do things to which one is already carried by one's inclination? You naturally love the pleasure of taste, and this can be applied to all the other pleasures; you cannot abstain from it, not even in the times intended for fasting and for penance, in these times in which the Church—in which propriety itself requires of you more mortification. When, by a good use of the things that gratify your senses, you will have added, to this penchant that attracts you, the weight of the bad habit, how will you be able to resist? When one obeys passion, says Saint Augustine, a habit soon forms, and this habit, if you let it get a foothold, will change into necessity: "By servitude to passion, habit is formed, and habit to which there is no resistance becomes necessity."[12] One speaks of a queen of the Assyrians, of whom even Scripture makes mention, that, having obtained from her husband that she was permitted to reign in his place only one day, she began to exercise her sovereign authority by having the royal crown taken from him, as if she thought only to have fun. Then, seeing that he did not stand up for himself, she stripped him of all his signs of royalty, she made demand of him even to his sword, finally, she had his head cut off and thus took from him, with his life, a crown that he had thought to be able to reclaim after twenty-four hours of servitude.[13]

This is precisely what happens almost to everyone who grants something to passion, under the pretext that this is only for a time and that reason and virtue soon will reclaim their first rights. One continues to do by force that which one first began by pleasure and by indulgence. It is in this way that this religious of whom it is spoken in Saint Dorotheus, having stolen a few times by the pure necessity in which he was to eat, did not fail to do it still when there no longer was necessity and that, these spoils having become entirely unnecessary to him, the bread went bad and rotted away in the mattress of his bed.[14] It is thus that one sometimes[15] sees old men, in whom age has almost extinguished even the feeling of sensual pleasure, to be led along, as though despite themselves, to shameless actions, without either the love of their reputation or the fear of the death that they expect at every moment capable of restraining them.

Please God, Christian auditors, that there were fewer examples of this invincible necessity, and that one did not hear every day those who have made themselves slaves moan vainly in their chains and render useless the insights, the inspirations, the desires to do the good; [those insights, inspirations, and desires that are] capable of sanctifying several souls to whom some freedom still remains. Ah! Poor man, how I feel sorry for you, how I find you worthy of compassion! At the beginning how you gave yourself over to debauchery, to gambling, to malicious gossip, to anger: debauchery seemed to you a vice appropriate and as though proper to your age; gambling, a respectable occupation; malicious gossip, a necessary conversation; anger, an understandable passion, in view of the reasons that one has every day to put one in a bad mood. But today it is not the same thing. Your reason [having] matured with age, your conscience enlightened with a thousand supernatural lights, you point out all these things as faults—as shameful, unjust, pernicious, detestable vices—and nevertheless you will not fail to fall into them. "You see that your behavior is wrong," says Saint Augustine, "that it is detestable and makes you unhappy, yet you go on behaving in the same way."[16]

You know that to drink to the point of losing your mind is a brutality of which a gentleman ought to blush for all those who indulge in it; you are ashamed of it yourself, when you are sober; and nevertheless you get drunk at the first opportunity. You are convinced that you risk your good to gamble—that beyond the money, you waste there your time, your soul, paradise; you criticize yourself in this for your weakness; you quite would like to cure yourself of it—you have asked help for that—you have tried some means—and you have gained nothing: "You did so yesterday, and you will today."[17] You swore yesterday [on] the name of God; you are in despair from it, you confessed it today—you have wept bitterly over it; you cannot understand how you were able to consent to a sin that you hate, it seems to you, with all your heart; and notwithstanding all that, you will swear even today—you will do it again tomorrow—you will accuse yourself of it a hundred times and always with tears, but always in vain.[18]

The thing sometimes goes still further. The natural necessities ordinarily attract us only to things that are pleasant: [there is] some need that one has to take food, [yet] one feels pressed to do it only for as much time as one finds some pleasure there; from the moment that one has taken distaste for foods, one no longer feels the need that one has to eat. The burning of thirst once forced soldiers to drink their own blood mixed with the mud of a stream; but this ghastly concoction[19] was to them at that time a very delicious drink. Habit produces a necessity stronger and more invincible than all that. It forces us to sin, even when we have no pleasure to do it. Saint John Chrysostom was right to compare it to an old tyrant whose unjust domination is still extremely cruel, who is not content to impose great tributes but who demands them in a hard and ruthless way, who does not want only to be served but who asks for shameful and painful services. If I told you, Christian auditors, that, if you did not hurry to change your life, your bad habits would grow stronger in such a way that you could not restrain yourself from offending God as many times that sin will have for you some sweetness, it seems to me that this would be enough to make you desire a prompt conversion. But I go still further: a time will come perhaps that evil will present itself to you without any charms—that you will have disgust of it, that you will find there even bitterness—and yet you will be as though constrained to do it. I do not know how it happens, but all the same I know that this happens, the attraction that brought us to the sin beginning to lack, one still loves the sin in which one no longer finds anything that does not repulse. It seems that this is an effect of the justice of God, which blinds us in order to punish us and which permits that we do for a long time, with difficulty and despite ourselves, that which we have done for some time despite him and with pleasure.

I know that this seems incredible to those who have not experienced it. But I entreat them in the name of God not to trust their judgment, to believe those whom experience has instructed and who, so to speak, see every day [and] who touch the bonds with which the bad Habit holds its slaves enchained.[20] Certainly one will not be able to reject on this subject the witness of Saint Augustine who himself had experienced it; he still was young when God began to reveal to him the danger in which he was and to inspire in him the desire of a more orderly life. What sinner has ever received greater graces! And what would be our presumption if, engaging in sin with such knowledge, we hoped to have graces as strong to help us get free of it! However all these graces were useless for many years. Not only did he defend himself against the exhortations and tears of his mother, against[21] the zeal and the eloquence of the most learned prelates, of the greatest saints of his century; but for a long time he withstood himself to himself. Persuaded—convinced—of the truth, filled with admiration for the life of virtuous persons and even with love for virtue, he throws himself still into the pleasures that he so often detested, he plunges into these sins in which he no longer finds pleasure, in which he even finds a thousand pains: "while I plunged into pleasures," these are his words, "I plunged into miseries."[22]

But how easy would it be for man to leave a habit of several years, if Jesus Christ himself made it known that it was difficult for him to draw him out of it after some days? All the Fathers [of the Church] agree it was to indicate this extreme difficulty that, wanting to resurrect Lazarus, who represented the state of a sinner who has grown old in sin, he wept, he shuddered, he raised his voice and gave all the signs of an action that demanded an effort and an extraordinary power: "yet he showed you a certain sense of difficulty. He groaned in spirit, he showed that loud shouts of censure and disapproval are required for people who have become hardened in bad habits."[23] That is Saint Augustine. However, Gentlemen, we have taken so little advantage of this lesson that I know not if, of all the people, either who throw themselves into a worldly life or who persevere there with some knowledge of the danger in which they are, I know not, I say, if there is a single one of them who makes plans of retreat and of amendment for the future, and who takes account of all this as if they were absolute masters of their will or of the help that will be needed for them in order to make [this worldly life] yield.

But what, Christian soul—you already have such a great inclination to vanity, to sloth, to pleasure, to anger, to intemperance, to ambition, that you cannot resist them. And, when all these passions will be established and fortified in your heart by several years of dissoluteness, you hope to be able to conquer them?[24] Today, when God touches you, when he puts pressure on you, when he offers you his grace, you do not have the strength to obey him; and you believe that you will be stronger after ten or twenty years of weakness and of constant relapses![25] And me, I believe to the contrary—and it is on the word of God that I believe it—that, if at present you habituate yourself to do evil, one will sooner exonerate a Moor than one will make you practice the good: "If the Ethiopian can change his skin, and the leopard his spots: you may also do well, when you have learned badly."[26] You promise yourself an old age completely different from this vain, idle, depraved youth; and me, I predict to you that age will carry new vices to you and that it will increase still the former ones.

Today you give yourself over to the sensual pleasure that you pursue; it flees you for the moment and you run after it. Beauty corrupts you and then you will kiss cadavers.[27] You sin at this time by interest and in order to please others; a day will come that others[28] themselves will condemn you and you will not fail to sin. After having loved apparel, in order to make yourself pleasing to the world, you will continue to love it, when it makes you ridiculous. You let yourself be tempted presently by the first one who invites you to drink or to gamble; you will tempt others later—you will become a corrupter of youth and you will go everywhere looking for people who want to keep you company in your debauchery. Finally Christians, if I said to you that you will lie even in dying—that even on your deathbed you will blaspheme, you will make love, you will dream of vanity and of revenge—I would tell you nothing that has not happened to many people who for a long time had deluded themselves with the same hopes that your weakness entertains today. But no, I content myself with foreshadowing to you that you will die in the same habits in which you presently live, which is to say that at the last confession that you will make, you still will accuse yourself of this same weakness—of this same sin that you do not want to give up so soon—that you will fall there two days before your last illness—that you will die before having the consolation of having spent fifteen days or a month of time without falling back there and before ever having carried out the intention that, all the same, you repeat every time you go to confession.

What do you think of this death, Christian auditors? For me, I admit to you that I would not be able to think of it without shuddering. To die in a malicious Habit, to die before having mended one's ways, before having changed one's life—to die miserly, vain, ambitious, drunk, given to sensual pleasure, irascible, vindictive—although that be after having gone to confession and having received all the sacraments of the Church! O my God, do not permit that I die such a death! Do you know to what it is that I compare this kind of death? I compare it to that of that unfortunate man whose tragic end came at the time of Saint Peter Damian, who recounts it in a letter to Pope Alexander.[29] This man having gone into a forest with another to cut down a tree, at the first strike of the axe that he gave, there came out of the trunk a snake of an enormous girth and length. As this monster was coming to devour him, with the two heads that it had, he cut one of them off. But, his axe having at the same time slipped from his hands, he remained in the grip of the revenge of the snake which, having seized him by the middle of the body, dragged him into its hole despite his cries and his futile resistance. He asked in vain for help from his companion; he pleaded with him in a pitiful way to come at least to give him his axe—but he pleaded with him in vain; he had to follow the dragon and to endure all its fury. The news of this fatal accident filled the whole world with fright and with sadness; the saint above all says of himself that he could not hold back his tears all the times that he imagined that unfortunate man at the bottom of a cave and in the power of this horrible foe, no matter that one only could think of these last circumstances of his death and that one was unaware if he had been strangled by this monster, or poisoned by his venom, or eaten completely alive, or smothered by his fearsome stranglehold.

There, Christian auditors, is what I think of a soul who dies in a malicious Habit. I do not know if the last contrition she[30] had was sincere, if in dying she formed a more effective intention than all those preceding that still had never produced anything. I do not know if, after she has received absolution,[31] the demon will not have presented once again the objects to which she had such attachment, and if, in the weakness that she found herself, she will have made more resistance than she had the habit of doing in full health. I know that many have died in this way, after having received extreme unction.[32] What is certain is that she breathed her last in the hands of a horrible monster. God knows what treatment she received from it; but there is only too much appearance that she was treated cruelly by it.

Let us anticipate this misfortune, Christian company, and let us not make, if it is possible, a questionable death. Let us hasten to tear out from our heart these habits that otherwise would accompany us up to the last moment of life—that seemingly would make this moment dire for us. But, if these habits already are formed, is it still in our power to destroy them? Yes, Gentlemen, this is still in our power. This is difficult, in truth, but it is not absolutely impossible. This is my second part.

Second Point

Saint Bernard, in the eighty-first sermon on the *Canticles*, speaking of the necessity that the habit of offending God imposes on the soul, says that it is a necessity that the will makes for itself—a free necessity that pressures it, but that does not excuse it. It is a violence that [the will] suffers, but that it does not mind to suffer; it is an intention so strong that it excludes all opposing intention; in a word, it is a powerlessness that one wants and that one loves. "Your will is not diminished because it is in bondage; your will is strong to do what you cannot refuse to do, even if you struggle; now where there is will, there is freedom."[33] Not only do you want the evil that you do, but you want it emphatically, since you want it necessarily. One must want a thing when one cannot not want it. And yet, wherever there is intention, there is choice and consequently freedom.[34]

This reasoning, however unassailable, perhaps will appear obscure to those who are not accustomed to the subtleties of the School.[35] But everyone will understand what I am going to say. However strong, however deeply entrenched be the Habit to which our heart has submitted,[36] it is certain that we sin when we obey it. Consequently we can refuse to obey it, since all sin is an action free and done with deliberation, and that to act freely is to do a thing that one would be able not to do.[37] If all the times that I give in to the violence of a vicious Habit, I can resist it if I really want to do so, I will be able to resist it so often that I will lose the custom that I had made myself to give in to it—which is nothing other than to destroy it itself and to destroy it entirely.[38] Much more, I can practice, as many times as it pleases me, acts opposed to those that have served to form this Habit. One can fast in order to amend for the excesses that one has committed, work[39] in order to restore what idleness had spoiled, affect to speak well of everyone, in order to correct the inclination to speak badly of others, and in this way to make for myself a contrary Habit[40]—a habit that makes the good as easy to me as the evil was necessary to me before.[41] I know this does not always happen all at once: first one avoids the occasions in which one knows that one ordinarily falls; one prepares oneself for those [occasions] that one cannot avoid; one takes precautions, one keeps on guard, one arms oneself with good thoughts, one does violence to oneself in the encounters that one has foreseen; and, in part by fleeing, in part by fighting with an advantage, one spares oneself plenty of relapses, one allows grace to establish itself; one feels strength and courage return, one no longer despairs of victory, one develops a strong intention to win completely. This strong and sincere intention conquers everything; and it is only because we lack it that the bad Habit is so difficult to overcome.

Yes, a good intention is all-powerful;[42] there is nothing that it does not conquer. Indeed, what does one not do, when one really wants to do it? One bends iron, one melts bronze, one makes marble figures as delicate and as tender as if the marble itself were soft and made no resistance to the hand of the sculptor. We see such people all the time, says Saint Augustine, who, having left very wicked Habits, live better than those who reprimanded them in their dissoluteness and who were scandalized by them. Magdalene rose more perfectly from her dissolute life than Lazarus, her brother, rose from the tomb where he was half-decomposed.[43] We see many of them, says this [Church] Father; we know many of them who have imitated this great saint: "We see many, we know many."[44] He himself could offer himself for example; it sufficed to establish this doctrine and to confound our weakness; for finally he softened this iron will, as he calls it, that seemed so uncompromising and so rigid. Not only did he cut back to sin more rarely, but never to sin again, not even slightly with consideration. Not only did he win this over himself little by little and by force of patience, but he won it all at once: from the time that he had resolved to drive away sensual pleasure, it was banished forever; there was no longer any way back for it. He was not bound with only one chain—ambition, pride, greed reigned in his soul, as well as incontinence: one same day delivered him from all these tyrants. But in what way was he freed and how perfect was the liberty that he obtained for himself? He makes a vow of chastity—he who could not resign himself to the bond of marriage; he had not been able until then to go without the most criminal pleasures, [and now] he makes himself crimes of the most innocent [pleasures];[45] he would like to be able to lose the taste for food; he fears to be attracted to the Church by the sweetness of the singing; he criticizes his eyes even to the pleasure that the light causes them. He who, in order to acquire some property, came to risk his life in the university of Milan, raises the standard of voluntary poverty that still had not had an example in Africa. The most vain of all men accepts the function of priest despite himself and laments bitterly the need in which he finds himself to obey in that the one who has the power to order him. Glory was one of his greatest passions: he confesses to the whole universe—to all the ages to come—and writes a book in order to render immortal the memory of his most shameful dissoluteness.[46]

Of what is our will not capable, Gentlemen, when, sustained by grace, it is pleased to turn toward an object and to embrace it all the best? What obstacles—what such strong chains can stop a person who has a genuine desire to go to God? What difficulties is she not capable of overcoming? What is so great, so hard in the most elevated counsels of divine providence![47] What have the most renowned—the most magnanimous—saints done that I do not undertake today, that even today I do not overcome, if I really want to do so?

Why do we take pleasure in deceiving ourselves and in concealing with empty excuses the weakness and the little sincerity of our good desires? "I would like to correct myself," we say, "if I could do it;[48] I would like to become better; for that I will do all that I will be able." And me, I tell you that, if you did only the tenth part of what you are able in this, the thing would be done in less than twenty-four hours. "I would not be able to defeat myself in the occasion [of sin], if I am carried away despite myself; I do what I would not like to do."[49] My God, do we very well dare say this in your presence! You[, auditor,] cannot do without this pleasure! And you would do without it so easily, if there were a witness—if important business called you away! If you were certain to have a burning fever upon returning from this gathering, from this rendezvous, you would not consider even to go there. If the person whom you love most in the world begged you to do for her what you cannot do for God; if you were certain that, in abstaining either from drinking, or from swearing, or from speaking ill, or from taking revenge, you, who are only a simple gentleman, you would become peer of the realm with one hundred thousand pounds of pension,[50] would you find some one of these things impossible?

Do you really know what is the true sense of these words that so often we have in the mouth: "I would like to serve God, if I could do it"? This means that I would like that one could serve God, please others, and satisfy oneself at the same time. I would like to be devout, that is to say, I would like to find as much readiness, as much pleasure to fast, to pray, to read books of piety as I find at gambling and at the theater. I would like to be holy, if that could be done without difficulty, without care, without pressure; I would like that it were fashionable to be dressed simply, that the world let each one live according to his whim, that one split up all the gatherings, that one no longer gave me reason to get into a bad mood; I would like to be able to watch, to listen to everything, to take all kinds of liberties without being affected by anything, or at least being forced to practice all the good that I know, without it being in my power to refrain from it. What illusions! And can we say that we seriously form similar desires? Do we really dare make this feeble excuse at death, when our Judge criticizes us for our negligence? I really would have wanted, if I could have? What are you saying, if you could have? And what was there then of impossibility in the practice of the most perfect piety? Has there never been either a male or female saint in your state or temperament? This man, who had been plunged in all sorts of vices, has completely withdrawn from them; this woman who was possessed, so to speak, with seven demons, whose rashness and bad conduct you have so rebuked, this woman, I say, has changed in your eyes, in six months' time; she has left nothing to reform—she has become a model of all virtue, and you have not been able to get rid of a single vice to which you had some connection! A preaching has melted this heart of bronze; a word has opened—has shattered—this rock—has moved this mountain; and you, after so many instructions, so many lights, so many graces—you have remained hardened and immovable, and you claim that you have not been able to do otherwise! You really would have liked to correct yourself; and me, I would have liked also to save you, and you know enough what I have done for that; but how is it that heaven, which cannot admit one sole sin, could admit of a bad Habit, which is to say, a pile and a source of sins?[51]

Oh! Christian company, may a soul who has a genuine desire to convert speak truly in another manner. "Lord," she says with Saint Paul, "what will you have me do?"[52] Lord, what do you want that I do? Here I am, completely ready to obey you, and I feel strength for all things. Can you really drink the cup that the world is preparing for you and as it prepared it for me myself—suffer the persecutions, the ridicule, the judgments that one will make of you? "We can."[53] And why could we not do it, since so many others were able to do it with your grace?[54] But this is only to begin—one must persevere to the end. That is also what I want, Lord—to love you and to serve you until death; and who will be able to separate me from you, if once I am yours? "Who will separate us from the love of Christ?"[55] Yes, Lord, I want to be yours—I want to tear out these Habits that I have nurtured only too much; and I will do it, whatever it costs me, should I die from the effort. I will try at least what so many others have so happily achieved: I will see if the thing actually is impossible, and I will believe it only after I have put all sorts of means to use in order to succeed. I know that I will have battles to wage and obstacles to overcome, but I am resolved to everything. I do not intend to spare relatives, nor friends, nor property, nor honor, nor holiness, nor life; I consider an enemy whoever opposes my intention, and from now on I recognize, neither good, nor evil on the earth except that which can either harm me or help me to serve God. Gentlemen, when one wants the good in this way, one no longer finds either powerlessness or weakness in oneself; one no longer finds difficulty, even in difficult things: vices, wicked inclinations, the most ancient habits, the world, the demon—everything flees, everything disappears before a soul so resolved;[56] she searches everywhere for the obstacles that one had represented to her—the enemies with whom one had threatened her—and she finds all the paths united and all the passages clear. It is then that she cries out with the prophet: "I have seen an end to all persecution: your commandment is exceedingly broad."[57] Hey! Lord, where then are these monsters and these giants who were to oppose our holy desires,[58] with which one frightened us so? Ah! How miserable I would have been had I let myself be frightened by these ghosts—if I had no longer trusted in your grace and if I did not distrust my own strength! Oh! What joy for me to have embarked on such a wide and beautiful road, which will lead me so gently and so surely to the end for which I long, which is the everlasting happiness that I wish for you, in the name of the Father, and of the Son, and of the Holy Spirit.

9

On Confession[1]

Prepare the way of the Lord, make straight the paths by which he will come.

(Luke 3:4)[2]

Two errors, into which almost all of us fall, make most of our confessions useless: we believe ourselves more innocent than we are; we believe ourselves truly repentant, although we are not at all.

HERE WE FINALLY ARE ON THE EVE of our joy.[3] The Desire of nations comes to us,[4] and our hearts begin to open up to the odor of his fragrance. It is unnecessary to observe the sky in order to know that the hour of his birth is very near;[5] we have a definite omen of it in this joy so gentle and so pure that is in the habit of preceding it and of spreading itself in the soul of all the faithful. I do not know, Gentlemen, if you ever have tried to look for the cause of such a great happiness. It is obvious that the faith of the Redeemer[6]—that the remembrance of a mystery as dear and as devout as that which we soon are going to celebrate—is the first source of it; but I do not doubt that [this happiness] also come from the holy disposition of most Christians at this time to reconcile themselves with God.[7] How could the peace and consolation of the Holy Spirit not spread itself over the whole Church, on a day when almost all its children consider purifying themselves by penance and tearing out from their hearts sin, this bitter root of all evils and of all the sorrows of life?

These are my thoughts, Christian auditors; and I admit to you that from this perspective I have ascended the pulpit today much more willingly than usual! Of all those who will hear me, I told myself, there is hardly one sole of them who be not planning to go to confession, either as early as tonight, or tomorrow, or at least before the celebrations be over. What more helpful disposition could one wish in one's auditors? When will the word of God bear fruit, if it is sterile at such a favorable time? But what subject could I choose, either more pleasant or more useful to people who prepare themselves to go to confession than Confession itself? That is the way by which Jesus will come to them—it is this way that he orders me to prepare for him and to straighten out, if possible: "Prepare the way of the Lord, make straight the paths by which he will come."[8]

How I would consider myself happy, Christian company, if, by the instruction that I am going to give, I could help you to approach worthily at least one time the sacrament of penance! Besides, this word of instruction ought not to discourage you; I know that I speak of people who know their catechism; that is why I will try to say nothing too ordinary; I dare promise myself that, if one sees fit to listen to me with some attention, there will be few of my auditors who do not benefit from this discourse and who after do not confess a little better than they did. Holy Virgin, I commit myself only in the confidence that I have in your protection. I humbly ask you for it in the name of this whole assembly: *Hail, Mary.*[9]

To hear the awful threats that God makes to the sinner on almost every page of Scripture—to see the tortures that he keeps right at hand to punish us, it seems, as soon as we have committed some sin—there is no one who have not reason to believe that he is lost without recourse, if he is unfortunate enough to offend him. But is it not something quite worthy of admiration, Christian auditors, that while the Lord rages—while he seems on the one hand completely ready to strike down—while he lights the furnaces, the lakes of fire, for the rebellious man—he prepares for him at the same time a bath beyond price in order to heal him of all the evils that his disobedience could cause him?

When, in spite of all these threats—all this system of terror—we come to fall into some sin, he does not fail to find himself close to us in order to help us—to raise us back to our feet with gentleness—to wash us in his own blood! O love! O mercy! O harshness itself full of tenderness! It seems to me like seeing a good mother who, in the fear that she has that her child not hurt himself, tears in anger the knife from his hands, forbids him under serious penalties to take it back. You would say then that she has neither tenderness, nor friendship; but if, despite these precautions, the poor child happens to injure himself, she feels as though stricken herself: she runs to him completely emotional, and quite far from carrying out her threats, she thinks only of washing the wound, only of dressing it, only of consoling him herself and of drying his tears. What would become of us, Christian auditors, if one treated us in another way—if we did not receive the cure for our transgressions from the same One whom we offend!

The demon—who is not unaware that we, being fragile as we are, could not fail to die without this cure—the demon, I say, does not neglect anything, either to steal it from us, or to make it useless to us. He has managed to steal it entirely from those who are outside the Roman Church;[10] he leads our Catholics to make use of it only rarely; and when they have recourse to it, he tries to turn it into poison for them by the little preparation that they bring to it. It is a great misfortune, without a doubt, that in the same sacrament that was established for our reconciliation we find the subject of a greater disgrace—that the same thing happens to us as to those who drown in taking the bath that was prescribed to them for their health. But what can be the source of such a great misfortune? It is not ordinarily that one lacks sincerity; there are few penitents whose mouth confusion closes at the tribunal of penance. No, if I am not mistaken, it is rather that one deludes and that one blinds oneself; but it happens very often that we mislead our confessors, because we first are misled.

There are then two errors into which almost all of us fall and that make most of our Confessions useless to us. In order to force you to avoid them, Christian auditors, it is enough to reveal them to you; and that is what I will try to do in this discourse. The first error is that we attribute much more innocence to ourselves than we actually have; and the second is that we pride ourselves in a repentance that we do not have. We believe ourselves more innocent than we are: that is the first point; we believe ourselves truly repentant, although we are not at all: that will be the second point. This is the whole subject of our discussion.

First Point

One sometimes sees Christians who excuse themselves from confessing often, on the basis that they do not find anything of which to accuse themselves unless they let a considerable space of time go by after each Confession. And, in fact, it may happen that, after having received absolution from the priest, one spends several days in a great enough innocence by virtue of the grace that one has received in this sacrament, which[11] later beginning to slacken, one falls back into the same faults.[12] If this is [the case,] by this same reason that one has nothing to say after some days, it would be necessary to repeat Confession often in order always to have nothing to say, and in this way to spend one's life in a perfect distance from sin.[13] But it is much more probable, according to the word of the learned abbot of Celle,[14] that those who find no sins in themselves be in this difficulty only because there are too many [such sins]: "Truly abundance has made such persons paupers."[15] These are persons who, in their self-examination, do not get to the heart of the soul, because in this heart they glimpse a pile of corruption that they are afraid to reveal completely, for fear that a greater knowledge obligate them to reform themselves. That is why one is happy to pass quickly over what one has done since the last examination; one applies oneself only to the faults that one can remove without undermining a certain life plan that he has outlined for himself on the rules of the world and that one has no desire to change.

This plan that one does not change when one examines oneself contains a thousand maxims adverse to the maxims of Jesus Christ. Miserliness, ambition, vanity, the love of pleasure determine there all the actions of the day; one must forget nothing in order to enrich oneself, to rise in status, to please, to pass the time pleasurably; one must have the reputation of a gentleman, of a gallant, of a kind-hearted man, in some sense that it pleases the corrupt world to take these terms; one must appear in the gatherings, there to stand out, there to outshine, if it is possible, the rest of the world; and for that one must ignore nothing: one must use all the tricks that the world habitually puts to use. Finally, one must try to lead a cheerful and comfortable life, and to taste all the gentleness that it presents to us. All that cannot be done unless one runs a thousand risks of sinning, unless one actually sins in a thousand ways; all that is formally opposed to the holiness of Christianity to which each Christian is obliged to aspire according to his state.[16] This here is not a life simply to reform, but to change from top to bottom. However, for fear of being obligated in fact to change one's life or to awaken the criticisms of the conscience, which[17] then would disturb all the entertainment, one closes the eyes to all this dissoluteness, one tells oneself that it is nothing, that if one sins sometimes in living this way, these are the effects of weakness rather than occasions in which one engages oneself; in a word, that it is a necessity to live like this.

This assumed, Christian auditors, one need not be surprised that one have few things to say in Confession. When one has set down as principle that it is a necessity to live as one lives in the world, and that to be Christian it suffices to have the name [of Christian], I understand how it is that one finds oneself quite innocent and that one is embarrassed when one has to go to confess. But if one wanted to act sincerely there—if one wanted to examine deeply the life that one leads, to see a little on what principles, on what maxims it runs, what it has of conformity or of opposition with the life of Jesus Christ; if, I say, one wanted to stir up this cesspool—to lance this abscess—where it makes of itself such a great mass of rottenness, one soon would be out of this supposed trouble, to fall into a completely contrary trouble, where the sight of an almost infinite number of disorders would strike us.

To get out completely from such a dangerous error, it seems to me that, when one prepares to go to Confession, one only would have to cast the eyes over the life of some male or female saint in the same condition as us—for there are such in all conditions—and to remark in how many things our conduct finds itself diametrically opposed to their conduct. Compare yourself a little, Christian auditors, with some person of eminent virtue and of exemplary piety. See how many things give her scruples that you do not confess. Compare her prayers with your prayers, her speech with yours, her meals with your meals, her habits with your habits, her occupations with your idleness. If this person had lived only one day in the way that you live, she would think herself the most miserable of all creatures—she would believe herself lost—and however, you do not believe yourself guilty of anything. You are Christian, however, as well as she, and consequently you have the same obligations.

But it is not only those who are exceedingly worldly who blind themselves deliberately in this way. There are sometimes people who believe themselves scrupulously sensitive, who fail to accuse themselves of their principal faults because they cannot resolve to believe that they be faults. For example, one owes the shopkeeper, one owes the workmen, the servants, one owes others, from whom in the past one either had borrowed or perhaps even had taken property; and nevertheless one does not want to deduct anything from the expense, to put oneself in the state of paying; or, although one could pay at once, one postpones to another time; one believes that it is enough to intend to do it. One deceives oneself: it is an obvious injustice. One suspects it; and if one is not completely certain of it,[18] it is that one is delighted to be unaware of it. However, one racks one's mind in order to state one's sins, where one hardly finds matter for absolution, and one says nothing of these things that are altogether essential. There are entire families, completely divided, that do not want to hear speak of reconciliation. These are, for the rest, decent people; but they have convinced their conscience that they are not obligated to take any initiative; that one has reasons not to see one another, to complain eternally about each other, and to let the whole world know these reasons. One confesses them twice, three times, four times; but finally, as one really senses that one has no desire to mend one's ways, one does not confess them anymore and one deludes oneself into believing that there is no obligation to confess them. How many people, given to devotion, are subject to episodes of impatience, of which they claim to make a merit before God; who, quite far from accusing themselves of the trouble they cause at home, want to pass off their ill-humor as an effect of their vigilance and of the care they take of their servants. How many zealous people, under pretext of having religion and justice at heart—of not being able to suffer anything that not be in order—under pretext of instructing the weak and the ignorant or of consoling themselves with the good at the misfortune of those who perish, indulge in cruel, malicious gossip that they prefer to color and to disguise in that way only to fight the inclination that they have to this vice?

What if these defects, though coarse, elude those who do not have much desire to know them? How many interior movements will be omitted in the examination of conscience, if one does not make every effort to probe the heart in order to discover all the wounds? You say that, thank God, you are without passion. What! Without love, without hatred, without envy, without any desire for revenge, without loathing?[19] Whence comes, then, this secret eagerness that you have to see I know not what person, to please her and to do good to her? It is an effect, you will tell me, of your friendship. Yes, but you well know that in all these supposed friendships there always is something impure and sensual, and, if you really want to tell us what it has come to, it is no longer friendship but a very dangerous love. What does it mean, this joy that your heart feels, when some little misfortune happens to this man? Whence does it come that you take so much pleasure to see this woman humiliated?[20] Whence does it come that you suffer—that you are tortured—when one speaks well of this other? I want this not to go further; it is certain that these sentiments are contrary to Christian charity.[21]

What if you tell me that you have examined yourself on all these points and with the best faith in the world, that you have gone back even to the source—even to the motives—of your actions, that you have gone down even to the bottom of your soul and that you have told everything to the confessor, God be praised a thousand times for it. If you continue to do justice to yourself in this way, I answer back to you that in little time you will draw great fruit from the use of Confession. But after having asked yourself again for such an exact account of what you had done, have you had the courage to cast your eyes on what you had not done? I ask if you have had enough courage for that, because I fear that this not be for you an abyss—an inexhaustible sea. For each action that one does and that one ought not to do, it is certain that there are a hundred of them that one ought to do and that one does not do. Have you taken care that your subjects, that your servants do nothing unjust in your name and under your authority? Do your servants know what they need to know in order to be saved? Do they pray to God, both at morning and at night? Do they observe the fasts of the Church? Do they confess? Are they reserved in their actions and in their words? You know nothing about it, you tell me. Well good, this ignorance is a matter for Confession. When all things find themselves happily to be well-arranged, you would not fail to be guilty for not having informed yourself of the state in which they are. If you have no care for those who are in your service, what will they become, above all in a country where they have neither bishop, nor pastor, nor catechist—where they can learn the duties of Christianity only from yourself or from those to whom you will give responsibility for it?[22] You are not unaware of the obligations that you have regarding your children; you know that it is not enough that they be instructed in the humanities or in physical exercises, but that you need to teach them to know God, to fear him, to love him with all their heart. To whom do you entrust them, these children? Are you quite aware that they have no principle of piety—that one dreams of nothing less than of setting them on the path of salvation?

Furthermore, there are occasions in which you are obliged to correct your brothers—to counsel them charitably. Have you not failed to do so in some encounter? The principal use that you are obliged to make of your authority, of your goods, of your prudence, is to prevent that the Lord be offended. You ought, when it is in your power, to anticipate disputes, subdue them, repress unjust and violent persons, impose silence on the ungodly and on the malicious. Have you really fulfilled all these duties? This young lady, who listens so patiently to talk that offends Christian decency, this young lady, I say, knows well that in assuming a certain tone she would shut the mouth of all those who dare speak in that way in her presence. If she has not done it, she has neglected her duty—she has made herself guilty of all the faults that she could have prevented. You have not fixed your attention on this painting, you have not read this offensive book— that is not enough: you had to burn the one and the other and not worry about sacrificing a furnishing, of whatever price it may be, for the salvation of the souls for whom Jesus Christ gave his blood even to the last drop.

More: when you would not have done evil since your last Confession, you still would have to examine what good it is that you have practiced, what use you have made of your spare time and of your goods. It is an article of faith that you will be accountable to God for all your idle words: "He will render an account for every idle word."[23] But, if God is so rigorous to search for your useless words, do you believe that he will forgive you your useless spending, your useless finery, your useless actions, your whole life which you spend entirely in a useless idleness? I serve my prince, someone will tell me, in an occupation that keeps me extremely busy.—And me, another will say, I render justice with all kinds of fairness.—And me, I have engaged in an important business that I exercise in good faith. One can have all these occupations and lead a pointless and completely useless life. How is that? If it is vanity, or ambition that you attach to the service of your master; if you are fair only because you like glory or because you naturally have an upright spirit; finally, if desire for the good is the motivation that makes this whole business run, not only do you do nothing, but also you are unjust toward God, who ought to be the goal of all the thoughts of human beings[24]. All that which does not relate to him lacks some essential element in order to be good. You offer to God, beginning in the morning, all the actions of the day—see here what is good. But this offering is only a routine, only a vain compliment, if at bottom it is not the desire to please him and to accomplish his will that makes you act—if you search for yourself in all your actions.

Finally, you should not forget that at the last judgment our trial will not be made for us only on our omissions. Go, cursed ones, the Savior of the world will say, go to the eternal fire.—But why, Lord? What was there in my actions contrary to your holy commandments?—It is not about your actions that I am complaining; but I was hungry and you did not give me to eat; I was sick, and you did not deign to visit me; I was cold, and you did not dress me; you preferred to gamble the silver with which you were able to help me; you preferred to squander it on decorations and on useless meals. See here what is the reason for my complaints and for your condemnation: "I was hungry, and you did not give me to eat; I was thirsty, and you did not give me to drink; I was a stranger, and you did not take me in; naked, and you did not cover me; sick and in prison, and you did not visit me."[25] It is then necessary that I tell my confessor if, being able to give alms, I refused it to only one person; if I neglected the poor sick, if I helped my brothers in some need to which Providence had reduced them. One must do it, I say, if I am not mistaken; one must do it, or I understand neither Jesus Christ nor the gospel. What convinces me completely that we delude ourselves, for the most part, in the examination that we make of our consciences, is that, when it happens that God touches us for the best—that he inspires in us a genuine resolution to change our lives—to live from now on only to die well, then, I say, there is no one who does not believe himself obligated to begin by making a general Confession and who, in this Confession, does not accuse himself of a hundred things of which he had made no mention in all the preceding Confessions.

This is what I had to tell you in order to give you some access to the knowledge of yourselves. But it is from you, O my God, that we await the genuine insight that we need in order to know ourselves perfectly. Without this insight, everything I just said will be only a vain and fruitless instruction. I will have taught my auditors to know others, to judge them, to censure them, but not in the least to judge themselves and to condemn themselves. Without this insight, we will see without seeing, as you have told it to us yourself;[26] we will see enough to be guilty, but not enough to recognize that we are [guilty]. Rather than admitting it, we will believe that one preaches exaggerations to us and that the truth itself makes use of overstatement; in a word, we always will make ourselves more innocent than we are; we even will believe ourselves genuine penitents, often without having any reason to believe it. This is the second error that can make our Confessions useless, and that I will reveal in the second part.

Second Point

Interior repentance, which is the kind in question here, consists in a bitter regret for having sinned, joined to a sincere resolution not to sin any more. It is of this repentance that Saint Ambrose indeed has dared to make this dreadful statement: "I have found more who had preserved their innocence than who had repented properly."[27] We rarely find people who have never lost the innocence of baptism; but, however, the number of those who, after having lost it, make a genuine repentance, is still much smaller.[28] And this is not a fantasy—it is a thing that I know from my own experience: I have found more truly innocent people than I have found genuine penitents—"I have found more who had preserved their innocence than who had repented properly." Now, how could this be true, if one had only to read in one's book an act of contrition and to strike his breast two or three times?

For repentance, which is the first part of penance:[29] a proof that most people do not even know what it is, is that one hardly fears to expose one-self to it.[30] There is nothing in the world more severe than authentic repen-tance; one must have great strength of mind to suffer this kind of grief and not be overcome by it. One sees every day people whom [this grief] carries to the point of despair. This must be something quite bitter, since God ac-cepts it in place of the eternal tortures that are due to our sins. It is for this reason that this grief is called *attrition* or *contrition*, because it not only wounds the heart: it breaks it, it in some way crushes it, it causes it, so to speak, as many wounds as there are atoms that make it up. But though that be so, does one imagine that anxiety about such a great pain diverts Chris-tians from offending God? On the contrary, does one not make up one's mind every day to offend him in the hope of entering again by this way into grace? I will confess it, one says. I believe it: if there were only that to do, I understand how it is that to satisfy a passion one would expose oneself willingly to all the shame that consent to sin could bring about. But it is not enough to confess it: one must repent of it.—I will repent of it as well, you respond.—You will repent of it, and you do not fail to commit it? Tell me, Christian auditors: outside of sin have you done nothing in your life of which you were quite certain to repent? Is not the fear of repentance alone the strongest motive for diverting a man from whatever action it may be? How then is the assurance that you have to suffer this same pain a motive for you to act against your conscience, if it is not, because it is not in effect the same pain, because the repentance that you have of the sin is of another nature than the others—that it only has the name of genuine repentance.

The second reason that I have to believe that this grief is feigned or at least that it is very weak is the feebleness with which one behaves ordinar-ily, be that to confess one's sins, be that to ask or to receive penance for them. If this fault caused us as much pain to the spirit as it has caused plea-sure to the flesh—which is the rule that Saint Augustine gives to determine authentic contrition—not only would we not hesitate to declare it—this fault—but we would have trouble to hold it back. Would we hesitate to re-ject a burning coal that we would have in the breast, or an asp that cruelly would bite us? The same Saint Augustine undoubtedly felt this authen-tic regret. Neither is he happy to accuse himself in secret of his youthful dissoluteness; he publishes it openly, he wants that all the world, that all posterity know that he was subject to a hundred passions, and above all to the most shameful of all the passions, too happy if, thus making the confusion both public and immortal, he himself can take revenge on himself and soften a little the grief that the memory of his sins causes him.[31]

We read, in the *History of the Councils of Toledo*, that a bishop of Braga, named Potamius—venerable for his age, famous in all of Spain for his virtue and above all for the zeal with which he had spoken out several times against the immodest—having himself fallen, by a strange weakness, in a secret act of fornication, was touched so deeply by it that he never could stop himself from venting his grief. But what occasion did he take—God of heaven!—in order to relieve himself? Gentlemen, this was in a council where he himself presided! This council was composed of fifty bishops, of a great number of abbots, of doctors, and of other ecclesiastics. This was in the presence of an assembly so numerous and so illustrious that this great man, this public protector of chastity, prostrated himself on the ground, confessed his incontinence aloud, everyone trembling at this spectacle and unable to understand what such urgent motive could have led him to endure willingly such a horrible embarrassment.[32]

What does one not do, Christian company, in order to pacify a pain so sharp? Decide then, if you please, what is the weakness of our own [pain]. Not only one excuses, one masks, one plays down one's sins by weak and ambiguous expressions; but still, after having just confessed them, one fights with the confessor over a fast of two or three days, one refrains from giving alms, one cannot consent to deprive oneself of a minor satisfaction! What penance! What repentance is this? One sometimes sees some of them, real penitents, come to throw themselves at the feet of the priest; but it is quite easy to distinguish them. It seems to me like seeing sick people who no longer can endure the illness that is killing them and who want to heal at whatever the price.[33] That one should pierce, that one should cut, that one should burn—provided that one relieve me, it does not matter by what agony one brings my torture to an end. One is obliged to reprimand others in order to make them aware of their own evils: these [evils] draw from us ourselves tears from the eyes; they must be consoled instead of criticizing them. They have never expressed strongly enough the malice of their sins; however rigorous be the punishment that one imposes on them, they would never be able to be satisfied with it!

I understand, Christian company, how it is that Jesus Christ prevails and that all the angels quiver with joy at the sight of a man who makes a similar penance. I understand how it is that God forgets his dissoluteness, that he embraces him, that he showers him with favors, that he loves this child even more tenderly than he did before his disobedience. But that this insensitive Christian who, after having sinned mortally, had the courage to fall asleep in the arms of the demon, who could endure the hatred of God for a month—for several months—and wait coldly for the celebrations to arrive in order to come out of a state so dire and dangerous; that this man,

I say, for having come to recount his life to me, as he would relate a story, without tears, without feeling, have made this wonderful penance which drives out the demons, which brings down the Holy Spirit, which extinguishes the flames of hell, which compels heaven, which disarms the anger of the Almighty—no, Gentlemen, I cannot convince myself of that, and I am sure that you doubt it yourselves.

What I said about repentance, I say it still about the resolution not to sin again. Everyone knows that [this resolution] ought to be firm and sincere; but, alas! How few people put into practice what they know on this point! It does not suffice, Christian auditors, that the mouth speak certain formulas that express this resolution in three or four words; the heart must speak and it must agree with the tongue. Let us reflect a little on this point, this evening, when we will prepare ourselves to confess; let us try to enter into this heart and to discover what are its true sentiments. We will find perhaps that it hardly participates in all the good intentions that we have to be converted. You promise then no longer to take revenge on your enemies; you promise no longer to lie, above all about certain people of whom you often speak ill by a spirit either of vengeance or of envy. You promise it, you say; watch what you say—the heart does not get engaged at all in all of that; on the contrary, it senses very well that in the future it will treat them as it did before. What way to receive an insult without drawing revenge from it? And of what would one speak, if one no longer spoke ill of others?[34] You accuse yourself of having been found at entertainments, in gatherings where all things—at least in your opinion—do not happen in an innocence as great as one wants to have us believe it. You accuse yourself of having cast lascivious glances there, of willingly having entertained impure thoughts there, of having seen things there, of having heard conversations there that were in your soul like the seed of several sins that you have committed even in solitude.[35] Have you quite resolved to correct yourself of all that? Have you not completely resolved, on the contrary, to spend Carnival in the same entertainments, in the same company where your weakness exposes you to so many dangers of offending God?[36] You did not fast yesterday; there were no ember days for you.[37] You say that you will mend your ways; but why do you say it? You did not observe the last Lent, and you know well that you will find a pretext in order not to observe this coming one. It already has been several years since you treat it this way, and you have not resolved completely to change so soon. You promise to correct yourself of your fits of rage, of your blasphemies; but, in good faith, do you believe that this promise should have an effect other than that which you had made at the last Confession? Are you not completely persuaded that, the first time that you will return, you still will have the same sins to confess?

I am not surprised, Christian auditors, that of all the resolutions that one makes in life, there be not one of them of which we recall less than of those that we make when we go to Confession. It is that, in truth, when one confesses, one makes no resolution. On the contrary, one is very resolved to live as one has done up until then; and, whatever one say, one does not doubt that things ought always to go the same. From thence comes, that on the first occasion that will present itself, and perhaps it will present itself two days later, not only will one be conquered, but one will not even see fit to fight, one will not deliberate to turn himself over. If one had developed a genuine desire to mend one's ways, one would be very wary of going on one's own accord to seek out danger where one is not unaware that it be found. On the occasions that one would not have sought out, one would recall the intention that one had formed; the fear to irritate God by such a great act of treachery would fight in our heart against the attraction of sin; one would consent at least with more difficulty than one did in the past. And do not say that one is fragile, that it is impossible to resist temptations, as I know a hundred people who, after having complained ten and twenty years of their impotence and of their fragility, finally made a resolution no longer to offend God that they never have violated since—that I dare affirm that they never will violate.

But what is it necessary to search so far for evidence of our little sincerity in the intention we make to change our life, since, in the time itself that one forms this intention, one is still quite often in the dissoluteness of which one accuses oneself? You have in yourself a person at whom everyone is scandalized; you are in a house where you have an impending occasion to offend God: you say that you have in mind to remove this scandal, to go out from this danger, but why have you not done it before coming to confess? How dare you appear before the eyes of your judge without having given to him this proof of your repentance? How dare you say that you no longer will fall back into the sin after having confessed, since you do not leave it even in order to confess? Was it no longer an intention—was there no longer the decency to begin by reconciling yourself with your enemy, by restoring this money that is not yours, by repairing the wrong that you did to the reputation of your brother? Why do you want to wait until after the Confession to fulfill these essential obligations? Do you want me to tell you? It is because you have a secret desire to do nothing about all this. Without a doubt, it was more natural to destroy before all things the work of iniquity. But it still pleases you, this work, and you cannot decide to destroy it; the heart hopes that it will remain, if only it can save it until after Confession.

See, Ladies, in what state Magdalene threw herself at the feet of the Son of God, when she resigned herself to repentance.[38] She was very careful not to wear the same jewelry there that had made her virtue suspect to the whole town of Jerusalem; she appeared there completely sloppy, completely unkempt; she would not have dared show herself to Jesus Christ in the state in which up to then she had been seen; she would have been quite ridiculous, quite extravagant to do it; it would not have been a very good way of having her luxury and her former vanity forgotten, to go make a show of it in the eyes of the Savior. But how many men and women will fall tomorrow[39] into a fault completely similar to that which they would have condemned in this holy penitent. It is to be mistaken oneself, Gentlemen, to think that one ought to forgive the sins that we love, where we still have some attachment; it is to scorn God, to make him a promise that one fails to keep at the time itself that one makes it. "He is a mocker," says Saint Isidore, "and no penitent, who continues to do what he has repented."[40]

For the conclusion and for the fruit of this discourse, you will ask me perhaps by what means one can arouse in one's heart both this regret for having sinned, and this resolution not to sin again? Whence comes, you will ask me, that we are so insensitive on an occasion when we ought to die of grief? Saint Chrysostom says that sin is the only evil that one can heal with tears;[41] one even can say that it is the only evil that deserves to be lamented. Whence comes then that it is the only one that is not lamented? Is it possible that one knows well all the reasons that one has to be grieved about it? Yes, Christian company, one knows them; but one does not understand them. This little child knows well that he has lost his father, that death comes to take him away from him; he does not fail to play however and to laugh in the greatest mourning of his family, because the poor child is not aware of the loss he just had. This eldest one, in whom age has already matured reason, cannot get over it. Every time that we commit this mortal sin, we do to ourselves about as much harm as Saint Peter did to himself in renouncing Jesus Christ, as Magdalene had done to herself in becoming too attached to the world. The tears of this great penitent did not dry up until his death,[42] although he could not doubt the forgiveness that he had received;[43] and we, who know neither if one has forgiven us, nor if one ever will forgive us, we are in no way touched by our disorders! Those who are in this disposition have need perhaps of a greater cure than I can give in so little time. I will tell you nevertheless that those who are in this disposition, after having taken a reasonable time in order to examine their conscience, ought to take a much longer time in order to ask God earnestly for the grace to feel their pain. They must—out of respect for this infinite Majesty that they have dared offend gravely, out of respect for Jesus Christ crucified for their love, in sight of the paradise they have renounced, of the hell that one is preparing for them—try to arouse in their heart this genuine compunction, without which there is no grace for them.

If all the considerations of the greatness, of the goodness, of the justice of God are not capable of moving them, may they test a little if the sight of their own hardness might not soften them. Poor wretch that I am! Have I then lost reason and feeling in losing grace? Nothing touches me—neither love, nor fear, nor kindnesses, nor punishments? Is it not that I have taken my unfaithfulness to the limit and that the Lord has abandoned me? An earthworm dared to rise up against the Creator of the universe, and he would not be able to repent of his treachery? I have despised, I have insulted a thousand times the One who has given me life, the One who has given his life for me, and I have no horror of such an enormous ingratitude? I see myself on the edge of hell, I can die in the dire state in which I find myself, and I do not tremble, and I do not die of fear! I did not make these reflections at the time when I was offending God, and when I would have made them, the passion then was so strong that one would not have found [it] so strange if I had not been sensitive to that. But, at this hour, it is without passion that I consider these truths, and they make no impression on my mind! What is it then, O my lovable Redeemer? Am I lost with no means of support? My God, would there be no longer any mercy for me? Would it really be possible that you had rejected me forever? Alas! What would I become if you abandoned me in this way?

These same motives still can help us to form a sincere intention of amendment. One also can arouse oneself to it by the justifiable fear that we ought to have of pushing the patience of our Judge to the limit—of closing to ourselves, by the first relapse, all return to clemency.[44]

But what ought to have, it seems to me, more force than all that, at least on hearts that are not completely hardened, is the surprising readiness with which we see that God graces us after so many acts of treachery. "You have prostituted yourself to many lovers,"[45] he tells us through the mouth of the prophet Jeremiah: Christian soul, you have offended me cruelly, and not only one time, but a hundred, but a thousand, but two thousand times. "Lift up your eyes on high, and see where you have prostituted yourself."[46] Cast your eyes over your past life: you hardly will find one year, one day or even one hour of innocence. You have had regard neither for time, nor for place; you have sinned even in the days intended for my service, and even in the temples where I made my dwelling. "You have polluted the land with your fornications and with your wickedness."[47] You have abused all my creatures; you have degraded my servants, you have corrupted them by your scandals. "Therefore the showers were withheld, and there was no late rain."[48] In order to oblige yourself to enter back into your duty, I sent you afflictions, I made your work useless, I confounded your plans—all that was pointless. "You had a harlot's forehead, you would not blush."[49] Quite far from feeling ashamed of your dissoluteness, you have gloried in it before all;[50] I have not even been able to make you blush from them in my presence. "Nevertheless return to me, says the Lord."[51] Return however, poor stray; here I am, completely ready to welcome you. "At least at this time call to me, your Father."[52] Is it not time that you finally return to me? Do you not know that I am your Father? Why do you want to ignore it, although you receive from me each day both life and all the goods of life?

This is, Gentlemen, the way in which the Creator of heaven and earth treats us, instead of scorning us, destroying us, damning us, as he has damned so many others much more innocent and less stubborn than we are. He has waited for us until today, and here is he who lovingly presses us himself to ask his forgiveness: "at least at this time"—at least at these celebrations, may all Christians consider giving me some sign of their piety; at these celebrations when everyone is reconciled, that the most hard-hearted are affected by the memory of my birth,[53] call me your Father; I will let myself be swayed by such a tender name, I will come to you, I will recognize you as my child,[54] "At least at this time call to me, your Father."

No, Lord, I am not worthy to be counted among your children; it is quite something that you are so good as to welcome me among the number of your servants.[55] But I vow today, in the presence of all heaven that I have annoyed, that you never will have a more faithful servant. It is too much to take advantage of such an excessive mercy; there is no longer a way to resist you, O my God; I confess that all my hardness of heart would not hold any longer against such a paternal tenderness. How good you are, Lord, not to have made me die in my sin, although it seemed that I had intended to force you to do it by my boldness and stubbornness! How I am obliged to you that you call me back yet again! But how much more grateful to you I ought to be that you finally called me back, never to abandon you again! I have promised it to you a hundred times, my good Master, and a hundred times I have broken my promise. But I never have promised it as I do presently, and I feel certain that from now on I am going to be faithful to you. This desire that I have to avoid not only sin, but all the occasions and even the appearances of sin; this distaste in which I find myself of all that enchanted me before; this courage that you inspire in me to declare an everlasting war against my passions; this love of retreat, of prayer, of mortification that your love is beginning to produce in my heart; all these are graces that respond to me in some way about my steadfastness. Rejoice boldly, blessed spirits; no, this is not a false joy that I give you. I no longer am what I was, and if you are so good as to help me with your prayers, I forever will be what I am [now].

If you are in this disposition, Christian auditors, go, in good time, go plunge yourself into the blood of Jesus Christ; go recapture in this holy bath a beauty that will delight the angels and win for you the heart of God himself. Go, filled with faith, with grief, and with confidence, to prostrate yourself at the feet of the priest, open your conscience to him with humility and with courage. Accept with joy the penance that he will want to impose on you; force him to give you one that be a little more fitting to your sins and to your grief, and do not doubt that the absolution that you then will receive be confirmed in heaven. *So be it.*

On the Mercy of God toward the Sinner[1]

Here is your King who comes to you full of gentleness. (Matt 21:5)[2]

God is not repelled by the treachery of the sinner, and he does not repel him in his
repentance: he runs after him in his flight; on his return he comes before him.

IT IS A COMMON ENOUGH SENTIMENT among the masters of
Christian eloquence that preachers ought to speak only with reserve about
the Mercy of God, for fear that sinners, who already are only too disposed
to exercise delay and postponement, take occasion from the discourse to
postpone their repentance even more.[3] It is not that one not be well aware
that there is nothing more unreasonable than deciding to displease God,
because he is good. One knows moreover that there is no sinner more
hopeless than the one who sins in the hope that one will forgive him, and
that to make use of the thought of Mercy as a motive for persevering in evil
is, in fact, to close all return to this same Mercy.[4] One knows it, Christian
auditors; but how difficult it is to make everyone understand it well; one
fears scandalizing the weak by speaking to them of a thing that they do not
understand; one fears leading them to offend God, by pointing out to them
his readiness to forgive our offenses.

But what, Lord, will we then be mute on the most lovable of your divine
perfections? Will we say nothing of this Mercy of which the whole world is
full, according to this word of David: "the earth is full of the mercy of the
Lord"?[5] This Mercy appears in all that you have done and in all that you do;
it is itself the most admirable of all your works: "his tender mercies are over
all his works."[6] And it will be the only one that we will not be allowed to
praise! It anticipates us, it accompanies us everywhere, we are completely
surrounded by it; we owe to it all that we are; we await from it all that we
hope: and we will not make it known to the whole universe—and we will
not even dare to speak of it! No, Christian company, I cannot stop myself
from telling you my thoughts on this subject. I would not be able to hold
back the admiration that this infinite goodness causes me; and since our

gospel gives me the occasion to speak with you about it, I am resolved to be satisfied. Quite far from risking something, in endeavoring this plan, I have reason to promise myself much fruit from it. I will speak of Mercy to people, either who already have obtained it, or who presently ask for it, or, at least, who seriously consider to ask for it. Now, for all these kinds of people, nothing could be more helpful, more edifying than the discourse that I am going to begin. Help me, divine Spirit, to display the riches of this infinite love that you have for sinners. I ask you this grace in the name of Mary, who is your Spouse and their Advocate: *Hail, Mary*.[7]

Sin is like a lost route by which, in distancing himself from the law of God, man distances himself at the same time from God himself, and distances himself from him to an infinite extent. Repentance is like a completely opposite path, by which one tries to return from this fatal distraction. In the first of these two paths, the sinner is a madman who runs after sickly creatures to whom he pays more attention than to the Creator; in the second, he is a poor wretch who, having noticed his error, would like, if it were possible, to make it right. It is certain that, in his flight, he deserves the most rigorous punishments, because [his flight] is extremely insulting to God, and because, even upon his return, he is unworthy of the Mercy he asks, because he has sinned with a malice extreme and against an infinite Majesty. Such that, if the Lord were not infinitely good, the gentlest treatment that I would have reason to expect would be to be left to myself when I withdraw and to be rejected when I return. But consider the love of this good Shepherd, of this good Master! He is not repelled by the treachery of the sinner and he does not turn him away in his repentance. Much more: be that we distance ourselves or that we seek to come closer, we always find him on our path; either he pursues us, if we flee him, or he makes himself present, if we seek him. This, Gentlemen, is what I intend to make you see in the two parts of this discourse. I want to show you with what goodness our God treats the sinner, in whatever disposition that he find him: how, in his flight, he runs after him—this will be the first point; how, upon his return, he comes before him—this will be the second. This is all that I have to say.

First Point

In the separation that sin makes between the soul and God, no tongue can express, no mind can understand the loss that we bring about, since we lose the friendship of God, since we lose God himself. However, it is a wonder to see with what indifference one brings about this loss of the greatest of all goods. That hardly surprises me—it is that we know not what we do—we almost do not know God; and passion smothers in us the little knowledge that we have of him. What surprises me is that God, to whom our nothingness is perfectly known, who brings about no real loss when we separate ourselves from him, that God, I say, evinces, at this separation, such a great grief, and that he so strongly hastens to have us return. And this, Gentlemen, is not a dream; it is from the Gospel—it is from Jesus Christ himself—that we learn it. Do you want to know, Christian soul, what are the sentiments of the Savior of the world every time that you lose the grace of God? He is grieved about it to the depths of the soul; he is as bothered by it as a poor shepherd who has lost one of his sheep—as much as a poor woman who, having only ten pieces of gold in all her property, notices that she is missing one of these pieces.[8] These are the two comparisons that the Son of God uses in order to make us understand the regret he has of losing us.

Imagine then, if you please, the distress of a poor shepherd whose sheep has strayed. In all the surrounding countryside, one hears only the voice of this poor wretch, who, having abandoned the main body of the flock, runs in the woods and on the hills, combs through the thickets and the bushes, in bemoaning and crying with all his might, and unable to resign himself to give up until he found his sheep and brought it back to the fold. This is what the Son of God did, says Saint Cyril: when human beings[9] had escaped, by their disobedience, the supervision of their Creator, he came down to earth and spared neither care nor tiring efforts to restore us to the state from which we had fallen.[10] It is what he still does every day for those who distance themselves from him by sin: he tracks them, so to speak, not ceasing to call them back until he have set them back on the way of salvation. And certainly, if he did not treat us in that way, you know that it would be done for us after the first mortal sin: it would be impossible for us to return from it. It must be he who makes all the overtures—that he offer his grace to us, that he pursue us, that he invite us to have Mercy on ourselves, without which we never would consider to ask Mercy of him.[11]

It is for this reason that David said to God: "Lord, I have strayed like a lost sheep—have the goodness to look for your servant. 'I have gone astray like a sheep that is lost: seek thy servant.'"[12] This prayer seems at first rude enough—it is for the servant to look for his master whose good graces he has lost, and not for the master to look for the servant who has been unfaithful to him. But we are so wretched that, after having made so much progress in so little time only to go astray, we would not be able to take a single step in order to get ourselves back on the path, and, if our God has not the goodness to run after us in order to stop us in our flight, we will flee forever and never return to his service.

But admire, if you please, the zeal and the love of this good Master. No sooner have we lost his friendship, in offending him, that, completely alarmed by this misfortune that has happened to us all the same by our fault, he sets out to pursue us with cries that indicate to us marvelously well the feeling of his heart. This conscience that is troubled suddenly breaks out in a thousand complaints, in a thousand reproaches. This conscience, this is not the voice of the demon, since it leads us to the good;[13] it is not our own voice, since it speaks despite us and against us.[14] It then must be the voice of God. And it is for this [reason] that everything that it says is as though infallible—that [everything that it says] is like so many laws against which we will be judged. What does it not tell you, this secret voice? If God had some great interest in saving you—if in losing you, he had, so to speak, lost half of his kingdom, would he be either more prompt in calling you back or more diligent in pointing out to you the extreme danger in which you are, or more agile for insinuating himself into your heart, or more steadfast in seeking your friendship? Is it not true that he never ceases to put before your eyes all that is capable of affecting you: the uncertainty of death, the punishments of the next life, his benefits, his rewards, his justice, his love, his Mercy?[15] Is it not true that he pursues you at all times and in all places—in the sermon, at Mass, in solitude, even in the midst of gatherings; that he is found everywhere, that everywhere he renews his moaning and his complaints? Is it not true that he takes the opportunity of everything that presents itself to you—either edifying or dreadful—in order to speak to you of reconciliation? Are you sick? There he is at your bedside, to make you recall that he can both give you health and also take life away from you, but that you run a still greater danger, by the sin with which your soul is mortally wounded, than by the fever that devours your body. If some accident upsets the course of your affairs—if some disgrace happens to you—he finds himself immediately before you, in order to make you hear that the source of all your woes is in you yourselves and that you never will be happy unless you return to him, who is the source of all goods. Finally, it seems to me that he takes no rest and that he gives you no respite.

My God, is it then so important to you to recover this useless servant? Would you be unable to do without me? When you would abandon me to my bad will and to my degenerate sensibility, would you be more unhappy for having done that? For one lost soul could you not create ten thousand whom you would sanctify and whom you would attach to your service by indissoluble bonds?

This ardor with which he pursues us is without doubt an effect of a very great Mercy. But the gentleness with which this zeal is accompanied indicates a still more admirable goodness. Notwithstanding the extreme desire that he has of making us return, he never makes use of violence, he uses nothing for that but the ways of gentleness. I see no sinner, in the whole history of the Gospel, who was invited to repentance other than by affection and by kindnesses. He attracted Saint Matthew, Zacchaeus,

and the other publicans by inviting himself to eat in their homes and wit-
nessing that he did not flee them, as did the Pharisees, who saw them as
loathsome.[16] He touched Magdalene, not in permitting her to approach
him, as disparaged as she was, [but][17] in speaking well of her and taking her defense in all encounters.[18] Another would have ordered that one
observed, against the adulterous woman, the law that condemned her to
death. Jesus Christ, on the contrary, saved her by a miracle: he obliged
the judges and accusers to withdraw, and, seeing her all alone, Woman,
he said to her, no one then has condemned you?—No, Lord.—Go: I will
not condemn you either; do not fall back any more into your sin.[19] He did
not make the Samaritan woman blush in telling her first what he knew of
her scandalous life; he encouraged her skillfully to begin her confession
herself, after which he insinuated himself little by little so deeply into her
mind that she admitted everything to him, that she recognized him for
who he was and made him known to the whole town of Samaria.[20] What
did he not do in order to win over Judas? He did everything, outside of
confusing him and of treating him harshly. He told him that he knew his
crime, but he told him it in such a way that he could understand without
the others perceiving it; he washed his feet, he dried them, he let himself
be kissed by this traitor, he treated him neither as apostate, nor as traitor;
he called him his friend and then by his name, as a sign of familiarity and
tenderness.[21] In order to lead Saint Peter to repentance, he was happy to
look at him; and it was not with a dreadful eye that he looked at him: it
was a gaze full of gentleness and of love.[22] Finally, in order to conquer the
stubbornness of Saint Thomas, he himself took his hand and directed it
into the wound in his side.[23]

If, when God wants to convert us, he worked for his own interests, I
would not be surprised that he exercised such moderation and such goodness. But it is admirable that, his zeal having nothing for goal but to draw
us out from death and from hell, he keeps such means, that he spare us,
that he show consideration for us in this way. When a father sees his son
who is drowning or who is in danger of being enveloped in a fire, he does
not consider if it is by the foot or by the hand, if it is by the clothes or by
the hair that he grabs him in order to pull him from this danger; he believes
that he will have done much if he can save his life, even though he would
wound him a little. But our God has consideration for our weakness, even
in these urgent occasions. He studies our moods, our inclinations, even
our passions, and our bad habits, in order to take us by the route that he will
make for us the least trouble. To this man who loves money he offers the
treasures of heaven, he makes him recall the extreme poverty in which he
will find himself in the next life, if he does not deliver there, by the hands of
the poor, what he possesses in this one here. He proposes to this sensual one
the delights and the peacefulness of a life pure and distant from all kinds of

crimes. To this person, who is very sensitive to the slightest pains, he puts the tortures of the damned before her eyes. To this other, who has heart and friendship, he points out everything that she has done and everything that she still does for him.

David had taken away the wife of Uriah and, in addition, he had had her husband killed.[24] Here are two great crimes, above all for a man exceedingly enlightened and favored of God. God sends Nathan to him in order to force him to recognize himself, for the poor prince[25] in no way was considering repentance.[26] What one will do in order to awake him from this drowsiness and to give him a great horror of sin! David loved equity very much and consequently he had a great horror of the contrary vice: it is necessary then to represent his fault to him as the most unjust action that ever have been done and, for fear that one not make for him too much trouble if one goes to tell him openly in what his injustice consists, God wants that the prophet expose his crime to him under a kind of parable, pretending that one of his subjects very rich in flocks had abducted from his neighbor the only sheep that he had—the one that made all his pleasure and all his treasure—so that, David himself having condemned himself to death, as he did it in the person of this unjust rich man, he have no difficulty recognizing that he was guilty and worthy of punishment.

I am certain, Gentlemen, that if we reflected a little on what happens in ourselves, on what has happened there before, when we have withdrawn from dissoluteness or from a lukewarm and imperfect life; if you wanted to examine a little the means of which [God[27]] has made use in order to conquer you; with what gentleness he has disposed you to repentance; how imperceptibly he has softened for you the practice of virtue; how, without effort and without noise, he has made himself the master of all your desires; how he has taken advantage of your minor adversities; how he even has made use of your faults and of your passions in order to enlist you in his service: I am certain that you would notice that everything that I have said has happened to you, and may be something still more pleasant than all that I could tell you.

Only if you have not reflected upon the wonderful gentleness that he used to attract you to himself can you not have noticed his steadfastness. We cannot deny that[28] for the most part we strangely have tested it. For a long time you did not condescend even to listen to God. Then you deliberated a long time whether you ought to give yourself over to his insistent and loving appeals. And when you were persuaded that the best option for you was to give yourself completely to him, how much has he had to deliver more battles to your heart in order to oblige it to follow the insights of your mind? How many extensions taken, one after the other?[29] How many promises made and betrayed? How many commitments broken? How many years of obstinacy and of relapses, before you surrendered in good faith and forever?

My God, your love has found itself tested by this long and excessive resistance. All of that has not been capable of putting you off. You have continued to pursue me, to call me, to attract me, to love me. What does one
know, you have said to yourself,[30] what does one know, if this heart will not
let itself be swayed after having been unyielding for so long? I see well that
this will not be so soon; that he will not keep for me the word that he gives
me today any more than that which he gave me six months ago; that after
this delay he will ask of me yet another; that this tomorrow, to which he
postpones me, will not come perhaps for several years. But perhaps also, if
I do not weary of following him, he finally will weary of fleeing from me. I
would like that, from this moment, he were all mine; but I prefer still better
to wait for him a long time than to give up on him forever.

Behold what is the love that our God has for sinners. Nothing more
urgent, nothing more gentle, nothing more constant than the entreaties
that he makes to them in order to draw them out of the misfortune into
which they have thrown themselves. When, after having examined atten-
tively this zeal tireless and full of tenderness, I cast the eyes on this same
sinner who is the object of it, I confess to you, Gentlemen, that I fall into an
amazement from which I cannot return. David, considering our meanness
and in his mind setting it against the infinite Majesty of God, cried out,
Alas! Lord, what is man, that you see quite fit to remember him? "What
is man, that you are mindful of him?"[31] But here is yet another subject for
admiration! God remembers man, when man has forgotten him entirely!
Even more, he seems to forget all the rest, in order to recall only this in-
grate; he leaves the ninety-nine sheep in the desert, and runs after the one
that has strayed, preferring to expose the whole flock than to abandon this
unfortunate one! He loves us, all sinners that we are, which is to say, although we hate him and, what is still more admirable, although he hates
infinitely our sins!

Yes, Gentlemen, God naturally hates sin; and the soul who is dirtied
with it is something so dreadful to his eyes, that a decomposing dog—this
is the comparison of Saint Augustine—that a decomposing dog causes infinitely less horror to the most sensitive people: "How much more toler-
able a stinking, decayed dog to men than a sinful soul to God!"[32] Judge
then what should be the force of his love, since it can conquer such a great
loathing. That makes me recall these insane lovers that one says to have
themselves dug up the half-corrupted bodies of the people whom they had
loved and to have attached themselves to these rotten and disfigured cadavers, with the same passion as if they had been living, the passion smoth-
ering in them the horror that we all naturally have of this decomposition.[33]
All these ideas of cadaver and of rottenness express so imperfectly the
hideous state of a soul who is in mortal sin that it is only with regret that
I use these weak comparisons. And however, God does not fail to love

her in that state—to reach out his arm to her, to present to her the kiss of peace, to run after her, as after the most perfect beauty in the world!

"Whom do you pursue, King of Israel," David once said to Saul; and we well can say it to God, with regard to the love that he witnesses us: "Whom do you pursue? You pursue a dead dog."[34] "After whom do you run, King of Israel, King of heaven and of earth? You run after a dead dog who, quite far from deserving your over-attentiveness, is not even worthy of your anger and can cause you only horror? But we, Christian auditors, who is it that we flee? How do we think to despise God, to mock his love, to try his patience for so long, to refuse his friendship that he offers us and that he presses us to receive? We believe that this secret voice that we hear in the bottom of the heart, that invites us to repentance, that points out to us with such gentleness and such force the danger in which we are of perishing eternally, we believe, I say, that this voice is the voice of God, and we attach no importance to it, and we even dare to silence him? What! We do not fear to repulse this infinite Majesty! We do not recall either what he is, or what we are! We are not frightened to see the Master of the universe, after having been offended a hundred times, come himself to our door to look for our friendship! We let him knock, we make him wait for such a long time without seeing fit to open to him or to respond to him! What should I admire more here, O my God—either your patience, or our obstinacy; either your love, or the hardness of our heart? What will be the confusion of this ungrateful and daring soul, if ever you open her eyes? Will she dare appear in your presence, after having treated you in this way? But when we would have the boldness to present ourselves before him, would he wish to welcome us, after having been rejected in such a shameful manner?

Yes, Gentlemen, he does not fail to receive the sinner, when after a long distraction—after much contempt—he wants finally to return to his duty. I say much more: the same love that leads God to run after him in his flight binds him to go before him upon his return. This is my second part.

Second Point

When I say that God goes out after the sinner who returns to him through repentance, I do not want to say another thing, Christian company, if it is not that he forgives the greatest crimes with an unbelievable readiness. He forgives them quickly, he forgives them with joy, he forgives them in good faith and without reservation, he even causes new graces instead of punishing. I am going to touch in passing upon each one of these points.

On his swiftness to forgive, I note that he treats the sinner in a way opposed to that in which he himself has been treated by the sinner. The sinner let him knock for a long time, he left him to moan, to cry at the door of his heart. It would be quite fair that God recalled these rejections and that he left the penitent in turn to sigh and to worry. But no, he cannot resolve himself to treat him in this way. As soon as I have admitted my crime, I immediately receive forgiveness for it. The Lord does not even always wait for this confession; hardly have I developed the desire to enter back into grace than I am welcomed there at once, without deposit, without assurance for the future, although I have broken my word a hundred times and though this be any day to resume. It seems that our God lets himself be blinded by the desire that he has to reconcile himself with us; he prefers to expose himself to an infidelity, which he so often has tested, than to postpone his grace a moment in order to take his precautions; in a word, Saint Augustine says that he is in a greater impatience to forgive the sinner than the sinner is to receive forgiveness. "He is swifter in offering forgiveness to a sinner than the sinner is in accepting it."[35] My God, how well you have made us understand this truth in the Parable of the Prodigal Son![36]

The prodigal son was a young libertine, who had treated his father in the most disgraceful manner possible.[37] He had forced him to divide up all his goods and to give him the part that he had right to claim for himself. Next, he had left the paternal home and had gone to spend his days in a region so remote that it was clear that his intention was then never to return: "went into a far country."[38] I would not dare tell you the loathsome and scandalous life that he led in this foreign country; he squandered all his property there in shameful debauchery; and a horrible famine having occurred, he saw himself reduced to keeping pigs, wishing every day to appease his hunger with acorns; but he wished it in vain—no one wanted to give him any. Such a great disgrace made him come to his senses. He recalled the abundance in which he had lived, when he had kept to his duty. How many, he said to himself, how many people does my father have in his service, who lack for nothing, who even have everything in abundance, while I die here of hunger! I must resolve to go find him and tell him, My father, I have sinned against heaven and against you; I no longer am worthy to be called your son; but take me into your house as a servant and treat me as the others whom you employ. "I am not worthy to be called your son: make me as one of your hired servants."[39] There is nothing more appropriate than this story to express the aberrations of the sinner, the evils that his licentiousness attracts to him, the vile and shameful condition to which he is reduced, the little satisfaction that he finds in sensual pleasures, as he is always hungry for them, as he is more carnal and more miserable than the animals, as, after many falls and relapses, finally being touched by God, he begins to envy the innocence and the peacefulness of good people, to be disgusted with his dissolute life and to develop the desire to bring an end, by whatever way possible, to his misfortune and to his dissoluteness.

Here then is this young man who leaves in order to journey back, but who leaves in a condition quite different from the one in which he had come, not only on foot and without money, but half-naked, weak, exhausted, completely filthy, completely covered with dirt. How do you think that having squandered, as he had, his father's goods in all kinds of dissoluteness, he ought to be received at his arrival? He still was quite far, says the Gospel, when his father, having seen him in the pitiful state in which he was, he felt moved with compassion; and, without waiting that he come to throw himself at his feet, he runs quickly before him, he throws himself on his neck, he embraces him, he kisses him, he cries over him, while this poor wretch gives him the speech that he had prepared. This speech was quite short, but however the good father does not give him the time to finish it. That is enough—half of what he had to say is too much: "Quickly, quickly, bring forth quickly the first robe, and put it on him."[40] Quickly, quickly, bring me the most beautiful robe from my wardrobe and dress him in it; bring the fatted calf, kill it, and may only joy and good food be spoken of today, because this poor child was dead and he has come back to life; I had lost him, and here I find him again: "He was dead, and is come to life again: was lost, and is found."[41] Gentlemen, I know what is the tenderness of a father; I know that it is difficult to smother it in such a way that it does not soon awaken, when a child submits himself and recognizes his fault. But however there are certain errors so significant and so important that one forgives them only with difficulty. Another father, as easy, as loving as he were, not only would have awaited this prodigal at his house, but he would have at least pretended to be angry; he would have hidden his eagerness, he would have received him only at the urging of his friends, he would have given him lessons and criticisms upon receiving him, and prudence would have, it seems, demanded that he treat him in this way. But our God, represented by this father of whom we speak, has too much love to be able to hide it a single moment.

The impatience in which he is to see his son in the same state in which he was before does not permit him to keep calm. *Cito, cito*—quickly, quickly. On that occasion one would not be able to serve him promptly enough for his liking; the son is far from wishing for his recovery with as much enthusiasm as the father desires it: "He is swifter in offering forgiveness to a sinner than the sinner is in accepting it." Behold, Gentlemen, how it is that Jesus Christ himself wanted to depict the readiness and the swiftness with which he receives the greatest sinners to repentance.

For the joy that this same repentance causes him, it seems that he lacked both symbol and terms to express it. What would be the joy of a mother from whom death would have taken her child if, in the deepest moment of her pain, one replaced this dear child in her arms, full of life and of health? See there, more or less, that [this joy] is the joy that God feels at our conversion: "He was dead, and is come to life again"; it is as if he were dead and then come back to life. I say nothing of the rejoicing that was made for the prodigal son—of the music, of the dances, of the good fare[42] at which the whole day was spent. But nothing touches me as this emotion of the good Shepherd, when having found his sheep, he returns triumphant and, not being able to contain all his joy, he calls all his friends and all his neighbors and begs them to take part in it: "Rejoice with me," he tells them, "because I have found the sheep that was lost."[43] Rejoice with me, for I have found[44] the sheep that I had lost. Would one not say, Gentlemen, that our God has made some great conquest—that he has become master of a new kingdom?[45] It is only a poor soul who withdraws from dissolution, and [God] wants that all the angels congratulate him for it—that one celebrate it in paradise and, what seems unbelievable and full of an excessive exaggeration, he appears to be more satisfied with the repentance of this sinful soul than with the perseverance of ninety-nine righteous people who have never done anything of which they have reason to repent.

We would have difficulty to believe all these things, if every day we did not have tangible evidence of them in the conversions of the most dissolute Christians. This need not be only tears, only mourning, only bitterness; and however, this is not only happiness, this is not only gentleness and only consolation. God first makes there for the sinner a delicious feast that makes him forget all the past sensual delights. If grief sometimes makes tears flow there, repentant souls, I call you to witness that in the greatest joy in the world there is nothing more pleasant than these tears. Have you never had a more beautiful day than that when you unburdened your conscience of the heavy load that weighed it down—where you said an everlasting farewell to sin and to all the creatures that kept you subjected there?

I have said, in the third place,46 that God forgave completely and without reserve. Because he loses even the memory of the greatest insults, he takes no revenge from them. When the Good Shepherd has found the sheep, he does not mistreat it, says Saint Gregory of Nyssa: he does not force it at all, by pursuing it with great blows, to return to the flock; on the contrary, he takes it on his shoulders, he spares it the fatigue of the path and puts it back gently with the others.47 I already had you notice, some time ago, in what way the Savior of the world had treated Saint Peter and all the other disciples who had been unfaithful to him at his Passion.48 He had predicted to all of them their cowardice; but he did not hold it against any of them, he did not fail to see them, to instruct them, to fawn over them after the Resurrection. Saint Peter, who had renounced him, did not fail to be the first of the apostles and the visible head of all the Church; one can say that he was no less holy for having been a sinner. No, Christian auditors, our God does not do like men—he does not forgive half-way. When one has betrayed us—has offended us very bitterly—whatever peace, whatever reconciliation that be made; although, on the outside, things are restored well enough; although one wanted to forgive in good faith and made efforts of himself for that; although one has much difficulty to return to this same tenderness, to this same confidence; despite that one have some of this, there remains at the bottom of the soul I know not what bitterness that makes itself felt from time to time, when one remembers what one has done to us. Our good Master is not subject to this weakness. I would like that all sinners, who repent of their dissoluteness, could see in his heart the feelings that he has for them—as there remains no resentment there, no bitterness; with what sincerity he forgives them, with what exemption he forgives them all the punishment that he could impose on them.

He does not stop there: he does not content himself with forgetting our faults, with returning to us all the merit of our good works that we had lost in losing his grace; but he returns to us both this grace and these merits, with a notable increase; he puts us into a more advantageous state than the one from which we had fallen. From there comes this fervor of the penitents, which, as the great Saint Gregory has seen it, often surpasses that of the most innocent souls. "The penitents are often more fervent than the innocent."49 It is in this view that the Holy Spirit has said these lovely words of the repentant soul under the figure of Jerusalem: "Be comforted, be comforted, my people; speak to the heart of Jerusalem: her evil is come to an end, her iniquity is forgiven; she has received of the hand of God double for all her sins."50 Be consoled, my people, and make Jerusalem hear the reasons that she has to rejoice: it is true that her malice had arrived at its height; but all these sins have been forgiven her and, for all vengeance, she has received double the goods that she possessed before: "she has received of the hand of God double for all her sins."

After that, I am not surprised that, during the space of thirty years, Magdalene did not cease to mourn her depravities, although she could not doubt that they had been forgiven her.51 I am not surprised that Saint Peter was inconsolable, until his death, to have been unfaithful to Jesus Christ, whatever assurance he had of the forgiveness of his crime. Can one remember that one has offended such a good Master, without having the heart pierced with grief and without developing a mortal hatred against oneself? Can one think that one has offended him gravely in cold blood, for no reason, having, on the contrary a thousand reasons to love him; that for so long one has taken advantage of his goods, of his patience, of his love, without dying of regret and of sorrow?52

But all that has been forgiven you. The Lord has given you his word that he never will remember it: quite far from resenting it, he loves you even more than he did before your fall. And it is even this that embitters and increases my grief: to have so cruelly offended a God who forgives me so easily, so perfectly, who returns to me good for evil and all kinds of goods for all kinds of evils! Could it happen that I never forget the acts of ingratitude that he has so soon forgotten, that I forgive myself the acts of treachery for which he has accorded me, for which he has offered me—for which he even has urged me to receive—forgiveness; finally, that I console myself from having hated him so long—he who loves me no less today, who loves me still more than he did before I had never offended him? My God, how cruelly you take revenge, it seems to me, in not taking any revenge for so many infidelities! How your Mercy seems much more severe to me than your justice could be! To what torturer would you have been able to deliver me, who would have been crueler to me than the displeasure that I feel to have offended this infinite Mercy? How much this excessive goodness makes me hateful to myself, who has forgotten nothing to bring your anger upon me—to push your patience to the limit? Must it be, O my God, that I have treated you so shamefully—you who do not treat me with less gentleness for that—you who do not even complain about my past conduct![53]

How hard you are, sinner, whomever you be, that such a great readiness does not touch, that it does not attract you to repentance! But how unreasonable you are, if it leads you to commit new sins! It is an inhumanity that one cannot suffer, to take advantage of the weakness of a man in order to mistreat him—to strike him because he cannot defend himself. But what will one say of those who offend God because he does not want to punish us, because we know that he loves us dearly, and that he dreads losing us! One has reason to expect much from such a great Mercy; but misery for those who distrust [this mercy], in whatever state that they themselves be reduced by their obstinacy, however enormous that their sins be, however great that the number of them be, when there would remain only a moment of time—when one would no longer have but a breath of life. But misery and double misery for those who postpone taking recourse to [this mercy], because it awaits them with patience; who do not want to hurry to ask grace of it because it is always ready to give it;[54] who are wicked, because God is good; who sin easily, because he forgives easily; who resolve themselves to displease him, because it is only with difficulty that he resigns himself to punish them!

How is it that mercy would save people to whom [mercy] is a motive of persevering in sin—to whom it is an occasion of condemning oneself? Mercy ought to save us, it is true; but is it by sin or by repentance that it ought to do it? It saves those who want to take advantage of it, but will it save those who do not take advantage of it—those who abuse it, those who change it into a deadly poison, by the improper use that they make of it? It ought to defend the sinner from despair, I admit: but it is certain that there is no sinner more desperate than the one whom it leads to unrepentance.

Lord, accomplish in us, if you please, the work of this infinite Mercy. Do not permit that it become harmful to us or that it be useless to us. Do not allow that we lose our way in this source of salvation. Make that the infinite love that you have for the sinner force him to hate sin with a hatred in some way infinite—that it force him to love you continually in this world, so that he love you forever in the next. *Amen.*

On Submission to the Will of God[1]

Whoever will have done the will of my Father who is in heaven, that one will take
the place for me of brother, of sister, and of mother. (Matt 12:50)[2]

The will of God tends only to make us eternally happy in heaven, and our
Submission makes us happy starting in this life.

ALTHOUGH THE GOSPEL, by inviting us to want everything that God
wants of us, seems to imply that it is within our freedom to subject ourselves
to or to elude the direction of Providence, it is true, however, that one must
obey by preference or by force, and that the will of the Lord will be accomplished equally for those who resist it and for those who submit to it: "My
counsel will stand, and all my will will be done,"[3] he tells us through Isaiah:
My plans will prevail, and your rebellion will not prevent that my orders be
carried out; if you do not approve of what I ordain, I will do despite you that
which it pleases me, and you will be taken along, when you will refuse to follow.[4] What then does the Son of God hope, when he exhorts us to do the will
of his Father, since it always is done necessarily, and it is in no way in human
power to oppose it? He wants to enlist us to carry gladly a yoke that we would
not be able to shake off. He wants to lead us to love our chains, so that they be
lighter for it, and that he have reason to reward our obedience. In such a way
that, when one preaches to us conformity to the good pleasure of our Master, or we consider in ourselves if we ought to abandon ourselves entirely to
his divine Providence,[5] are you quite aware of what it entails, Gentlemen? It
entails knowing if, in the necessity in which we are of going where it pleases
him, it is better to make of oneself with him a merit of an essential Submission than to draw his anger by a useless resistance; if it is better that our heart
be in the law of God, as the Prophet says,[6] or that it groan against this law; if
it is better to bind oneself to it like zealous servants and obliging friends or to
be tied to it like slaves: in a word, if it is better to do the will of the Lord in the
way that it is done in heaven, as we ask it every day in the Lord's Prayer,[7] or as
it is carried out in hell. I am certain that of all those who hear me no one will
hesitate between two such uneven courses of action; and so it is to confirm
you in your feelings, rather than to inspire new ones in you, that I am going

to exhort you to prefer a free and loving Submission [rather than] forced and involuntary obedience.[8] The Holy Virgin, whose life was a constant exercise of this virtue, will obtain for us the lights we need in order to discover the benefits of it. Let us ask this grace of her with confidence. *Hail, Mary.*[9]

If all men guided themselves by the light of reason, it is certain that between their wills and that of God there always would be a very perfect conformity. For can it be that there is in the world a person unreasonable enough to deny that it is fair that God be the master and that everything bend under the orders of his Providence? When his desires are found opposed to our desires, is there anyone who dares affirm that it is for the Lord to give way and to adjust himself according to our whims? Has the madness of men ever gone to the point of thinking that two contrary wills can be equally correct and, supposing that one of the two be necessarily out of order, who was ever so presumptuous as to believe that it is the will of God that has strayed and that ought to be reformed according to our blind and fickle will? The whole world is therefore convinced that man must obey and that he find good all that comes from the part of his Creator. "It is just to be subject to God," said the wretched Antiochus: it is just that man be submitted to God.[10] Whence, then, comes that in spite of this belief one has such difficulty to submit oneself? Whence comes that one complains, that one is distressed, that one despairs, when something happens that is not in conformity with our desires? It is not that the dispositions of God seem unfair to us; no, we have too much insight to form a judgment so false and so ridiculous; but it is that we believe that they are not worthwhile for us. That is why one does not condemn them, these holy dispositions, but one cannot resolve oneself to love them; it is not the reason, it is the heart that revolts. In a word, one calms the mind easily enough; all the difficulty is to moderate the will. But will one be able to refuse to submit it, this will, and to submit it even with pleasure, if I make you see that [the will] of God is as favorable to us, in all things, as it is fair in itself; if I prove that it is no less in our interest than in our duty to subject ourselves?

I am going to convince you of it, Gentlemen; and for that I have only two reasons to propose to you, of which the first is drawn from the will itself of God, and the second from our Submission. I say that we have an interest to submit ourselves perfectly to what God wants, because his will tends only to make us eternally happy in heaven: that is the first point; in the second place, because our Submission makes us happy starting in this life: that is the second.

First Point

First, I presuppose one of the best established and most consoling truths that have ever been revealed to us: it is that, with the exception of sin, nothing happens to us here below unless because God wants it; it is he who gives riches and it is he who sends poverty. If you are sick, God is the cause of your illness; if you have recovered health, it is he who has returned it to you. If you live, it is only to him that you owe this great good; and when death comes to end your life, it will be from his hand that you will receive the mortal blow: "Good things and evil," says Ecclesiastes, "life and death, poverty and riches are from God."[11]

The libertines, who attribute to chance the majority of life events, are blind people who feel sorry for whoever applies oneself a little to investigate the causes of the most unexpected effects. In order to render them silent on this point, I need only the example of Saul. You know that this prince was elected king by lot,[12] which of all elections is that in which reason and human will have the least part. Lots were cast first on the twelve tribes [of Israel], and that of Benjamin won. One then cast them on the families of this tribe; the family of Matri was the lucky one. One came to those who composed this family; and the lot fell on Saul, who was to lead,[13] and whom his appearance and his size made more worthy of the throne than any other of the Israelites. They did not fail to cry out at once, What luck! What fortune! And however, there was so little luck in all that, as Saul had already been consecrated by the prophet Samuel seven days before they assembled for the election.[14] All this was only a ceremony by which God wanted to declare to all his people the choice that he had made of this man: "Lots are cast into the lap," says the Wise Man, "but they are disposed of by the Lord."[15] It is quite often a child who puts the slips of paper into the tail of his coat and who takes them out blindly and without knowing what he is doing; but it is the Lord who guides his hand as he deems it more appropriate in order to have emerge this prince or that magistrate as it pleases him. "Lots are cast into the lap, but they are disposed of by the Lord."

But when the wicked persecute us with injustice, ought we still then to blame God and to accuse him of the evil that we endure? Yes, Christian auditors, you ought to accuse him exclusively of it. He is not the cause of the sin that your enemy commits by mistreating you, but he is the cause of the evil that this man, by sinning, makes you suffer.[16] This unjust man is like a flood that from the top of a rock is cast down onto a vast countryside: it is not the worker who gives to this rapid flood the movement that carries it away; but it is the laborer who, sometimes breaking a dike, sometimes filling a trench or raising an embankment, makes these waters enter into one field rather than into another, whether he wish, by this way, to nourish this field or to devastate it; or, if you prefer, this wicked man is, in the hands of God, like a poison in the hands of a skilled charlatan: it is not the charlatan who gave to this herb or to this mineral the malicious character that is proper to them, but it is he who mixed them into this drink that he presents to you, whether he have the intention to kill you or, as it may happen, to heal you.

In this way it is not God who has inspired in your enemy the malicious will that he has to harm you, but it is he who has given him the power to do it; it is he who has turned against you the malice of this person; who has disposed things in such a way that she has found herself in the condition to disturb your rest—that she in fact has disturbed it. The Lord indeed wished that you fell into this trap, since he has not prevented it—since he even has lent a hand to those who set it for you[17]; it is he who has delivered you to them without defense and who has guided, so to speak, all the blows that they have dealt to you: "Refer the scourge that falls on you," says Saint Augustine, "to God."[18] Have no doubt in the least, if you receive some wound, that is God himself who has wounded you. When all creatures would form a league against you, if the Creator did not want it, if he did not join them, if he did not give them both the strength and the means to execute their malicious plans, they would never manage: "You would not have any power against me, unless it were given to you from above," said the Savior of the world to Pilate.[19] We can say the same to demons, to men, and even to things that are deprived of reason and of feeling. No, you would not distress me, you would not disturb me as you do, if God had not so arranged it. It is he who sends you with power to tempt me and to make me suffer. "You would not have any power against me, unless it were given to you from above."

If from time to time we meditated a little on this article of our faith, no more would be needed in order to smother all our mutterings in all the losses, in all the misfortunes that happen to us. "The Lord gave, the Lord has taken away."[20] It is the Lord who had given me these goods; it is he himself who has taken them away from me; it is neither this litigant, nor this judge, nor this thief who has ruined me; it is not this woman who has blackened my reputation with her malicious gossip; if this child is dead, it is neither for having been mistreated, nor for having been poorly served: it is God, to whom all these things belong, who has not wanted that I enjoy them any longer: "The Lord gave, and the Lord has taken away."

It is therefore a truth of faith, that God does all the evil of which we complain in the world. I go further: I say not only that he does it, but even that he does it with reason, since everything that happens here below regarding us is an effect of his Providence, which is to say, of his divine wisdom administered to govern us. From this proposition it is easy to conclude that everything that happens to us is inevitably to our advantage—and here is how I prove it.

It is a principle of ethics, with which the whole world agrees, that all just and well-ordered government has for its end the happiness of those who are submitted to it. But of all governments, there is none more well-ordered than the one that God exercises over us by his Providence, which aims only to make us happy. Moreover, the faith teaches us that this Providence is universal, which is to say, that everything there is in the universe, everything that is done there by the absolute will or by the permission of

God, all of that relates to the good government of men, and consequently it relates to their happiness.

In such a way that we cannot doubt that all the evils that God sends us, of whatever nature that they may be, we cannot doubt, I say, that they be very helpful to us, without suspecting God himself either of tyranny or of imprudence, without accusing him of having ideas contrary to those that a good ruler ought to have, or of lacking the insight to discern what is worthwhile for us. How much more does it appear that it is we who deceive ourselves, who are unaware of both who is good to us and who is bad to us; who often desire everything that we ought to fear and who fear everything that we ought to desire! It is a sign of an unbearable pride, says Saint Basil, to believe that in one's own affairs one does not need to take anyone's advice and that one has from oneself enough prudence to choose the best option. But if, in the things that we regard, anyone sees better than we what is most helpful for us, what madness to think that we see it better than God himself—that God, I say, who is free from the passions that blind us, who sees into the future, who foresees the events and the effect that each cause ought to produce! You know that the most unfortunate accidents sometimes have happy results, and that on the contrary the most favorable successes can end finally in disastrous outcomes. It is even a rule that God keeps ordinarily enough, to attain his ends by ways completely opposed to those that human prudence habitually chooses.

But not knowing, as we do, what will happen subsequently, how dare we mutter about what we suffer by the permission of God? Do we not fear to complain falsely, and when we would have the greatest reason to be very happy with Providence? Joseph is sold, he is led into slavery, he is thrown into a prison; if he is distressed about these apparent misfortunes, he is in fact distressed with his good fortune, for these are so many steps that raise him imperceptibly even to the throne of Egypt.[21] Saul lost the she-asses of his father; he had to go look for them quite far and quite in vain; this is much time and effort wasted: it is true; but if this effort bothers him, there never was a more unreasonable grief, considering that all this was permitted only to lead him to the prophet who will anoint him on God's behalf to be the king of his people.[22]

How embarrassed we will be, when we will appear before God and when we will see the reasons that he will have had to send us these crosses, for which we are so ungrateful to him! I missed my only child who died in the flower of his life; alas! If he had only lived a few months, a few years, he would have been killed unfortunately and would have died in mortal sin! I was unable to console myself from the break-up of this marriage: if God had never permitted that the affair were ended, I was going to spend my days in mourning and in misery. I owe thirty or forty years of life to this illness that I have suffered with such impatience. I owe my eternal salvation to this confusion that has cost me so many tears. My soul was lost, if I had not lost this money. What business is it of ours, Christian auditors! God takes care of our supervision, and we are worried; one abandons oneself to the good faith of a doctor, because one figures that he understands his profession; he orders that one drill a hole in your skull, that one cut you, that one cut off your arm or leg, in order to stop the gangrene that could end up reaching all the way to your heart; one suffers all these cruel operations, one is grateful to him for it, one rewards him liberally for it, because one judges that he would not do it if it was not quite necessary and because we have to trust each one at his art; and we do not want to give the same honor to our God! One would say that we mistrust his wisdom and we fear that he leads us astray, in thinking to lead us to our end. What! You turn over your body to a man who can make a mistake and whose least errors could cost your life, although he torture you, though he cause you horrible pains, you let him do everything as he understands it; and you cannot let God act; you mean to instruct him in an art in which he is so knowledgeable and in which men nor angels themselves see a thing!

But it is for this itself that we complain, because we never have entered into the mysteries of his Providence, because we are unaware of the motives that he has to exercise it as he does. If we saw all that he sees, we inevitably would want everything that he wants; one would see us ask of him with tears the same afflictions that we try to turn away by our vows and by our prayers. It is for this that he tells us all in the person of the sons of Zebedee: "You know not what you ask."[23] Poor people, your blindness is pitiful; let me govern your destiny; I know better than you yourselves what is necessary for you; if until now I had guided you by your feelings and according to your tastes, you already would be lost without resources: "You know not what you ask." My God, how good you are to have no regard for our blind prayers! What would we become if, in order to punish our half-hearted submission, you decided finally to satisfy all our desires! What aberrations, what falls, what fatal and incurable wounds! Into what confusion, into what depths of evils would we not soon be plunged! Continue, Lord, to despise our wills and to let yours reign: we are quite unreasonable, if we refuse to submit ourselves to it, since it does all things with such wisdom, with such reason, that reason itself enlists it to do nothing against our genuine interests.

But, Gentlemen, God does not do only with reason all that he has done for us; he does it also with love. Yes, Christians, everything that happens to us in this life happens by the order or the permission of a God who always has loved us, and who loves us still more than we love ourselves. He regards us as his creatures, as his children, as his heirs, as his reflections. The benefits that we have received from him have surpassed all our desires; they surpass even our imaginings, and those [benefits] that we receive from him every day are without measure and without number. He has drawn us out of the void, and he is constantly dedicated to save our being and life. He has washed us in the blood of his own Son, and he feeds us today with the flesh of his only Son. Could a heart so tender and so loving resolve to do us the slightest evil; could it even allow that it be done to us, being able to stop it, as he can? My God, rather than think it, I would believe that the greatest evils are very great goods and that your heaviest blows are very gentle and magnificent caresses.

Do you want therefore, Christian auditors, do you want to be persuaded that in everything that God allows to happen to you, he has in sight only your genuine benefits and your eternal happiness? Reflect a little on what he has done for you. You are presently in affliction; consider that the one who is the author of this is that One himself who was happy to spend his whole life in distress in order to spare you from eternal distress; that it is the One whose angel is always at your side, watchful, by his order, over all your ways and dedicated to turn away all that could harm your body or dirty your soul. Consider that the One who causes you this pain is the One who, on our altars, prays constantly and sacrifices himself a thousand times a day in order to atone for your sins and to appease the wrath of his Father to the extent that you irritate him; that it is He who comes to you with such goodness in the sacrament of the Eucharist, who has no greater pleasure than of uniting himself to you and conversing with you. What ingratitude, after such great signs of love, to distrust him still, to reject his gifts as suspicious, to doubt if it is to do us good, or to injure us that he visits us!—But he strikes me cruelly; he strengthens his authority over me.—What do you fear from a hand that has been pierced, that has let itself be fastened to the cross for you?—He makes me walk on a very spiny path.—And if there was no other path to go to heaven? Poor wretch that you are, do you prefer to perish forever than to suffer for a little while? Is it not this same path that he followed before you and for love of you? Will you find there one sole thorn that he did not trample, that he did not blunt, that he did not redden with his blood?—He presents me a chalice full of bitterness.—Yes; but consider that it is your Redeemer who presents it to you; that, loving you as much as he does, could he resolve to treat you in such a way, if he did not see there either an extraordinary usefulness or an urgent need? You have heard tell of this prince who preferred to expose himself to being poisoned than to refuse the drink that his doctor had ordered for him, because he always had shown gratitude for this doctor, very faithful and very dedicated to his person. And we, Christian auditors, we offend gravely our good Master, refusing the chalice that he has prepared for us himself! I beg you not to forget this consideration; it suffices, if I am not mistaken, to make us accept the most regrettable arrangements from the divine will.

When the demon will suggest to you thoughts of impatience and of blasphemy; when nature will revolt in you against the orders of the Lord; when people, as it sometimes happens, will want to carry you to complaining or to revenge—respond to these dangerous advice-givers what the Lord said to Saint Peter in order to make him put his sword back into the scabbard: "The chalice, which my Father has given to me, will I not see and drink it?"[24] What then, you mean to prevent me from drinking the chalice that my Father has given me; you would want that I refused it from his hand, from this hand that created me, that supports me, that guides me, that protects me, that always has been so gentle and so reasonable to me? "The chalice, which my Father has given to me, will I not see and drink it?" If it was an enemy who presented it to me, this chalice; if it came to me from a suspicious or unknown hand, you would be right to lead me to reject it; but he is my Father, he is the best, the most tender, the most passionate of all fathers; he is the One from whom I have received everything and from whom I await all things! "Go behind me, Satan, you are a scandal to me, because you savor not the things that are of God."[25] Be silent, rebellious and seditious thoughts; and you, false friends, carnal men, withdraw! You are an obstacle to me; one sees well that you have no judgment, no prudence; it is you who are my real enemies, since you want to separate me from the most generous, the most constant friend I have in the world; since you want to make my good Father suspicious to me. But say what you like, I am certain that he loves me, that he wants only my good, that he wants to make me eternally happy, and that I will be happy even beginning in this life, if I submit myself to everything that he wants.[26] This is my second point.

Second Point

Saint Augustine, in the twenty-second book of the *City of God*, speaking of the bliss of the saints, says that, in heaven, there will not be in all the blessed but one sole will, which will be accompanied by four prerogatives in which all their happiness will consist. In the first place, this will will be perfectly free and independent; in the second place, it will be freed from all evil; in the third place, it will enjoy all kinds of goods; finally, it will enjoy them forever and without fear of losing them: "In the Heavenly City, [then,] there will be freedom of will: one freedom for all, and indivisible in each. That city will be redeemed from all evil and filled with every good thing; constant in its enjoyment of the happiness of eternal rejoicing."[27] This is without a doubt all that one can wish in order to make bliss complete. But is it really true that on earth, in this valley of tears, in this region so fertile in evils and in pains, where chance and fickleness reign, in this life that is nothing but temptation, but constant war; is it true, I say, that one can

gather these benefits there? Yes, Gentlemen, perhaps. But in order to manage this, there is but one path to take: that is to submit one's will perfectly
to that of God.

I suppose then that a Christian person, being disabused, by her reflections and by the insights that she has received from God, of all the illusions
of the world; seeing that all is but vanity,[28] that nothing can satisfy her
heart, that what she desired most eagerly is often what causes her the most
difficulty; that one almost would not be able to distinguish what is good
for us from what is harmful to us, the good and the evil being found nearly
everywhere mixed together,[29] and what was yesterday the best being found
today the worst; seeing that her desires do nothing but torture her, that the
care that she takes to succeed consumes her and sometimes even hinders
her plans instead of advancing them; that after all, it is a necessity that
the will of God be carried out; that nothing happens to us except by his
orders and that he can command nothing in our regard that not be to our
advantage: I suppose, I say, that after all these plans a person throw herself
blindly into the arms of God, that she turn herself over to him without
condition and without reserve, so to speak, quite resolved to rely upon him
in all things from then on and no longer to desire anything, no longer to
fear anything; in a word, no longer to want anything except what [God] will
want and also to want all that he will want: I say that, from this moment,
this happy creature gains for herself a perfect freedom, that she no longer
can be either bothered or constrained by anyone; that there is no authority,
no power on earth, that be capable of doing her violence or of causing her
a moment of anxiety.[30]

How is it that you will force me to do what I do not want? said a holy man
whose sentiments an ancient reports: "Nothing can compel me more than
God himself."[31] In order to be able to make me do something against my liking, one would need to be able to force God himself; for while God will do
whatever he wants, I cannot fail to be quite free, since I want only what he
does.[32] Does God want that I be sick? Sickness is more pleasant to me than
health. That I be poor? I would not want to be rich. That I be everyone's out-
cast? I grant that the world despise me; I put all my glory in that. Must it be
that I live here or elsewhere, that I spend my days in rest or in the confusion
of business, that I die very young or very old? I would be unable to say what I
prefer of all these things. But from the moment that God will have made his
choice and that he will have let me know to which side his heart leans, mine
will be able to embrace this course of action and will find its bliss there.[33]
"Nothing can compel me more than God himself."

I say, in the second place, that this person is beyond reach of all kinds
of evils, both of the one called "moral," which is nothing other than sin,
and of the one called "natural."[34] Sin is nothing other than a rebellion of
our will against the will of God. And yet, it is obvious that there can be no

rebellion where there is a perfect Submission. All the other evils are evils for us only by the opposition that they have with our own will; for from the moment that we want a thing, however bad that it be in the estimation of other people, it is good with regard to us. It is in this sense that one can take the words of Saint Bernard, when he says that there would be no hell, if there were no self-will: "Let the individual's will cease, and hell will not be,"[35] because the great difficulty of the damned is in that they forever will have everything that they do not want—that they never will have anything that they would like to have. So that, if I want everything that God wants, I inevitably will be exempt from all evils, nothing being able to happen in life that be opposed to the will of God or, consequently, to my own. But is this not an illusion, a man on whom goods and evils make an equal impression? No, this is not an illusion; I know several people who find themselves equally well in sickness and in health, in riches and in destitution; I even know some who prefer destitution and sickness to riches and to health.[36] And how many of them are there who go even further—who make a pleasure of distress and who are more jealous of their poverty than the most miserly are of their treasures?

It is a great deal, for this miserable life, no longer to have anything to suffer. And yet it is not enough. For complete bliss one still must have nothing to desire; this is the state of those who want blindly everything that God wants. As their desires are the same as those of God, they cannot fail to have all that they want, since God desires nothing in vain. But, furthermore, there is nothing so true as what I am going to say: to the extent that we have Submission for the will of God, so does God have acquiescence for our wills; it seems that from the moment that one endeavors only to obey him, he does not apply himself any longer but to make us happy. Not only does he grant our prayers, but he anticipates them—he goes to search even to the depths of the heart for these same desires that one tries to suppress for love of him, and he carries them out, he fulfills them, he surpasses them all by far.

Finally, the happiness of the one whose will is submitted to that of God is a happiness constant, unchanging, everlasting. No fear troubles his bliss, because no accident can destroy it. I think of him as a man seated on a rock in the middle of the ocean: he sees, without being frightened, the most furious waves coming toward him; he takes pleasure in considering them and in counting them as they come to break at his feet. That the sea be calm or rough, that the wind push the waves from one side or that it drive them back from another, he is equally still, because he has affixed himself to something firm and solid.

From there comes this peace, this calm, this face always serene, this temperament always balanced that we notice in the true servants of God. You are quite right, holy souls, to be without worry: you have found in the will of your God a retreat inaccessible to all the adversities of life: "You have made the most High your refuge. No evil will come to you, nor will the scourge come near your dwelling."[37] You have raised yourselves quite high above the region of storms: there is no arrow that can go up to there. You ought to fear neither men nor demons. Whatever one do, whatever happen, you always will have your way, or God himself will find himself far from his: "You have made the most High your refuge. No evil will come to you, nor will the scourge come near your dwelling."

It remains to see how it is that we will be able to gain this happy Submission. This cannot be done, Gentlemen, but by the frequent exercise of this virtue. And because the great opportunities to practice it are rare enough, the whole secret consists in taking advantage of the minor ones which are daily and of which the good use soon would have put us in a state of meeting with the greatest setbacks without being affected by them in the least.[38] There is no one to whom, each day, there do not happen a hundred minor things contrary to one's desires and to one's inclinations, be that our carelessness or slow-wittedness attracts them, be that they happen to us by the thoughtlessness or by the malice of others, be finally that this be a pure effect of chance and of the unforeseen combination of certain necessary causes. However that may be, all our life is strewn, so to speak, with these tiny thorns, which produce in our heart a thousand involuntary movements of hatred, of envy, of fear, of impatience, a thousand little passing sorrows, a thousand minor worries, a thousand disturbances, which at least for a moment affect the peace of the soul. For example, a word slips out that one would not want to have said; one says to us another one that shocks us; a servant serves you poorly or too slowly; a child bothers you, a bore stops you, a scatterbrain bumps into you; a horse covers you with mud; the weather displeases you; your work does not go as you would like; a little piece of furniture breaks; a dress gets stained or tears. I know well that this is not the matter to practice a great heroic virtue; but I say that this would be enough in order to acquire it without fail, if we wanted to do so. I say that a person who would be on her guard to offer to God all these little annoyances and to accept them as being ordained by Providence, besides acquiring by this practice a great number of merits, besides in this way disposing herself imperceptibly to a very great union with God, I say that in little time, she would be capable of withstanding the most sad and the most disastrous accidents of life.[39]

One can add to this exercise, which is easy and nevertheless more useful for us and more pleasing to God than I can tell you; one can, I say, add to it still another of them. Although great disgraces do not arrive every day, one can offer oneself to God every day in order to endure them, when it will please him. If God wanted to take from you either this son or this spouse, if he permitted that you lose this trial or this money that you have invested, you would need great strength in order to withstand such harsh blows.

You still do not know what will be his will on this point. Anticipate his orders and, from here, submit yourself to everything that he has resolved to do. Renounce often in his presence all the desires that you may have to increase or to conserve your goods, your health, your reputation, and affirm to him that you are ready to do without all things, if he wants it so. Think every day, from the morning, about all the most regrettable things that might happen to you during the course of the day. It may well be that, on this day, one will bring to you news of a shipwreck, of a bankruptcy, of a fire; perhaps before night you will receive some remarkable insult, some horrible confusion; perhaps death will take from you the person whom you love most in the world. You do not know if you yourself will not die suddenly and in a tragic way. Accept all these misfortunes in case it please God to permit them; restrain your will to agree to this sacrifice, and do not give it rest until you feel it disposed to want or not to want all that God can want or not want.

Finally, when some one of these misfortunes actually will have befallen you, instead of wasting time on complaining, either about people, or about luck, go to throw yourself at the feet of your good Master in order to ask him the grace of enduring it steadfastly. A man who has received a mortal wound, if he is wise, he does not run after the one who wounded him; he goes right away to the doctor who can heal him. But when, in similar encounters, you would search for the author of your evils, it still would be to God that you would have to go, since there is only he who could be the cause of them.

Go therefore to God, but go there quickly—go there at once; let that be the first of your concerns; go bring back to him, so to speak, the arrow that he shot at you, the scourge he used to beat you: "Ascribe your chastisement to your God."[40] Kiss a hundred times the hands of your crucifix, these hands that have struck you, that have done all the evil that grieves you. Tell him often these lovely words that he himself said to his Father in his cruelest agony: "Not mine, but your will be done":[41] Lord, may your will be done and not mine. I bless you with all my heart; I thank you that your orders be carried out for me; and when it would be in my power to resist them, I would not fail to submit to them: "not as I will, but as you will."[42] I accept this disaster, both in itself and in all these circumstances; I do not complain of the evil that I suffer, or of the people who cause it for me, or of the way that it has happened to me, or of the circumstances of time or place in which it has surprised me. I am certain that you have wanted all these things, and I would rather die than oppose in any way your very holy will: "Your will be done."[43] Yes, my God, all that [you] will want in me and in all men, today and at all times, in heaven and on earth; may it be done, your will; but may it be done on earth, as it is carried out in heaven. *So be it.*

On Confidence in God[1]

It is your confidence that has healed you. (Luke 17:19)[2]

God is strictly committed to help those who put their Confidence in him,
and, when he would not have committed to this himself, this Confidence
would commit him to it.

GENTLEMEN, I DO NOT KNOW if I ought to admire more, either the infinite virtue of this Confidence, which works so many miracles, or the unyielding hardness of men, in whom so many miracles cannot arouse this Confidence. This second wonder seems to me even more worthy of admiration that one cannot attribute it, at least universally, to certain natural fear that leads timid spirits to distrust everything and to believe that the firmest supports are fragile. On the contrary, we are, for the most part, of an entirely conflicting opinion; the weakest supports seem solid to us: the sages of the world rely on their prudence, as if it were unerring; the rich count on their gold, the young people on their age, the strong people on their health, as on very solid foundations; one makes such a great provision on favor, on authority, on friends, that one thinks with that to be able to manage without God himself. We experience every day the powerlessness and the infidelity of creatures, without that being able to weaken the confidence that we have in them; we do not fail to go back to these reeds that have bent, that have broken so often in our hands. Whence comes then that we have so little faith in the Lord, in him, I say, whose power is immense and whose faithfulness so steadfast? Whence comes that, although nature have put into our hearts the seeds of this virtue, as it seems to the most ungodly who, in great dangers and at unexpected accidents, cannot stop themselves from raising their hands to heaven and from calling God to their rescue; whence comes, I say, that, despite this instinct, we have such difficulty putting our Confidence in the Creator? As this is completely unreasonable, it is impossible to offer any reason for it; what one can say is that we never have considered well those [reasons] that we would have to treat him completely differently. I am going to propose them to you, these reasons, Christian auditors, with this firm hope that the Holy Spirit will give me the insights that I need in order to do it with some usefulness, and which I ask of him in the name of Mary. *Hail, Mary.*[3]

We must admit that the Christian religion demands quite lofty and quite heroic virtues of those who profess it: to believe blindly what one cannot conceive, to love with all one's strength what one never has seen, to hope firmly against all kinds of hope—this is to what Christianity calls us and what God demands of each one of us.[4] He is the Master, Christian auditors, and it is right that all bow beneath the orders of such an absolute Majesty. But have you never considered that, although on the one hand he asks for an entirely blind submission, he otherwise exercises such deference in order to lead us there that he seems to distrust his supreme authority and to want to persuade us rather than to force us to submit to him. So, although the mysteries that he obliges us to believe be extremely obscure, nevertheless he establishes the truth of them by such strong and convincing proofs that unless having renounced all reason we cannot doubt them. He does the same thing in order to engage us in his love: although he want to be loved without being seen, nevertheless he does not want to be loved without having convinced us that he is lovable. That is what he does by the diverse portraits that he has traced, in creatures, of his infinite perfections, and by the actual signs that he gives us every day of his goodness. I am going to make you see that he keeps the same behavior with regard to hope. He wants that it be firm and unwavering, even when all its supports seem wrecked and when we no longer see any means. But then, although he hide from us the paths by which help will come to us, he does not hide the reasons that persuade us that it will come without fail; in such a way that, quite far from there being situations in which the exercise of this virtue be impossible, it is impossible that one not exercise it in all encounters, for the little effort that one makes to consider these reasons. I mention them both together, which will be the two parts of this discourse: the first, it is that God is strictly committed to help those who place in him their Confidence; this will be the first part; the second, it is that, when he would not have committed to this himself, this Confidence would commit him to it without fail; this is the second part. There is everything that I have to say.

First Part

Men commit themselves in several ways, be that to do, be that to give; there they commit something: their honor, in promising; their conscience, in promising it with an oath; their goods, in giving real pledges of their word;

finally, their freedom and their life, in turning over their own persons, up until they be released from their promise. And yet, Gentlemen, God has committed himself to help us in all our needs, to protect us in all our perils, to grant us all that we will want to await from his goodness, and he has committed himself to this in all the ways that I just said. He has promised it to us; the God of heaven and earth, the Almighty has given us his word; and he has given it in terms so clear and so strong that one cannot doubt the effect of his promise, without suspecting him of the most vile infidelity and of the most remarkable treachery. I am certain, Christian auditors, that we do not reflect enough on this reason; for, if we had penetrated the force of it a little, we would not hesitate, as we do, between the hope of obtaining and the fear of not obtaining. The Lord has said that, in the divine nature, there is a Trinity of Persons that does not destroy the unity of essence.[5] Although this goes beyond all our conceptions, we do not fail to believe it as firmly as if we see it with our eyes, because we are convinced that God would not be able to lie. The same God says, in still clearer terms, that he will grant to us all that which we will ask of him; that, without expecting even that we pray to him, he watch over all our needs in order to provide for them. The thing is not more incredible than the mystery of the Trinity, and God cannot lie on this point any more than on all the others. Why then would we refuse to add a perfect belief to these latter [points]? He declares, in a hundred places in Scripture, that whoever hopes in him will not be disappointed in his hope— that there is no danger so great, no necessity so urgent from which he does not pull those who will have recourse to his goodness. Ought this not to suffice in order to give us a complete Confidence, unless we have the most extravagant and shameful opinion in the world of him?

Abraham had a barren wife and, in addition, her age, which was quite advanced, had removed from him all hope of having children. However, God promised to this patriarch to populate the earth with his descendants.[6] He believed him without difficulty, and soon after he was confirmed in his belief by the birth of Isaac.[7] Then he received the order to slit the throat of his only son.[8] He prepares to obey and does not cease hoping for an abundant posterity by the same son that he is going to sacrifice with his own hand.[9] I do not know, Gentlemen, if you admire this faith; for myself, although to me it seems very great, I am otherwise not surprised.—But how reasonable that a dead child could be the father of an entire nation?—But is it more likely that the King of the living and of the dead have deceived his servant or that he would break his word?—Isaac must then be brought back to life?—When he would have to annihilate the universe and to create a new world, the Lord will not disappoint: he can do everything, and he will do everything rather than commit an act of treachery.

Do you want to see a truly admirable Confidence? It is that of the Canaanite woman.[10] The Son of God forgets nothing, it seems, in order to plunge her into despair. Quite far from promising her something, he gave her responses that seemed to indicate a will intended to deny her to the end. He treated her as a dog, he pretended not to want to understand her, he discouraged the apostles who wanted to speak for her; all that was not capable of killing in her heart the hope that she had conceived in the goodness of Jesus Christ. Jesus Christ himself too was charmed with her and, no longer able to hold back his admiration, he was as though compelled to make it burst out in these words: "Oh woman, I must confess that you have a great Confidence! 'O woman, great is your faith!'"[11] Yes, without a doubt, there is good reason to be surprised that this poor pagan woman have been able to withstand this refusal without being shaken. That truly is called to hope against hope: "in hope, against hope."[12] But, for us, is there reason to be surprised that we expected everything from God after the words that he has given us; after he not only has permitted us, but even ordered us to go to him; after he complained so often that we did not ask anything of him or even that we did not ask enough of him?[13]

When an honest man promises us to perform a good deed or to perform some other favor for us, that he gives us his word on it, it is as though we already had the thing in hand. We would not dare to ask him for greater assurances, and we do not even believe that they be necessary in his regard. Would I trust less in the promise of my God, and would I not feel as confident of his word as of that of the most honest man in the world? All the more that the word that he has given to us is not an idle word that he was able to disavow—really, he would be subject, like us, to change his will; it is a promise in writing and inserted into the same book on which he will judge us someday, which is to say in the book of the Gospels. If he had failed to carry out his promise with complete fidelity, how, on judgment day, would he dare to produce this holy book in order to condemn our disobedience, since he would find there at the same time the condemnation of his infidelity? What likelihood that this God, who demands with such strictness, the fulfillment of the vows and of the promises that we make to him, however difficult be the things that one has vowed to him,[14] although one be committed without any knowledge of the future and without having been able to foresee the difficulties that would go through the execution, how, I say, could this same God let himself be convinced to have lacked faith and poorly kept his word, he for whom all things are so easy and who cannot have today any reason to refuse us that he not have foreseen from the time of his promise? Now, he has given me the means to convince him of it, in case he refused me something of what I will ask of him or that I will expect from his munificence, without even that I ask him. "I have a signed attestation," says Saint John Chrysostom, "that vouches for all that he has promised me and that makes my Confidence unshakable."[15]

After these guarantees, all other precaution is unnecessary from God's side. Nevertheless, as the vow is something more inviolable among people than all other commitments, the Lord has wanted to add it to his word, in order to make us see, says Saint Paul, with more certainty, the unchanging firmness of his promises, and that being supported by these two things by which it is impossible that God deceive us, we develop a hope firm and solid.[16] What happiness for us, says Tertullian on this subject, that God be happy to swear for love of us! Could he better make us understand how sincere is the desire that he has of giving us what he promises us? "O blessed are we for whose sake God binds Himself by oath; most wretched, if we believe not [God], even on His oath."[17]—Wretched Man, will nothing be capable of giving you confidence? I give you my word, says the Lord; remember that it is the word of a God; I give you my word that I will take care of you and that I will provide for all your needs. May it be enough for you that I am your Father and that I am not unaware of your needs. Ask me whatever you want, I leave nothing out; I am ready to grant it to you. This is much to promise; but, once again, it is God who commits himself. Is this still not enough? I swear to you, by myself who am the Way and the eternal Truth, by myself who hate untruthfulness and who punish perjury with eternal penalties, by myself who neither can lie nor deceive anyone, to cease to be what I am; I swear to you that I will serve you as shield against all your enemies, as doctor in all your illnesses, as guide in all your ways, as advisor in all your doubts, as refuge in all your dangers, as unfailing resource in the greatest plights and when you will be abandoned by all creatures.

I do not think, Gentlemen, that our little faith can resist such great assurances. After that, if God could refuse us something, he would be able to renounce himself and make himself guilty of a horrible perjury. But how is it necessary to produce so many reasons in order to fight against our defiance? Do we fear, Christian auditors? Do we not have real and effective pledges of his word? Every day we see people who go back on the words that they have given; we find some who disavow their writing; there are some who dare even to break the most solemn vows; but there is not one of them whose fickleness or treachery can be feared, when one has good evidence in hand or the person herself has given herself as hostage to her word. I often have admired, in Holy Scripture, the prayer that Moses makes to God in order to obligate him to forgive his people.[18] In order to obtain from him this grace, he makes a long, precise description of all those that he already has allotted to this thankless nation; he makes him remember the wounds of Egypt, the crossing of the Red Sea, and all the wonders that accompanied or that followed this memorable journey. It seems, first of all, that [Moses] sets about doing it very badly, as after all, the way to soften an offended master is not to point out to him what he did for the servant whose thanklessness makes him angry; the more his benefits are notable, the greater the crime; and consequently, the care that one takes to exaggerate to him the size and number of his favors seems much more capable of irritating than of subduing his resentment. However, the complete opposite happens: God was disarmed by the memory of the immense goods that he had done to his people; he cannot refuse to this consideration the forgiveness that one asked of him. Whence does that come, Christian auditors? It is that the graces that we receive from God are like so many pledges of those that we can ask and for which we can hope subsequently; although we have angered him, he cannot resolve to lose us, because he would lose at the same time all his graces. Moreover, propriety does not allow him to refuse anything to people to whom he already has witnessed his love by great, generous liberalities, for fear that there appeared in this some fickleness, above all if what one asks is much less than what he has given of his own accord or that it be necessary in order to accomplish the first gifts.

This being assumed, Gentlemen, I ask you yourselves to review at leisure the benefits that you have received from God and to consider if, after such great abundance, there is something that you ought not to expect from his goodness. In the first place, the majority of what you wish is like a continuation and of secondary importance to what he already has given freely to you; and consequently, he is so committed to give it to you that one can say that in doing it he will settle a debt rather than practice his lavishness; and thus, by giving you life, he is as though forced to give to you the means to survive; in multiplying your children, he has taken upon himself the care of feeding them and of obtaining reasonable housing for them. He has created you for heaven; he owes you in some way all the means that are necessary to achieve it—assistance to observe the commandments, strength to resist temptations, insights to know his will, courage to carry it out; in short: steadfastness in all the evils of life, and perseverance in the practice of Christian virtues. In the second place, all that you can desire is infinitely below what you already have received, such that it is to do him wrong to think that his love—which has led him to do for you such great things—can refuse you such small things.

What! Christian auditors, this God, who has created for you heaven and earth, will not take care to provide for you a hovel in some corner of the world for your dwelling? He has drawn you out of nothingness, and he will not draw you out of poverty? He has done such wonders for the pleasure of your eyes and of all your other senses, and you fear that he leaves you to lack what is necessary! He adorns so magnificently the earth that serves you as a stepping stone, and he will not at least cover your nakedness![19] But where do I stop? "The Lord is my refuge, and my God the help of my hope."[20] My God himself has become the support of my Confidence; he has been happy to commit to me, so to speak, his own person, so that there were nothing so great, nothing so precious, nothing so extraordinary that I expected of him with complete certainty; indeed, as the pledge is an assurance that leaves no place for restlessness, as one believes already to possess all that is promised under such a fine guarantee, not only do I hope, but I believe already to have all things in a trust of such great price. "He who did not spare his own Son but delivered him up for us all, how has he" says the apostle Saint Paul, "not also, with him, given us all things."[21] I do not say that you ought to expect everything from the one who has given you his own Son; I say that he already has given to you all things with him, since, after this commitment, you ought no longer to distrust his munificence unless you were already in possession of all that you can expect of him.

But, in what way has he given himself to us, this immortal Son? He has given us his blood, his qualities, his distress, his life, his death, and, after his death, his blood, to serve us as drink, and his flesh, to take the place for us of food. However much God shouted that he is our Father, that it is he who created us, that we are no less dear to him than the birds that he feeds in the worst weather, that he even accounts for our hair, that one cannot pull out a single one from us that he not be aware of it:[22] all of that is unlikely not to strengthen us. He promises us that he will perform miracles rather than mislead our hope. Yes, he tells us, the mountains will move at your word, the most deadly poison will have no strength to harm you, serpents will be without venom and lions without ferocity; you will have only to touch the sick in order to heal them; you will be fearsome to all the demons; all nature will obey you. You can take my word for it, I vow it to you; I have done all that for a hundred others, I have done for you yourself more than that.[23] Such great promises, such great oaths made, both for us, and for others, all of that cannot reassure us against the least danger, cannot make us put ourselves into his hands and help us to hope in him, and make us understand well that he can refuse nothing to us; in a word, in order to make our confidence unshakable. "The Lord is my refuge, and my God the help of my hope." What, therefore, ought to be the firmness of this confidence that is supported on such powerful commitments? What calm, what peacefulness ought not such well-founded hopes produce in our hearts? How can it be that we hesitate still in our demands, and that there be accidents that frighten us? However, it is only too true that worries, mistrust, and fear reign almost universally in all hearts.

The one fears for one's health, the other for one's reputation, the other for one's property, another for one's life or for that of one's friends; who dreams of investing one's money, who of setting up a daughter, who of saving for retirement; and all that with much grief, with an intense anxiety; this mother trembles constantly for her only son and fears that at each moment one is going to announce to her some misfortune that will have happened to him; the least wind bothers this captain, the least cloud alarms this plowman. But, what is quite strange and completely offensive to God, is that at the same time that one scorns in this way the help that he offers us, one appeals to mortal and powerless creatures; one has recourse to weak, self-seeking, fickle people, who never have done anything in our favor, who have been against us, who have deceived us in a thousand encounters, in a word, from whom we have as much reason to distrust as we would have reason to rely only on our good Master.

That, Christian company, is what pushes the patience of the Lord to the limit. That is what forces him not only not to help us with our plans, but even to oppose them with all his might. It is in order to take revenge on this, such unjust scorn that he takes these human supports from us, that he uproots these hedges by which we believe ourselves well-defended, that he cuts at the base these trees, in the shadow of which we thought to sleep in safety; in a word, that he turns everything against us, even our carnal prudence, and reduces us to the point of dreading all the things in which we had most Confidence, according to this word of the prophet: "You have broken down all his hedges: you have made his strength fear."[24] Let us go to the second part.

Second Part

When God would not be committed to help those who have placed in him their Confidence, I say, Gentlemen, that this Confidence will commit him to them sufficiently by itself. I would mention two reasons for this that I will be happy to address briefly. The first, it is that one cannot do more honor to God than by expecting from him all things; the second, it is that God would be infinitely dishonored if you thwarted this initiative.

For the first, it is so clearly expressed in Scripture by the mouth of the prophet that one cannot doubt it: "Call upon me in the day of trouble," says the Lord; "I will deliver you, and you will glorify me":[25] Call me to your help on the day of your affliction; I will deliver you, and you will do me honor. But what honor, Christian company? The greatest, if I am not mistaken, the most sensitive, the most worthy of God that he can receive from a creature. It is an honor that makes public at the same time all his perfections and that places them in their greatest light. For finally, it is not possible that one trust in God unless one believe him very true in his words; very enlightened to see our needs; very good to want to help us; very strong to execute, in our favor, what goes beyond all the strengths of creatures; very wise to do it by ways gentle and easy, unknown to all human prudence; very faithful to help us quickly, continually, and without ever tiring; very magnificent to grant us all that we ask of him; finally, very merciful not to be prevented from doing it by all our sins. I know that all Christians ought to have these sentiments, but by no means do all have them engraved so foremost in the heart.[26] A man full of Confidence believes these things in a real way; he is so convinced of them that he risks all on his belief, or rather, that he depends entirely on them without believing to risk anything.

It is quite easy to give to the Lord, in a prayer, the status of "Father" and to praise him for his generosity and for his omnipotence: one does it often without knowing what one does.[27] But to be happy to depend for everything on his paternal Providence; to wait, without unease and in the most urgent occasions, for the help that he has promised to us; to do more fundamentally on his word than on all human means; to rely on him for all our cares; to sleep, so to speak, in his arms in the strongest of horrible storms—this is what is called to believe truly that there is a God, and to have from him an idea corresponding to his infinite grandeur. It is for this that, as in the Old Testament he glorified himself to be the God of Abraham, of Isaac, and of Jacob, because he had not had such worshippers so faithful, nor so submissive; also is he called by Saint Paul the God of hope: "God of hope,"[28] in order to make us understand that of all the virtues there is no one of them that honors him more, and that treats him more truly as God.[29]

But when this virtue would do less honor to God, one cannot deny that he would dishonor himself strangely if he did not respond by his kindness to the sentiments with which [this virtue][30] would have inspired us by his munificence. It would be said, then, that the confidence of a creature would have surpassed the generosity of the Almighty, and that a man would have found the divine goodness less liberal, in fact, than he would have conceived it in his mind! I leave you to judge what stain this would be to the name of the Most High, and if there is some indication that he allows it. It is on this foundation that the Fathers [of the Church] taught that our hope is the measure of the graces that we receive from God. Saint Thomas says that [our hope][31] is in us the principle of impetration, as charity is of merit;[32] in such a way that, as we merit in proportion to the love that makes us act, we also obtain always in proportion to the Confidence that leads us to ask.[33] It is even for this same reason that Saint Gregory of Nazianzus says that, from the moment that one has prayed, God believes himself committed by gratitude to give what one demands of him; this is no longer a grace that he grants, it is a kindness that he recognizes: "When a kindness is asked of God, He thinks himself blessed with a kindness."[34] How therefore, Christian auditors, could God let fall into confusion a man who honors him so perfectly? How could he refuse to protect us, if it is true that we cannot glorify him more than in asking his protection?

It is a movement so natural and, at the same time, so reasonable—the one that encourages us to love and to help those who take recourse to us—that one would judge unworthy of the name of "man" whoever would deal differently with [those who take recourse to them].[35] We read, in Greek history, that a senator of the Areopagus, having brutally driven away a sparrow that had thrown itself onto his chest in order to save itself from a vulture that was pursuing it, this action seemed so weak to all his colleagues that they chased him from their company, as if he had dishonored it by his callousness.[36] What would these judges have done, if, instead of a bird, it had involved either a man or a woman? But what would it be if the Lord behaved in this way with regard to his own children, to his poor creatures, when, full of Confidence, they go to him as to the source of all goodness? How unworthy that would be of his greatness and of his infinite mercy! No, Gentlemen, do not fear that he reject you. Whatever danger that threaten you, whatever enemy that persecute you, whatever grief that oppress you, in whatever weakness that you find yourself, rely on your God, throw yourself boldly into his arms—he will not withdraw to make you fall on your face: "Cast yourself upon him. . . . He will not withdraw himself so that you fall."[37]

For myself, my God, I am so convinced that you watch over those who hope in you and that one cannot lack for anything, when one expects from you all things, that I have resolved to live in the future without any worry and to offload onto you all my anxieties:[38] "In peace in the selfsame I will sleep, and I will rest, for you alone, O Lord, have settled me in hope."[39] Men may strip me of possessions and of honor; illnesses may take from me the strength and the means to serve you; I even may lose your grace through sin; but never will I lose my hope; I will conserve it up until the last moment of my life, and all the demons of hell will make at that moment vain attempts to tear it from me: "In peace in the selfsame I will sleep, and I will rest." Others may await their happiness, either from their riches, or from their talents; others rely, either on the innocence of their life, or on the rigor of their penances, or on the number of their alms, or on the fervor of their prayers:[40] "you alone, O Lord, have settled me in hope." For me, Lord, all my Confidence, it is my Confidence itself. This Confidence never will mislead anyone: "no one, no one has hoped in the Lord and has been confounded."[41] I am certain therefore that I will be eternally happy, because I hope firmly to be so and because it is from you, O my God, that I hope for it: "In you, O Lord, have I hoped; let me never be confounded."[42] I know, alas! I know it only too well, that I am fragile and fickle; I know what temptations are capable of doing against the most strengthened virtues; I have seen fall the stars from heaven and the columns from the firmament.[43] But all that cannot frighten me while I will hope; I keep myself sheltered from all misfortunes and am sure to hope always, because I hope even for this unchanging hope. Finally, I am sure that I cannot hope too much in you and that I cannot have less than what I will have hoped from you. Thus I hope that you will maintain me on the steepest slopes, that you will sustain me against the most furious assaults, and that you will make my weakness triumph over my most fearsome enemies. I hope that you will love me always and that I will love you also without rest; and, in order to carry, once and for all, my hope as far as it can go, I hope for you yourself from yourself, O my Creator, both for time, and for eternity! *Amen.*

Abbreviations

Unless otherwise indicated, works are cited by volume, page, and line.

A: *Sermons prêchez devant Son Altesse Roîale Madame la Duchesse d'Yorck. Par le R. P. Claude La Colombière.* 4 vols. Lyon: Anisson, Posuel, and Rigaud, 1684.

ACW: Ancient Christian Writers. New York: Paulist Press, 1946–.

AE: Martin Luther. *Luther's Works. American Edition.* Edited by Jaroslav Pelikan and Helmut T. Lehman. 55 vols. Philadelphia: Fortress Press, and St. Louis: Concordia, 1955–86.

ANF: A Select Library of Ante-Nicene Christian Fathers. Edited by Alexander Roberts and James Donaldson. Revised by A. Cleveland Coxe. 10 vols. Peabody, MA: Hendrickson Publishers, 1994.

BA: Bibliothèque Augustinienne. Paris: Desclée de Brouwer, 1936–.

BCJ: Carlos Sommervogel. *Bibliothèque de la Compagnie de Jésus. Nouvelle édition.* 12 vols. Brussels: Oscar Schepens, and Paris: Alphonse Picard, 1890–1960. Cited by volume and column.

C: *Œuvres complètes du Vénérable Père Claude de La Colombière de la Compagnie de Jésus.* Edited by Pierre Charrier. 6 vols. Grenoble: Imprimerie du Patronage Catholique, 1900 (vol. 1); Imprimerie Notre-Dame, 1901 (vols. 2–6).

CCE: *Catechismus Catholicae Ecclesiae.* Vatican City: Libreria Editrice Vaticana, 1997. Cited by paragraph number.

CCL: Corpus Christianorum, series latina. Turnhout: Brepols, 1954–.

CF: Cistercian Fathers. Trappist, KY: Cistercian Publications, 1970–.

COGD: *Corpus Christianorum, Conciliorum Oecumenicorum Generaliumque Decreta.* Turnhout: Brepols, 2006–. Cited by council, session, title, part, chapter, and number of document, and by volume and page of this work.

CSEL: Corpus scriptorum ecclesiasticorum latinorum. Vienna: Verlag der Österreichischen Akademie der Wissenschaften, 1866–. Cited by volume, part, and page.

CW: *Philonis Alexandrini opera quae supersunt.* Edited by Leopold Cohn and Paul Wendland. 7 vols. Berlin: George Reimer, 1962–63.

DEC: *Decrees of the Ecumenical Councils.* Edited by Norman P. Tanner. 2 vols. London: Sheed and Ward, and Washington, DC: Georgetown University Press, 1990.

DH: *Enchiridion symbolorum, definitionum et declarationum de rebus fidei et morum.* 41st ed. Edited by Heinrich Denzinger and Peter Hünermann. Freiburg: Herder, 2007.

DRA: *Douay-Rheims Bible.* 1899 ed. N.p.: n.p., 1899. BibleWorks, v.8.

DSAM: *Dictionnaire de spiritualité, ascétique et mystique, doctrine et histoire.* 17 vols. Paris: Beauchesne, 1932–95. Cited by volume and column.

EJF: *Les établissements des jésuites en France depuis quatre siècles.* Edited by Pierre Delattre. 5 vols. Enghien: Institut supérieur de théologie, and Wetteren: Imprimerie De Meester frères, 1949–57.

EP 2: *The Essential Peirce: Selected Philosophical Writings, Volume 2 (1893–1913).* Edited by the Peirce Edition Project. Bloomington, IN: Indiana University Press, 1998.

ES: Claude La Colombière. *Écrits spirituels.* Edited by André Ravier, SJ. 2nd ed. Paris: Desclée de Brouwer, 1982. Cited by page.

FC: Fathers of the Church. Washington, DC: Catholic University of America Press, 1947–.

FCM: Fathers of the Church: Medieval Continuation. Washington, DC: Catholic University of America Press, 1989–.

Furetière: *Dictionnaire Universel Contenant généralement tous les mots François. Recueilli et compilé par Messire Antoine Furetière, Abbé de Chalivoy, de l'Académie Françoise.* La Haye: Leers, 1690.

GCS: Die Griechischen Christlichen Schriftsteller der ersten [drei] Jahrhunderte. Berlin: Walter de Gruyter, 1897–.

GL: *Grand Larousse de la langue française.* 6 vols. Paris: Librairie Larousse, 1971.

GNO: Gregorii Nysseni Opera. Edited by Werner Jaeger et al. Leiden: Brill, 1952–. Cited by volume, part, page, and line.

GNT: *The Greek New Testament.* 4th rev. ed. Edited by Barbara Aland, Kurt Aland, Johannes Karavidopoulos, Carlo M. Martini, and Bruce M. Metzger in cooperation with the Institute for New Testament Textual Research, Münster/Westphalien. Stuttgart: Deutsche Bibelgesellschaft, 1993. BibleWorks, v.8.

HL: Henri Bremond. *Histoire littéraire du sentiment religieux en France, depuis la fin des guerres de religion jusqu'à nos jours.* Edited by François Trémolières. 5 vols. Grenoble: Jérôme Millon, 2006.

L: Claude La Colombière. *Lettres.* Edited by Claude Bied-Charreton. Paris: Desclée de Brouwer, 1992. Cited by page.

MHSI: Monumenta Historica Societatis Iesu. Madrid and Rome, 1894–.

MHSSC: Monumenta Hispaniae Sacra. Serie Canónica. 6 vols. Madrid: Consejo Superior de Investigaciones Científicas, Instituto Enrique Flórez, 1966–2002.

NCE: New Catholic Encyclopedia. 2nd ed. 15 vols. Washington, DC: Catholic University of America, 2003.

NPNF[1]: A Select Library of the Nicene and Post-Nicene Fathers. First Series. Edited by Philip Schaff. 14 vols. Peabody, MA: Hendrickson Publishers, 1994.

NPNF[2]: A Select Library of the Nicene and Post-Nicene Fathers. Second Series. Edited by Philip Schaff and Henry Wace. 14 vols. Peabody, MA: Hendrickson Publishers, 1994.

OED: The Oxford English Dictionary. 2nd ed. Prepared by J. A. Simpson and E. S. C. Weiner. 20 vols. Oxford: Clarendon Press, 1989.

OPD: Opere di Pier Damiani. Rome: Città Nuova Editrice, 2000–.

PBSK: Patrologia: Beiträge zum Studium der Kirchenväter. Frankfurt am Main: Peter Lang, 1991–.

PG: Patrologia Graeca. Edited by Jacques Paul Migne. 165 vols. Paris: 1857–58.

PL: Patrologia Latina. Edited by Jacques Paul Migne. 221 vols. Paris: 1844–55.

PO: Claude La Colombière. *Prolusiones oratoriae.* Lyon: Anisson, Posuel, and Rigaud, 1684. Cited by page.

SB: Spircilegium Bonaventurianum. Grottaferrata (Rome): Editiones Collegii S. Bonaventurae ad Claras Aquas, 1963–. Abbreviations of works generally follow the respective volumes.

SBO: Sancti Bernardi Opera. Edited by Jean Leclerq, Charles H. Talbot, and Henri-Marie Rochais. 8 vols. Rome: Editiones Cistercienses, 1957–77. Abbreviations of works follow those appearing in the index (SBO 9:XV–XVI).

SC: Sources chrétiennes. Paris: Éditions du Cerf, 1955–.

SLS: Acta Universitatis Stockholmiensis. Studia Latina Stockholmiensia. Stockholm: University of Stockholm, 1952–.

ST: Thomas Aquinas. *Summa theologiae.* Cited by part, question, article, and division.

VUC: Michael Tweedale, ed. *Biblia Sacra juxta Vulgatam Clementinam.* N.p.: n.p. <http://vulsearch.sf.net/html>. BibleWorks, v.8.

WSA: The Works of Saint Augustine. Translated by Edmund Hill. Edited by John E. Rotelle. Brooklyn, NY: New City Press, 1990–. Cited by part, volume, and page.

Notes

Introduction

1. For a cultural history of the devotion in modern France, see Raymond Jonas, *France and the Cult of the Sacred Heart* (Berkeley: University of California Press, 2000).

2. This prayer of consecration or *offrande* appears at the end of the *Retraitte* [*sic*] *spirituelle du R. P. Claude La Colombière* (Lyon: Anisson, Posuel, and Rigaud, 1684), which volume was republished in *Écrits Spirituels*, with an introduction and notes by André Ravier (Paris: Desclée De Brouwer, 1982), 173–75; hereafter *ES*. Ravier speculates that the *offrande* probably dates from Claude's London retreat of 1677 but that he had pronounced a primitive form of it as early as 1675 (*ES* 75).

3. These biographical notes follow Georges Guitton, *Le Bienheureux Claude La Colombière, son milieu et son temps* (Lyon: Librairie Catholique Emmanuel Vitte, 1943), with occasional reference to Pierre Charrier, *Histoire du Vénérable Père Claude de La Colombière, de la Compagnie de Jésus, complétée à l'aide de documents inédits*, 2 vols. (Paris: Delhomme et Briguet, 1894).

4. Since 1429, the great-grandson of Gaude, named Jean or Jeannet, had held the office of notary (*notaire*) at Saint-Symphorien. Antoine Furetière, in his *Dictionnaire Universel* (La Haye: Leers, 1690), defines a *notaire* as an "official depository of public faith." As such, Jean would have kept track of contracts, including those dealing with marriages and real estate. His son Philippe followed in his profession, as did Philippe's son, Benoît, and grandson, Pierre. The second wife of Pierre then gave birth to Bertrand, who married Marguerite Coindat, the mother of Claude. For the complete genealogy, see Charrier, *Histoire*, 1:1–7, 255–65.

Note that in a French surname, the particle *de* traditionally signified membership in the aristocracy or noble class that comprised the Second Estate before the Revolution. The noble status of Gaude would have entitled his descendants to use this particle. Furthermore, nearly all notaries were placed in the noble class during the fifteenth century, although they seem to have lost that privilege by virtue of an edict adopted in 1573 in the former Dauphiné province to which Saint-Symphorien belonged (Charrier, *Histoire*, 1:266). In any case, the particle no longer appears after 1562 in the name of Benoît, the great-grandfather of Claude, although it does appear as late as 1600 in the name of his son Odet. Neither does it appear in the name of Pierre, who served as both notary and *procureur d'office* at the court of the marquisate of Saint-Symphorien.

As for Bertrand, son of Pierre and father of Claude, his name and the names of his family do not appear in the nobility lists furnished for the region in 1666; Bertrand demanded recognition of the nobility of his ancestors, which recognition his eldest son, Humbert, obtained. However, there exist no records that Claude used the particle, although today his name often appears as "Claude de la Colombière." On this point, while the catalogs of the Society of Jesus for 1666–73 and 1674–75 print the name of Claude with the particle, neither the extant autograph letters nor the first editions of his writings, published posthumously, contain it. For these reasons, the present edition follows Guitton in omitting the particle from Claude's surname.

5. The subsequent editions appeared in 1687, 1689, 1692, and 1697 (*BCJ* 2:1311, 9:94).

6. For an index of the esteem in which former generations held Claude's pulpit oratory, see the title page of Migne's multi-volume *Collection intégrale et universelle des Orateurs sacrés* (Paris, 1844–66), which organizes into three "orders" the names of the preachers whose work appears in that edition. While the first order includes only Bourdaloue, Bossuet, Fénelon, and Massillon, La Colombière appears along with Fléchier and Lingendes in the second rank, ahead of such greats as Camus, Castillon, and Coton, all relegated to the third order.

7. For an account of these developments, see Thomas Worcester, "The Catholic Sermon," in *Preachers and People in the Reformations and Early Modern Period*, ed. Larissa Taylor (Leiden: Brill, 2001), 3–33, and Larissa Taylor, "The Influence of Humanism on Post-Reformation Catholic Preachers in France," *Renaissance Quarterly* 50 (1997): 115–30.

8. For the sake of convenience, I have translated the French word *collège* throughout this book as "college," despite the fact that the term meant something much broader in the Jesuit culture of yesteryear than in the American and even French contexts today.

9. Michael A. Mullett, *The Catholic Reformation* (New York: Routledge, 1999), 94–95. For a recent translation and bibliography, see *The* Ratio Studiorum: *The Official Plan for Jesuit Education*, trans. and annotated by Claude Pavur (Saint Louis, MO: The Institute of Jesuit Sources, 2005). Citations of the *Ratio* in the present volume reference paragraph numbers of the Pavur translation.

10. See William P. O'Brien, SJ, "Une 'manière' de prêcher: Rhétorique et sainteté chez Claude La Colombière," *Archivum Historicum Societatis Iesu* 79, no. 157 (Spring 2010): 125–70. Having analyzed Claude's sermons according to the Ciceronian categories of invention, division, and elocution, this article demonstrates that his preaching represents a "holy practice" of rhetoric aimed at the conversion of the listener (164–69).

11. For the role of the College of the Trinity as an expression of the cultural activity of the Jesuits in the modern city, see Stéphane Van Damme, *Le Temple de la sagesse: Savoirs, écriture et sociabilité urbaine (Lyon, xviie–xviiie siècles)* (Paris: Éditions de l'École des hautes études en sciences sociales, 2005).

12. *Sermons prêchez devant Son Altesse Roîale Madame la Duchesse d'Yorck. Par le R. P. Claude La Colombière*, 4 vols. (Lyon: Anisson, Posuel, and Rigaud, 1684), hereafter indicated by the letter A. Pierre Charrier reedited these sermons and Claude's other extant writings in *Œuvres complètes du Vénérable Père Claude de La Colombière de la Compagnie de Jésus*, vol. 1 (Grenoble: Imprimerie du Patronage Catholique, 1900), vols. 2–6 (Grenoble: Imprimerie Notre-Dame, 1901), hereafter indicated by the letter C. André Ravier reedited the Meditations on the Passion in *ES* 177–266. For convenience, citations of the sermons in the notes generally refer to the

more readily-available Charrier edition, except when a note deals with a verification against the earlier text.

13. On this point, see John W. Donohue, *Jesuit Education: An Essay on the Foundation of Its Idea* (New York: Fordham University Press, 1963), 67–69, 150–51.

14. "Laus panegyristae," in *Prolusiones oratoriae* (Lyon: Anisson, Posuel, and Rigaud, 1684), 12; hereafter *PO*. This collection of three Latin discourses, which appears in the last eighty-nine pages of the editio princeps of the *Réflexions chrétiennes*, was reedited in C 5:441–519.

15. Donohue, *Jesuit Education*, 146.

16. James M. May and Jakob Wisse, "Introduction," in Cicero, *On the Ideal Orator* (New York: Oxford University Press, 2001), 26.

17. Donohue, *Jesuit Education*, 130–32. For the moral dimension, see André Schimberg, *L'Éducation morale dans les collèges de la Compagnie de Jésus en France sous L'Ancien Régime (xvie, xviie, xviiie siècles)* (Paris: Champion, 1913).

18. Donohue, *Jesuit Education*, 121.

19. Ibid., 149. For the philosophy of education implicit in the *Ratio*, see the *Humanist Educational Treatises*, trans. and ed. Craig W. Kallendorf (Cambridge, MA: Harvard University Press, 2002).

20. Allan Peter Farrell, SJ, *The Jesuit Code of Liberal Education: Development and Scope of the* Ratio studiorum (Milwaukee, WI: Bruce Publishing Company, 1938), 352.

21. Ibid., 356.

22. *PO* 68–89/C 5:501–19.

23. Worcester, "The Catholic Sermon," 21–22; cf. Marc Fumaroli, *L'Âge de l'éloquence*, Titre courant 24 (Geneva: Droz, 2002), 116–61.

24. J. Giffon, *Relation de tout ce qui s'est passé de plus mémorable, en la sollennelle octave de la canonisation de sainct François de Sales, evesque, et prince de Geneve, célébrée dans l'église du premier monastère des religieuses de la Visitation Ste-Marie, de la ville et cité d'Avignon, depuis le 29 may 1666 jusques au 6 juin inclusivement. Avec une sommaire description, de tout le superbe appareil que ces dignes religieuses ont dressé* (Arles: François Mesnier, 1667); Ms. 2446/3 at the Municipal Library of Avignon. The convent in question was built between 1631 and 1638 at rue de la Philonarde, today place Pignotte. Note that, although Francis was canonized April 19, 1665, the liturgical celebrations related to his feast would not have begun until the following year, viz., 1666—the year indicated in the *Relation*. Furthermore, the week in which a given community celebrated the canonization varied depending upon circumstances: for examples, see Viviane Mellinghoff-Bourgerie and Frieder Mellinghoff, *Bibliographie des écrivains français: François de Sales* (Paris: Éditions Memini, 2007), 527–32.

25. Judg 14:14.

26. References to Francis de Sales appear in six of Claude's sermons (C 1:390; 2:300, 452, 482; 3:210; 4:394), in four of his letters (*L* 66, 92, 95, and 109), and in his retreat notes (*ES* 171). He appears to have known the *Introduction à la vie dévote*, the *Combat spirituel*—of which Francis made use (C 2:452; 4:394)—his *Lettres*, and his *Vie* (*L* 92). Unless otherwise noted, citations of Claude's correspondence refer to Claude La Colombière, *Lettres*, ed. Claude Bied-Charreton (Paris: Desclée de Brouwer, 1992), abbreviated *L*.

27. For a description of this practice, see Peter Bayley, *French Pulpit Oratory, 1598–1650: A Study in Themes and Styles, with a Descriptive Catalogue of Printed Texts* (Cambridge: Cambridge University Press, 1980), 56–60.

28. *EJF* 1:459–62.

29. Emmanuel Bury, "Bossuet Orateur," in Gérard Ferreyrolles, Beatrice Guion, and Jean-Louis Quantin, *Bossuet* (Paris: Presses Universitaires Paris Sorbonne, 2008), 231–34. For his preaching, see *Œuvres oratoires de Bossuet*, ed. Joseph Lebarq, rev. Charles Urbain and Eugène Levesque, 7 vols. (Paris: Desclée de Brouwer, 1914–26).

30. "Oraison funèbre de très noble et très vertueuse dame Françoise Magdeleine de Nérestang, abbesse du Monastère royal de la Bénissons-Dieu, décédée le 21 Mai 1675" (C 4:455–88).

31. The story that Claude functioned as tutor to the sons of Colbert, and that the minister subsequently dismissed him after having discovered two satirical verses that Claude had composed about him, has entered so deeply into the tradition concerning Claude that many simply accept it as historical fact. Yet the only known textual evidence both for Claude's serving as tutor and for the ensuing scandal appears in a single exchange of letters, dating from 1738, which did not come to light until the late nineteenth century (Guitton, *Le Bienheureux Claude La Colombière*, 97–100). Furthermore, I have found no mention of La Colombière in any of the literature associated with either Colbert or his sons.

32. Guitton, *Le Bienheureux Claude La Colombière*, 63.

33. Ibid., 68.

34. An autograph letter of La Colombière to Bouhours, kept in the *Bibliothèque publique de Grenoble*, appears in *ES* 501–02. For a historical analysis of this document, see Michel de Certeau, "Un maître spirituel: La confiance, conversion du cœur chez le Père La Colombière (1641–1682)," in G. de Broglie et al., *Fête du Sacré-Cœur* (Paris: Saint-André/Cerf, 1967), 66–76.

35. Nicolas La Pesse offers this commentary in a biographical note introducing the first edition of the *Sermons* (C 1:iii).

36. *PO* 51–55/C 5:486–90. Noting that Vaugelas referred to Patru as the *Quintilien François*, La Colombière indicates that Quintilian himself, had he read Patru, would not have hesitated to refer to him as *notre Tullius* (*PO* 52/C 5:487).

37. *Augusti Caesaris aetas* (1671) and *Laus oratoris galli* (1672) (*PO* 3–67/C 5:443–500).

38. Dominique de Colonia, *Histoire littéraire de la ville de Lyon, avec une bibliothèque des auteurs lyonnais, sacrés et profanes, distribués par siècles* (Lyon: François Rigollet, 1728–30), 2:750–51.

39. For examples and discussion of this style, see Thomas Worcester, "The Classical Sermon," in *Preaching, Sermon and Cultural Change in the Long Eighteenth Century*, ed. Joris van Eijnatten (Leiden: Brill, 2009), 133–72.

40. On the symbolic value of his heart, now preserved at the Monastery of the Visitation in Treviso, see *I Leave You My Heart: A Visitandine Chronicle of the French Revolution—Mère Marie-Jéronyme Vérot's* Letter of 15 May 1794, trans. and ed. Péronne-Marie Thibert, VHM (Philadelphia: Saint Joseph University Press, 2000).

41. *ES* 101–08. The text of the vow also appears in the La Pesse introduction to the *Sermons* (C 1:viii–xx). To understand this vow in the context of Claude's spiritual life, see André Ravier, "L'Évolution spirituelle de saint Claude La Colombière, d'après ses notes personnelles," in *Claude La Colombière: Colloque public du Centre Sèvres, 5 et 6 mars 1993* (Paris: Médiasèvres, 1993), 57–65. For the place of the vow in "the internal logic of his biography," see Édouard Glotin, SJ, "Claude La Colombière: Le Sens d'une canonisation," *Nouvelle revue théologique* 114, no. 6 (1992): 816–38. On the vow in general, see Pinard de la Boullaye, SJ, "La Spiritualité ignatienne: Bibliographie sommaire,"

Revue d'ascétique et mystique 26 (1950): 282–83; *DSAM* 12:230. For probable allusions to the vow in his preaching as represented in the present volume, see "You Should Serve Only One Master" and "On Confidence in God."

42. Furetière, in his *Dictionnaire Universel*, gives *monial, -ale* only as an adjective, and defines it as follows: "Which is said in these phrases. St. Pierre *le Monial*. The *moniales* of such a place. A convent of *moniales*, [which is] to say, the religious. They are so named in canon law."

43. Francis de Sales and the Baroness de Chantal, the widow Jeanne-Françoise Frémyot (1572–1641), established the Order of the Visitation of Holy Mary, or Visitandines, at Annecy on June 6, 1610. They intended this community to represent a "new form of religious life . . . marked by simplicity" (*DSAM* 16:1003). Nevertheless, eight years later, their simple vows, moderate cloister, and visits to the sick were exchanged for solemn vows and perpetual cloister—the kind of religious life that Margaret Mary would have known. The definitive constitutions of the order appeared in print along with the Rule of Saint Augustine in 1622. For more information on the origin, expansion, and spirituality of the Visitation Order, see *DSAM* 16:1002–10.

44. The first biography of Margaret Mary appears in Jean-Joseph Languet, *La Vie de la vénérable mère Marguerite Marie, religieuse de la Visitation Sainte Marie, du monastere de Paray-le-Monial en Charolois* (Paris: La veuve Mazieres and Jean-Baptiste Garnier, 1729). See also Bernard Descouleurs and Christiane Gaud, *Marguerite-Marie Alacoque: La Mystique du Cœur* (Paris: Cerf-Saint-Augustin, 1996). Margaret Mary's writings appear in the *Vie et œuvres de sainte Marguerite-Marie Alacoque*, ed. Raymond Darricau, 2 vols. (Paris: Saint-Paul, 1990–91).

45. The expression *cœur de Jésus* appears in four sermons (C 1:263, 2:24, 3:212, 4:278) and in one meditation on the Passion (*ES* 205). It also appears once in an anonymous polemical text, traditionally dated 1679 and attributed to La Colombière. The passage in question reads: *Surtout on tâchera de ne rien dire qui choque la charité Chrétienne, à laquelle on ne peut donner atteinte, sans blesser le cœur de Jésus-Christ, et sans renoncer à toute vertu*; see the *Réponse à la* "Relation de l'affaire du P. S. Just, à Grenoble," 5. The copy that I consulted belongs to the Jesuit archives in Vanves (C 41/86) and appears in a bound volume entitled *Pour les Jésuites*, on the first page of which appears inscribed *Recueil de Pièces pour la Défense de la Compagnie de Jésus, Recueil U. 4. 1650–1761–1845*.

46. Although France had adopted the Gregorian calendar in 1582, England continued to use the Julian calendar until 1752. As a result, the dates in England varied with those on the continent according to the century, so that from March 1, 1500, to February 29, 1700, the discrepancy amounted to ten days. To indicate this difference here, the local (English) date appears first, followed by the French date. Thus, *October 3/13* signifies a day falling on October 3 in England and October 13 in France. On the question of date styles, see *A Handbook of Dates for Students of British History*, rev. Michael Jones (Cambridge: Cambridge University Press, 2000).

47. David Baldwin, "The Politico-Religious Usage of the Queen's Chapel, 1623–1688," thesis presented for the title of Master of Letters in the Department of Theology, University of Durham (1999), 133. On the career and origins of Edward Colman, see Andrew Barclay, "The Rise of Edward Colman," *The Historical Journal* 42, no. 1 (March 1999): 109–31.

48. The notes from this retreat were published for the first time in 1684 along with those from Claude's tertianship retreat (see n2 above).

49. Baldwin, "The Politico-Religious Usage of the Queen's Chapel," 124–28.

According to one hypothesis, the congregation met in Claude's private rooms.

50. For the history of this affair, see John Kenyon, *The Popish Plot* (London: Phoenix Press, 2001).

51. Larissa Juliet Taylor, "Dangerous Vocations: Preaching in France in the late Middle Ages and Reformations," in *Preachers and People in the Reformations and Early Modern Period*, 91–124.

52. See n45 above. For an analysis of this document, see William P. O'Brien, "Claude La Colombière. Rhétorique et spiritualité," unpublished doctoral dissertation (Université Paris-Sorbonne, 2008), 289–320.

53. Reedited in *ES* 79–80.

54. This includes both stylistic and thematic similarities, such as the fact that both Bossuet and Bourdaloue also delivered panegyrics to Francis de Sales. See "Panégyrique du bienheureux François de Sales," in Bossuet, *Œuvres oratoires*, 3:575–92, preached on December 28, 1660, the year before Francis was beatified, and "Sermon pour la fête de saint François de Sales," in *Œuvres complètes de Bourdaloue*, new ed. (Paris: Beauchesne, 1905), 6:116–36, composed for the canonization ceremony, which took place on April 19, 1665.

55. On these conventions, see Bury, "Bossuet Orateur," 222.

56. Alexander Bitzel, "The Theology of the Sermon in the Eighteenth Century," in *Preaching, Sermon and Cultural Change in the Long Eighteenth Century*, 61–62.

57. Worcester, "The Catholic Sermon," 26–29.

58. On this style in context, see O. C. Edwards, Jr., "Varieties of Sermon: A Survey of Preaching in the Long Eighteenth Century," in *Preaching, Sermon and Cultural Change in the Long Eighteenth Century*, 10–11.

59. In Lonerganian terms, this means establishing a foundational horizon within which to apprehend the meaning of doctrines. For discussion of this method, see Bernard J. F. Lonergan, *Method in Theology*, 2nd ed. (Toronto: University of Toronto Press, 2003), 128–32, 267–333. My use of Lonergan's method follows Donald L. Gelpi, SJ, "The Authentication of Doctrines: Hints from C. S. Peirce," *Theological Studies* 60 (1999): 261–93.

60. On this quest, see, for example, Hans Urs von Balthasar, "Theology and Sanctity," in *Explorations in Theology I: The Word Made Flesh*, trans. A. V. Littledale with Alexander Dru (San Francisco: Ignatius Press, 1989), 181–209.

61. Peter Bayley, *French Pulpit Oratory*, 6–8. This textual focus had characterized contemporary studies of modern spirituality in France, notably under the influence of philologist Jean Orcibal, for some time before Bayley. For a description of Orcibal's method, see Jean Orcibal, "Histoire du catholicisme moderne et contemporain," in *Problèmes et méthodes d'histoire des religions: Mélanges publiés par la Section des sciences religieuses à l'occasion du centenaire de l'École pratique des Hautes Études* (Paris: Presses Universitaires de France, 1968), 251–60.

62. Virtue ethics has experienced a resurgence in contemporary moral theory, thanks to the work of Philippa Foot, Alisdair MacIntyre, and others. For bibliography and a recent study in this vein, see Julia Annas, *Intelligent Virtue* (Oxford: Oxford University Press, 2011). For the influence of virtue theory in contemporary Roman Catholic theological ethics, see James F. Keenan, SJ, *A History of Catholic Moral Theology in the Twentieth Century: From Confessing Sins to Liberating Consciences* (New York: Continuum, 2010).

63. The *Ratio studiorum* specifies the teaching of "the main areas of moral science that are contained in the ten books of Aristotle's [Nicomachean] *Ethics*" (235) and

the explanation of "a few things . . . about habit and about virtue in general" (C77) as presented in *Summa theologiae* (hereafter *ST*) Ia-IIae. Note however that, in its "Rules for the Professor of Scholastic Theology," the *Ratio* qualifies the priority that it accords to Thomas for theological instruction: "Jesuits should entirely follow the teaching of Saint Thomas in Scholastic theology and they should consider him their own particular authority. And they should make every effort to ensure that the students are as well disposed toward him as possible. They should nevertheless realize that they ought not be so tied to Saint Thomas that they may not differ from that theology in any issue whatsoever, since even those very ones who most pointedly profess that they are Thomists differ from him now and then; and it is not right that Jesuits be bound more tightly to Saint Thomas than the Thomists themselves are" (175).

64. Peirce presented his mature thinking in a series of lectures delivered at Harvard University from March through May of 1903, and in a series of essays published in the *Monist* in 1905. For a recent edition of these materials, see *The Essential Peirce: Selected Philosophical Writings, Volume 2 (1893–1913)*, ed. the Peirce Edition Project (Bloomington, IN: Indiana University Press, 1998), 133–241, 331–97; hereafter *EP* 2.

65. "Épistre trente-uniesme, à un seigneur d'Église," in *Les Epistres spirituelles du bien-heureux François de Sales, d'heureuse et saincte memoire, evesque et prince de Geneue, Fondateur de l'Ordre de la Visitation saincte Marie* (Lyon: Vincent de Cœur-silly, 1628), 111–37. Reedited in *Œuvres de saint François de Sales*, ed. the Religious of the Visitation (Annecy: J. Niérat, 1892–1935), 2:299–325.

66. Worcester, "The Catholic Sermon," 18.

67. *Introduction à la vie dévote par François de Sales, Évesque et Prélat de Genève* (Lyon: Pierre Rigaud, 1609).

68. Claude recommends the *Introduction* explicitly to his listeners (C 2:452, 4:394) and writes from England in February 1678 that he soon will have a copy for himself (*L* 92). Claude's preaching treats many of the themes that Francis discusses in that book, notably the virtue of humility, the purging of evil inclinations, and the necessity of making a "spiritual retreat."

69. On his life and work, see Thomas Worcester, *Seventeenth-Century Cultural Discourse: France and the Preaching of Bishop Camus* (New York: Mouton de Gruyter, 1997).

70. Charrier, *Histoire*, 1:97. The treatise in question first appeared in René Rapin, *Réflexions sur l'usage de l'Éloquence de ce temps* (Paris: Claude Barbin and François Muguet, 1671), 75–175. Rapin reviewed, corrected, augmented, and republished these reflections in 1672 and again in 1679.

71. C 2:330–31.

72. C 1:29. Claude most likely preached this sermon in 1676.

73. C 1:163, 194, 230, 290; 2:123; 3:458; *ES* 121.

74. C 1:451–52, discussed at length below.

75. C 1:384.

76. C 1:180, 295; 3:78; 4:385.

77. Francis de Sales, "À Monseigneur André Frémyot," *Œuvres de saint François de Sales*, 2:305.

78. C 1:308–10.

79. C 1:7.

80. In his sermon for Trinity Sunday, Claude compares the incomprehensibility of the mystery of the Trinity to the incomprehensibility of the human person: "But we want to understand God, we who have not even understood the least of his works, we

who do not understand ourselves? Who will tell me by what powers the soul stirs the body that it animates and how the body communicates to the soul, which is completely spiritual, the passions by which it is troubled?" (C 1:495).

81. For an approach along these lines, which builds on Peirce, see Donald L. Gelpi, SJ, *The Gracing of Human Experience* (Collegeville, MN: The Liturgical Press, 2001), 282–301.

82. On this theme, see "On the Vicious Habit," n1.

83. I am using the terms *esthetics, ethics,* and *logic* as Peirce uses them in his fifth Harvard lecture (1903; *EP* 2:196–207), which is to say, as all dealing with kinds of goodness. For the development of Peirce's thought on this matter, see Vincent G. Potter, SJ, "Peirce's Analysis of Normative Science," *Transactions of the Charles S. Peirce Society* 2, no. 1 (Spring 1966): 5–32.

84. Peirce situates the sign relation at the center of his philosophy, which in turn serves as the keystone of his scientific structure. For an overview of this structure and its development in Peirce's thought, see Richard Kenneth Atkins, "Restructuring the Sciences: Peirce's Categories and His Classifications of the Sciences," *Transactions of the Charles S. Peirce Society* 42, no. 4 (Fall 2006): 483–500. For an introduction to Peirce's sign theory, see T. L. Short, *Peirce's Theory of Signs* (Cambridge: Cambridge University Press, 2007).

85. See Peirce, "A Letter to William James," in *EP* 2:493–94.

86. For a study of this debate as it played out in Claude's day, see the anthology *La Querelle des anciens et des modernes: xviie–xviiie siècles,* ed. Anne-Marie Lecoq (Paris: Gallimard, 2001).

87. For an important caution against strictly textual treatments of sermons, see Larissa Taylor, *Soldiers of Christ: Preaching in Late Medieval and Reformation France* (New York: Oxford University Press, 1992), 52.

88. Gérard Ferreyrolles, "Rhétorique et christianisme: Esquisse d'une problématique, de Platon à Bossuet," *Rivista di Storia e Letteratura Religiosa* 44, no. 1 (2008): 70.

89. This passage recalls Chrys. *Hom. in Rom 12:20* 2 (PG 51:174.39–49); trans. W. R. W. Stephens, "To Those Who Had Not Attended the Assembly" (NPNF[1] 9:224):

> And this is the reason why he called you leaven (Matt 13:33): for leaven also does not leaven itself, but, little though it is, it affects the whole lump however big it may be. So also do you: although you are few in number, yet be you many and powerful in faith, and in zeal towards God. As then the leaven is not weak on account of its littleness, but prevails owing to its inherent heat, and the force of its natural quality, so you also will be able to bring back a far larger number than yourselves, *if you will* [italics added], to the same degree of zeal as your own.

Chrysostom here implies, as apparent in the expression translated "if you will" (Greek *an thelēte* "if you are willing"), that Christians do not automatically function as salt, leaven, and light to the rest of the world but must *want* to do so. In the context of this sermon, he is exhorting the congregation to refute the arguments, which he considers weak, that friends and family members might have offered for not attending the worship service.

90. La Colombière clearly thinks that Chrysostom understands the leavening effect in general in terms of a duty rather than as a natural result of the indwelling of the Spirit. While the passage quoted in n89 supports this understanding, cf. Chrys. *Diab.* 3:2 (PG 49:266.48–63) where, again with reference to Matt 13:33, Chrysostom suggests

a less willful interpretation. Chrysostom uses the metaphor elsewhere with reference to Eustathius, archbishop of Antioch, who "fermented everyone into the true faith, and . . . didn't give up until God provided Meletius to come and take the whole dough." He likewise refers to Moses and Aaron who, "by circulating like a yeast in the midst of the Egyptians, made many people enthusiasts of their own piety." See Chrys. *Pan. Eust. Ant.* 4 (PG 50:605.4–7, 9–11); trans. Wendy Mayer, "On Saint Eustathius," in *St. John Chrysostom: The Cult of the Saints*, trans. and ed. Wendy Mayer with Bronwen Neil, Popular Patristics Series 31 (Crestwood, NY: St. Vladimir's Seminary Press, 2006), 61.

91. This broad notion of preaching recalls the maxim attributed to Francis of Assisi, "preach the gospel, and if necessary, use words." For the sentiment, see *RegNB* 17 (SB 36:268); trans. Regis J. Armstrong, OFM Cap. et al., "The Earlier Rule (The Rule Without a Papal Seal) (1209/10–1221)," in *The Saint: Volume I of Francis of Assisi: Early Documents*, ed. Regis J. Armstrong, OFM Cap. et al. (New York: New City Press, 1999), 75: "Let no brother preach contrary to the rite and practice of the Church or without the permission of his minister. Let the minister be careful of granting it without discernment to anyone. Let all the brothers, however, preach by their deeds"; cf. *Adm* 6 (SB 36:360); trans. Regis J. Armstrong, OFM Cap. et al., "The Admonitions," in *The Saint*, 131: "Let all of us, brothers, consider the Good Shepherd Who bore the suffering of the cross to save his sheep. The Lord's sheep followed him in tribulation and persecution, in shame and hunger, in weakness and temptation, and in other ways; and for these things they received eternal life from the Lord. Therefore, it is a great shame for us, the servants of God, that the saints have accomplished great things and we want only to receive glory and honor by recounting them."

92. C 1:451–52.

93. For a similar view of reality, see Sang Hyun Lee, *The Philosophical Theology of Jonathan Edwards*, 2nd ed. (Princeton, NJ: Princeton University Press, 2000).

According to Lee, American puritan theologian and philosopher Jonathan Edwards (1703–58) "departed from the traditional Western metaphysics of substance and form and replaced it with a strikingly modern conception of reality as a dynamic network of dispositional forces and habits. Dispositions and habits, conceived as active and ontologically abiding principles, now play the roles substance and form used to fulfill" (4). For discussion of this "dispositionalism" in Edwards's thought, see Michael J. McClymond and Gerald R. McDermott, *The Theology of Jonathan Edwards* (Oxford: Oxford University Press, 2011), 5–6, 103–104, 529–32, 589–98, 646, 660–61.

94. For an introduction to Jansenism, see William Doyle, *Jansenism: Catholic Resistance to Authority from the Reformation to the French Revolution*, Studies in European History (New York: St. Martin's Press, 2000); and Alexander Sedgwick, *Jansenism in Seventeenth-Century France: Voices from the Wilderness* (Charlottesville: University of Virginia Press, 1977).

95. Owen Chadwick, *From Bossuet to Newman*, 2nd ed. (Cambridge: Cambridge University Press, 1987), 16.

96. Robin Briggs, *Communities of Belief: Cultural and Social Tension in Early Modern France* (Oxford: Clarendon Press, 1989), 236.

97. Jean Dagens, "Le xviie siècle, siècle de Saint Augustin," in *Cahiers de l'Association internationale des études françaises* 3, nos. 3–5 (1953): 31–38. For discussion, see Philippe Sellier, "Le Siècle de saint Augustin," *xviie siècle* 135 (1982): 99–102; and Briggs, *Communities of Belief*, 289.

98. See Robin Briggs, *Communities of Belief*, 344; and Jean-Pascal Gay, "Voués à

quelle royaume? Les Jésuites entre vœux de religion et fidélité monarchique: À propos d'un mémoire inédit du P. de la Chaize," *xviie siècle* 57, no. 2 (2005): 285–314.

99. See, for instance, the ending of "On Confession," as well as "On Confidence in God," in the present volume.

100. At least two English-language translations of the Meditations on the Passion have appeared (London, 1876 and 1933), as well as a selection of sermons and meditations, entitled *The Servant of the Sacred Heart* (London: Sands and Company, 1933). More recently, Patricia Fontaine defended a doctoral dissertation for the University of Ottawa entitled "A Translation of Selected Sermons of Father Claude de la [*sic*] Colombière as an Adjunct to James Joyce Scholarship" (PhD diss., University of Ottowa, 1978), <http://www.ruor.uottawa.ca/fr/handle/10393/3763>. Note that the translator appears to have worked from the Charrier edition alone and does not provide notes for the sermons she translated, two of which, entitled "One Master" and "Conscience," respectively, appear retranslated in the present volume.

101. Call number: BX1756 .L22 1684 v.1–4 CRC SMR. This book belongs to both the Counter Reformation Collection (CRC) and the Saint Michael's College Rare Books Collection (SMR). Note that the Kelly Library owns a second copy of Volume 1 (BX1756 .L22 1684 v.1–4 SMR), which contains an engraving of La Colombière that does not appear in the first copy. A reproduction of this engraving appears on p. ii of the present volume.

102. This microfilm is now cataloged in the Kelly Library at BX1756 .L22 1684 v.1–4 mfm SMC.

103. Edgar Swift, "Introduction," *The Vulgate Bible: Douay-Rheims Translation: Volume I: The Pentateuch*, Dumbarton Oaks Medieval Library 1 (Cambridge, MA: Harvard University Press, 2010), ix.

104. For an electronic edition, see Michael Tweedale, ed., *Biblia Sacra juxta Vulgatam Clementinam* (n.p.: n.p.), <http://vulsearch.sf.net/html>. BibleWorks, v.8. The BibleWorks abbreviation vuc associated with a quotation in the notes indicates the text of this edition.

105. Douay-Rheims Bible, 1899 ed. (n.p.: n.p., 1899), BibleWorks, v.8. The Bible-Works abbreviation dra associated with a quotation in the notes indicates the text of this edition.

106. Edgar Swift, "Introduction," xxii.

107. See *The SBL Handbook of Style: For Ancient Near Eastern, Biblical, and Early Christian Studies*, ed. Patrick H. Alexander et al. (Peabody, MA: Hendrickson Publishers, 1999), 73–74.

108. For a bibliography of these editions, see Dominique Bertrand, "The Society of Jesus and the Church Fathers in the Sixteenth and Seventeenth Century," trans. Antoinina Bevan, in *The Reception of the Church Fathers in the West: From the Carolingians to the Maurists*, ed. Irena Backus (New York: Brill, 1997), 2:889–950.

109. The *JECS* style sheet can be accessed through the Johns Hopkins University Press website, <press.jhu.edu/journals>. In accord with *JECS* style, abbreviations of patristic authors and sources follow Albert Blaise, *Dictionnaire latin-français des auteurs chrétiens*, ed. Henri Chirat (Turnhout: Éditions Brepols, 1954), 9–29; and *A Patristic Greek Lexicon*, ed. G. W. H. Lampe (Oxford: Clarendon Press, 1961), xi–xlv.

110. *The Oxford Classical Dictionary*, ed. Simon Hornblower and Antony Spawforth, 3rd ed. rev. (Oxford: Oxford University Press, 2003), xxix–liv.

111. On this point, Wendy Mayer notes that La Colombière probably knew

Chrysostom's works from the Church-endorsed Latin translations available at the time, given that the first modern Greek edition, which Sir Henry Savile (1549–1622) published in 1612–13, fell under the politically-motivated suspicion of the Roman Catholic Church. On this point, see Jean-Louis Quantin, "Du Chrysostome latin au Chrysostome grec: Une histoire européenne (1588–1613)," in *Chrysostomosbilder in 1600 Jahren: Facetten der Wirkungsgeschichte eines Kirchenvaters*, ed. Martin Wallraff and Rudolf Brändle, Arbeiten zur Kirchengeschichte 105 (Berlin: Walter de Gruyter, 2008), 267–346. For the influence of Chrysostom on preachers at the time of La Colombière, see Simon Icard, "Saint Jean Chrysostome: un modèle d'exégèse pour la prédication classique?," in *L'Éloquence de la chaire à l'âge classique*, ed. Anne Régent-Susini, supplement, *Revue Bossuet*, no. 2 (2011): 89–103.

112. *Dictionnaire Universel Contenant généralement tous les mots François. Recueilli et compilé par Messire Antoine Furetière, Abbé de Chalivoy, de l'Académie Françoise* (La Haye: Leers, 1690), hereafter "Furetière." The version of the *Dictionnaire* that I have consulted appears in Gallica, a digital library accessible through the web site of the *Bibliothèque nationale de France* at <gallica.bnf.fr>. As this edition has no page numbers, my citations refer to the entries themselves.

113. On this distinction, see Eugene A. Nida, *Toward a Science of Translating: With Special Reference to Principles and Procedures Involved in Bible Translating* (Leiden: Brill, 1964), 159.

114. *The Chicago Manual of Style*, 16th ed. (Chicago: The University of Chicago Press, 2010), online at < http://www.chicagomanualofstyle.org/home.html >.

1: On the Flight from the World

1. A: *De la fuite du monde* (A 3.57/C 3.57). Little in the text suggests either the audience or the occasion for this discourse, apart from an analogy to a plague victim entering London—an analogy that may allude to the Great Plague (1665–66) of just ten years earlier, which had killed some twenty percent of the city's population. This lack of evidence might suggest that La Colombière did not deliver the sermon before the Duchess of York but rather at his other primary preaching venue, viz., the College Church in Lyon. In fact, the terms *Messieurs* and *Madame* both appear in some sermons, including this one, in the form of direct address, suggesting either that he edited Lyon sermons for London or that he addressed the congregation generally by *Messieurs*, even in the presence of the duchess. This might suggest, for example, that originally he may have addressed a given sermon to the members of a Marian congregation or sodality.

2. vuc: *Tunc Jesus ductus est in desertum a Spiritu*; cf. Mark 1:12–13; Luke 4:1–2. A quotation such as this, presumably taken from the gospel of the day—here, of the First Sunday of Lent—appears in Latin and then in French translation at the head of each sermon. The present edition gives an English translation of only the French version of the quote, placing in the notes the Latin version, taken from the Clementine Vulgate and indicated by the abbreviation. For more on the scripture quotes that appear in the present translation, see the Introduction.

3. With reference to the example of Jesus, Claude introduces the notion of *la retraite* ("the retreat"). Note that *faire retraite* and *se retirer* (Latin *retrahere* "to draw or pull back" [*GL* 6:5153]), both imply movement from one realm into another—a

movement that we can express formally as an *ex* opposed to an *in*. What these terms mean for La Colombière appears gradually as the sermon develops. Note too that the pessimistic idea that one must leave the world so as to live in a Christian manner seems more in keeping with the sensibilities of Port-Royal than with the Jesuits. In this vein, Henri Bremond describes Claude's holiness as "not sad, as one too often says, but more serious than joyful" (*HL* 2:968). Yet Bourdaloue develops the same point in "On the Passion of Christ," viz., that Christ "knew too well that his doctrine could not be relished in a place where one follows only the rules of a worldly wisdom"; and also in "On the Distancing and the Flight from the World" (Bourdaloue, *Œuvres complètes*, 8:173; 7:39–82). Even Francis de Sales, a great promoter of lay spirituality, recognizes the difficulty of living untainted in the world and insists on the importance of making frequent spiritual retreats in the midst of worldly affairs. On this point see Saint Francis de Sales, *Introduction à la vie dévote*, in *Œuvres* (Paris: Gallimard, 1969), 23–24, 96–98.

4. Bernard of Clairvaux expresses sentiments of this sort in his letters to the prior and religious of the Grande Chartreuse (SC 425:216, 246). With reference to Bernard, La Colombière here juxtaposes "the retreat" with "the world." Through an analysis of the preacher's language, I will explore the practical implications of this *fuga mundi* for the preacher's audience, i.e., what La Colombière means by telling his listeners that they must withdraw from the world. Note too that the pair commotion/trouble (*tumulte/ embarras*) introduces a rhetorical *repetitio* (see nn49, 64), which provides formal continuity in the discourse while reinforcing La Colombière's contention that social interaction effectively blocks conversation with God.

5. This qualification underscores the importance for La Colombière of the *fuga mundi*, which provides a key to interpret his preaching.

6. See the Parable of the Sower (Matt 13:1–9; Mark 4:1–9; Luke 8:4–8, 5:1–3).

7. This indicates that La Colombière understands preaching as collaboration between God and the preacher; see the Introduction on this point. La Colombière presents his theology of grace in the second part of this sermon.

8. A: *Ave Maria*, etc. The first exordium of La Colombière's sermons typically concludes with an intercessory prayer, almost always addressed to Mary, the mother of Jesus.

9. A: *des premiers hommes du monde*.

10. A: *n'a pas peu contribué depuis à les corrompre*. One of many examples of litotes, a form of rhetorical understatement that involves denial of the opposite. I have here, as in most cases, translated such figures literally.

11. On this trend, see William Harmless, SJ, *Desert Christians: An Introduction to the Literature of Early Monasticism* (Oxford: Oxford University Press, 2004).

12. As above (n3), La Colombière again speaks in terms that suggest a juxtaposition of spaces, here "civil life" as opposed to "the most distant places." He presents this idea explicitly in the *divisio* at the end of the paragraph.

13. In the second point, La Colombière seems to suggest an apparent contradiction, viz., that one could be converted *in* the world by retreating *from* the world. This suggestion recalls the Johannine theme of being in the world, but not of the world, as in John 17:15–16. On this theme, see also Rom 12:2; 1 Cor 5:9; 2 Cor 6:17; cf. 1 Cor 9:22, 10:32–33.

14. Here La Colombière introduces explicitly the notion of a world-within-a-world, "even among Christians." This idea challenges a conception of the world as a place apart, in that "the world" can appear where one does not expect it to appear—or even in a context that seems to exclude it by definition, e.g., "even among Christians." The mutu-

ally exclusive *in/ex* categories (n3) cannot account for this interpenetration of realities.

15. John 14:17.

16. A: *Mundus me priorem vobis odio habuit*; cf. John 15:18 VUC: *Si mundus vos odit, scitote quia me priorem vobis odio habuit.*

17. La Colombière here identifies "the world" with "reprobates" who live among the God-fearing—a notion that renders thinkable the idea of a world within a world. This notion correlates with the interpretation of the Parable of the Weeds that follows the parable itself: the field is the world and the good seed is the children of the kingdom, while the weeds are the children of the wicked one (Matt 13:38). La Colombière develops this understanding at length in the following paragraph.

18. John 17:9 VUC: *Non pro mundo rogo, sed pro his quos dedisti mihi.*

19. A: *pour ses crimes.* Here and throughout this volume, I generally translate *crime* as "sin" when La Colombière's usage seems to follow the second entry in Furetière: "Crime, in terms of Devotion, is said of all those sins [*pechez*] that one has committed against God, be they great or small. The man most darkened by sins [*crimes*] obtains absolution for them by true repentance. The devout often make sins [*des crimes*] of petty things."

20. Gal 6:14; 1 Cor 6:2.

21. A: *Quicumque voluerit esse amicus saeculi hujus, inimicus Dei constituitur*; cf. Jas 4:4 VUC: *quicumque ergo voluerit amicus esse saeculi hujus, inimicus Dei constituitur.*

22. This reference to *les lois du faux honneur* calls to mind the principle of "honor among thieves." It also suggests the practice of following through on a promise so as not to lose face, even when that promise obliges one to sin, e.g., as when Herodias demands that Herod make good on his public vow by delivering to her the head of John the Baptist on a plate (Matt 14:9–11; Mark 6:26).

23. La Colombière juxtaposes two contexts: religious life, which the founders of the various religious orders established in order to facilitate the acquisition of virtue; and the world, which the demon arranges so as to inspire vice. This juxtaposition suggests two realms, of which we can conceive using the same, mutually-exclusive categories *in/ex*. According to this model, either a person is in the world or has left the world. La Colombière then explains that in the world, the demon tries to introduce certain stimuli through the senses in order to provoke a change in the individual.

24. La Colombière introduces here a major motif in his preaching, viz., the theme of corruption or contagion, i.e., the idea that people take on the negative characteristics of their environment (see nn29, 34 below).

25. A: *galanterie.* La Colombière seems to mean the exercise of social skill, especially by a man toward a woman, in order to gain favor.

26. A: *on sent Dieu qui se retire et on s'accoutume déjà à son absence.* The notion of habituation (*l'accoutumance*), which plays a central role in La Colombière's preaching, comes to the fore in his discussions of vice, e.g., in "On the Vicious Habit."

27. For a development of this theme, see "On Venial Sin."

28. This observation calls into question the interpretation of a retreat as a place apart from the world (see n13 above). Furetière defines *cloistre* ("cloister") first as an "enclosed dwelling where canons and religious live." He then notes that *cloistre* "is said more particularly of enclosed monasteries of religious men or women," and that "people who have renounced the world retreat into a *cloistre*." This latter definition effectively establishes "cloister" in opposition to "the world." Yet the fact that La Colombière

affirms that "there is good reason to fear even in cloisters" suggests that the flight from the world into a sanctuary is not enough to keep one safe. Indeed, he seems to be saying that whatever characterizes the world as such has the ability to enter into spaces defined in opposition to the world. For this reason, it seems more coherent to interpret *monde* ("world"), as La Colombière employs the word, not in spatial terms but in terms of actualized tendencies, e.g., as Bourdaloue refers to *l'esprit du monde* ("the spirit of the world") (Bourdaloue, *Œuvres complètes*, 8:187). Claude's discussion of the world in terms of vice supports this reading. For an analysis of this explanation in contemporary philosophical categories, see the Introduction.

29. La Colombière develops the image of evil as contagious (see n24 above and n34 below).

30. Presumably Solomon, "the son of David, king of Israel" (Prov 1:1 DRA), whom Proverbs indicates as its author (Prov 10:1, 25:1; cf. 30:1, 31:1). According to tradition, Solomon's request for wisdom rather than for long life, riches, or the lives of his enemies pleased God, who in turn gave him the wisdom for which he had asked, while also giving him the riches, honor, and long life for which he had not asked (Prov 3:9–14).

31. A: *Ne ambules cum homine furioso, ne forte discas semitas ejus*; cf. Prov 22:24–25 VUC: *neque ambules cum viro furioso: ne forte discas semitas ejus*.

32. A: *Et cependant on peut dire que de tous les vices la colère est celui dont l'exemple a le moins de malignité*. Furetière defines *malignité* as the "bad quality of something that causes evil." He illustrates this definition by using the word in the following sentence: "the plague only comes from the *malignité* of infected air." This suggests that La Colombière associates the evil of the world with malicious humors or temperaments that could spread like a disease from person to person—as indicated at nn24, 29 above, and n34 below. Based on this analysis, we can conclude that, for La Colombière, "the world" refers not so much to a particular place as to a worldly spirit or spirits that coincide with those communicable, general tendencies he calls "vices" (n28 and "On the Vicious Habit"). Such an interpretation makes it easy to see how "there is good reason to fear even in cloisters," given that vices, not being particular and circumscribed—like a space—but rather general and communicable—like a disease— can cross boundaries and thus inhabit multiple realities. Given this interpretation, the question arises: is it possible to retreat from a general, communicable reality, e.g., from anger, pride, or mendacity? And if so, then what might this mean? The answer that emerges from his preaching as a whole seems to be *no*: freedom from vicious realities comes not from moving about in space but from taking on divine habits, i.e., virtues.

33. 1 Cor 5:6–8; cf. Gal 5:9.

34. See nn24, 29 above.

35. Gen 19; cf. Luke 17:28–30; Gen 11–14.

36. Gen 6:5–8.

37. A: *le premier dans un païs, & le second dans un siécle extrémement corrumpu*; cf. C: *le premier, dans un palais, et le second, dans un siècle extrêmement corrompu*. Although Lot did not live in a palace, except arguably during captivity (Gen 14:11–12), the singular *corrompu* indicates that *corrompu* modifies only *siècle*, which would render the unmodified *païs* less intelligible, in context, than *palais*, for which reason I read with the Charrier edition.

38. In fact, scripture says only that Noah did "all things which God commanded him" (Gen 6:22 DRA); the Bible makes no issue of the behavior of others during the time at which Noah fulfilled God's commandments.

39. Cf. Chrys. *Hom. in Gen.* 43.1 (PG 54.396); trans. Robert C. Hill, "Homily 43," in *Saint John Chrysostom: Homilies on Genesis 18–45*, FOTC 82 (Washington, DC: Catholic University of America Press, 1990), 437–38: "The extraordinary degree of this good man's virtue is really remarkable in that, though living in the midst of such villains, he not only had grown more indifferent but even gave evidence of much greater virtue. . . . Where now are those who say that it is not possible for someone growing up in the environment of the city to keep one's virtue, but for this is required retreat and a life in the mountains, and that it is not possible for the man of the house, with a wife and with children and servants to look after, to be virtuous? . . . I say this, not to oppose retreat from the cities nor to discourage life in the mountains and deserts, but to show that for a person intent on remaining vigilant and alert none of these things proves an obstacle."

40. While La Colombière seems to return to the spatial metaphor, suggesting a "middle course" (*milieu*) between the "desert" and the "great world" where one can find salvation, we can interpret this "middle course" in non-spatial terms, as an idea, attitude, or disposition. This interpretation has the advantage of accounting for cases such as those of Lot and Noah, who found salvation in the midst of the world.

41. Periodic sentences like this one, more effective in the hearing than in the reading, again reveal the influence of La Colombière's formation in classical rhetoric.

42. A: *tribunal de la pénitence*. The first entry that Furetière gives for *pénitence* suggests something more like repentance than punishment—*Amendement de mœurs, conversion, satisfaction qu'on fait à Dieu pour les pechez qu'on a commis*; the second entry specifies sacramental reconciliation or "confession"—*un vray Sacrement, par lequel Dieu pardonne aux pecheurs les fautes qu'ils ont commises, quand ils en sont bien reprenants, après les avoir confessées au Prestre qui en absoud*; the third refers to the punishment itself that the penitent receives—*la peine que le Confesseur impose pour la satisfaction des peches dont il absoud*. The translations for *pénitence* appearing in this volume follow Furetière, specifying the meaning of *pénitence* according to the context of the sermon.

43. A: *la règle du monde la plus austère*, i.e., one would have an easier time following the most strict monastic rule than living in the world while resisting its temptations.

44. A: *Quid tibi necesse est in ea versari domo, in qua necesse habeas quotidie, aut perire, aut vincere? Quis unquam mortalium juxta viperam securos somnos capit, quae, et si not percutiat, certe sollicitat?* Cf. Hier. *Ep.* 117.3.20–23 (CSEL 55:425–26): *quid tibi necesse est in ea uersari domo, in qua necesse habeas cotidie aut perire aut uincere? quisquamne mortalium iuxta uiperam securus somnos capit? quae ut non percutiat, certe sollicitat*; trans. William Henry Fremantle, George Lewis, and William Gibson Martley, "To a Mother and Daughter Living in Gaul" (NPNF[2] 6:216).

45. The point, however, is not to retain one's innocence but to become holy—a process that God facilitates. The sermon "On the Mercy of God toward the Sinner" makes clear that God treats sinners with kindness, pursuing them in whatever state he finds them and preceding them upon their return (see: below). For the circumstances attending genuine penance, see "On Relapsing."

46. La Colombière understands grace in terms of divine initiative that "clarifies the mind and . . . warms the will" (p. x). As the preacher describes it, God brings this about either directly within the person or, more often, by influencing external circumstances. As regards the theme of the sermon, La Colombière points out that the many distractions of the world make it difficult both for God to bring about graced circumstances there and for people living there to fall under their influence.

47. The text reads *ce*, which could refer either to *conversion* or to *grâce sur-*

naturelle, from the preceding sentence. While substituting "supernatural grace" makes the sentence incoherent, substituting "conversion" complements the reference to "change" (*changer*) at the end of the phrase. The passage then presents conversion as carrying out the plans that God indicates.

48. A: *il faut que ses conseils soient exécutés*. This does not specify whether La Colombière indicates a moral or a physical necessity, i.e., that man ought to do what his heart suggests, or that he in fact cannot do otherwise. However, the description, in the following paragraph, of grace as "a light that clarifies the mind and . . . warms the will" suggests the former.

49. See n4 above and n64 below.

50. Note that the action of God through the senses opposes that of the demon described in the first part of the sermon (n23).

51. La Colombière seems to understand the qualifier *efficace* as a post-factum judgment that divine activity has in fact come to bear in a given case. Of course, one can make this judgment only if the individual already has converted.

52. The question of what it means to call this grace "effective" lies at the heart of the late sixteenth-century controversies *de auxiliis*, which have to do with how to think of the human person as both under divine guidance and free to choose. On the Jesuit perspective at the time, see Philippe Lécrivain, "Liberté et grâce au XVIIe siècle et la part prise par la Compagnie de Jésus dans ce débat," in *Dieu au XVIIe siècle: Crises et renouvellements du discours*, ed. Henri Laux and Dominique Salin (Paris: Éditions facultés jésuites de Paris, 2002), 191–212. La Colombière seems here to define "effective" or "efficacious" grace as God's choosing circumstances advantageous for the individual's progress. This grace leaves one free not to take advantage of the circumstances and thus absolves God from any responsibility for sin and failure.

53. See, for example, Cant 3:2.

54. John 1:23 vuc: *Ego vox clamantis in deserto*; cf. Matt 3:3; Mark 1:3; Luke 3:4; Isa 40:3; Claude's sermon "On Conscience" takes Luke 3:4 as its epigram. Note that John the Baptist does not, as La Colombière suggests here, identify himself with the voice of God. For the story of John's death, see Matt 14:1–12 and Mark 6:14–29.

55. This unknown source seems to be speculating upon both the implication that the Israelites had not engaged in worship of the Lord while in Egypt (Exod 3), and the explanation of Moses: "now if we kill those things which the Egyptians worship, in their presence, they will stone us. We will go three days' journey into the wilderness: and we will sacrifice to the Lord our God, as he has commanded us" (8:26–27 DRA). On this point, see Carol L. Meyers, *Exodus* (Cambridge: Cambridge University Press, 2005), 83. On the history of sacrifice in Israel, see Roland de Vaux, *Ancient Israel: Its Life and Institutions* (Grand Rapids, MI: Eerdmans, and Livonia, MI: Dove Booksellers, 1997), 424–32.

56. Death, judgment, and hell represent three of the four "last things" of the Christian tradition, the fourth being heaven: La Colombière devotes sermons to each of the three former themes (A 3.48/C 3.49; A 3.52/C 3.53 and A 3.53/C 3.54; and A 3.54/C 3.55, respectively). An overview of these themes might begin with *NCE* 5:332; for a collection of interdenominational studies, see *The Last Things: Biblical and Theological Perspectives on Eschatology*, ed. Carl E. Braaten and Robert W. Jensen (Grand Rapids, MI: Eerdmans, 2002).

57. A: *Cor meum conturbatum est in me, et timor mortis cecidit super me; dolores inferni circumdederunt me, et contexerunt me tenebrae, et dixit: Quis mihi dabit pennas ut columbae, et volabo, et requiescam?* Cf. Pss 54:5, 17:6, 54:6b-7 vuc: *Cor meum*

conturbatum est in me, et formido mortis cecidit super me. . . . Dolores inferni circum-dederunt me. . . . et contexerunt me tenebrae. Et dixi: Quis dabit mihi pennas sicut columbae, et volabo, et requiescam?

58. A: *un lieu propre.* La Colombière appears to play on the multiple meanings of *propre* in use at the time, viz., essential to some particular being, necessary to succeed, clean and neat, belonging to someone, etc.

59. In other words, those who leave the world during their active life have time to enjoy being apart from the world.

60. This probably refers to Alphonse-Louis du Plessis de Richelieu (1582–1653), the older brother of Armand Jean du Plessis de Richelieu, Cardinal-Duc de Richelieu (1585–1642), Minister of State under Louis XIII. Having spent twenty years in a Carthusian monastery, Alphonse-Louis was made to accept the archepiscopal chair of Lyon, where he died in 1653.

61. While Charrier, in a footnote to his edition of the sermons, attributes this sentiment to Louis XIII (1601–43), Lloyd Moote, author of *Louis XIII: The Just* (Berkeley: University of California Press, 1991), wrote me that he does not think the passage could refer to his subject. Note too that the only other French king reigning "at the beginning" of the seventeenth century is Henry IV (1553–1610), who was assassinated.

62. Ps 10:7 VUC: *Pluet super peccatores laqueos.*

63. Note that in speaking to the members of his audience (*vous-même*), La Colombière focuses on the heart and its passions, inclinations, and habits (*les passions, les inclinations, les habitudes*). These notions of tendency and disposition constitute the central theme of his preaching and suggest a fundamentally dynamic vision of the human person. For a philosophical interpretation of this theme, see the Introduction.

64. The pair difficulty/confusion (*trouble/embarras*) picks up on the *repetitio* from earlier (nn4, 49 above), providing rhetorical closure while driving home the main point of the sermon.

65. Matt 5:28.

66. Col 3:3.

2: One Should Serve Only One Master

1. A: *On ne doit servir qu'un maître* (A 3.58/C 3.58).

2. VUC: *Nemo potest duobus dominis servire*; cf. Luke 16:13. This verse also appears as the epigraph for Bourdaloue's sermon "On the Distancing and the Flight from the World" (Bourdaloue, *Œuvres complètes*, 7:39–82).

3. The term *monde* ("world") in this sermon is best interpreted in light of the commentary that accompanies "On the Flight from the World."

4. A: *Ave Maria.*

5. On this point, see the Message to Laodicea (Rev 3:14–22).

6. Furetière (1690) defines *Carnaval* as the "Time of merrymaking that is counted from the Kings [Epiphany] until Lent." To illustrate the events of this time, he writes that "Balls, parties, and marriages take place primarily during *Carnaval*." This period would correspond roughly to the contemporary celebration in the United States of Mardi Gras, a celebration known for its excess and traditionally understood as a precursor to the austerity of Lent, the latter with its practices of fasting and abstaining from meat. Scholarly interpretation of the meaning of Carnival differs. While Bakhtin

explains that "carnival celebrated temporary liberation from the prevailing truth and from the established order," marking "the suspension of all hierarchical rank, privileges, norms, and prohibitions" (*Rabelais and His World*, trans. Hélène Iswolsky [Blooming-ton, IN: Indiana University Press, 1984], 10), Ingvild Salid Gilhus argues that the mean-ing of certain Carnival forms "must be sought in relation to the Catholic Church and to the religious universe of that Church" ("Carnival in Religion: The Feast of Fools in France," *Numen* 37, fasc. 1 [June 1990]: 25). Four discourses on "The Last Days of Car-nival" appear in the first edition of La Colombière's *Sermons* (A 3.44–47/C 3.45–48).

7. This calls to mind the moral standard of Jesus: "You have heard that it was said to them of old: You will not commit adultery. But I say to you, that whoever will look on a woman to lust after her, has already committed adultery with her in his heart" (Matt 5:27–28 DRA).

8. Matt 26:41.

9. This recalls the Aristotelian definition of virtue as "a kind of middle state, in that it is something which aims at and hits the mean" (*Nic. Eth.* 2.6.1106b 27–28; trans. C. C. W. Taylor, *Nicomachean Ethics: Books II–IV* [Oxford: Oxford University Press, 2006], 9). For the gospel ideal, see Matt 7:13; Luke 13:24.

10. Matt 5:43–46; Luke 6:27–28, 32–36.

11. Matt 6:25–34; cf. Luke 12:22–32. This passage follows the admonition of Je-sus in Matthew that one cannot serve two masters (Matt 6:24).

12. Matt 5:48 VUC: *Estote ergo vos perfecti, sicut et Pater vester caelestis perfectus est*; cf. Matt 19:21 VUC, which also uses a form of *perfectus*.

13. Quite likely an allusion to the vow that La Colombière professed during ter-tianship (*ES* 101–08). Regarding this vow, see the Introduction. For another probable reference to this vow, see "On Confidence in God."

14. Here La Colombière introduces his understanding of *sainteté* ("holiness"). The text reads: *Or la perfection, la sainteté et surtout celle de Dieu . . . renferme tout; c'est un dévouement entier de tout ce qu'il y a dans l'homme . . . un assemblage de toutes sortes de vertus. Vous ne sauriez lui en ôter une seule sans la détruire.* In this sentence, *en* refers to *vertus*; *lui* refers either to the "collection" (*assemblage*) of virtues, to the virtuous man, or to his holiness; and the final object pronoun *la* indicates *sainteté*. For La Colombière, holiness consists of virtues in the same way that a chain is made up of links: just as the removal of one link would break the chain, so would the removal of one virtue destroy the integrity of one's holiness. Because holiness expresses itself in virtue, the presence of holi-ness implies that virtue will appear in the various areas of the holy person's life. For this reason, a saint by definition could not remain habitually angry, since holiness manifests itself necessarily in virtue and as such precludes such vices as habitual anger; La Colom-bière develops this theme in the following paragraphs. For a discussion of the unity of the virtues in Thomas Aquinas, see Eleonore Stump, "The Non-Aristotelian Character of Aquinas's Ethics: Aquinas on the Passions," *Faith and Philosophy* 28, no. 1 (2011): 33–34.

15. Cf. Mark 9:23 DRA: "I do believe, Lord: help my unbelief."

16. A: *il ne lui donne.*

17. Mark 12:30 VUC: *ex tota anima tua, et ex tota mente tua, et ex tota virtute tua*; cf. Matt 22:37; Luke 10:27; Deut 6:5, 26:16; Sir 7:33.

18. Luke 10:42 VUC: *porro unum est necessarium.*

19. For context, see *Witness of the Body: The Past, Present, and Future of Christian Martyrdom*, ed. Michael L. Budde and Karen Scott (Grand Rapids, MI: Eerdmans, 2011), 3–60.

20. Matt 27:28–31; Mark 15:17–20; John 19:1–5.

21. Cf. the admonition of Jesus to pay the temple tax (Matt 17:24–27) and Paul's discussions of not causing scandal by what one eats (Rom 14:13–23; 1 Cor 8, 10:23–33), both of which suggest a contrary attitude toward appearances.

22. This kind of pretense would contradict the gospel admonition to "love your enemies" (Matt 5:44; Luke 6:27 DRA).

23. The ancient idea that repeated actions form habits plays a central role in Claude's notion of holiness as the sum total of all virtue. For more on these themes, see "On the Flight from the World" and "On the Vicious Habit." Note that, as La Colombière puts it here, to expect a certain behavior of a saint is practically equivalent to expecting it of the corresponding habit, which supports an understanding of the human person as a network of dispositions (Introduction).

24. For the most part, La Colombière here follows the account in Luke 23. For a study of, and select bibliography concerning, the passion and trial of Jesus, see Gerard S. Sloyan, *Jesus on Trial: A Study of the Gospels*, 2nd ed. (Minneapolis: Fortress Press, 2006).

25. A: *parricide*. Furetière gives the following as the second of two entries for *parricide*: *se dit aussi du meurtre d'une personne sacrée, comme celle des Rois & des Prelats. On a commis d'horribles parricides en la personne de nos Rois. Les Juifs firent le plus grand des parricides en crucifiant le Messie.*

26. A: *absous*. Furetière defines *absous* as *Affranchy ou delivré de crime* and goes on to say that *se dit aussi en matiere civile*, giving the following illustration: *Un defendeur conclut toûjours à être renvoyé quitte & absous de la demande qu'on luy a faite.*

27. Luke 23:16 VUC: *Emendatum ergo illum dimittam.*

28. Matt 27:19.

29. A: *Quamobrem hoc parum non est parum, imo vero est fere totum.*

30. 1 Kgs 11:1–13.

31. Cf. Job 31:1 VUC: *Pepigi foedus cum oculis meis, ut ne cogitarem quidem de virgine*; DRA: "I made a covenant with my eyes, that I would not so much as think upon a virgin."

32. See the story of David and Bathsheba (2 Sam 11–12).

33. On mortal and venial sin, see the sermons consecrated to those themes in the present volume.

34. Acts 17:28.

35. A: *sa.*

36. Matt 6:24 VUC: *aut unum sustinebit, et alterum contemnet.*

37. The idea is that everything that human beings possess, they have received from God; and that everything that God possesses, he has given to them. This passage recalls the *Contemplatio ad amorem*, which La Colombière would have used for meditation during his long retreats; see Ignatius of Loyola, *Ejercicios espirituales* 230–37 (MHSI 100:306–11).

38. Sanctifying or habitual grace, that permanent disposition by which God perfects the soul and enables it to live and act with God, can be lost by serious sin but recovered through perfect contrition or sacramental reconciliation. Actual grace, as distinct from habitual grace, refers to those transient interventions by which God helps the individual to act. La Colombière would have learned these concepts from his study of scholastic theology. For discussion of grace in Thomas Aquinas, see Stephen J. Duffy, *The Dynamics of Grace: Perspectives in Theological Anthropology* (Collegeville, MN: Liturgical Press, 1994), 121–70. In the current edition, see also "On the Relapse."

39. See n17 above.

40. John 20:28 vuc: *Dominus meus et Deus meus.* La Colombière cites the profession of faith that Thomas makes in the divinity of Jesus.

41. Phil 2:5–8.

42. Matt 11:28–30.

43. On God's answering of prayer, see Matt 7:7–8, 21:22; Mark 11:24; Luke 11:9–10; John 14:13–14, 16:24.

3: On Care for Salvation

1. A: *Du soin du salut* (A 3.59/C 3.59). Although the title suggests that La Colombière plans to focus on salvation, he spends more than half the discourse discussing success in temporal concerns. God's sovereignty operates as the unifying principle in both areas, meaning effectively that all success depends upon God's intervention.

2. vuc: *filii hujus saeculi prudentiores filiis lucis in generatione sua sunt.*

3. La Colombière follows Thomas Aquinas in asserting that true prudence implies both the proper goal and the means to reach that goal (C 1:17; *ST* IIa-IIae q.47). In this sense, worldly prudence, which lacks the first element, is merely skill.

4. Perhaps an allusion to Pierre Charron, *De la sagesse* (Bordeaux: S. Millanges, 1602); 2nd ed., ed. G.-M. de La Rochemaillet (Paris: D. Douceur, 1604). Jesuit François Garasse (1585–1631) vigorously attacked this work for its secularism. For his part, La Colombière identifies *sagesse* as the "particular character of the second person" of the Trinity (C 1:106, 3:118), thus associating it closely with holiness, which he casts as "true wisdom" in contrast to worldly wisdom (C 1:1–3, 372). On the secularization of the ancient idea of wisdom and its transformation on the threshold of the modern era from an intellectual to a moral virtue, see Eugene F. Rice, *The Renaissance Idea of Wisdom*, Harvard Historical Monographs 37 (Cambridge, MA: Harvard University Press, 1958), 149–77.

5. Rom 8:5–8. Aquinas discusses sham prudence in *ST* IIa-IIae q.55.

6. A: *Ave Maria.*

7. A: *hommes.*

8. Wis 9:14 vuc: *incertae providentiae nostrae.*

9. On the relationship between nature and grace, see "On the Flight from the World."

10. A: *Prudentia est amor, ex quibus adjuvatur, ab eis quibus impeditur sagaciter eligens*; cf. Aug. *Mor. eccl.* 1.15.25 (CSEL 90:29–30): *prudentia amor ea quibus adiuuatur ab eis quibus impeditur sagaciter seligens*; trans. Roland J. Teske, *The Manichean Debate* (WSA 1.19:43). Aquinas cites this passage in *ST* IIa-IIae q.47 a.1 obj.1.

11. A: *la.*

12. Ps 32:10 vuc: *reprobat consilia principum.*

13. Ibid.: *reprobat autem cogitationes populorum, et reprobat consilia principum.*

14. Jdt 5:24 vuc: *perquire si est aliqua iniquitas eorum in conspectu Dei eorum: ascendamus ad illos, quoniam tradens tradet illos Deus eorum tibi.*

15. Ps 32:16 vuc: *Non salvatur rex per multam virtutem.*

16. Ibid.: *et gigas non salvabitur in multitudine virtutis suae.*

17. Ps 32:17 vuc: *Fallax equus ad salutem.*

18. 2 Sam 18:9.

19. A: *ce juge qui prétend se faire des amis en faisant des malheureux.* To render the second part of the phrase "by making people miserable" would make more sense in English, but it would lose the rhetorical effect of the parallel structure: the judge wants to make one thing by making another, incongruous thing.

20. See Ezek 23, esp. vv. 40, 48, which, although not dealing with legal proscriptions, express this sentiment. For the vanity of ornamentation and cosmetics, see Jer 4:30.

21. Gen 3.

22. Gen 37, 42:6.

23. Exod 1:12 VUC: *Quantoque opprimebant eos, tanto magis multiplicabantur, et crescebant.*

24. For the story of Saul's campaign against David and David's rise to the throne of Judah, see 1 Sam 18:5–2 Sam 2:7.

25. John 11:47–57.

26. Aug. *Ev. Io.* 49.26 (CCL 36:432): *Temporalia perdere timuerunt, et uitam aeternam non cogitauerunt, ac sic utrumque amiserunt*; trans. John Rettig, *St. Augustine: Tractates on the Gospel of John, 28–54* (FC 88:258): "They were afraid of losing temporal possessions and gave no thought to eternal life, and so they lost each."

27. La Colombière makes a running commentary on Psalm 51, beginning here with v. 3.

28. A: *Propterea Deus te in finem, & emigrabit te de tabernaculo tuo, & radicem tuam de terra viventium*; cf. Ps 51:7 VUC: *Propterea Deus destruet te in finem; evellet te, et emigrabit te de tabernaculo tuo, et radicem tuam de terra viventium.*

29. Ps 51:8 VUC: *Videbunt justi, et timebunt; et super eum ridebunt.*

30. Ps 51:8–9 VUC: *et dicent: Ecce homo qui non posuit Deum adjutorem suum; sed speravit in multitudine divitiarum suarum, et praevaluit in vanitate sua.*

31. I.e., the strength of God.

32. A: *Ecce homo.* The most famous occurrence of this expression appears in John 19:5 VUC. Alluding to this particular passage seems strange, however, given that in it Pilate presents Jesus to the people, declaring that he finds no reason to execute him. For the same expression elsewhere in the VUC, see Ps 51:9; Matt 11:19, 12:10; Luke 2:25, 7:34, 14:2.

33. Ps 51:10 VUC: *Ego autem, sicut oliva fructifera in domo Dei; speravi in misericordia Dei, in aeternum et in saeculum saeculi.*

34. La Colombière develops this theme at length in "On Confidence in God."

35. Prov 23:4 VUC: *prudentiae tuae ponde modum.*

36. Ps 120:2 VUC: *Auxilium meum a Domino, qui fecit caelum et terram.*

37. On this theme, see "On the Flight from the World."

38. A: *c'est assez on n'en demande pas davantage?* C: *c'est assez; on n'en demande pas davantage.*

39. A: *une chimère.*

40. A: *Nous faisons les habiles où il ne s'agit de rien.* The point seems to be that we come up with brilliant plans but for trivial projects.

41. Luke 10:25 VUC: *quid faciendo vitam aeternam possidebo?*

42. A: *Quid haec ad vitam aeternam?* This quote, which sometimes appears in the form *quid hoc ad aeternitatem?*, is often attributed to, among others, Italian Jesuit Aloysius Gonzaga (1568–91). The first biography of Aloysius is Virgilio Cepari, *Vita del Beato Luigi Gonzaga della Compagnia di Giesu* (Rome: Luigi Zannetti, 1606), French

and Latin translations of which appeared in 1608 (*BCJ* 2:957–60). While the quote does not appear in that edition, Cepari writes in chapter 27: "When the Father [Robert Bellarmine, the confessor of Aloysius,] told [Aloysius] that the desire of death in order to be united with God, was not wrong of itself, provided there was due resignation, and that many ancient and modern saints had a like desire, Aloysius gave himself up entirely with a new earnestness to the thought of eternal life." See Virgil Cepari, SJ, *Life of Saint Aloysius Gonzaga*, ed. Francis Goldie, SJ (New York: Benziger Brothers, 1891), 220. For commentary on the cult of Saint Aloysius, see Oliver Logan, "San Luigi Gonzaga: Princeling-Jesuit and Model for Catholic Youth," in *Saints and Sanctity*, Studies in Church History 47, ed. Peter Clarke and Tony Claydon (Woodbridge, Suffolk: Boydell Press for the Ecclesiastical History Society, 2011), 248–57.

43. Matt 16:26 vuc: *Quid enim prodest homini, si mundum universum lucretur, animae vero suae detrimentum patiatur?*

44. In all likelihood, La Colombière had in mind such missionaries as Isaac Jogues (1607–46) and Jean de Brébeuf (1593–1649), French Jesuits who were martyred while working among the native peoples of North America. For accounts of the Jesuit missions in New France, see MHSI 96, 116, 130, 135, 138, 144, 146, 149, 154.

45. A: *que je l'aime autant que vous l'aimez, afin que je donne tout pour elle, &.* This phrase does not appear in the Charrier edition.

4: On Mortal Sin

1. A: *Du péché mortel* (A 4,61/C 4,60). Since mortal or serious sin sets the norm for sin, I have followed Charrier in ordering this sermon before the one on venial sin. The word *mortal* comes from the Latin *mortalis*, "subject to death," from the root *mors*, "death." According to tradition, mortal sin causes the death of the soul by separating the sinner from God completely (1 John 5:16–17).

2. vuc: *Ecce ascendimus Jerosolymam, et filius hominis tradetur principibus sacerdotum, et scribis, et condemnabunt eum morte*; cf. Mark 10:33; Luke 18:31–33. The Anisson edition has *Hierosolimam* and *Sacerdotam*.

3. Matt 20:19 vuc: *et tradent eum gentibus ad illudendum, et flagellandum, et crucifigendum.*

4. Luke 18:34 vuc: *Et ipsi nihil horum intellexerunt.*

5. Heb 6:6. Scholars in general today reject Pauline authorship of Hebrews and question which audience the text addresses. For commentary, see Alan C. Mitchell, *Hebrews*, Sacra Pagina 13, ed. Daniel J. Harrington, SJ (Collegeville, MN: Liturgical Press, 2007), 2–6, 11–13.

6. 1 Cor 2:8. Paul does not specify "the Jews" here, referring generally to "the princes of this world" (*tōn archontōn tou aiōnos toutou*). In fact, recent scholarship suggests that Paul had a much more balanced opinion of the Jewish people than La Colombière implies. On this point, see Edward Kessler, *An Introduction to Jewish-Christian Relations* (Cambridge: Cambridge University Press, 2010), 40–44.

7. A: *Ave Maria.*

8. A: *Aequum est subditum esse deo*; 2 Macc 9:12 vuc: *Justum est subditum esse Deo.* La Colombière develops this theme at length in "On Submission to the Will of God." The king in question is Antiochus IV Epiphanes (ca. 215–164 BCE), ruler of the Seleucid Empire (175–164 BCE), whom scripture characterizes as "impious" (2 Macc

9:9 VUC: *ita ut de corpore impii vermes scaturirent, ac viventis in doloribus carnes ejus effluerent, odore etiam illius et foetore exercitus gravaretur*). La Colombière also references him in "On Conscience" and "On Submission to the Will of God."

9. On being subject to authorities, see Rom 13:1–7; on paying taxes, see Mark 12:13–17; cf. Matt 22:15–22; Luke 20:20–26.

10. Ps 126:1 VUC: *Nisi Dominus custodierit civitatem, frustra vigilat qui custodit eam.*

11. A: *Est dictum, factum vel concupitum contra legem aeternam*; cf. Aug. *Faust.* 22.27 (CSEL 25.1:621): *Ergo peccatum est factum uel dictum uel concupitum aliquid contra aeternam legem*; trans. Roland Teske, *Answer to Faustus a Manichaean* (WSA 1.20:317): "A sin, therefore, is a deed, word, or desire contrary to the eternal law."

12. 2 Cor 3:5; cf. Rom 13:1; 1 Cor 2:12, 6:12, 7:7, 11:11–12; Eph 2:4–10.

13. An allusion to the story of Joseph and Potiphar's wife: Joseph is sold into slavery to Potiphar, who makes Joseph head of his household, and Potiphar's wife tries to seduce Joseph (Gen 39).

14. Gen 39:9 VUC: *quomodo ergo possum hoc malum facere, et peccare in Deum meum?*

15. In 16 BCE, Cornelius Cinna, grandson of Roman triumvir Pompey, was accused of conspiring to kill the Roman Emperor Augustus, who pardoned him and later allowed him to be consul. See Mark Everson Davies and Hilary Swain, *Aspects of Roman History 82 BC–AD 14: A Source-Based Approach* (New York: Routledge, 2010), 282. Cinna is the main character in the tragedy of the same name, appearing in 1639 and published in 1643, by the Jesuit-educated dramatist Pierre Corneille (1606–84). La Colombière may have expected his audience to be familiar with the story of Cinna, if not from the ancient sources then from this contemporary work.

16. A: *Auguste, son successeur, ayant pardonné à Cinna le complot qu'il avait formé contre sa vie.*

17. This story appears in the *Legenda sanctorum* (ca. 1260). Committed to "the denunciation of vice and all iniquity," Saint Ambrose (ca. 340–98) took the emperor Theodosius (ca. 346–95) to task for ordering the bloody and indiscriminate suppression of a riot in Thessalonica. In punishment for his war crimes, Ambrose would not permit him to enter the Milan cathedral. Finding the emperor in tears, his army commander Rufinus offered to speak with Ambrose. Upon seeing him, however, Ambrose said: "You act like an impudent dog, Rufinus! You, the perpetrator of such a slaughter, you don't wipe the shame from your face, you don't blush while you bark at the divine majesty!" Theodosius later received public penance from Ambrose and was reconciled to the Church. See Jacobus de Voragine, *The Golden Legend: Readings on the Saints*, trans. William Granger Ryan (Princeton, NJ: Princeton University Press, 1995), 1:236–37.

18. Charrier notes: "If it was certain that this town is Paray[-le-Monial], this passage would prove that the province imitated only too much the dissoluteness of the large cities at the time of Carnival" (C 4:10n1). On the pre-Lenten celebration of carnival, see "One Should Serve Only One Master," n6.

19. Ps 48:13 VUC: *Et homo, cum in honore esset, non intellexit. Comparatus est jumentis insipientibus, et similis factus est illis*; cf. Ps 48:21. Anisson leaves out *et*.

20. A: *il faut encore que le cœur soit favorable à celui qui découvre l'objet de la foi et qu'il pousse l'esprit, qui n'est attiré que faiblement par des vérités obscures en elles-mêmes.* Theologians traditionally have affirmed that God prepares the heart (Ps 10:17), and they speak of this preparation as grace. On this theme, see "One Should Serve Only One Master."

21. A: *c'est que.*

22. A: *Signatum est, &c*; cf. Ps 4:7 VUC: *Signatum est super nos lumen vultus tui, Domine.*

23. Ps 92:5 VUC: *Testimonia tua credibilia facta sunt nimis.*

24. Ps 118:96 VUC: *latum mandatum tuum nimis.*

25. A: *Quid tibi sum, Domine, ut amari te jubeas a me, et nisi faciam, irascaris mihi, et mineris ingentes miserias? Parva ne est miser a, si non amem te?* Cf. Aug. *Conf.* 1.5.5 (James J. O'Donnell, ed., *Augustine: Confessions* [Oxford: Clarendon Press, 1992], 1:4): *quid tibi sum ipse, ut amari te iubeas a me et, nisi faciam, irascaris mihi et mineris ingentes miserias? parvane ipsa est si non amem te?*; trans. Henry Chadwick, *Saint Augustine: Confessions*, Oxford World's Classics (Oxford: Oxford University Press, 1991), 5.

26. A: *al fin*, probably meaning *fin* ("end") in the sense of "telos."

27. A: *elle*, referring to *une de vos créatures* ("one of your creatures").

28. Acts 5:1–11. Ananias and his wife Sapphira sold a piece of property, for which they decided that Ananias would bring only a part of the proceeds to the apostles. When Peter accused him of lying to God about what he had received for the land, Ananias fell down and died. He was buried, and about three hours later his wife appeared, not knowing what had happened. Peter accused her as well, after which she too dropped dead and was buried beside her husband.

29. Cf. Or. *Philoc.* 27.8 (SC 226:294) and *Comm. in Mt.* 15.15 (GCS 10:392–393), neither of which makes reference to a "ray of light."

30. La Colombière plays on the word *lumières*, which he uses here in the figurative sense of "spiritual knowledge" or "insight." For this meaning, see the seventh entry under *lumière* in Furetière.

31. The word *lucifer* (Latin "morning star," literally "light-bringing") appears once in the Latin Vulgate (Isa 14:12), where it refers to the king of Babylon. For Christian use of the term in referring to Satan, see "Devil," *New Catholic Encyclopedia Supplement 2010*, ed. Robert L. Fastiggi (Detroit: Gale, 2010), 1:403–05.

32. For the image, see Gen 2:7; 2 Cor 4:7.

33. A: *toutes les facultés de leurs corps, toutes les puissances de leur âme!* As this passage indicates, La Colombière expressed himself using the conceptual grammar of faculty psychology that he appropriated from his study of Aristotle and Thomas Aquinas. For studies of this model as it developed through the High Middle Ages into the early modern period, see *Transformations of the Soul: Aristotelian Psychology, 1250–1650*, ed. Dominik Perler (Leiden: Brill, 2009). I have written the notes in the present volume from the perspective that the thought of Charles Peirce interprets La Colombière's spiritual insights coherently and adequately, and in so doing avoids some of the conceptual difficulties arising from Aristotelianism.

34. In *Pensées* 663, Blaise Pascal (1623–62) juxtaposes the account of history that emerges from the Pentateuch with that recounted in Martino Martini, *Sinicae Historiae Decas Prima* (Munich: Lukas Straub, 1658): with reference to this comparison, the editors note that "whereas, according to the usual interpretation during the seventeenth century, the biblical chronology placed the creation about four thousand years before Christ, one reported that the Chinese chronicles clearly went back earlier in time" [*Pascal: Les Provinciales, Pensées et opuscules divers*, ed. Gérard Ferreyrolles and Philippe Sellier (Paris: Le Livre de poche/Classiques Garnier, 2004), 1193n3].

35. A: *Ignis accensus est in ira ejus et ardebit usque ad inferni novissima*; cf. Deut 32:22 VUC: *Ignis succensus est in furore meo, et ardebit usque ad inferni novissima.*

36. On this theme, see "On Hell" (A 3.55/C 3.55).

37. Cf. Aug. *Civ.* 15.25 (CCL 48:493); trans. R. W. Dyson, *The City of God Against the Pagans*, Cambridge Texts in the History of Political Thought (Cambridge: Cambridge University Press, 1998), 686: "But God's anger is not a disturbance of His mind; rather it is a judgment according to which punishment is visited upon sin."

38. Judg 16:28–30.

39. As printed in the Anisson edition (1684), the sermon ends here. In his own edition (1901), Charrier (C 4:20–22) reproduces the ending that appears in *Sermons prêchés devant S. A. R. Mme la duchesse d'Yorck, par le R. P. Claude La Colombière . . . Nouvelle édition mise en meilleur françois* (Lyon: Pierre Bruyset-Ponthus, 1757).

5: On Venial Sin

1. A: *Du péché véniel* (A 4.60/C 4.61). As venial sin takes mortal or serious sin as its norm, I have followed Charrier in ordering this sermon after the one on mortal sin. The word *venial* comes from the Latin *venialis*, "pardonable," from the root *venia*, "forgiveness, indulgence, pardon." According to tradition, venial sin, unlike mortal sin, does not separate the sinner from God completely; see 1 John 5:16–17.

2. VUC: *Homo quidam [descendebat ab Jerusalem in Jericho, et] incidit in latrones, qui etiam despoliaverunt eum: et plagis impositis abierunt semivivo relicto.* The part in brackets does not appear in the Anisson text.

3. A: *l'éclat déporable [sic]*; cf. C: *l'état déplorable.*

4. A: *légèrement.*

5. A: *Ave Maria.*

6. For a discussion of traditional opinion regarding the sinfulness of first movements, see Simo Knuuttila, *Emotions in Ancient and Medieval Philosophy* (Oxford: Oxford University Press, 2006), 172–204.

7. La Colombière here makes reference to the theme of habituation, which he develops at length in "On the Vicious Habit."

8. In his entry for *actuel*, Furetière makes the traditional theological distinction between *un peché* actuel, *par opposition à* originel. On this distinction, see *ST* Ia-IIae q.81 a.1.

9. While this naturally calls to mind Jean Gerson (1363–1429), a search of the literature has not found a corresponding reference. For Gerson's analysis of sin, see D. Catherine Brown, *Pastor and Laity in the Theology of Jean Gerson* (Cambridge: Cambridge University Press, 1987), 116–70.

10. By "in themselves" (*en eux-mêmes*), La Colombière seems to mean as abstract moral principles involving offenses against God, rather than as case studies drawn from human experience.

11. See, for instance, Matt 18:23–35; 22:2–14.

12. This refers generally to the destruction of Sodom and Gomorrah, and specifically to what happened to Lot's wife when she disobeyed the command to flee Sodom and not to look back (Gen 19:17, 26; Luke 17:28–32; cf. Judg 19:22–24; Luke 9:62). La Colombière's interpretation is extreme regarding the attitude of God both toward the disobedient and toward venial sin, the latter of which by definition is not serious (see n1), although it can have serious implications. We might understand La Colombière, motivated primarily by concern for his listeners, as here using rhetorical technique

in order to move them to act. Note that contemporary scholarship regarding Genesis 19:26 focuses not on the sinfulness of what Lot's wife does but on the general prohibition on looking back, which appears as a motif throughout ancient narrative. For a summary of opinions, see Claus Westermann, *Genesis 12–36: A Commentary*, trans. John J. Scullion, SJ (Minneapolis: Augsburg Publishing House, 1981), 307. Westermann affirms the interpretation of Walther Zimmerli that the wife's turning to salt expresses "the whole horror of the disaster" that befell Sodom and Gomorrah.

13. This refers to the incident at Meribah, where the Lord told Moses to speak to the rock in order to bring forth water for the people (Num 20:1–13). Instead of speaking to the rock, however, Moses struck the rock twice with his staff, for which offense God punished both Moses and Aaron by having them die before entering the promised land (Num 20:29, 27:12–14; Deut 32:49–52, 34:1–12); the incident is memorialized in Ps 95 (vv. 7–11).

14. See 1 Chr 21; cf. 2 Sam 24. While commentators differ in their interpretations of this incident, they generally agree that David made the census in order to evaluate the strength of his army, thus representing a lack of trust in God and ultimately causing God to punish Israel with a plague.

15. 1 Kgs 13. In the larger narrative context, the passage represents a commentary not on the prophet's credibility but on Jeroboam's cultic innovations.

16. 2 Kgs 2:23–24.

17. This suggests Paul's warning that all those who do not keep the law perfectly will suffer the curse (Gal 3:10; cf. Deut 27:26).

18. Rev 3:14–16.

19. This may refer to the period of her life during which, under the pretense of humility, Teresa ceased to pray. See *Vida* 7.1–2, 8.1–2, in Santa Teresa de Jesús, *Obras Completas*, 5th ed., rev. Enrique Llamas et al. (Madrid: Editorial de Espiritualidad, 2000), 32–34, 44.

20. Matt 25:14–30; Luke 19:12–28. Again, La Colombière seems more interested in moving the audience to act than in providing an accurate representation of the Father-God of Jesus, who actively seeks and rejoices over the lost (Luke 15:1–10). The point here seems to be not that God will not welcome back the repentant sinner, but that God will leave the willful, as the story of the Prodigal Son (Luke 15:11–24) illustrates, to see how poorly they manage without divine help.

21. Possibly a reference to the following, probably Pseudo-Augustine fragment (PL 39:1947): *Quibus peccatis licet occidi animam non credamus; ita tamen eam velut quibusdam pustulis, et quasi horrenda scabie replentia deformem faciunt, ut eam ad amplexus illius sponsi coelestis aut vix, aut cum grandi confusione venire permittant.*

22. The notion of intention plays a major role in Chrysostom's understanding of sin, as in *Hom. 19 in Mt.* (PG 57:274.12–22), where Chrysostom explains that Christ determines the penalty or reward for an action by the agent's intention; cited in *ST* Ia-IIae q.20 a.4. On this theme in Chrysostom, see Raymond Laird, *Mindset, Moral Choice and Sin in the Anthropology of John Chrysostom*, Early Christian Studies 15 (Banyo, Queensland: Centre for Early Christian Studies, 2012).

23. A: *une douleur sincère d'y être tombé et une ferme résolution de n'y retomber pas à l'avenir.* This sentiment parallels, in both form and content, the teaching of the Council of Trent regarding *contritio* ("contrition"). See Conc. Trid., sess. XIV, 25 Nov. 1551, *Doctrina de ss. poenitentiae et extremae unctionis sacramentis*, cap. 4 (*COGD* 3:64.1759–61), trans. Norman P. Tanner (*DEC* 2:705): "Contrition, which holds the first place among the above-mentioned acts of the penitent [viz., contrition, confession, and satisfaction], is a grief and detestation of mind at the sin committed, together with the

resolution not to sin in the future"; quoted in *CCE* 1451.

24. On this point, see Conc. Trid., sess. XIV, 25 Nov. 1551, *Doctrina de ss. poenitentiae et extremae unctionis sacramentis*, cap. 4 (*COGD* 3:64.1761–65), trans. Norman P. Tanner (*DEC* 2:705): "This movement of sorrow [*contritio* 'contrition'] has been necessary at all times to obtain the pardon of sins and, in a person who has fallen after baptism, it finally prepares for the forgiveness of sin if it is linked with trust in the divine mercy and the desire to provide all the other requirements for due reception of the sacrament." This understanding is consistent with contemporary Church teaching (*CCE* 1452–53).

25. Ps 31:10 vuc: *Multa flagella peccatoris.*

26. I follow Charrier in adding a paragraph break here, which I do in order to emphasize La Colombière's announcement of the end of the first part of the sermon.

27. Here we have implicit the idea of a sort of act (viz., venial sin) that creates a disposition to a qualitatively different sort of act (viz., mortal sin). This idea relates directly to the concept of habituation, which I argue plays a central role in La Colombière's anthropology. For an analysis of this process in modern philosophical categories, see the Introduction.

28. *ST* Ia-IIae q.88 a.3 ad 1. The idea is that because venial sin remains always venial, it cannot of itself dispose directly to mortal sin unless a preexistent mortal sin draw it beyond its sphere; but venial sin can dispose to mortal sin by a kind of consequence. See Thomas Pègues, OP, *Commentaire français littéral de la Somme théologique de Saint Thomas D'Aquin, VIII: Les Vertus et les vices* (Paris: Pierre Téqui, 1928), 789.

29. For more on the theme of habit formation, see "On the Vicious Habit." For the concept of habit in La Colombière's preaching, see the Introduction.

30. The contagion metaphor also appears in "On the Flight from the World."

31. While La Colombière speaks here of "habituation" (*l'accoutumance*) as that which misleads the uneducated soul, note that the problem appears not in habituation itself, given that moral education is itself a kind of habituation, but in the quality of the habits that govern the soul.

32. Jesus contrasts God with "the world" throughout the Fourth Gospel, e.g., John 1:9–10; 7:7; 15:18–19; 17; 18:36.

33. A: *Hinc amor, inde stupor;* cf. HUM 21.51 (SBO 3:55.6): *In altero amor, in altero stupor laborem non sentit.* Bernard here describes those in the midst of either the climb toward humility or the descent toward pride, respectively.

34. 1 Thess 4:3 vuc: *Haec est enim voluntas Dei, sanctificatio vestra.* The word *enim* does not appear in the Anisson edition.

35. A: *nous;* cf. C: *vous,* which I follow here for consistency.

36. Cf. Gal 3:27.

37. The term "nature," here and in the following paragraph, refers to human nature; which is to say, to that part of the human person that resists transformation according to divine grace. For an overview of the distinction, see "Grace and Nature" in *NCE* 6:411–13; for in-depth study, see Stephen J. Duffy, *The Dynamics of Grace,* op. cit.

38. Addressed to the auditors.

6: On Conscience

1. A: *De la conscience* (A 4.62/C 4.62).

2. A: *Vox clamantis in deserto: Parate viam Domini, rectas facite semitas eius;* this verse appears verbatim in Mark 1:3 and Matt 3:3; cf. John 1:23.

3. Isa 40:1–5.

4. John 1:23.

5. The Second Vatican Council (1962–65) uses similar imagery in speaking of the conscience; see Conc. Vat. II, const. past. De ecclesia in mundo, *Gaudium et spes*, pars I, cap. I, n. 16 (*COGD* 3:563), trans. Norman P. Tanner (*DEC* 2:1077): "conscience is the most intimate centre and sanctuary of a person, in which he or she is alone with God whose voice echoes within them."

6. Cf. Conc. Vat. II, Decl. De libertate religiosa, *Dignitatis humanae*, cap. I, n. 3 (*COGD* 3:477), trans. Norman P. Tanner (*DEC* 2:1003): "People grasp and acknowledge the precepts of the divine law by means of their own consciences, which they are bound to follow faithfully in all their activity, so as to come to God, their end."

7. See n2.

8. A: *Ave Maria.*

9. Isa 48:22; cf. Isa 57:21.

10. This passage appears in French in both the Anisson and the Charrier editions. With an allusion to Mark 9:48 (cf. Isa 6:24), La Colombière introduces the theme, which he will develop through the peroration, of conscience as torturer. However, Wendy Mayer notes that these images taken together are not consistent with the picture of conscience in Chrysostom, who prefers to speak of an unbribable judge or a harsh prosecutor, as in *Laz.* 4 (PG 48:1011), *Pecc.* (PG 51:357.34–37), or *Sac.* 3.14 (SC 272:222.46–47). For the conscience as torturer, see *Ep.* 13 (SC 13bis:336.52–59), *Dimiss. Chan.* (PG 52:450.23–27). *Hom. 17 in Gen.* (PG 53:135.30–59) brings the two ideas together, torture playing an essential part in the questioning of witnesses in the classical and late antique Greek judicial systems; cf. *Exp. in Ps.* 48 (PG 55:235). And while Chrysostom generally does not speak of worms to characterize the operation of the conscience per se, see *Hom. 73/74 in Mt.* (PG 58:676.2–6) for a discussion of those who appear beautiful but are rotten within, where he explains that to smash open a conscience would reveal worms, ichor, and a horrible stench, representing unnatural desires and evils that are themselves more unclean than worms.

11. A: *Parturiit injustitiam, concepit dolorem*; cf. Ps 7:15 VUC: *Ecce parturiit injustitiam; concepit dolorem, et peperit iniquitatem*; cf. Job 15:35.

12. A: *Introspice, si libet, falso jurantis animum*; cf. Philo *De Dec.* 17.86 (CW 4:288).

13. A: *Aspicies eum non quiescere, sed plenum tumultu trepidationeque, accusatum a se ipso et sibi ipsi facientem convitium*; cf. Philo *De Dec.* 17.86 (CW 4:288).

14. Chrys. *Laz.* 4 (PG 48:1012.2–16); cf. John 16:21.

15. Ps 50:5 VUC: *Quoniam iniquitatem meam ego cognosco, et peccatum meum contra me est semper.*

16. Which is to say, being reminded of one's sins would be easy if conscience made them look attractive, just as greed makes them appear attractive before one commits them; instead, conscience makes sins one already has committed look repulsive.

17. A: *excès de fureur.* For the story, see Georgius Cedrenus, *Corpus scriptorum historiae*, ed. Imannuel Bekker (Bonn: n.p., 1838–39), 1:762; reprinted in PG 121:834. Fearing that his younger brother, Theodosius, might take the throne from him, Constans II (630–68), Roman (Byzantine) emperor from 641 until his assassination at the age of thirty-seven, forced him into holy orders and later had him killed.

18. The idea here seems to be that by failing to forgive, one forfeits one's own forgiveness. On this dynamic, see the Lord's Prayer (Matt 6:9–13; cf. Luke 11:2–4).

19. For an illustration of this point, see the Parable of the Unforgiving Servant (Matt 18:23–35).

20. For the sentiment, see Chrys. *Laz.* 4 (PG 48:1013.28–38).

21. A: *Nihil est . . . quod tam summo dolori sit, quam si unusquisque positus sub captivitate peccati recordetur unde lapsus sit*; cf. Ambr. *Paen.* 2.11.102 (SC 179:196): *Nihil autem est quod tam summo dolori sit quam ut unusquisque positus sub captivitate peccati recordetur unde lapsus sit*; trans. *Concerning Repentance* (NPNF² 10:358).

22. Job 29:2, 4–5 VUC: *Quis mihi tribuat ut sim juxta menses pristinos, secundum dies quibus Deus custodiebat me? . . . sicut fui in diebus adolescentiae meae, quando secreto Deus erat in tabernaculo meo: quando erat Omnipotens mecum . . . ?*

23. Job 29:8 VUC: *Videbant me juvenes, et abscondebantur: et senes assurgentes stabant.*

24. Job 29:11 VUC: *Auris audiens beatificabat me, et oculus videns testimonium reddebat mihi.*

25. A: *Nunc autem derident me juniores, nunc in eorum canticum versus sum et factus sum illis in proverbium; aboninantur me*; cf. Job 30:1, 9–10 VUC: *Nunc autem derident me iuniores tempore. . . . Nunc in eorum canticum versus sum, et factus sum eis in proverbium. Abominantur me.*

26. This description suggests a type of edema aggravated by the drinking of alcoholic beverages. While the entry for *hydropisie* in Furetière makes no allusion to alcohol, nineteenth-century French physician Étienne Bergeret (1814–93) writes: "Very frequently one sees persons who have abused alcoholic drinks succumb at a still young age to what one commonly calls a hydropsy of the chest—an illness characterized by horrible fits of breathlessness and accompanied by a general swelling of the body that produces an effusion of serous water seeping under the skin. It is on the occasion of this end, so common of drunkards, that this famous proverb was born: *Qui vivit in vino morietur in aquâ; the one who lives in wine will die in water.*" See Étienne Bergeret, *De l'Abus des boissons alcooliques, dangers et inconvénients pour les individus, la famille et la société, moyens de modérer les ravages de l'ivrognerie* (Paris: J.-B. Baillière et fils, 1870), 90.

27. 1 Sam 16:14–23.

28. Exod 8:1–14.

29. In fact, the writings of Epicurus present a more nuanced understanding of pleasure than that often associated with him. See, for instance, *Ep. Men.* 129.4–130.4 ("Epistula ad Menoeceum," in Epicuro, *Opere*, 2nd ed., ed. Graziano Arrighetti [Turin: Giulio Einaudi, 1973], 113); trans. Cyril B. Bailey, "Epicurus to Menoeceus," in *Epicurus: The Extant Remains* (Oxford: Clarendon Press, 1926), 87–89: "And since pleasure is the first good and natural to us, for this very reason we do not choose every pleasure, but sometimes we pass over many pleasures, when greater discomfort accrues to us as the result of them: and similarly we think many pains better than pleasures, since a greater pleasure comes to us when we have endured pains for a long time. Every pleasure then because of its natural kinship to us is good, yet not every pleasure is to be chosen: even as every pain also is an evil, yet not all are always of a nature to be avoided. Yet by a scale of comparison and by the consideration of advantages and disadvantages we must form our judgment on all these matters. For the good on certain occasions we treat as bad, and conversely the bad as good."

30. Ps 84:11 VUC: *justitia et pax osculatae sunt.*

31. Gen 42:21, 22 VUC: *Merito haec patimur, quia peccavimus in fratrem nostrum. . . . en sanguis ejus exquiritur.*

32. 1 Macc 6:12 VUC: *Nunc vero reminiscor malorum quae feci in Jerusalem.* The Anisson edition leaves out *vero.*

33. Antiochus IV Epiphanes (ca. 215–164 BCE), who ruled the Seleucids from 175 BCE until his sudden death from disease, sacked Jerusalem in 167, desecrating the Temple and siding with the Hellenists in persecuting the Jews (2 Macc 5–6).

34. This refers to the breaking wheel and the gridiron, two forms of torturous execution associated with Catherine of Alexandria and Lawrence of Rome, respectively. For descriptions of these methods, see Geoffrey Abbott, *Execution: The Guillotine, the Pendulum, the Thousand Cuts, the Spanish Donkey, and 66 Other Ways of Putting Someone to Death* (New York: St. Martin's Press, 2006), 39–50, 123–24. The breaking wheel continued in use through the modern period in Europe, as indicated in Lisa Silverman, *Tortured Subjects: Pain, Truth, and the Body in Early Modern France* (Chicago: University of Chicago Press, 2001), 3, 36–37, 48, 94, 158, 227.

35. A: *Quocunque fugerit, se talem trahit post se, et quocunque talem traxerit se, cruciat se*; cf. Aug. *Psal.* 45.3 (CCL 38:519): *Quocumque fugerit, se trahit post se; et quocumque talem traxerit se, cruciat se de se*; trans. Maria Boulding, *Expositions of the Psalms 33–50* (WSA 3.16:312): "Wherever we run, we drag this self after us, and wherever we drag a self in this state, we make it our tormentor."

36. 1 Sam 1:8 VUC: *Anna, cur fles? et quare non comedis? et quam ob rem affligitur cor tuum?*

37. Ibid.: *numquid non ego melior tibi sum, quam decem filii?*

38. Job 15:21 VUC: *Sonitus terroris semper in auribus illius.*

39. Job 15:22 VUC: *Non credit quod reverti possit de tenebris ad lucem, circumspectans undique gladium.*

40. See Chrys. *Stat.* 8 (PG 49:99.10–17), which addresses the paranoia of sinners conscious of their own sin.

41. Wis 17:10 VUC: *Cum sit enim timida nequitia, dat testimonium condemnationis: semper enim praesumit saeva, perturbata conscientia.*

42. Job 15:25 VUC: *Tetendit enim adversus Deum manum suam, et contra Omnipotentem roboratus est.* The Anisson text has *adversus* in place of *contra.*

43. A: *d'un trés-petit nombre d'hommes*; cf. C: *d'un petit nombre d'hommes.*

44. Of course, this opinion would have seemed more self-evident—and would have met with more widespread acceptance—before the Enlightenment. For analysis, see Michael J. Buckley, *At the Origins of Modern Atheism* (New Haven, CT: Yale University Press, 1987).

45. Probably a reference to Peter Chrysologus, who wrote a sermon on Christian fearlessness of death (Luke 12:4–6); see *Chrysol.* Serm. 101 (CCL 24A:620–26).

46. Matt 27:3–8; Acts 1:18–19.

47. For the image, see n34.

48. Or. *Princ.* 2.10.3–5.

49. Hier. *Ruf.* 2.7 (SC 303:114), *Ep.* 124.7 (CSEL 56.1:104–05). For Jerome's role in the Origenist controversy, see Elizabeth A. Clark, *The Origenist Controversy: The Cultural Construction of an Early Christian Debate* (Princeton, NJ: Princeton University Press, 1992), 121–51, 221–27.

50. Cf. Hier. *Ep.* 22.30 (CSEL 54:190); trans. Charles Christopher Mierow, "To Eustochium" (ACW 33:165–66): "Upon being asked my status, I replied that I was a Christian. And He who sat upon the judgment seat said: 'Thou liest. Thou art a Ciceronian, not a Christian. *Where thy treasure is, there is thy heart also* (Matt 6:21).' I was

struck dumb on the spot. Amid the blows—for He had ordered me to be beaten—I was tormented the more by the flame of conscience. I repeated to myself the verse: *And who shall confess thee in hell?* (Ps 6:6)."

51. Ambr. *Off.* 1.12.45 (Ambrose, *De officiis*, ed. and trans. Ivor J. Davidson, Oxford Early Christian Studies [Oxford: Oxford University Press, 2001], 2:142–43): *Licet ipsa quae videtur, etiam dum vivunt, impiorum requies in inferno sit: viventes enim in inferna descendunt.* The Anisson edition has *tamen* in place of *enim*; Davidson's translation appears verbatim in the text.

52. La Colombière dedicates a sermon each to the themes of the world ("On the Flight from the World," in the present volume) and death (A 3.49/C 3.49).

53. Jer 2:12–13 VUC: *Obstupescite, caeli, super hoc, et portae ejus, desolamini vehementer, dicit Dominus. Duo enim mala fecit populus meus: me dereliquerunt fontem aquae vivae, et foderunt sibi cisternas, cisternas dissipatas, quia continere non valent aquas.*

54. Cf. Matt 7:13–14.

55. Ps 94:8 VUC: *Hodie si vocem ejus audieritis, nolite obdurare corda vestra;* cf. Heb 3:7–8, 15; 4:7.

56. I follow Charrier in placing a question mark at the end of this sentence.

7: On the Relapse

1. A: *De la rechute* (A 4.63/C 4.63).

2. A: *Fiunt novissima omnis ullius pejora prioribus;* cf. VUC: *fiunt novissima hominis illius pejora prioribus.* This verse appears verbatim in Matthew 12:45.

3. Chrys. *Serm. 1 in Gen.* (SC 433:138–40). Preaching at the beginning of Lent, Chrysostom says that seasonal spring pleases sailors and farm workers not nearly as much as the time of fasting—the spiritual spring of souls—the true calm of rational thoughts—pleases those who wish to lead a life of Christian meditation. Note that the French word *carême* derives from the Latin *quadragesima*, which refers to the forty days preceding Easter (*GL* 1:600); however, in Teutonic languages apart from English, forms of the words "Lent" and "Lenten" simply mean "spring" (*OED* 8:828–29). For an overview of the origins of the liturgical season of Lent, see Maxwell E. Johnson, "Baptismal Preparation and the Origins of Lent," in *The Rites of Christian Initiation: Their Evolution and Interpretation* (Collegeville, MN: Liturgical Press, 1999), 159–76.

4. A: *Les travaux du laboureur.* The referent for *laboureur* is unclear.

5. A: *homme;* cf. Luke 15:10.

6. A: *a une véritable pénitence.* Here La Colombière introduces the theme of the sermon, viz., the distinction between genuine and feigned repentance.

7. On Carnival, see "One Should Serve Only One Master," n6.

8. A: *fermeté;* cf. C: *fierté.*

9. A: *Ave Maria.*

10. La Colombière again uses the metaphor of physical illness to describe moral vice (see "On the Flight from the World," nn24, 29, 34). By this analogy, vicious habits relate to sinful acts as causes relate to their effects, and can transmit themselves among carriers. The concept of habit formation, which plays a central role in classical French oratory, introduces the philosophical question of the ontological status of a habit. A fundamental thesis of the present study is that the importance of habituation in La Colombière's preaching can serve as a basis for understanding the human person not as a

substantial reality undergoing accidental changes but as a nexus of habits or dispositions from which a distinct, evolving identity emerges. On this point, see the Introduction.

11. A: *il est à craindre du moins lors que ce sont des pechez considérables.* This does not appear in the Charrier edition.

12. A: *compendium ignium aeternorum.* Regarding the outward manifestations of repentance *(exomologesis)*, see Tert. *Paen.* 9 (316:180): *Haec omnia exomologesis, ut paenitentiam commendet, ut de periculi timore Dominum honoret, ut in peccatorem ipsa pronuntians pro Dei indignation fungatur, et temporali afflictatione aeterna supplicia, non dicam frustretur, sed expungat*; trans. William P. Le Saint, *Treatises on Penance* (ACW 28:32): "Exomologesis does all this in order to render penitence acceptable and in order to honor God through fear of punishment, so that in passing sentence upon the sinner it may itself be a substitute for the wrath of God and, by temporal punishment, I will not say prevent eternal torments but rather cancel them." Nicolas La Pesse (1646–1724), who lived with La Colombière during two different periods (1665–66, 1679–80), and who is said to have written the preface to the first edition of La Colombière's sermons, explains in one of his own sermons that "Tertullian called [contrition for sin] *compendium ignium aeternorum*, a shortening of the fires of hell: because your repentance ought to compensate in some manner for the eternal punishments you have deserved." See "Sur la Douleur du Pénitent," in *Sermons du P. La Pesse* (Lyon: Louis Declaustre, 1708), 3:76.

13. A: *aurait peu exiger*; I follow Charrier in reading *aurait pu exiger.*

14. Along these lines, see Gr. Nyss. *Or. Catech.* 8 (GNO 3.4:34.13–17); trans. William Moore and Henry Austin Wilson, *The Great Catechism* (NPNF² 5:142): "Accordingly, which was the better way?—never to have brought our nature into existence at all, since He foresaw that the being about to be created would fall away from that which is morally beautiful; or to bring him back by repentance, and restore his diseased nature to its original beauty?"

15. A: *d'éttuit*; I follow Charrier in reading *détruit.*

16. Cf. ASSP 4:4 (SBO 5:246.24–247.5); trans. Ailbe J. Luddy, "Fourth Sermon for the Feast of the Assumption," in *St. Bernard's Sermons for the Seasons and Principal Festivals of the Year* (Westminster, MD: The Carroll Press, 1950), 3:250–51: "Now what is the mystical meaning of the Savior's command to 'take away the stone,' and a little later to 'loose him and let him go'? (John 11:39–44). Are we to suppose, my brethren, that after being visited by the grace of consolation our Lazarus will cease to 'do penance, because the kingdom of heaven is at hand' (Matt 3:4), or will renounce 'discipline, and so perchance the Lord be angry and he perish from the just way' (Ps 2:12)? God forbid! No, let the stone indeed be taken away, but let penance remain, penance that no longer burdens and oppresses the sick soul, but rather gives fresh life and vigor to the already revived and vigorous soul; for that which before she would not touch is now become her food, namely, to do the will of the Lord (Job 6:7; John 4:34)."

17. Regarding this distress, cf. "On Venial Sin," n23.

18. The tradition attributes many such miracles to the Spanish Dominican Vincent Ferrer, known for his preaching and holiness. For his biography, see Marc Antoine Bayle, *Vie de S. Vincent Ferrier de l'Ordre des Frères-Prêcheurs (1350–1419)* (Paris: Ambroise Bray, 1855).

19. This could refer to Nestorius or to one of the patriarchs from the iconoclastic period.

20. A: *au sentiment près.* This expression seems to function in the same way as does, for example, the English expression "right to the inch" when measuring something closely.

21. On this dynamic, see the first and second rules for the discernment of spirits for the first week, in Ignatius of Loyola, *Ejercicios espirituales* 314–15 (MHSI 100:374–75).

22. A: *Ita plerique mali . . . inutiliter compunguntur ad justitiam, sicut plerique boni innoxie tentantur ad culpam*; Greg.-M. *Past.* 3.30 (SC 382:480): *ita plerumque mali inutiliter compunguntur ad iustitiam, sicut plerumque boni innoxie temptantur ad culpam*; trans. George E. Demacopoulos, *St. Gregory the Great: The Book of Pastoral Rule*, Popular Patristics Series 34 (Crestwood, NY: St. Vladimir's Seminary Press, 2007), 184. Bossuet reproduces this passage in his sermon "On the Integrity of Repentance" (Bossuet, *Œuvres oratoires*, 4:339), as does Bourdaloue in "On the Relapse into Sin" (Bourdaloue, *Œuvres complètes*, 7:221).

23. A: *avec autant de sens froid*; cf. C: *avec autant de sang-froid*.

24. A: *Peccatum quod poenitentia non deletur, mox suo pondere ad aliud trahit*; cf. Greg.-M. *Mor.* 25.9.22 (CCL 143B:1247): *Peccatum namque quod paenitentia non diluit ipso suo pondere mox ad aliud trahit*; Hom. *Ez.* 1.11.24 (CCL 142:179). Peter Lombard (*Sent.* 2.36.3 [SB 4:539]), Peter of Celle (*Serm.* 58 [PL 202:0816D]), and Thomas Aquinas (*ST* Ia-IIae q.109 a.8) all reference Gregory on this point.

25. La Colombière alludes to Luke 11:21–22, which precedes the verse that appears at the head of this sermon: "When a strong man armed keeps his court, those things are in peace which he possesses. But if a stronger than he come upon him, and overcome him, he will take away all his armor wherein he trusted, and will distribute his spoils" (DRA).

26. On these categories, see "One Should Serve Only One Master."

27. On Pauline authorship of Hebrews, see "On Mortal Sin," n5.

28. Heb 6:1–12 deals with the danger of apostasy. La Colombière does not reference the conclusion to this passage, which tempers the warning; nevertheless, the ending of the present sermon echoes this hopeful turn with a prayer for mercy.

29. La Colombière broadens the message of Heb 6:4–6 to apply to any moral slip a Christian might commit. For a discussion of this passage, see Mitchell, *Hebrews*, 124–25.

30. Rom 6:11; cf. Rom 7:8, 8:10.

31. Rom 6:2 VUC: *Qui enim mortui sumus peccato, quomodo adhuc vivemus in illo?*

32. A: *ressuscite*.

33. Luke 9:62 VUC: *Nemo mittens manum suam ad aratrum, et respiciens retro, aptus est regno Dei*.

34. Luke 11:24–26; Matt 12:43–45; cf. Mark 16:9; Luke 8:1–2.

35. Cf. Ignatius of Loyola, *Ejercicios espirituales* 327 (MHSI 100:386–87); trans. George E. Ganss, SJ, *The Spiritual Exercises of Saint Ignatius* (Saint Louis, MO: Institute of Jesuit Sources, 1992), 125: "the enemy acts like a military commander who is attempting to conquer and plunder his objective. The captain and leader of an army on campaign sets up his camp, studies the strength and structure of a fortress, and then attacks at its weakest point. In the same way, the enemy of human nature prowls around and from every side probes all our theological, cardinal, and moral virtues. Then at the point where he finds us weakest and most in need in regard to our eternal salvation, there he attacks and tries to take us."

36. On the theme of habituation, see the Introduction and the sermon "On the Vicious Habit."

37. The theme of loving one's enemies, which plays a central role in the ethical teaching of Jesus (Matt 5:43–48; Luke 6:27–28, 32–36), appears in the dying prayers

of both Jesus (Luke 23:34) and Stephen (Acts 7:59–60). For commentary on these passages, see Shelly Matthews, "Clemency as Cruelty: Forgiveness and Force in the Dying Prayers of Jesus and Stephen," *Biblical Interpretation* 17 (2009): 118–46.

38. See, for example, the story of Saint Ignatius ministering to a plague-stricken man, as recounted in Luís Gonçalves da Câmara, *Acta P. Ignatii* 83 (MHSI 66:476); trans. Joseph N. Tylenda, SJ, *A Pilgrim's Journey: The Autobiography of Ignatius of Loyola*, rev. ed. (San Francisco: Ignatius Press, 2001), 151–52: "After he had consoled and encouraged the man a bit, he departed alone. He began to feel pain in his hand, and it seemed to him that he had the plague. This fantasy was so strong that he could not banish it until he thrust his hand into his mouth, turning it around this way and that, and said: 'If you have the plague in your hand, you will also have it in your mouth.' And as soon as he had done this the fantasy vanished as did the pain in his hand." Tylenda comments that, while this action may have revealed heroic virtue in the young Ignatius, he would not have acted so imprudently later in life.

39. Contemporary Roman Catholic teaching on hell has evolved from the harsh perspective that La Colombière presents here. For instance, in his General Audience of July 28, 1999, Pope John Paul II explains that *"hell* is the ultimate consequence of sin itself. . . . Rather than a place, hell indicates the state of those who freely and definitively separate themselves from God, the source of all life and joy." See *"*Hell Is the State of Those Who Reject God," in *L'Osservatore Romano* (Vatican City) 31, August 4, 1999, Weekly Edition in English, 7.

40. Probably a reference to Heb 10:26, discussed below (n43); cf. Matt 18:21–22 (Luke 17:4), where Jesus preaches what amounts to unlimited forgiveness. For an overview of forgiveness in the New Testament, see Anthony Bash, *Forgiveness and Christian Ethics*, New Studies in Christian Ethics 29 (Cambridge: Cambridge University Press, 2010), 79–100.

41. A: *la confussion qu'il a souffert en confessant ses crimes fait assez voir qu'il en a reconnu l'énormité*; cf. C: *la confusion qu'il a soutenue en confessant ses crimes fait assez voir qu'il en avait reconnu l'énormité.*

42. Charrier leaves out *notre.*

43. Heb 10:26 ᴠᴜᴄ: *Voluntarie enim peccantibus nobis post acceptam notitiam veritatis, jam non relinquitur pro peccatis hostia.* As in Heb 6:1–12, discussed above (n28), La Colombière is referring to apostasy, as Heb 10:29 suggests: "How much more do you think he deserves worse punishments, who has trodden underfoot the Son of God and has esteemed the blood of the testament, by which he was sanctified, unclean, and has offered an affront to the Spirit of grace?" (ᴅʀᴀ). For commentary, see Mitchell, *Hebrews*, 215–18.

44. See Heb 10:29.

45. Probably a paraphrase of Tert. *Paen.* (SC 316:162); trans. Le Saint, *On Penitence* (ACW 28:22–23): "But does he sin venially against the Lord who, in penance, renounces His adversary, the devil, and thus subordinates him to the Lord, but who then, falling back into sin again, exalts him once more and is a cause of his joy, so that the evil one, recovering his booty, laughs in the face of the Lord? Does he not—it is a dangerous thing to say, but for edification I must speak out—prefer the devil to the Lord? For after he has known them both, he seems to have instituted a comparison [*comparationem*] between them and to have pronounced judgment that he is the better whose possession he has again elected to be. Therefore the man who began to satisfy the Lord by repenting his sin will satisfy the devil by repenting his repentance, and he will be as hateful to

the Lord as he is dear to his adversary."

46. Rom 1:25.

47. 1 Sam 15:11 VUC: *Poenitet me quod constituerim Saul regem.*

48. A: *Porro triumphator in Israël non parcet; neque enim homo est, ut agat poenitentiam*; cf. 1 Sam 15:29 VUC: *Porro triumphator in Israël non parcet, et poenitudine non flectetur: neque enim homo est ut agat poenitentiam.*

49. Charrier infers from this line that the present sermon was preached during the season of Lent in 1677 or 1678.

50. A: *comme au paralytique de trente-huit ans.*

51. A: *Vade et noli amplius peccare, ne quid deterius tibi contingat*—apparently a conflation of John 8:11 and 5:14. Note that John does not mention a paralytic, but rather "a great multitude of sick, of blind, of lame, of withered" (John 5:3 DRA)—a group that included "a certain man there, that had been eight and thirty years under his infirmity" (John 5:5 DRA).

52. A: *couper ce bras qui vous a scandalisé.*

53. See Matt 5:29–30; Mark 9:43–47.

54. On this theme, see "On the Flight from the World."

55. La Colombière develops this point in "On Confidence in God."

56. Matt 8:25 VUC: *Domine, salva nos, perimus*; cf. Mark 4:38; Luke 8:24. La Colombière alludes to the Calming of the Storm. The two subsequent quotations, both of which appear in Latin, both reference this verse.

57. A: *je ne puis pas vous répondre pour une heure de ma constance.*

8: On the Vicious Habit

1. A: *De l'habitude vicieuse* (A 4.64/C 4.64). This sermon provides the conceptual key to La Colombière's preaching by presenting the idea of habituation (*l'accoutumance*) that governs his thinking about both vice and virtue. From this perspective, the human person evolves both morally and spiritually through habituation to virtue, and degenerates through habituation to vice; for an interpretation of this process, see the Introduction.

In addition to their theological significance, vice and virtue also function as the topics of the epideictic or ceremonial branch of rhetoric to which pulpit oratory belongs. According to the conventions of that genre, the orator blames vice and praises virtue, both in general and as exemplified in the lives of vicious or virtuous people. Note that the majority of La Colombière's sermons focus explicitly on virtue, extolling the saints as models of holiness (*sainteté*) and virtuous behavior. Regardless of the subject matter, however, La Colombière understands the primary goal of his preaching as the sanctification of his audience—an intention that he makes clear when addressing the Duchess of York in what appears to be the first sermon he delivered in her presence: "I know, Madam, that when your royal highness ordered me to ascend this pulpit, she had no other design than to give to those who will hear me a means to sanctify themselves. And I declare, in the presence of Jesus Christ, that in obeying your orders I will never have any intention other than to work for the sanctification of my auditors" (C 1:29).

2. VUC: *invenietis asinam alligatam, et pullum cum ea: solvite, et adducite mihi*; cf. Mark 11:2 and Luke 19:30, both of which specify only a colt. Significant for La Colombière's interpretation of this verse, the Greek text of Matt 21:2 does not give an object for the double order of Jesus (GNT: *lusantes agagete moi*), which makes it un-

clear whether Jesus means to untie both the ass and the colt or exactly what he wants brought to him.

3. The point here is that, although one cannot expect to lose a vicious habit as easily as one adopts it, one can in fact leave it if one has the *bonne volonté*—good intention, or willingness—to do so. The sermon divides according to these two points.

4. PALM 3.2 (SBO 5:53): *Solutus est ad mandatum Domini qui antea tenebatur, aut non valens, aut non volens facere bene, aut, utroque fortius vinculo alligatus, nec volens scilicet, nec valens.* For an analysis of this passage as it relates to the question of conversion, see William P. O'Brien, SJ, "Une 'manière' de prêcher: Rhétorique et sainteté chez Claude La Colombière," *Archivum Historicum Societatis Iesu* 79, no. 157 (Spring 2010): 168–69.

5. A: *Ave Maria.*

6. La Colombière returns to the idea, introduced in "On Care for Salvation," of grace or divine help. While he insists here on the need for human effort, using both reason and emotion to move his listeners to act, he never loses sight of the role that grace plays in both conversion from sin and the eradication of vicious habits. In this way the theme of divine providence, which comes to the fore in "On the Mercy of God toward the Sinner" and "On Confidence in God," effectively balances the apparent voluntarism of the present sermon. On this point see his analysis of Chrysostom, discussed in the Introduction.

7. A: *combine il vous sera malaise de vous défaire d'un vice. . . . lorsque l'habitude s'en sera formée en vous.* This phrase suggests a distinction between the vice and the habit to practice or activate that vice. In this sense, La Colombière seems to understand *vice* and *virtue* either as (1) kinds of habits, such that *habit* represents any general tendency, while *vice* and *virtue* indicate the moral valence of that tendency; or as (2) kinds of actions considered according to their moral value.

8. A: *secundam et quasi affabricatam naturam*; cf. Aug. *Mus.* 6.7.19 (SLS 47:46): *Non enim frustra consuetudo quasi secunda et quasi adfabricata natura dicitur*; trans. Martin Jacobsson (SLS 47:47): "For it is not without reason that habit is called a 'second' nature, 'added by art.'"

9. The medical practices of inoculation and vaccination rely upon this principle.

10. A: *nos premières années*, a metonym for "us, during our first years."

11. Judg 16. The words *la plus-mince &* do not appear in the Charrier edition.

12. Aug. *Conf.* 8.5.10 (O'Donnell, 1:92): *dum servitur libidini, facta est consuetudo, et dum consuetudini non resistitur, facta est necessitas*; trans. Chadwick, *Confessions*, 140.

13. This refers to the mythical queen Semiramis, whose name appears as Semiramoth in the VUC version of 1 Chronicles (15:18, 20; 16:5) and 2 Chronicles (17:8). The legend as recounted in *Diod. Sic.* 2.20 (*Diodorus of Sicily*, trans. C. H. Oldfather [Cambridge, MA: Harvard University Press, 1933], 1:416–18) gives the time frame as five days.

14. For the story, see Alphonsus Rodriguez, *Exercicio de Perfecion, y virtudes cristianas por el Padre Alonso Rodriguez, de la Conpañia [sic] de Jesus natural de Valladolid*, 3 vols. (Seville: Matias Clavijo, 1609); trans. *The Practice of Christian and Religious Perfection* (Dublin: James Duffy, 1861), 2:44–46. Note that this translation was made from the French translation of Regnier des Marais, *Pratique de la Perfection Chretienne*, 3 vols. (Paris: Sebastien Marbre-Camoisy, 1675–79). In total, seven French editions of this book appeared, beginning with that of Paul Duez (1621), to any of which La Colombière may have had access.

15. The word *quelquefois* does not appear in the Charrier edition.

16. Aug. *Psal.* 30.2.s.1.13 (CCL 38:201): *Vides quam male facias, quam detest-*

abiliter, quam infeliciter; et facis tamen; trans. Boulding, *Expositions of the Psalms 1–32* (WSA 3.15:332). In the Anisson edition, the verb forms appear as *facies . . . facies.*

17. Aug. *Psal.* 30.2.s.1.13 (CCL 38:201): *fecisti heri, facturus es hodie*; cf. PL 36:238: *fecisti fieri, facturus es hodie*; trans. Boulding, *Expositions of the Psalms 1–32* (WSA 3.15:332). This phrase concludes the quotation cited in n15 above.

18. A: *inutilement.* This description recalls the inner conflict as Saint Paul recounts it in Rom 7:14–25.

19. A: *mas ce béevage affreux.*

20. This line seems to imply that La Colombière himself has experienced, either directly or indirectly—e.g., while presiding at the sacrament of penance—habituation to destructive behavior, e.g., what today goes by the name of *addiction.*

21. A: *les exortations, & les larmes de sa mere, contre.* This does not appear in the Charrier edition.

22. A: *Dum irruebam in voluptates . . . irruebam in dolores*; cf. Aug. *Conf.* 1.20.31 (O'Donnell, 1:15): *hoc enim peccabam, quod non in ipso sed in creaturis eius me atque caeteris voluptates, sublimitates, veritates quaerebam, atque ita inruebam in dolores, confusiones, errores*; trans. Chadwick, *Confessions,* 22–23: "My sin consisted in this, that I sought pleasure, sublimity, and truth not in God but in his creatures, in myself and other created beings. So it was that I plunged into miseries, confusions, and errors." Chadwick notes that here Augustine fuses Romans 1 with Plotinus *Enn.* 1.6.8.

23. Aug. *Serm.* 98.6 (PL 38:594): *difficultatem quamdam ostendit tibi. Infremuit spiritu, ostendit multo clamore objurgationis opus esse ad eos qui consuetudine duruerunt*; trans. Edmund Hill, *Sermons (94A-147A) on the New Testament* (WSA 3.4:46–47).

24. La Colombière's use of the word *passion* effectively defines it as equivalent to *vice,* where *vice* refers to a habit that results from a certain kind of action, viz., an action characterized as *déréglée,* "dissolute."

25. Regarding this theme, see "On the Relapse."

26. Jer 13:23 VUC: *Si mutare potest Aethiops pellem suam, aut pardus varietates suas, et vos poteritis benefacere, cum didiceritis malum.* The adverb *male* appears in the Anisson edition in place of *malum.*

27. Regarding necrophilia, see also "On the Mercy of God toward the Sinner."

28. A: *hommes.*

29. *Ep.* 57.17–18 (OPD 1.3:262–64); trans. Owen J. Blum, OFM, "Letter 57" (FCM 2:380–81). The translator identifies the recipient not as Alexander II, to whom Italian Benedictine Peter Damian (ca. 1007–72) had written a number of letters, but as Gerard, bishop of Florence—then Pope Nicholas II elect—and Hildebrand, noting that the name of the pope-elect does not appear in the oldest manuscripts.

30. A: *elle,* referring to "soul."

31. A: *après avoir reçu l'absolution.* I accept the correction of Charrier *après qu'elle a reçu l'absolution* so as to clarify the subject as *une âme,* for which I use feminine pronouns here.

32. Today, the Catholic Church refers to this sacrament as "anointing of the sick," as explained in *CCE* 1512.

33. SC 81.9 (SBO 2:289): *Non ergo parum firmiter vis quod et necessario vis. Multum vis quod nolle nequeas, nec multum obluctans. Porro ubi voluntas, et libertas*; trans. Irene Edmonds, *Bernard of Clairvaux: On the Song of Songs IV* (CF 40:165). In the Anisson text, the word *obluctaris* appears in place of *obluctans*—probably a typographical error.

34. The argument turns on the definitions of both *necessario* and *voluntas* (French

volonté "will" or "intention"). La Colombière assumes that intention implies the possibility to choose otherwise, which logically contradicts the idea of necessity.

35. I.e., scholasticism, viz., the critical method that predominated in medieval European universities from about 1100 to 1500.

36. A: *Quelque forte, quelque enracinée que soit l'Habitude qui s'est assujetti notre cœur.*

37. La Colombière thinks of sin as a free action, and a free action as a thing that one could choose not to do. This raises the question of when and to what extent the dispositions and habits that govern one's behavior mitigate one's ability to choose a different course of action, as in the case of the alcoholic who, once having taken a drink, appears to lose the ability to choose not to take another.

38. Regarding the ontological status of habits, see "On the Relapse," n10.

39. A: *pour réparer les excez qu'on a commis, travailler.* This does not appear in the Charrier edition.

40. The words *une habitude contraire* do not appear in the Charrier edition.

41. The Jesuits, with whom La Colombière had studied, adopted this approach to character development, which today falls under the general rubric of virtue ethics, from Aristotle and Aquinas (see Introduction).

42. A: *Oui, une bonne volonté est toute-puissante.* This use of the expression *bonne volonté*—the only time that the expression occurs in the present sermon—allows for a nuanced interpretation of the preceding paragraph, in which La Colombière describes what seems to be a show of will. In contrast, *bonne volonté* suggests a readiness to take instruction for the sake of the good, even should this readiness mean acting against one's own judgment and natural inclination. La Colombière develops this perspective in the final paragraph of this sermon. He discusses *bonne volonté* explicitly in his first sermon "For Christmas Day" (A 1.5/C 1.5), which takes as its point of departure Luke 2:14.

43. La Colombière seems to conflate the sinful woman from Luke 7:37–47 with both Mary of Bethany (John 11:1–2)—the sister of Lazarus—as Augustine had done (PL 35:1748; NPNF[1] 7:271), and with Mary Magdalene. Note however that none of the four canonical gospels identifies Mary Magdalene as Mary of Bethany or connects her in any way with dissolute living. Although she appears in the gospels primarily as a witness to the crucifixion, empty tomb, and resurrected Christ, writers from at least the third century have tended to conflate her with a number of New Testament figures, including Mary of Bethany, the sinful woman from Luke, the Samaritan woman (John 4:1–42), and the woman caught in adultery (John 8:1–11). This may owe in part to the identification of Mary Magdalene as the woman out of whom Jesus had cast seven demons (Luke 8:2). The number seven from this story connects in later exegesis to the seven deadly sins, which would have included the sin of lust. See Susan Haskins, *Mary Magdalen: Myth and Metaphor* (New York: Harcourt Brace and Company, 1993), 3–32. The reference to Lazarus appears in John 11:39–44.

44. Aug. *Ev. Io.* 49.3 (CCL 36:421): *Videmus multos, nouimus multos*; trans. Rettig, *St. Augustine: Tractates on the Gospel of John, 28–54* (FC 88:241).

45. I.e., after his conversion, he scrupulously finds sin in even the most innocent pleasures.

46. For the Latin text of the book in question, see *Augustine: Confessions*, ed. James J. O'Donnell (Oxford: Clarendon Press, 1992); for a recent translation, see *Saint Augustine: Confessions*, trans. Henry Chadwick, Oxford World Classics (New York: Oxford University Press, 1991).

47. A: *les conseils les plus relevés*. Furetière offers a theological definition for *conseil*, with the following illustrations: *Les* conseils *de Dieu sont impenetrables. Les* Conseils *Evangeliques sont les avis utiles à nostre salut que conseille l'Evangile, mais qui ne sont pas d'obligation.*

48. A: *Je voudrais bien me corriger, disons-nous, si je le pouvois.* This does not appear in the Charrier edition.

49. An allusion to Paul's confession in Rom 7:14–25; cf. n18 above.

50. These references to British culture indicate that some stage of the redaction of this sermon probably took place in England.

51. A: *un amas et une source de péchés.* Here La Colombière makes explicit the general nature of the vicious habit, in that a habit produces particular acts of a certain quality. In so doing, he affirms that to enter into heaven requires not only absolution from the sinful acts one has committed but also transformation of the sinful tendencies and dispositions that lead to such acts. Theologians traditionally have distinguished between these two operations as "justification" and "sanctification," respectively. For discussion of these categories, see Dawn DeVries, "Justification," in *The Oxford Handbook of Systematic Theology*, ed. John Webster et al. (Oxford: Oxford University Press, 2007), 203–7.

52. Acts 9:6 VUC: *Domine, quid me vis facere?* By developing the theme of good intention, or willingness, understood as a readiness to disregard one's own will and ideas in favor of God's, La Colombière establishes a connection between habituation to virtue and dependence on God. Regarding dependence on God, see "On Submission to the Will of God."

53. Mark 10:39; Matt 20:22 VUC: *Possumus*; cf. John 18:11 DRA: "Jesus therefore said to Peter: Put up thy sword into the scabbard. The chalice which my Father hath given me, shall I not drink it?"

54. See n6 above.

55. Rom 8:35 VUC: *Quis ergo nos separabit a caritate Christi?* This passage recalls the epigraph discussed in the first paragraph of the sermon.

56. For La Colombière this shift in attitude brings about a change in perspective on the world, such that everything now appears as an opportunity to serve God.

57. Ps 118:96 VUC: *Omnis consummationis vidi finem, latum mandatum tuum nimis.*

58. A: *qui devoient s'opposer.* With Charrier I read *devaient*, as the verb *devoyer* does not appear in Furetière and for this reason alone seems not to have been the writer's idea.

9: On Confession

1. A: *De la confession* (A 4.65/C 4.65).

2. Luke 3:4 VUC: *Parate viam Domini: rectas facite semitas ejus;* this allusion to Isa 40:3 appears verbatim in Mark 1:3 and Matt 3:3, and slightly altered in John 1:23.

3. Charrier notes that La Colombière delivered this sermon in England on the fourth Sunday of Advent, which, following the Julian calendar, fell on December 24, 1676. The later remark about not fasting (see n37) supports this claim, given that the Feast of Saint Lucy (December 13) would have fallen on a Wednesday that year, making the following Wednesday (December 20), Friday (December 22), and Saturday (December 23) ember days and thus days of fasting.

4. A reference to the antiphon *O Rex Gentium, et desideratus earum*, traditionally sung at evening prayer on December 22.

5. An allusion to the star that revealed to the magi the birth of Jesus (Matt 2:1–11; see also the prophesy in Num 24:17).

6. A: *la foi du Rédempteur*, i.e., the faith "associated with" or "linked to" the Redeemer.

7. Here we see the same emphasis on dispositions or governing tendencies that La Colombière treats thematically in "On the Vicious Habit." Conceptually, an acquired habit has the same effect as a natural disposition in that both determine the way we behave. Our actions in turn both reinforce and establish dispositions and habits. For commentary on this dynamic, see the Introduction.

8. See n2 above.

9. A: *Ave Maria*.

10. Quite possibly an allusion to the religious context in England at the time.

11. I.e., the grace received from the sacrament.

12. On this theme, see "On the Relapse."

13. Going to confession while "in a great enough innocence" (*dans une assez grande innocence*) or having "nothing to say" (*rien à dire*) implies confessing either venial sin or previously-confessed mortal sin—a practice known as "devotional confession." Regarding this practice, which contemporary Catholic teaching strongly recommends (*CCE* 1458), see Catherine Dooley, "A Theology of Devotional Confession," *Questions Liturgiques* 66 (1985): 109–24.

14. A: *abbé de Celles*. French Benedictine Pierre de la Celle (Peter Cellensis, ca. 1115–83) may have received his surname from having spent time as abbot of Montier-la-Celle, near Troyes. He later served at Reims as abbot of Saint-Rémy (1162), then as bishop of Chartres (1181).

15. A: *Revera tales inopes copia fecit*; cf. "172. To John of Salisbury and his brother Richard," in *The Letters of Peter of Celle*, ed. Julian Haseldine, Oxford Medieval Texts (New York: Clarendon Press, 2001), 664–65: the correspondent exclaims, with reference to "certain persons who when they are admonished to confess say that they have nothing to confess," *Reuera tales copia inopes facit, uel solis claritas eos excecauit*—"Truly abundance makes such persons paupers, or the brightness of the sun has blinded them."

16. Holiness (*sainteté*)—the habituation to virtue—constitutes the central theme of La Colombière's preaching. On this point, see "On the Vicious Habit," n1, and the Introduction.

17. I.e., the criticisms.

18. A: *& si l'on n'en est pas tout-à-fait certain* (A 4:9); C: *et si l'on n'est pas tout à fait incertain* (C 4:125).

19. This passage recalls the description in Luke 18:11–12 of the Pharisee, obsessed with his own virtue.

20. Cf. the injunction in Prov 24:17–18. For a philosophical treatment of the issues, see John Portmann, *When Bad Things Happen to Other People* (New York: Routledge, 1999).

21. Aristotle analyzes these sentiments in *Eth. Nic.* 2.7.1108a35–1108b6 (*Aristotelis: Ethica Nicomachea*, ed. Ingram Bywater [Oxford: Clarendon Press, 1894]), 36–37; trans. C. C. W. Taylor, *Aristotle: Nicomachean Ethics, Books II–IV*, Clarendon Aristotle Series (Oxford: Clarendon Press, 2006), 11–12: "Indignation is a mean between spite and joy in misfortune, and they are concerned with pleasure and distress at what happens to oth-

ers; the indignant person is distressed at those who do well undeservedly, but the spiteful person exceeds him in being distressed at everyone's good fortune, while the person who rejoices in misfortune falls so short of being distressed as actually to rejoice."

22. Although both the Duchess of York and her husband were Catholic, note that, in addition to the hardships mentioned here, Catholics could not hold public office under Protestant rule, which included La Colombière's time at court (1676–78). For historical context, see John Spurr, "Politics, Piety and Toleration," in *England in the 1670s: "This Masquerading Age"* (Oxford: Blackwell Publishers, 2000), 214–40.

23. A: *rationem reddet de omni verbo otioso*; cf. Matt 12:36 VUC: *Dico autem vobis quoniam omne verbum otiosum, quod locuti fuerint homines, reddent rationem de eo in die judicii.*

24. A: *des hommes.*

25. Matt 25:42–43 VUC: *esurivi enim, et non dedistis mihi manducare: sitivi, et non dedistis mihi potum: hospes eram, et non collegistis me: nudus, et non cooperuistis me: infirmus, et in carcere, et non visitastis me.*

26. Matt 13:10–17; Mark 4:10–12; Luke 8:9–10; cf. Isa 6:9–10; John 12:40; Acts 28:26–27; Rom 11:8.

27. A: *Plures reperi qui innocentiam servaverint, quam qui recte paenitentiam egerint*; cf. Ambr. *Paen.* 2.10.96 (SC 179:192): *Facilius autem inveni qui innocentiam servaverint, quam qui congrue egerint paenitentiam*; trans. H. De Romestin, *Concerning Repentance* (NPNF² 10:357).

28. La Colombière alludes here to the traditional understanding of sacramental reconciliation as a "second conversion." For a contemporary restatement of this thinking, see *CCE* 1427–29. On the question of genuine repentance, see "On the Flight from the World."

29. A: *Pour le repentir, qui est la première partie de la pénitence.* The French noun *repentir* ("repentance") here refers to contrition, which, according to Trent, "holds the first place among the above-mentioned acts of the penitent," viz., contrition, confession, and satisfaction (*COGD* 3:64.1759; trans. Norman P. Tanner [*DEC* 2:705]; see "On Venial Sin," n23), while the term *pénitence* ("penance") here seems to refer strictly to sacramental confession (see "On the Flight from the World," n42).

30. I.e., if one understood what true contrition entails, e.g., its severity, then one would fear it.

31. See Aug. *Conf.* 2.1.1–2.3.8 (O'Donnell, 1:16–26). For a corrective to the modern view of Augustine as sexually wayward and obsessed with lust, see William Harmless, SJ, *Augustine in His Own Words* (Washington, DC: Catholic University Press, 2010), 17.

32. This account, which relates an incident that took place at the Tenth Council of Toledo (656), most likely derives from the *Decretum pro Potamio episcopo* included in the *Hispana* collection of ancient canons (MHSSC 5:537–44).

33. The feeling of hopelessness, born of pain, here gives way to the willingness to turn oneself over to the care of another: having come to the realization, which experience forces one to accept, that one cannot manage one's own life, one either devolves into despair and self-destruction or begins to cast about for help. Regarding willingness, see "On the Vicious Habit."

34. A: *si l'on ne médisait plus?* La Colombière expounds on this theme in "On Malicious Gossip" (*De la médisance*, A 4.78/C 4.78).

35. This passage quite possibly refers to masturbation, maybe with a play on the word *semence* ("seed"). For historical context regarding masturbation, see Michael

Stolberg, *Experiencing Illness and the Sick Body in Early Modern Europe* (New York: Palgrave Macmillan, 2011), 195–218. Note that a decree of the Holy Office, dating from March 2, 1679, affirms earlier Catholic doctrine prohibiting masturbation (DH 2149). Contemporary Church teaching quotes the Congregation for the Doctrine of the Faith, *Declaration on Certain Questions Concerning Sexual Ethics* (December 29, 1975), par. 9, in maintaining that "masturbation is an intrinsically and gravely disordered action" (*CCE* 2352).

36. Regarding the season of Carnival, see "One Should Serve Only One Master," n6.

37. A: *Vous ne jeûnâtes pas hier; il n'y a point eu de quatre temps pour vous.* The term *quatre temps* (Latin *quatuor tempora* "four periods") refers to the ember days—a quarterly observance of fasting and abstinence in the West that fell from the Roman Catholic universal calendar in 1969. The observance consisted of four groups of three days each, viz., the Wednesdays, Fridays, and Saturdays after the feast of Saint Lucy (December 13), the first Sunday of Lent, Pentecost Sunday (fifty days after Easter), and the Exaltation of the Holy Cross (September 14). See *The Oxford Dictionary of the Christian Church*, ed. F. L. Cross, 3rd ed. rev., ed. E. A. Livingstone (Oxford: Oxford University Press, 2005), 546.

38. On the tendency to conflate the identity of Mary Magdalene with the identities of other women from the canonical gospels, see "On the Vicious Habit," n43.

39. A: *demain*. Perhaps a reference to people dressing up for the Christmas celebrations the following day.

40. A: *Irrisor est, non poenitens, qui adhuc agit quod poenitet*; cf. Isid. *Sent.* 2.16.1 (CCL 111:128): *Inrisor est, non paenitens, qui adhuc agit quod paenitet.*

41. Chrysostom firmly believes in the power of tears to wash away sin in connection with repentance: in *Laz.* 4 (PG 48:1012.19–24), he affirms that nothing destroys sin so effectively as accusation and contrition with repentance and tears; see also *Poenit.* 3 (PG 49:298.38–45), in which he holds up Peter as an example of how weeping can erase sin.

42. For the story of Peter's tears, see Jacobus de Voragine, *The Golden Legend: Readings on the Saints*, trans. William Granger Ryan (Princeton, NJ: Princeton University Press, 1993), 1:341.

43. Perhaps an allusion to John 21:15–19.

44. Theologians traditionally have distinguished between contrition, as a feeling of sorrow for sin where that feeling arises from love of God, and attrition, as the same feeling resulting from some other motive, e.g., fear of punishment. On these concepts as understood in Early Modern Europe, see Jean Delumeau, *L'Aveu et le pardon: Les Difficultés de la confession (XIII–XVIIIe siècle)* (Paris: Fayard, 1990), 51–78; and the published doctoral thesis of Gordon J. Spykman, *Attrition and Contrition at the Council of Trent* (Kampen, Netherlands: J. H. Kok, 1955), 90–221. Contemporary Catholic teaching affirms the Tridentine understanding (*CCE* 1451–53).

45. Jer 3:1 VUC: *Tu autem fornicata es cum amatoribus multis.* This paragraph applies God's words to unfaithful Israel (Jeremiah 3:1–4) and the individual sinner, both of whom God calls to repentance.

46. Jer 3:2 VUC: *Leva oculos tuos in directum, et vide ubi non prostrata sis.*

47. Ibid.: *et polluisti terram in fornicationibus tuis, et in malitiis tuis.*

48. Jer 3:3 VUC: *Quam ob rem prohibitae sunt stillae pluviarum, et serotinus imber non fuit.*

49. Ibid.: *Frons mulieris meretricis facta est tibi; noluisti erubescere.*

50. A: *tu t'en est glorifiée devant les hommes.*

51. Jer 3:1 VUC: *tamen revertere ad me, dicit Dominus.*

52. Jer 3:4 VUC: *Ergo saltem amodo voca me: Pater meus.*

53. Presumably a reference to the Christmas season, as the epigraph suggests.

54. A: *je te reconnaîtrai pour mon fils.*

55. Luke 15:18–19.

10: On the Mercy of God toward the Sinner

1. A: *De la Miséricorde de Dieu envers le pécheur* (A 4.66/C 4.66).

2. VUC: *Ecce rex tuus venit tibi mansuetus;* cf. Zech 9:9; John 12:15.

3. On the urgency of repentance, see Gr. Naz. *Or.* 40.13 (SC 358:224–26); Chrys. *Catech.* 1.3–5 (SC 366:118–22); Aug. *Ep.* 2*.3–7 (BA 46B:62–74), *Serm.* 224.3 (PBSK 16:376–78).

4. This passage recalls Luther's frequently-misunderstood exhortation to Philip Melanchthon, "Be a sinner and sin boldly, but believe and rejoice in Christ even more boldly, for he is victorious over sin, death, and the world" (Martin Luther, "To Phillip Melanchthon, August 1, 1521," AE 48:281); for commentary, see Jane E. Strohl, "Luther's Spiritual Journey," in *The Cambridge Companion to Martin Luther*, ed. Donald K. McKim (Cambridge: Cambridge University Press, 2003), 157–58.

5. Ps 32:5 VUC: *misericordia Domini plena est terra;* cf. Ps 118:64.

6. Ps 144:9 VUC: *miserationes ejus super omnia opera ejus.*

7. A: *Ave Maria.*

8. Luke 15:1–10.

9. A: *les hommes.*

10. For the sentiment, although lacking the pastoral imagery, see Cyr. *Chr. un.* (SC 97:339).

11. La Colombière here insists on the primacy of grace—that God must take the initiative in our salvation. This sentiment balances the apparent voluntarism apparent elsewhere in his preaching, e.g., in "On the Vicious Habit."

12. Ps 118:176 VUC: *Erravi sicut ovis quae periit: quaere servum tuum.*

13. An application of Matt 7:16 DRA: "By their fruits you shall know them." Philosopher Charles Peirce considers this logical rule the antecedent of the experimental method (*EP* 2:401).

14. Cf. Rom 7:14–25.

15. La Colombière develops these themes in his sermons devoted to the "last things," viz., death and preparation for death (A 3.48–51/C 3.49–52), judgment (A 3.52–53/C 3.53–54), and hell (A 3.54/C 3.55).

16. Matt 9:9–13; Luke 19:1–10.

17. C: *mais.* I follow Charrier in adding this clarification.

18. Regarding the tendency to conflate other New Testament women with Mary Magdalene, see "On the Vicious Habit," n43.

19. John 8:1–11.

20. John 4:1–42.

21. Matt 26:25, 47–50; Mark 14:43–45; Luke 22:47–48; John 13:2–20.

22. Luke 22:54–62. While Luke does not qualify the feelings that Jesus had in looking at Peter, Mark says, in the story of the rich man—who also had not lived up to

the gospel ideal—that Jesus, looking at the rich man, "loved him" (10:17–21 DRA). The story of Peter's restoration (John 21:15–19), in which the resurrected Jesus gives Peter an opportunity to reverse his triple denial by making a triple affirmation of love, further supports La Colombière's interpretation.

23. John 20:24–29.

24. 2 Sam 11.

25. I.e., David.

26. 2 Sam 12:1–14.

27. A: *il.*

28. A: *Nous ne pouvons pas nier que*; cf. C: *Nous ne pouvons nier que.* I read with the Anisson edition, which seems to make more sense in context.

29. A: *Combien de termes pris les uns après les autres?* La Colombière seems to mean this in the sense of asking God for a delay in responding to the call to give oneself completely to him.

30. For the remainder of the paragraph, La Colombière imagines the interior discourse of God who contemplates the resistance of the sinner.

31. Ps 8:5 VUC: *Quid est homo, quod memor es ejus?* This appears verbatim in Heb 2:6.

32. A: *Quam tolerabilius canis putridus foetet hominibus quam anima peccatrix Deo!* Migne attributes this pseudonymous quotation either to Augustine (PL 40:0946), to Anselm of Canterbury (PL 40:0946, 158:0722C), to Bernard of Clairvaux (PL 184:0528A), or to "uncertain" (PL 185:1959).

33. It is unclear exactly what specific case or cases, if any, La Colombière has in mind. For accounts of this sort from Greek mythology through the middle ages, see Anil Aggrawal, *Necrophilia: Forensic and Medico-Legal Aspects* (Boca Raton, FL: CRC Press, 2011), 4–13.

34. 1 Sa 24:15 VUC: *Quem persequeris, rex Israël? quem persequeris? canem mortuum persequeris.*

35. *Spir. et an.* 6 (PL 40:0784): *Tardius siquidem ei videtur peccatori veniam dare, quam ipsi peccatori accipere*; trans. Erasmo Leiva and Sr. Benedicta Ward, SLG, "Treatise on the Spirit and the Soul," in *Three Treatises on Man: A Cistercian Anthropology*, ed. Bernard McGinn (Kalamazoo, MI: Cistercian Publications, 1977), 188. Scholars now consider the *De spiritu et anima*, long attributed to Augustine, to be a late twelfth-century compilation; on this point, see Bernard McGinn, "Introduction," in *Three Treatises on Man*, 63–74.

36. A: *dans la parabole de l'enfant prodigue.* The story appears in Luke 15:11–32.

37. A: *de la manière du monde la plus indigne.*

38. Luke 19:12 VUC: *abiit in regionem longinquam.* La Colombière appears to have conflated this verse, which comes from the Parable of the Ten Pounds, with the one that appears in the Parable of the Prodigal Son (Luke 15:13), which reads, *adolescentior filius peregre profectus est in regionem longinquam* (VUC). Nevertheless, his interpretation still fits.

39. Luke 15:19 VUC: *jam non sum dignus vocari filius tuus: fac me sicut unum de mercenariis tuis.*

40. Luke 15:22 VUC: *Cito proferte stolam primam, et induite illum.*

41. Luke 15:24 VUC: *mortuus erat, et revixit: perierat, et inventus est.*

42. A: *chere*; cf. C: *chair.*

43. Luke 15:6 vuc: *Congratulamini mihi, quia inveni ovem meam, quae perierat.* The Anisson text lacks *meam.*

44. A: *j'ai récouvert*; cf. C: *j'ai recouvré.*

45. Which is to say, that only such a conquest could explain the apparent joy that God, represented by the master, expresses.

46. At the beginning of the second part of the sermon, La Colombière announces four points, viz., that God forgives sinners (1) quickly, (2) with joy, (3) in good faith and without reservation, and (4) causing new graces instead of punishing them for their offenses.

47. Although the image of Christ the Good Shepherd plays an important role in the thought of Gregory of Nyssa, the wording of this particular passage recalls Chrys. *Thdr.* 1.7 (SC 117:112.17–34); trans. W. R. W. Stephens, "An Exhortation to Theodore after His Fall: Letter 1" (NPNF[1] 9:96): "Now that sheep which had got separated from the ninety and nine (Luke 15:4–5), and then was brought back again, represents to us nothing else than the fall and return of the faithful; for it was a sheep not of some alien flock, but belonging to the same number as the rest, and was formerly pastured by the same shepherd, and it strayed on no common straying, but wandered away to the mountains and in valleys, that is to say some long journey, far distant from the right path. Did he then suffer it to stray? By no means, but brought it back *neither driving it, nor beating it, but taking it upon his shoulders* [italics added]. For as the best physicians bring back those who are far gone in sickness with careful treatment to a state of health, not only treating them according to the laws of the medical art, but sometimes also giving them gratification: even so God conducts to virtue those who are much depraved, not with great severity, but gently and gradually, and supporting them on every side, so that the separation may not become greater, nor the error more prolonged."

48. La Colombière might be referring to his sermon "On Confession."

49. A: *Saepe ferventiores poenitentes innocentibus*; cf. Greg.-M. *Past.* 3.28 (SC 382:464–66): *Saepe entim nonnulli ad Dominum post carnis peccata redeuntes, tanto se ardentius in bonis operibus exhibent, quanto damnabilores se de malis uident. Et saepe quidam in carnis integritate perdurantes, cum minus se respiciunt habere quod defleant, plene sibi sufficere uitae suae innocentiam putant, atque ad feruorem spiritus nullis se ardoris stimulis inflammant*; trans. Demacopoulos, *The Book of Pastoral Rule,* 178: "For often, there are some who return to the Lord after having committed sins of the flesh, and these show themselves to be ardent doers of good works because they see themselves as being all the more damnable for their evil deeds; whereas some of those who preserve the integrity of their flesh believe that they have little in their past that needs to be deplored and think that their life is sufficiently innocent, and therefore do not inflame themselves by striving to be fervent in the spirit."

50. Isa 40:1–2 vuc: *Consolamini, consolamini populo meus. . . . Loquimini ad cor Jerusalem, et advocate eam, quoniam completa est malitia ejus, dimissa est iniquitas illius: suscepit de manu Domini duplicia pro omnibus peccatis suis.*

51. See above, n18.

52. This sort of reaction implies conscience, which La Colombière treats in "On Conscience."

53. Cf. Prov 25:21–22: "If thy enemy be hungry, give him to eat: if he thirst, give him water to drink: For thou shall heap hot coals upon his head, and the Lord will reward thee"; Paul quotes this passage in Rom 12:20. For judgment on the variety of interpretations, see Robert Jewett, assisted by Roy D. Kotansky, *Romans: A Commentary,* ed.

Eldon Jay Epp, Hermeneia: A Critical and Historical Commentary on the Bible (Minneapolis: Fortress Press, 2007), 777–78: "This verse . . . illustrates what might be involved in being 'at peace with all persons'" (12:18).

54. The feminine gender markers appearing here and in the preceding clause indicate that La Colombière is either personifying *Miséricorde* ("mercy") as waiting patiently to dispense grace, or using the term *Miséricorde* as a metonym for God. Considering this usage in relation to the God whom Paul calls the "Father of mercies" (2 Cor 1:3 DRA; *Pater misericordiarum* [2 Cor 1:3 VUC]) suggests the Spanish honorific *vuestra merced*, literally "your mercy," from which derives the third-person pronoun *usted*, today in use as a term of formal address.

11: On Submission to the Will of God

1. A: *De la soumission à la volonté de Dieu* (A 4.67/C 4.67). A line in the exordium of the first sermon "For the Day of the Dead" (A 1.3/C 1.3), which reads, *Je fis voir il n'y a pas longtemps le bonheur qui accompagne la vie des gens de biens* (C 1:59), seems to allude to the present sermon. This would mean that Claude preached the present sermon sometime before the Commemoration of the Dead, which falls the day after the Feast of All Saints. And because the exordium of the second sermon "For the Feast of All Saints" (A 1.2/C 1.2) suggests that sermon to have been the first one that La Colombière preached before the Duchess of York (1:29–30), which he would have done sometime in 1676, we can infer that he must have preached the present sermon the following year, i.e., in 1677.

2. VUC: *Quicumque enim fecerit voluntatem Patris mei, qui in caelis est, ipse meus frater, et soror, et mater est*; cf. Mark 3:31; Luke 8:21. The Anisson text does not include *enim*.

3. Isa 46:10 VUC: *Consilium meum stabit, et omnis voluntas mea fiet.*

4. The attribution of all outcomes to God, which forms the basis of La Colombière's spirituality, grounds his argument for submission to the divine will. This submissive attitude coincides with the *bonne volonté* described in "On the Vicious Habit." From this perspective, to accept God's providence develops a habit of trust that reorients the will, which otherwise tends to control and manage. La Colombière suggests that this reorientation disposes us to want what we get rather than to get what we want.

5. In the Anisson text, the paragraph ends with this sentence fragment and the next paragraph begins with the apostrophe, *Savez-vous bien de quoi il s'agit, Messieurs.* I follow Charrier in running the two sentences together, thus eliminating both the sentence fragment and the paragraph break. Note that, in this sermon, I reproduce the paragraph breaks as they appear in the Charrier edition.

6. Perhaps a reference to 1 Esdras 7:10 (DRA): "For Esdras had prepared his heart to seek the law of the Lord, and to do and to teach in Israel the commandments and judgment."

7. Matt 6:9–13; cf. Luke 11:2–4.

8. The reader may think of this sermon as a commentary on the Ignatian first kind of humility, which entails lowering oneself, insofar as possible, that in all things one might obey God's law. On this point, see Ignatius of Loyola, *Ejercicios espirituales* 165 (MHSI 100:260–61); cf. n36 below.

9. A: *Ave Maria.*

10. 2 Macc 9:12 VUC: *Justum est subditum esse Deo*. La Colombière also references Antiochus in "On Mortal Sin" and "On Conscience."

11. Eccl 11:14 VUC: *Bona et mala, vita et mors, paupertas et honestas, a Deo sunt.*

12. 1 Sam 10:17–27.

13. A: *qui en était.*

14. 1 Sam 9:27–10:8.

15. Prov 16:33 VUC: *Sortes mittuntur in sinum, sed a Domino temperantur*. According to scripture, the Lord had revealed to Samuel that the Lord would send to Samuel a man whom Samuel would then anoint prince over Israel (1 Sam 9:16). Then, when Samuel saw Saul, the Lord indicated that Saul was the man of whom the Lord had spoken (1 Sam 9:17).

16. La Colombière here introduces the distinction between *malum culpae* and *malum poenae*; see n34 below. Perhaps the most well-known example of this dynamic in scripture appears in the Lord's consent that Satan test Job (Job 1:12, 2:6).

17. A: *nous*; cf. C: *vous*: I read with Charrier.

18. Aug. *Psal.* 31.2.26 (CCL 38:243): *Prorsus ad Deum tuum refer flagellum tuum*; trans. Maria Boulding, *Expositions of the Psalms 1–32* (WSA 3.15:386). Augustine makes this comment with reference to Job 1:21, quoted below.

19. John 19:11 VUC: *Non haberes potestatem adversum me ullam, nisi tibi datum esset desuper*. In this vein, see the counsel of Gamaliel (Acts 5:38–39).

20. Job 1:21 VUC: *Dominus dedit, Dominus abstulit.*

21. Gen 37–41.

22. 1 Sam 9.

23. Matt 20:22; Mark 10:38 VUC: *Nescitis quid petatis.*

24. A: *Calicem, quem dedit mihi Pater, non vis ut bibam illum?* Cf. John 18:11 VUC: *Calicem, quem dedit mihi Pater, non bibam illum?*

25. Matt 16:23 VUC: *Vade post me Satana, scandalum es mihi: quia non sapis ea quae Dei sunt.*

26. La Colombière develops this theme at length in "On Confidence in God."

27. Aug. *Civ.* 22.30 (CCL 48:864): *Erit ergo illius ciuitatis et una in omnibus et inseparabilis in singulis uoluntas libera, ab omni malo liberata et impleta omni bono, fruens indeficienter aeternorum iucunditate gaudiorum*; trans. Dyson, *The City of God Against the Pagans*, 1180. The Anisson edition does not have *ergo*.

28. The book of Ecclesiastes takes this sentiment as its theme.

29. On this theme, see Matt 13:24–30.

30. In the first edition, as here, this whole paragraph consists of one single periodic sentence, which concludes with the promise of spiritual freedom that La Colombière offers his listeners as incentive to turn their will and their lives over to the care of God.

31. A: *Nulla res cogere me magis potest quam ipsum Deum.*

32. A: *puisque je ne veux que ce qu'il fait.*

33. This paragraph summarizes the notion of indifference from the principle and foundation of the Ignatian exercises, as expressed in Ignatius of Loyola, *Ejercicios espirituales*, 23 (MHSI 100:164–67). For an explanation of spiritual indifference in this context, see *The Spiritual Exercises of Saint Ignatius*, trans. and commentary by George E. Ganss, SJ (Saint Louis, MO: The Institute of Jesuit Sources, 1992), 151n20.

34. A: *Je dis, en second lieu, que cette personne est hors d'atteinte à toute sorte de maux, et à celui qu'on appelle moral, qui n'est autre chose que le péché, et à celui qu'on*

appelle naturel. This corresponds to Augustine's distinction between *malum culpae* and *malum poenae* (*Lib.* 1.1.1 [BA 6:190]; *Gen. imp.* 1 [CSEL 28.1:460]), which Aquinas treats in *De Malo*, q.1 a.4; cf. q.5 a.4 (*The De Malo of Thomas Aquinas*, trans. Richard Regan, ed. Brian Davies [Oxford: Oxford University Press, 2001], 94–104, cf. 424–30; for commentary, see Brian Davies, "Introduction," in *The* De Malo, 21–23).

35. PASC 3.3 (SBO 5:105): *Cesset voluntas propria, et infernus non erit.*

36. This distinction parallels the Ignatian second and third kinds of humility, as in Ignatius of Loyola, *Ejercicios espirituales*, 166–68 (MHSI 100:260–63); cf. n8 above.

37. Ps 90:9–10 VUC: *Altissimum posuisti refugium tuum. Non accedet ad te malum, et flagellum non appropinquabit tabernaculo tuo.*

38. La Colombière's theory of sanctification comes full circle here, where he identifies submission to the will of God as a virtue and then indicates how habitual practice of this virtue produces a state of spiritual freedom. On the process of sanctification, see "On the Flight from the World," "On Venial Sin," and "On the Vicious Habit."

39. On the taking of habits, see above, n4; see also "On the Vicious Habit." For a contemporary interpretation of this dynamic, see the Introduction.

40. See n18 above.

41. A: *Non mea, sed tua volontas fiat*; cf. Luke 22:42 VUC: *non mea voluntas, sed tua fiat*; cf. Matt 26:3; Mark 14:36.

42. Matt 26:39 VUC: *non sicut ego volo, sed sicut tu*; cf. Mark 14:36; Luke 22:42.

43. A: *Fiat voluntas tua.* This quotation appears verbatim in the Gethsemane scene (Matt 26:42) and in Matthew's version of the Lord's Prayer (Matt 6:10), to which La Colombière alludes in the final line of the sermon. In this vein, see also the *fiat* of Mary (Luke 1:38).

12: On Confidence in God

1. A: *De la confiance en Dieu* (A 4.68/C 4.68). This sermon presents a commentary on the theological virtue of hope: La Colombière uses the term *espérance* ("hope") in this context interchangeably with *confiance* ("confidence").

2. VUC: *fides tua te salvum fecit.* Charrier mistakenly gives the reference as Luke 11; this quotation appears verbatim in Mark 10:52 and Luke 18:42.

3. A: *Ave Maria.*

4. See n12 below.

5. The closest that the Jesus of the gospels comes to making such a clear affirmation of the doctrine of the Trinity is in the Matthean version of the Great Commission (Matt 28:16–20); cf. the triadic formulas in Paul (1 Cor 12:4–6; 2 Cor 13:13).

6. Gen 17–18.

7. Gen 21:1–7.

8. Gen 22:1–19.

9. From Abraham's response to Isaac that God will provide the lamb for a burnt offering (Gen 22:8), La Colombière apparently infers that Abraham "does not cease hoping." After the angel puts a stop to the sacrifice, the Lord reiterates his intention to bless Abraham with descendants, qualifying that he intends to do this precisely because Abraham did not withhold his son (Gen 22:16–18).

10. Matt 15:21–28; the same story appears in Mark 7:24–30.

11. Matt 15:28 VUC: *O mulier, magna est fides tua!*

12. A: *in spem contra spem.* Paul characterizes Abraham as he "who against hope believed in hope" (Rom 4:18 vuc: *qui contra spem in spem credidit*).

13. La Colombière treats this theme at length in "On Prayer" (A 4.69/C 4.69).

14. Perhaps an allusion to the vow that La Colombière professed during his tertianship (*ES* 101–8). Regarding this vow, see the Introduction and n39 below; for another probable allusion to this vow, see "You Should Only Serve One Master."

15. A: *J'ai une cédule de sa main, dit Saint Jean Chrysostôme, qui me répond de tout ce qu'il m'a promis et qui rend ma Confiance inébranlable.* According to Furetière, *cédule* refers primarily to memoranda but also, in the context of banking and commerce, to promissory notes, bills of exchange, and rescripts. Chrysostom often uses contractual language when expressing his confidence in God, as in *A. exil.* (PG 52:429.59–430.1); trans. Wendy Mayer: "I have his promissory note. Surely I am not confident in my own capability? I have in my possession his document. That is my staff, that is my assurance, that is my tranquil harbor."

16. Heb 6:13–20. For discussion of the Pauline authorship of Hebrews, see "On Mortal Sin," n5.

17. A: *O nos beatos quorum causa Deus jurat! O misserimos, si nec Deo juranti credimus?* Cf. Tert. *Paen.* 4.8 (SC 316:158): *O beatos nos, quorum causa Deus iurat; o miserrimos, si nec iuranti Domino credimus;* trans. Le Saint, *On Penitence* (ACW 28:21).

18. Num 14:10–20.

19. Matt 6:28–30; Luke 12:27–28.

20. Ps 93:22 vuc: *Et factus est mihi Dominus in refugium, et Deus meus in adjutorium spei meae.*

21. Rom 8:32 vuc: *Qui etiam proprio Filio suo non pepercit, sed pro nobis omnibus tradidit illum: quomodo non etiam cum illo omnia nobis donavit?*

22. Matt 6:25–26, 10:29–31; Luke 12:6–7, 24.

23. Matt 17:20, 21:21–22; Mark 11:22–24, 16:17–18; cf. 1 Cor 13:2; 2 Tim 4:17. Heb 11 chronicles the effects of the faith of the patriarchs, Moses, and other heroes of Israel.

24. Ps 88:41 vuc: *Destruxisti omnes sepes ejus; posuisti firmamentum ejus formidinem.*

25. Ps 49:15 vuc: *Et invoca me in die tribulationis: eruam te, et honorificabis me.*

26. A: *mais il s'en faut bien que tous ne les aient aussi avant gravés dans le cœur.*

27. La Colombière probably has in mind the practice of saying the Lord's Prayer (Matt 6:9–13; cf. Luke 11:2–4), which often is done in rote fashion.

28. A: *Deus spei;* cf. Rom 15:13 vuc: *Deus autem spei repleat vos omni gaudio, et pace in credendo: ut abundetis in spe, et virtute Spiritus sancti;* dra: "Now the God of hope fill you with all joy and peace in believing; that you may abound in hope, and in the power of the Holy Ghost."

29. Paul probably is thinking of a specific hope, viz., that God is the one to effect for the gentiles the conversion expected to precede their joining with Israel, which joining would in turn bring about the goal of history. For commentary, see Jewett, *Romans,* 897–99.

30. A: *elle.*

31. A: *elle.*

32. *ST* IIa-IIae q.83 a.2,13,15.

33. *ST* IIa-IIae q.83 a.2 ad 3; a.9 ad 5. Although Aquinas here does not explicitly mention *spes* ("hope"), he clearly indicates that prayer develops in us confidence (*fiducia*) in God.

34. A: *Cum a Deo beneficium petitur, beneficio affici se putat*; cf. Gr. Naz. *Or.* 40.27 (SC 358:260; PG 36:398): *cum ab eo beneficium petitur, ipse beneficio afficitur.*

35. A: *C'est un mouvement si naturel & si raisonnable en même-tems, que celui qui nous engage à aimer & à secourir ceux qui recourent à nous, qu'on jugeroit indigne du nom d'hôme quicôque en useroit autrement.*

36. This story appears in codex 279 of the 9th-century *Bibliotheca* of Patriarch Photios I of Constantinople, which references the fourth book of a *Chrestomathia* attributed to Helladius of Antinoopolis (4th c.), published in Utrecht in 1686 with notes by Joannis Meursius (Jan Van Meurs). The late date of this publication suggests that La Colombière knew the story from some other source, quite possibly from the *Bibliotheca*, of which Greek and Latin editions first appeared in 1601 and 1606, respectively. See Phot. *Bibl.* 279 (Photius, *Bibliothèque*, ed. and trans. René Henry [Paris: Belles Lettres, 1959], 8:183).

37. Aug. *Conf.* 8.11.27 (O'Donnell 1:100): *proice te in eum! . . . non se subtrahet ut cadas*; trans. Chadwick, *Confessions*, 151.

38. The latter sentiment echoes the invitation of Jesus in Matt 11:28–30 (DRA): "Come to me, all you who labor, and are burdened, and I will refresh you. Take my yoke upon you, and learn from me, because I am meek, and humble of heart: and you shall find rest for your souls. For my yoke is sweet and my burden light."

39. Ps 4:9–10 VUC: *In pace in idipsum dormiam, et requiescam; quoniam tu, Domine, singulariter in spe constituisti me.* This paragraph, which functions rhetorically as a peroration, summarizing and arousing sympathy for the orator's position, often appears excerpted as his "Act of Confidence in God." As such, it provides a fitting closure both to this particular sermon and to this volume, which is intended in part as an overview of La Colombière's spirituality. Note that this passage, which expresses the author's complete reliance on God, complements the perfectionism apparent in his vow of religious observance (see n14 above): recognizing his inability to save himself by any means, he develops and cultivates an attitude of trust in divine mercy. For a contemporary medical interpretation of a similar dynamic, see Ian Osborn, *Can Christianity Cure Obsessive-Compulsive Disorder?: A Psychiatrist Explores the Role of Faith in Treatment* (Grand Rapids: Brazos Press, 2008). Osborn develops his thesis with reference to the lives of Martin Luther, John Bunyan, and Saint Thérèse of Lisieux.

40. La Colombière here alludes to the traditional penitential practices of prayer, almsgiving, and fasting.

41. A: *Nullus, nullus speravit in Domine, et confusus est*; cf. Sir 2:11 VUC: *Respicite, filii, nationes hominum: et scitote quia nullus speravit in Domino et confusus est.*

42. Ps 30:2, 70:1 VUC: *In te, Domine, speravi; non confundar in aeternum.*

43. Cf. Matt 24:29.

Selected Bibliography

Abbott, Geoffrey. *Execution: The Guillotine, the Pendulum, the Thousand Cuts, the Spanish Donkey, and 66 Other Ways of Putting Someone to Death.* New York: St. Martin's Press, 2006.

Aggrawal, Anil. *Necrophilia: Forensic and Medico-Legal Aspects.* Boca Raton, FL: CRC Press, 2011.

Alacoque, Marguerite-Marie. *Vie et œuvres de sainte Marguerite-Marie Alacoque.* Edited by Raymond Darricau. 2 vols. Paris: Saint-Paul, 1990–91.

Annas, Julia. *Intelligent Virtue.* Oxford: Oxford University Press, 2011.

Atkins, Richard Kenneth. "Restructuring the Sciences: Peirce's Categories and His Classifications of the Sciences." *Transactions of the Charles S. Peirce Society* 42, no. 4 (Fall 2006): 483–500.

Bakhtin, M. M. (Mikhail Mikhaïlovich). *Rabelais and His World.* Translated by Hélène Iswolsky. Bloomington: Indiana University Press, 1984.

Baldwin, David. "The Politico-Religious Usage of the Queen's Chapel, 1623–1688." MLitt thesis, University of Durham, 1999.

Barclay, Andrew. "The Rise of Edward Colman." *The Historical Journal* 42, no. 1 (March 1999): 109–31.

Bash, Anthony. *Forgiveness and Christian Ethics.* New Studies in Christian Ethics 29. Cambridge: Cambridge University Press, 2010.

Bayley, Peter. *French Pulpit Oratory, 1598–1650: A Study in Themes and Styles, with a Descriptive Catalogue of Printed Texts.* Cambridge: Cambridge University Press, 1980.

Bergeret, Étienne. *De l'Abus des boissons alcooliques, dangers et inconvénients pour les individus, la famille et la société, moyens de modérer les ravages de l'ivrognerie.* Paris: J.-B. Baillière et fils, 1870.

Bertrand, Dominique. "The Society of Jesus and the Church Fathers in the Sixteenth and Seventeenth Century." Translated by Antoinina Bevan. In *The Reception of the Church Fathers in the West: From the Carolingians to the Maurists*, edited by Irena Backus, vol. 2, 889–950. New York: Brill, 1997.

Bossuet, Jacques-Bénigne. *Œuvres oratoires de Bossuet.* Edited by Joseph Lebarq, Charles Urbain, and Eugène Levesque. 7 vols. Paris: Desclée de Brouwer, 1914–26.

Bourdaloue, Louis. *Œuvres complètes de Bourdaloue.* New ed. 6 vols. Paris: Beauchesne, 1905.

Briggs, Robin. *Communities of Belief: Cultural and Social Tension in Early Modern France.* Oxford: Clarendon Press, 1989.

Brown, D. Catherine. *Pastor and Laity in the Theology of Jean Gerson.* Cambridge: Cambridge University Press, 1987.

Buckley, Michael J. *At the Origins of Modern Atheism.* New Haven: Yale University Press, 1987.

The Cambridge Companion to Martin Luther. Edited by Donald K. McKim. Cambridge: Cambridge University Press, 2003.

Cepari, Virgil, SJ. *Life of Saint Aloysius Gonzaga.* Edited by Francis Goldie, SJ. New York: Benziger Brothers, 1891.

Certeau, Michel de. "Un maître spirituel: La confiance, conversion du cœur chez le Père La Colombière. 1641–1682." In G. de Broglie et al., *Fête du Sacré-Cœur,* 66–76. Paris: Saint-André/Cerf, 1967.

Chadwick, Owen. *From Bossuet to Newman.* 2nd ed. Cambridge: Cambridge University Press, 1987.

Charrier, Pierre. *Histoire du Vénérable Père Claude de La Colombière, de la Compagnie de Jésus, complétée à l'aide de documents inédits.* 2 vols. Paris: Delhomme et Briguet, 1894.

Charron, Pierre. *De la sagesse.* 2nd ed. Edited by G.-M. de La Rochemaillet. Paris: D. Douceur, 1604.

Cicero. *On the Ideal Orator.* Edited by James M. May and Jakob Wisse. New York: Oxford University Press, 2001.

Clark, Elizabeth A. *The Origenist Controversy: The Cultural Construction of an Early Christian Debate.* Princeton, NJ: Princeton University Press, 1992.

Claude La Colombière. Colloque public du Centre Sèvres, 5 et 6 mars 1993. Paris: Médiasèvres, 1993.

Colonia, Dominique de. *Histoire littéraire de la ville de Lyon, avec une bibliothèque des auteurs lyonnais, sacrés et profanes, distribués par siècles.* 2 vols. Lyon: François Rigollet, 1728–30.

Dagens, Jean. "Le xviie siècle, siècle de Saint Augustin." In *Cahiers de l'Association internationale des études françaises* 3, nos. 3–5 (1953): 31–38.

Davies, Mark Everson, and Hilary Swain. *Aspects of Roman History 82 BC–AD 14: A Source-Based Approach.* New York: Routledge, 2010.

Delumeau, Jean. *L'Aveu et le pardon: Les Difficultés de la confession (xiii–xviiie siècle).* Paris: Fayard, 1990.

Descouleurs, Bernard, and Christiane Gaud. *Marguerite-Marie Alacoque: La Mystique du Cœur.* Paris: Cerf-Saint-Augustin, 1996.

Dieu au XVIIe siècle: Crises et renouvellements du discours. Edited by Henri Laux and Dominique Salin. Paris: Éditions facultés jésuites de Paris, 2002.

Donohue, John W. *Jesuit Education: An Essay on the Foundation of Its Idea.* New York: Fordham University Press, 1963.

Doyle, William. *Jansenism: Catholic Resistance to Authority from the Reformation to the French Revolution.* Studies in European History. New York: St. Martin's Press, 2000.

Duffy, Stephen J. *The Dynamics of Grace: Perspectives in Theological Anthropology.* Collegeville, MN: The Liturgical Press, 1993.

Farrell, Allan Peter, SJ. *The Jesuit Code of Liberal Education: Development and Scope of the Ratio studiorum.* Milwaukee, WI: Bruce Publishing Company, 1938.

Ferreyrolles, Gérard. "Rhétorique et christianisme: Esquisse d'une problématique, de Platon à Bossuet." *Rivista di Storia e Letteratura Religiosa* 44, no. 1 (2008): 47–71.

Ferreyrolles, Gérard, Beatrice Guion, Jean-Louis Quantin, and Emmanuel Bury. *Bossuet.* Paris: Presses Universitaires Paris Sorbonne, 2008.

Fontaine, Patricia. "A Translation of Selected Sermons of Father Claude de [sic] la Colombière as an Adjunct to James Joyce Scholarship." PhD diss., University of Ottawa, 1978.

Francis de Sales. *Les Epistres spirituelles du bien-heureux François de Sales, d'heureuse et saincte memoire, evesque et prince de Geneue, Fondateur de l'Ordre de la Visi-*

tation saincte Marie. Lyon: Vincent de Cœursilly, 1628.

——. *Œuvres*. Paris: Gallimard, 1969.

——. *Œuvres de saint François de Sales*. Edited by the Religious of the Visitation. Annecy: J. Niérat, 1892–1935.

Fumaroli, Marc. *L'Âge de l'éloquence*. 3rd ed. Titre courant 24. Geneva: Droz, 2002.

Gay, Jean-Pascal. "Voués à quelle royaume?: Les Jésuites entre vœux de religion et fidélité monarchique—À propos d'un mémoire inédit du P. de la Chaize." *XVIIe siècle* 57, no. 2 (2005): 285–314.

Gelpi, Donald L., SJ. "The Authentication of Doctrines: Hints from C. S. Peirce." *Theological Studies* 60 (1999): 261–93.

——. *The Gracing of Human Experience*. Collegeville, MN: The Liturgical Press, 2001.

Gilhus, Ingvild Salid. "Carnival in Religion: The Feast of Fools in France." *Numen* 37, fasc. 1 (June 1990): 24–52.

Glotin, Édouard, SJ. "Claude La Colombière: Le Sens d'une canonisation." *Nouvelle revue théologique* 114, no. 6 (1992): 816–38.

Guitton, Georges. *Le Bienheureux Claude La Colombière, son milieu et son temps*. Lyon: Librairie Catholique Emmanuel Vitte, 1943.

Harmless, William, SJ. *Augustine in His Own Words*. Washington, DC: Catholic University Press, 2010.

——. *Desert Christians: An Introduction to the Literature of Early Monasticism*. Oxford: Oxford University Press. 2004.

Haskins, Susan. *Mary Magdalen: Myth and Metaphor*. New York: Harcourt Brace and Company, 1993.

Hefele, Charles Joseph. *A History of the Councils of the Church*, vol. 4: 451–680. Translated by William R. Clark. Edinburgh: T. and T. Clark, 1895.

Johnson, Maxwell E. *The Rites of Christian Initiation: Their Evolution and Interpretation*. Collegeville, MN: Liturgical Press, 1999.

Jonas, Raymond. *France and the Cult of the Sacred Heart*. Berkeley: University of California Press, 2000.

Jones, Michael, ed. *A Handbook of Dates for Students of British History*. Cambridge: Cambridge University Press, 2000.

Kallendorf, Craig W., trans. and ed. *Humanist Educational Treatises*. Cambridge, MA: Harvard University Press, 2002.

Keenan, James F., SJ. *A History of Catholic Moral Theology in the Twentieth Century: From Confessing Sins to Liberating Consciences*. New York: Continuum, 2010.

Kenyon, John. *The Popish Plot*. London: Phoenix Press, 2001.

Kessler, Edward. *An Introduction to Jewish-Christian Relations*. Cambridge: Cambridge University Press, 2010.

Knuuttila, Simo. *Emotions in Ancient and Medieval Philosophy*. Oxford: Oxford University Press, 2006.

La Colombière, Claude. *Écrits Spirituels*. 2nd ed. Edited by André Ravier. Paris: Desclée De Brouwer, 1982.

——. *Lettres*. Edited by Claude Bied-Charreton. Paris: Desclée de Brouwer, 1992.

——. *Œuvres complètes du Vénérable Père Claude de La Colombière de la Compagnie de Jésus*. Vol. 1, Grenoble: Imprimerie du Patronage Catholique, 1900; vols. 2–6, Grenoble: Imprimerie Notre-Dame, 1901.

——. *Prolusiones oratoriae*. Lyon: Anisson, Posuel, and Rigaud, 1684.

——. *Retraitte* [*sic*] *spirituelle du R. P. Claude La Colombière*. Lyon: Anisson, Posuel, and Rigaud, 1684.

——. *Sermons prêchez devant Son Altesse Roîale Madame la Duchesse d'Yorck. Par le R. P. Claude La Colombière*. 4 vols. Lyon: Anisson, Posuel, and Rigaud, 1684.

La Pesse, Nicolas. *Sermons du P. La Pesse*. 6 vols. Lyon: Louis Declaustre, 1708.

La Querelle des anciens et des modernes: xviie–xviiie siècles. Edited by Anne-Marie Lecoq. Paris: Gallimard, 2001.

Laird, Raymond. *Mindset, Moral Choice and Sin in the Anthropology of John Chrysostom*. Early Christian Studies 15. Brisbane: Centre for Early Christian Studies, 2011.

Languet, Jean-Joseph. *La Vie de la vénérable mère Marguerite Marie, religieuse de la Visitation Sainte Marie, du monastere de Paray-le-Monial en Charolois*. Paris: La veuve Mazieres and Jean-Baptiste Garnier, 1729.

The Last Things: Biblical and Theological Perspectives on Eschatology. Edited by Carl E. Braaten and Robert W. Jensen. Grand Rapids, MI: Eerdmans, 2002.

Lee, Sang Hyun. *The Philosophical Theology of Jonathan Edwards*. 2nd ed. Princeton: Princeton University Press, 2000.

Lonergan, Bernard J. F. *Method in Theology*. 2nd ed. Toronto: University of Toronto Press, 2003.

McClymond, Michael J., and Gerald R. McDermott. *The Theology of Jonathan Edwards*. Oxford: Oxford University Press, 2011.

Mellinghoff-Bourgerie, Viviane, and Frieder Mellinghoff. *Bibliographie des écrivains français: François de Sales*. Paris: Éditions Memini, 2007.

Migne, J. P. (Jacques-Paul), ed. *Collection intégrale et universelle des Orateurs sacrés*. 67 vols. Paris, 1844–66.

Mullett, Michael A. *The Catholic Reformation*. New York: Routledge, 1999.

Nida, Eugene A. *Toward a Science of Translating: With Special Reference to Principles and Procedures Involved in Bible Translating*. Leiden: E. J. Brill, 1964.

O'Brien, William P. "Claude La Colombière. Rhétorique et spiritualité." Doctoral diss., Université Paris IV (Paris-Sorbonne), 2008.

———. "Une 'manière' de prêcher: Rhétorique et sainteté chez Claude La Colombière." *Archivum Historicum Societatis Iesu* 79, no. 157 (Spring 2010): 125–70.

Orcibal, Jean. "Histoire du catholicisme moderne et contemporain." In *Problèmes et méthodes d'histoire des religions: Mélanges publiés par la Section des sciences religieuses à l'occasion du centenaire de l'École pratique des Hautes Études*, 251–60. Paris: Presses Universitaires de France, 1968.

Osborn, Ian. *Can Christianity Cure Obsessive-Compulsive Disorder?: A Psychiatrist Explores the Role of Faith in Treatment*. Grand Rapids: Brazos Press, 2008.

Pavur, Claude, trans. and ed. *The* Ratio Studiorum: *The Official Plan for Jesuit Education*. Saint Louis, MO: The Institute of Jesuit Sources, 2005.

Peirce, Charles Sanders. *The Essential Peirce: Selected Philosophical Writings, Vol. 2 (1893–1913)*. Edited by the Peirce Edition Project. Bloomington: Indiana University Press, 1998.

Perler, Dominik. *Transformations of the Soul: Aristotelian Psychology, 1250–1650*. Leiden: Brill, 2009.

Portmann, John. *When Bad Things Happen to Other People*. New York: Routledge, 1999.

Potter, Vincent G., SJ. "Peirce's Analysis of Normative Science." *Transactions of the Charles S. Peirce Society* 2, no. 1 (Spring 1966): 5–32.

Preachers and People in the Reformations and Early Modern Period. Edited by Larissa Taylor. Leiden: Brill, 2001.

Preaching, Sermon and Cultural Change in the Long Eighteenth Century. Edited by Joris van Eijnatten. Leiden: Brill, 2009.

Rapin, René. *Réflexions sur l'usage de l'Éloquence de ce temps*. Paris: Claude Barbin and François Muguet, 1671.

Rice, Eugene F. *The Renaissance Idea of Wisdom*. Harvard Historical Monographs 37. Cambridge, MA: Harvard University Press, 1958.

Saints and Sanctity. Studies in Church History 47. Edited by Peter Clarke and Tony Claydon. Woodbridge, Suffolk: Boydell Press for the Ecclesiastical History Society, 2011.

Schimberg, André. *L'Éducation morale dans les collèges de la Compagnie de Jésus en France sous L'Ancien Régime: XVIe, XVIIe, XVIIIe siècles*. Paris: Champion, 1913.

Sedgwick, Alexander. *Jansenism in Seventeenth-Century France: Voices from the Wilderness*. Charlottesville: University of Virginia Press, 1977.

Sellier, Philippe. "Le Siècle de saint Augustin." *XVIIe siècle* 135 (1982): 99–102.

Short, T. L. *Peirce's Theory of Signs*. Cambridge: Cambridge University Press, 2007.

Silverman, Lisa. *Tortured Subjects: Pain, Truth, and the Body in Early Modern France*. Chicago: University of Chicago Press, 2001.

Sloyan, Gerard S. *Jesus on Trial: A Study of the Gospels*. 2nd ed. Minneapolis: Fortress Press, 2006.

Spurr, John. *England in the 1670s: "This Masquerading Age."* Oxford: Blackwell Publishers, 2000.

Spykman, Gordon J. *Attrition and Contrition at the Council of Trent*. Kampen, Netherlands: J. H. Kok, 1955.

Stolberg, Michael. *Experiencing Illness and the Sick Body in Early Modern Europe*. New York: Palgrave Macmillan, 2011.

Susini, Anne-Régent, ed. "L'Éloquence de la chaire à l'âge classique." Supplement, *Revue Bossuet*, no. 2 (2011).

Taylor, Larissa. "The Influence of Humanism on Post-Reformation Catholic Preachers in France." *Renaissance Quarterly* 50 (1997): 115–30.

———. *Soldiers of Christ: Preaching in Late Medieval and Reformation France*. New York: Oxford University Press, 1992.

Transformations of the Soul: Aristotelian Psychology, 1250–1650. Edited by Dominik Perler. Leiden: Brill, 2009.

Van Damme, Stéphane. *Le Temple de la sagesse: Savoirs, écriture et sociabilité urbaine (Lyon, XVIIe–XVIIIe siècles)*. Paris: Éditions de l'École des hautes études en sciences sociales, 2005.

Vaux, Roland de. *Ancient Israel: Its Life and Institutions*. Grand Rapids, MI: Eerdmans, and Livonia, MI: Dove Booksellers, 1997.

Vérot, Marie-Jéronyme. *I Leave You My Heart: A Visitandine Chronicle of the French Revolution—Mère Marie-Jéronyme Vérot's Letter of 15 May 1794*. Translated and Edited by Péronne-Marie Thibert, VHM. Philadelphia: Saint Joseph University Press, 2000.

Von Balthasar, Hans Urs. "Theology and Sanctity." In *Explorations in Theology I: The Word Made Flesh*, 181–209. Translated by A. V. Littledale with Alexander Dru. San Francisco: Ignatius Press, 1989.

Voragine, Jacobus de. *The Golden Legend: Readings on the Saints*. 2 vols. Translated by William Granger Ryan. Princeton: Princeton University Press, 1995.

Witness of the Body: The Past, Present, and Future of Christian Martyrdom. Edited by Michael L. Budde and Karen Scott. Grand Rapids, MI: Eerdmans, 2011.

Worcester, Thomas. *Seventeenth-Century Cultural Discourse: France and the Preaching of Bishop Camus*. New York: Mouton de Gruyter, 1997.

Index of Scriptural Passages

Index of Proper Names

General Index

Catholicism. *See* Roman Catholicism

cause, xxix, 28, 45, 66, 67, 72, 81, 100, 104, 117, 118, 126, 128, 132, 134; conscience as, 59, 60, 67, 69; of evil, 82, 97, 126, 135, 164n32; of fear, 59, 60, 67, 68, 69; God as, 28, 111, 126–27, 130, 132, 134–35, 159n90; of grief, 63, 67, 104, 105; of hate, 41, 42; of joy, 67, 71, 96, 120, 184n45; of pain, 61, 65, 104, 117, 126, 129, 130; of pleasure, 60, 93, 104; of sin, 38, 39, 74, 126, 181n10; sin as, 48, 53, 63, 65, 105, 117, 172n1

catechism, xviii, xix, 97, 101

chalice, 130–31, 189n53

chance, 126, 131, 134

charity. *See under* Christianity

chastity, 7, 16, 18, 41, 58, 75, 92, 105

children, 26, 31, 32, 35, 36, 50, 52, 61, 71, 74, 96, 97, 108, 126, 134, 138, 141, 163n17, 165n39; in biblical texts, 30, 51, 66, 67, 68, 120, 138; dead, 44, 120, 127, 128, 138; of God, 105, 110, 129, 145; having no, 66, 67, 138; making plans for, 31, 32, 35, 36; teaching of, xix, 13, 17, 49, 101

choice, xxiii, xxv, xxxiii, 11, 34, 35, 70, 81, 91; God's, 126, 132

Christianity, ix, xvii, xxiii, xxiv, xxv, xxix, 5, 16, 18, 19, 24, 27, 34, 67, 70, 96, 99, 101, 110, 121, 158n89, 162n14, 180n50, 181n3; auditor, xxxiii, 3, 7, 13, 15, 17, 18, 22, 26, 27, 28, 30, 31, 32, 34, 35, 36, 38, 40, 41, 42, 43, 44, 46, 48, 49, 50, 52, 53, 54, 56, 57, 58, 64, 66, 68, 69, 70, 71, 78, 85, 86, 87, 88, 90, 91, 96, 97, 98, 99, 104, 106, 110, 111, 118, 121, 126, 129, 130, 137, 138, 140, 141, 144; company, 9, 25, 35, 38, 40, 55, 57, 59, 69, 70, 74, 78, 79, 91, 94, 97, 105, 108, 111, 118, 143; and death, 13, 14, 90, 166n56, 180n45; early, 19; God of, xxviii, 22, 52, 80, 129, 132; living in the manner of, xxx, 3, 11, 13, 17, 35, 76, 162n3; obligations in, 100, 101, 143; offending God in, 38, 104, 105; repentance in, 72, 98; rhetoric and preaching in, xiv, xxvi, xxviii, xxix,

3, 10, 102, 111; and salvation, 17, 34, 81; sin in, 49, 51, 183n29; soul, 13, 58, 81, 89, 109, 113; virtues in, 137, 141; wickedness in, 4, 20, 61, 65, 84

church, xiii, xv, xviii, xix, xxi, xxix, 9, 19, 39, 71, 85, 93, 96, 159n91, 161n111, 192n35; Catholic, ix, xiii, 97, 161n111, 168n6; Peter as head of, 121; sacraments of, 54, 58, 86, 90, 173n17, 177n24, 187n32; seventeenth-century French, xxx; and state, xxi

Church Father. *See* Father of the Church

City of God. See under Augustine, Saint

cloister. *See* religious life

commandment, 17, 19, 40, 41, 44, 84, 95, 102, 132, 141, 164n38, 166n55, 175n12, 196n6; God's power in, 19, 25, 39, 182n16

Commemoration of the Dead, 196n1

commitment, 13, 33, 52, 92, 116, 137, 140, 173n17; of crime, 21, 56, 62, 74; of God to humans, 53, 136–45; of injustice, 17, 22, 31; of sin, 8, 14, 16, 17, 38–39, 41, 42, 45–46, 48–58, 61–62, 73, 75, 80, 97, 104, 106, 108, 123, 126, 163n19, 168n7, 176n23, 178n16, 183n29, 189n51, 195n49

communion, 16, 33, 53, 130, 142

concern, xxi, 13, 17, 20, 28, 33–36, 51, 69, 154n31, 191n21; for God, 28, 135; for worldly things, 26, 27, 28, 30, 32, 33, 170n1

concupiscence, 16, 57

condemnation, 3, 10, 11, 16, 19, 20, 50, 51, 54, 80, 103, 108, 110, 115, 125, 133, 139; of Jesus, 20–21, 38; of Lucifer, 45; of self, 61, 64, 68, 103, 116, 123; for sins, 50, 51, 89, 195n49

confession, xxx, 9, 13, 17, 26, 32, 53, 54, 69, 80, 90, 96–110, 119, 165n42, 176n23, 190n13, 190n15, 191n29; of beliefs, 21, 34, 40, 43, 48, 115, 117, 139, 189n49; final, 90; relapsing after, 71, 72, 76, 77, 78, 87, 90. *See also* penance; reconciliation; sacrament

confessor, xiii, xv, xxi, 34, 80, 81, 172n42

confidence, xxiii, 21, 32, 33, 68, 77, 110, 122, 198n1; in God, xx, xxi, xxiv, xxx,

confession, 97, 102; as harming God, 4, 70, 95; free from, 131, 132–33, 134; memory of, 60, 62, 65–66, 195n49; natural, 132–33, 179n29; persevering in, 75, 76, 111; sin as, 48, 49, 61, 96, 108, 119, 132; those who do to others, 16–17, 18, 52; withdrawal from, 75, 80, 84

examination of conscience, 36, 43, 102, 103, 116; complete, 64, 99, 101, 108; superficial, 13–14, 53, 56, 98, 100; when making plans, 33, 35

extreme unction, 91

fairness. *See* justice

faith, xxi, xxix, 18, 43, 96, 110, 136, 139, 140, 151n4, 158n89, 159n90; act in good, 29, 54, 101, 102, 106, 116, 118, 121, 129, 190n6, 195n46; article of, 102, 127; biblical examples of, 138–39, 170n40, 199n23; faithfulness, 51, 63, 66, 96, 100, 110, 130, 144, 178n6, 195n47; of God, 25, 85, 136, 143, 144; lack of, 18, 30, 31, 78, 109, 113, 121, 122, 195n45

fasting, 54, 71, 82, 92, 93, 105, 200n40; during times set by the church, 86, 101, 106, 167n6, 181n3, 189n3, 192n37

father, xxii, 17, 115, 119–20, 128, 138, 151n4; of the church, xxiii, xxix, 21, 48, 89, 92, 144; loss of one's, 50, 67, 79, 108

fault, 44, 51, 55, 98, 102, 113, 116; atoning for, 11, 71; confessing, 71, 100, 104; falling into, 73, 87, 98, 108; how God sees our, 42, 116, 122; minor, 13, 48–57; people without, 58, 64, 75; recognizing own, 6, 87, 120

fear, 5, 7, 8, 12, 20, 31, 32, 52, 68–69, 70, 71, 72, 79, 90, 93, 97, 109, 116, 128, 134, 136, 138, 140, 141, 142; caused by conscience, 35, 64, 67; in cloister, 7, 164n28, 164n32; evil, 22, 68, 81; free from, 109, 131, 133, 134; God, 7, 9, 12, 13, 22, 23, 32, 52, 53, 55, 56, 60, 101, 107, 118, 129, 130, 140, 141, 143, 145, 163n17; mortal, 12, 67, 69,

87, 180n45; one's enemy, 17, 76, 145; punishment, 55, 182n12, 192n44; true repentance, 98, 99, 101, 104, 111, 191n30; worldly things, 9, 15, 19, 20, 32, 64, 68, 82, 131, 142, 178n17

flesh, 17, 27, 104, 195n49

flight, 30, 66, 89, 95, 114, 175n12; from God, 111–13, 117, 118; from sin, 11, 51, 76, 92

force. *See* necessity; strength

forgetting, x, 16, 20, 41, 45, 51, 61, 70, 74, 99, 102, 117, 121, 130; of sins by God, 82, 105, 122, 138

forgiveness, 42, 79, 108, 120, 184n40; from God, 42, 53, 55, 62, 80–82, 102, 110, 111, 118–19, 120, 121–22, 123, 140–41, 195n46; in humans, 18, 23, 62, 121, 178n18; of self, 76, 122; of sin, 24, 47, 53, 55, 80–81, 108, 111, 118–19, 120, 121, 122, 177n24, 195n46

fornication, 18, 40, 105, 109

freedom, 11, 13, 15, 16, 69, 75, 138; of God, 25, 28, 128, 132, 141; in relation to habit, x, 84, 85, 87, 88, 91, 164n32; in sin, 22, 48, 91, 184n39, 188n37; in submission to God, 40, 70, 92, 124, 131, 132, 197n30, 198n38; of will, x, xxx, 7, 91, 131, 166n52

friendship, 5, 28, 31, 33, 52, 62, 66, 74, 97, 116, 136, 142; dangers in, 8, 16, 94, 100–101, 131, 158n89; with God, 23, 52–53, 67, 77, 112, 113, 114, 115, 118, 120, 121, 124, 131

gambling, 76, 86, 87, 90, 93, 102

gentile, 17, 19, 38, 43, 199n29

gentleness, 32, 96, 99, 121; of God, 25, 47, 97, 111, 112, 114–18, 123, 130, 131, 143

gifts, xxiii, xxvi, 46; of God, 20, 25, 33, 41, 45, 130, 141; supernatural, 46, 77

gridiron. *See* breaking wheel

glory, 12, 25, 62, 63, 67, 93, 102, 132, 159n91; of God, 29, 38, 50

God, 11, 12, 21, 32, 44, 50, 81, 124, 126, 133, 135, 139, 177n32, 198n9; abandoning, 23, 62, 64, 184n39, 187n22; allows evil, 29–30, 31–32, 48, 49, 55;

124, 144; to Christian life, 10, 11, 88,
103; from demon, 57, 153n23; divine,
10, 11, 20, 38–39, 88, 103, 110, 127;
to vice, 4–5, 7, 11, 16, 57, 163n23; in
world, 4–5, 10, 11
instruction, 10, 56, 88, 100, 121, 129,
188n42; of one's household, 9, 49, 101;
in preaching, xxii, xxiii, 94, 97, 103; in
religion, xix, 157n63
intention, 19, 62, 68, 78, 83, 119, 126,
176n22; to amend life, 75–78, 106,
107, 109, 165n39, 189n52; central-
ity of, 35, 36, 95; and freedom, 91,
188n34; of God, 46, 67, 198n9; good,
83, 92, 106, 107; and habit, 91–92,
186n3; in La Colombière's preaching,
xxiii, 41, 48, 185n1; malicious, 16,
31, 80; sincerity of, 28, 76, 78, 90, 91,
107, 109
Israelites, 30, 50, 192n45, 196n6, 199n23,
199n29; in Egypt, 12, 31, 166n55;
kings of, 81, 118, 126, 164n30,
176n14, 197n15

Jansenism, xxx, 162n3
jealousy, 21, 29, 133
Jerusalem, 17, 38, 65–66, 70, 107, 122,
180n33
Jesuit. *See* Society of Jesus
joy, 41, 71, 96, 101, 120, 191n22; in
children, 61, 67, 120; of God, 118,
120–21, 195nn45–46; God as source
of, 127, 184n39, 199n28; in heaven,
70, 131; in La Colombière's spirituality, 162n3; in penance, 105, 110, 118,
120–21, 195nn45–46; in reliance on
God, 36, 95; in retreat, 9, 12, 167n59;
in sin, 16, 184n45; in the world, 3, 11,
12, 17, 60, 67, 70
judgment, ix, xv, 4, 94, 115, 144–45,
196n6; based on exterior actions, 69,
75, 76; by conscience, 63, 68, 69, 114,
178n10; final, 12, 102, 139, 166n56,
180n50, 193n15; formation of, 18, 35,
44, 88, 103, 125, 129, 131, 179n29; by
God, 50, 57, 62, 68, 94, 107, 109, 139,
166n51, 175n37; of God by humanity,
26, 32, 81, 117, 144, 184n45, 188n42;

of Jesus, 21, 38; judicial, 20, 31, 127,
171n19; La Colombière's, xvii, xx,
xxiii; of Lucifer, 80; of preacher, 63,
72; of sin, 39, 47; in the world, 23, 33,
34, 39, 57
justice, 17, 41, 61, 64, 65, 100, 102; of
God, 43, 55, 67, 68, 73, 80–81, 88, 108,
114, 118, 123, 125; to self, 76, 101
justification, 6, 12, 63, 109, 189n51

kindness, 54, 99, 109, 114, 144, 165n45
kingdom, xxi, 8, 29, 31; of God, xv, 25, 79,
114, 121, 163n17, 182n16

Lent, 71, 106, 167n6, 181n3, 192n37;
preaching during, xix, xx, xxi, 161n2,
185n49
law, xxiv, xxvi, xxvii, 5, 36, 115, 195n47;
canon, 155n42; of God, 21, 31, 32,
39–40, 57, 73, 112, 114, 124, 173n11,
178n6, 196n6, 196n8; human, xiii,
xxii, 20, 21, 40; Jewish, 17, 176n17
libertine, 5, 8, 19, 21, 44, 63, 119, 126lib-
erty. *See* freedom
loathing. *See* hatred
logic, xv, xxiv, xxvii–xxviii, 158n83,
188n34, 193n13
Lord's Prayer. *See* prayer, Lord's
lots, 126
love, 43, 47, 52, 55, 57, 90, 93, 105,
109, 135; of enemies, 16–17, 18,
42, 169n22; of freedom, 15; of God,
19, 20, 23, 24, 25, 32, 37, 38, 40–42,
44–45, 47, 58, 59, 62, 63, 66–67,
69–70, 73, 79, 83, 85, 94, 97, 101, 112,
113, 114, 115, 116–18, 120, 122–23,
124, 129, 130, 131, 133, 135, 137, 140,
141, 145, 192n44, 194n22; of good, 10,
116; as motivation, 144; of neighbor,
18; as a passion, 26, 100; of penitential
practices, 71, 85, 110, 125; perfect, 57;
of pleasure, 52, 85, 86, 99; of reason,
23; of self, 3, 17, 18, 37, 129 (*see also*
pride); of sin, 32, 88, 91, 108; as virtue,
29, 57, 89; of the world, 5, 11, 12, 22,
49, 84, 87, 89–90, 115. *See also* charity
Lucifer. *See* devil
lust, 24, 168n7, 188n43, 191n31

intention to change life, 92, 103, 106,
107, 109; of penance, 54, 59, 74, 75,
77, 91, 98, 99, 103, 106
sinner. *See* sin
sister, 6, 124, 188n43
sloth, 89
Society of Jesus, xix, xxi, 152n11, 166n52,
173n15; contrasted with Jansenism,
xxx, 162n3; *Ratio studiorum*, xiv–xiv,
xviii, xix, 156n63; specific members of, xiv, 170n4, 171n42, 172n44;
theological instruction in, xiv, xxiv,
157n63, 169n38, 174n33, 188n41
sodomite, 8, 9, 175n12
solitude, 4, 9, 11, 13, 35, 106; God pursues in, 11, 114; retire into, 3, 12, 13
Son of God, 4–5, 37, 47, 58, 95, 107,
138–39, 184n43; Passion of, 20, 38;
sacrifice of, 113, 130, 142; teaching of,
15, 113, 124
sorrow, 42, 57, 60, 67, 75, 90, 96, 122,
134, 162n3, 177n24, 192n44; as punishment, 55, 60–61
soul, xv, xxvi, 12, 19, 39, 46, 51, 56, 59, 78,
80, 84, 85, 91, 113, 118, 122, 157n80,
177n31, 181n3; contamination of, 8,
45, 46, 48, 53, 54, 60, 61, 63, 66, 73,
130; conversion in, 94, 95, 121, 122;
danger to, 35, 36, 84; death of, 48,
49, 56, 91, 172n1; examination of, 98,
101; as form of address, 13, 58, 81, 89,
109, 113, 133; good in, 61, 66, 85, 96,
122; grace in, xx, xxix, 169n38; loss
of, 17, 36–37, 87, 114, 129; love God
with all, 19, 24; peace of, 134, 200n38;
repentance of, 10, 77, 121, 182n16;
salvation of, 5, 9, 37, 50, 87, 102; sin
in, 42, 46, 48, 49, 53, 55, 56, 67, 92,
106, 112, 114, 117, 121, 172n1
sovereignty, 27, 29, 36, 40, 86, 170n1
Spirit of God. *See* Holy Spirit
Spiritual Exercises. See under Ignatius of
Loyola, Saint
strength, xix, 8, 93, 109, 138, 158n89,
184n38; in army and weapons, 29,
176n14, 183n25, 183n35; biblical
examples of, 8, 21, 30, 41, 86, 176n14;
of conscience, 65, 118; of God, 20,

31, 33, 43, 52, 58, 113, 117, 127, 130,
134, 137, 141, 143, 144, 171n31; of
God's teaching and promise, 67, 79,
137, 138, 142; of grace, 75, 88, 141; of
grief, 74, 77, 79; of habit, xxvi, 56, 82,
86, 88, 89, 91, 92, 190n7; of hatred, 41,
42, 47; of illness, xxii, 72, 136, 145; of
intention, 36, 91, 92; to love God with
all one's, 19, 24, 137; in obedience to
God, 89, 94; in preaching, xvi, xxv,
xxix, 39, 70; of the relapse into sin, 77,
78, 79; reliance on one's own, 7, 30,
31, 32, 53, 86, 95, 143; of repentance,
77, 104, 105, 190n13; of sin, 32, 48, 49,
53, 68, 80; of temptation, 21, 41, 52,
53, 77, 141, 145; of the world, 9, 11,
12, 21, 23
submission, 41, 67, 91, 120, 129, 133,
137; to God's will, 27, 39, 44, 124–25,
129, 131–35, 137, 196n4, 198n38; to
government, 39, 127
suffering, 65, 70, 91, 100, 104, 123, 133,
176n17; choice of, 76, 79, 130; of
Christ, 159n91, 195n47; from conscience, 57, 70; from fear, 10, 15; God
allows, 66, 127, 128, 135; of good, 44,
75; from loss, 36–37, 67; from persecution, 94; from punishment, 12, 19,
45, 60, 61, 101; from sickness, xxi, 47,
128, 129; in sin, 48, 80, 126; of soul,
36–37, 45, 73

temptation, x, 5, 12, 55–56, 75, 76, 131,
145; giving in to, 78, 83, 90; God allows, 52, 127; resisting, x, 41, 53, 74,
77, 82, 107, 141, 159n91, 165n43
thanksgiving, 45, 58, 67, 100, 135, 140
theater, 5, 16, 35, 64, 93
theology, xv, xvii, xxviii, xxx, 80, 162n7;
scholastic, xiv, xxv, 157n63, 169n38
Toledo, Tenth Council of, 105, 191n32
treachery, 31, 61, 86, 138, 140; sin as act
of, 40, 107, 109, 111, 112, 122
Trent, Council of, xvi, xxiii, xxv, 176n34,
191n29, 192n44
tribes of Israel. *See* Israelites
Trinity, xxix, 138, 157n80, 170n4,
198n5; College of the Holy, xiv, xvii,

www.ingramcontent.com/pod-product-compliance
Lightning Source LLC
Chambersburg PA
CBHW030300100426
42812CB00002B/513